Virginia Colonial Abstracts
Volume 19 & 20

Northumberia Collectanea
1645-1720

A-Z

By:
Beverly Fleet

Southern Historical Press, Inc.
Greenville, SC

This volume was reproduced from
An 1943 edition located in the
Publisher's private library,
Greenville, South Carolina

All rights reserved. No part of this publication may be reproduced,
stored in a retrieval system, transmitted in any form, posted
on to the web in any form or by any means without the
prior written permission of the publisher.

Please direct all correspondence and orders to:

www.southernhistoricalpress.com
or
SOUTHERN HISTORICAL PRESS, Inc.
PO BOX 1267
375 West Broad Street
Greenville, SC   29601
southernhistoricalpress@gmail.com

Originally published: Richmond, VA 1943
Copyright 1943
By: Beverley Fleet
Reprinted by: Southern Historical Press, Inc.
Greenville, SC
ISBN #0-89308-945-1
All rights Reserved.
Printed in the United States of America

Preface.

The best friends of this work are genealogists. They like names and dates. Here is a great pot full of that unappetizing fare. The following for flavoring:

Two men. "Many abusive ill languages were rendered by both of them to each other".

Two women. "began to jarr and use very high termes".

And Jam Parker, 1666/7, who said "he must give the Widdow Hickman a spell of work for 3 small pigs about 2 dayes old which were brought up by and fed with a spoon". This prospect worse than a spell of illness and naturally put off since it was so much more fun to feed the pigs, who prospered and when last recorded were grown up and running at large.

Beverley Fleet.

15 August 1943.

Key.

Apl 17 1924. Under authority of the Acts of Assembly, 1918, chap. 231, the following were this day transferred to the Virginia State Library by the Circuit Court of Northumberland County:

Order Books.
	1	1650 - 1652
	2	1652 - 1665
	3	1666 - 1678
	4	1678 - 1698
	5	1690 - 1713
	6	1713 - 1719
	7	1719 - 1729
	8	1724 - 1726
	9	1729 - 1737
	10	1737 - 1743
	11	1743 - 1749
	12	1749 - 1753
	13	1753 - 1756
Record Books	14	1652 - 1658
	15	1658 - 1666
	16	1666 - 1672
	17	1706 - 1720
	18	1710 - 1713
	19	1718 - 1726
	20	1726 - 1729
	21	1738 - 1743
	22	1743 - 1749
	23	1747 - 1749

In regard to No.17 the following: "This Book containes the Records of Those papers which have been presented unto the County Court of Northumberland and by the Justices of the said Court admitted to record againe, they having been formerly recorded and the books of Records in which they had been recorded burned with the office the 25th day of October Domini One thousand seven hundred and ten Test Tho Hobson Cl Cur Com's per dicta ".

All items were taken from No.17. About one item in five from other books. See list of genealogists at ond of this volume if further data is desired.
My abbreviation St S is for St. Stephens, Wicco is for Wiccocomicoe, G and L Great and Little.   B.F.

Northumbria Collectanea
1649 - 1720

Adams, Kath: wife of John. 2 Jan. 1702/3.   17.161
 James Wit deed Jno Adams to Jno Shirley. 13 Feb 1701/2. 17.151
 John. Deed. 13 Feb. 1701/2. of N. Co., John Adams and Kath:
  his wife, sell Jno. Shirley of N. Co., for 2000 lb tobo.,
  60 a in N. Co. adj 'on left hand of main road from Cone
  mill toward Quntoncake'. Wit: Wm Mash, James x Adams,
  Tho Rout. Re rec 20 Feb 1711/12 by John Shirley. 17.151
 John of N Co planter. Sells Robt Harrison 241 a. 2 Jan 1702/3
  17.161
 Thomas. Admr of est of Henry Toppin decd. See entry Richd Rice.
  21 July 1660. 2.127
 Thomas. Land adj Tho Towers on Morattico path. 8 Sept 1668.
  16. 38
 Thomas. 300 a granted by escheat to him and Claudius Tulles.
  25 July 1680. 17.127
 Thomas. Sold land to Jno. Donaldson after 1680. 17.127
 Thomas. Land adj Geo Dawking 16 Dec. 1707. 17.114
 Dr. William. Owes a/c to John Lord of 'Harfort in New England
  mercht'. 12 Jan 1656/7. 14.101 Also referred to as
  'Wm Adams chirurgion' 19 March 1646/7. 14.103
 Dr. William. Now deceased. 20 Sept 1658. 2.94
 Dr. William. His widow now m. to Tho Brewer. 21 Oct 1658.
  2.94
 William. land adj. Geo Dawking. 16 Dec. 1707. 17.114
Agnew, Mr Basil. For some time past an inhabitant of this Co.
 Certificate for leaving the Colony. 1 July 1718. 6.359
Aires, John App. guardian of Steph: Landman. 21 Jan 1660/1. 2.137
 John. m the widow of Robt Smith. 6 June 1661. 2.141
 John. His widow Anne Aires. Deed of Gift to her children. This
  entry mutilated. To son Robert Smyth. To son Nicholas
  Smyth. To dau Elizabeth Smyth. To dau Jane Smyth.
  (They were orphans of Robt Smith. p 104. Vol.15)
  Date gone for this entry but recorded 16 June 1663.
  15. 100
Alderson, John Wit deed Conclin to Hutson. Signed with mark. 17 May
  1708. 17.143
Alderidge, William. Died from accidental gun shot. Jury of Inquest
  called. He exonerated all persons before his death.
  17 Nov. 1662. 15.84
Aldwell, Thomas. Bequest from Tho. Edwards 9 March 1669/70. 16.71
Algood, Edm: On Jury to div. land Saffin and Hull. 29 Nov. 1669.
  16. 63
Allen, James Formerly sold land to Ralph Waddington Sr. 20 Oct. 1678
  17.118
 James Land adj Ralph Beckley 2 July 1707. 17.24
 John. Wit will of Roger Walters 29 Dec 1669. 16.69

Allen, John Wit will of Jno. Webb 4 June 1709. 17.102
    John. Fined for ab from church in St. Stephens Par. 23 Sept. 1715. 6.137
    Teige Wit deed of gift Oldam to Oldam 15 Jan 1700/1. 17.185

Allerton, Mr Isaac. m. Mrs Ursula Colclough widow of Major George Colclough in 1664. A person of this name referred to as "our Loveinge Brother" by Tho and Sarah Willoby. 20 Feb 1663/4. 15. 124

Allinson, Debora Left stock by Richd. Eaton 13 March 1677/8. 17.158

Alloway, John His wife Dorothy rec bequest from Roger Walters. 29th Dec. 1669. 16.69

Alversone, Backnell (?) wit bond Churchill to Harrison 19 Dec 1705. 17.161

Alverson, Teliffe of St. S. Par. Deed from Langhly Conclin and Sarah his wife. 41 acres. 21 July 1703. Re rec 16 May 1711. 17.96

Alverson, Teleife Cath: Hughs bound to him till 18, which time is expired. 17 Sept 1714. 6.87

Alverson, Toleiff Jr. Wit bond Churchill to Harrison. 19 Dec 1705 17. 161   His land adj Saml Churchill on road to Totoskey Ferry. Same date, same Vol and page.

Amey, Eliz Wit Dan'l Neale's will 4 Nov. 1700 17.249

Andrewes Creek. In pat to Col. Rd. Lee 4 March 1656/7 17.66

Apes hole St. S. Par. adj Hulls Creek and Wm Wildey's land. 19th Nov. 1706. 17. 224-229

Ashburn, John chosen as guardian by Eliz Million 21 Jan 1718/19 6. 297

Ashburne, Tho. Walter Sterling, age 13, his servant. 23 July 1714. 6.65

Ashburn, Thomas chosen guardian by Sarah Webb 17 Jan 1716/17. 6.191

Ashe, John Age 26. 4 Aug 1665. 15.165

Ashley, Thomas Wit deed Rd Smith to Jas White 20 March 1677/8. 17.120

Ashton, Ann Relict of Charles, decd, swears he left no will etc. 16 June 1714   6.39

Ashton, Charles Aged 40 years 4 Aug 1665. 15.165
    Eliz: dau of Charles Ashton 4 Aug 1665. 15.161

Ashton, Col Peter Pat. 400 acres 17 Nov 1654. Pat. 485 acres 26th Sept 1668. 17.137
    Col. Peter High Sheriff 26 July 1658. 15.4
    Col. Peter "for his Burgesse charges two Assembly sessions men provision and boate hire" 11289 lb tobo. 14 Nov. 1660 2.134

Ashton, Capt Peter app guardian for Tho Claiborne an infant. 17th Dec 1660. 2.135

Ashton, Peter his servant John Lewis age 11. 20 Jan 1661/2. 2.149
    Peter see entry Wm Wildey. Atty of Henry Corbin prior to 21 Jan 1664/5. 17. 224-229

Ashton, Capt Peter see entry Jno LeBriton, letter from him. 24 May 1664. 15.146

Ashton, Col. Peter Assig: 485 acres in Wicco Par to John Cockrell. 20 Nov. 1668. 17.137

Ashton - Lindsey scandle. Depo of Mrs Isabel Ashton, wife of Charles
    Ashton, concerning David Lindsey and Mrs Susanna Lindsey
    his wife. Other depos. 4 Aug. 1665. 15. pp 158-166
Arbuthnot, David Merchant in Weymouth. Had business with Thomas
    Urquhart dec'd. 17 Feb 1714/15. 6.99
Archbell, John and Frances his wife, late Francis Clifford relict of
    Robt Clifford decd. 18 March 1713/14. 6.24
Arledge, Clement Deed to Patrick Maley 7 July 1703. 17.127
    Mary wife of Clement. Widow of Jno Donaldson. 7 July 1703
    17.127
    William of Wicco Par. Fined for ab from Church 2 mos. Prob.
    a Quaker. 23 Sept 1715. 6.138
Armsteed, Mrs Anne Dau of Hancock Lee. 31 Dec 1706. 17.29
Arnold, Mary Left a cow when she is free. 20 Jan 1676/7. 17.109
Atkins, Edw. Wit Jno Robinson's will. 13 Jan 1700/1 17.108
    John. Orph son of James Atkins, chooses Jno Blundle as his
    guardian. 20 Feb 1717/18. 6.256
    Thomas. As wit proves will of Patrick Keeve. 18 June 1718
    6.268
    William, deceased. Mary his relict swears he left no will.
    Admr granted. 20 Aug 1718. 6.276
Auckland, Saml. 'aged 19 years' 20 July 1670. 16.77
Austin, Elizabeth Keeps ownership of her two cows when she marries
    William Jeffers. Is not going to have the Fiddler's wife
    milking them. 7 July 1656. 14.89
Austen, James Deceased. Grandfather of Thos Webb the son of Thos
    Webb. 11 Sept 1702. R.B. 1706-20 p.4.
Auveling, Ann Orph dau of Peter Auveling deceased. Chooses William
    Metcalfe her guardian. 16 June 1714. 6.38
    Ann Swears she wit will of Edw Woolridge decd. 16 March
    1714/15. 6.100
Auvelyne, Catherine deceased, her dau Anne wife of Edw Barnes.
    20 Feb 1717/18 6.258
Auvelin, Hen: Div land with Ruth Wooldridge 15 June 1715. 6.110
Averett, George Age 24. - 1665. 15.172
Aylett, Richd. Bought land from Roger Walter 1659 and sold it to
    Dan'l Crosby 30 July 1662. 17.192

Bacon, Wm. Francis Clay his admr. 21 July 1660. 2.128
Badger, James Wit will of Jno Webb. 4 June 1709 17.102
    Sarah Exhib inv of est of her dec'd husband James Badger
    20 Jan. 1713/14 6.14
Bailes or Bayles.
    John. Age 33 or th-abts. Depo re Eliz Kaye. 20 Jan 1655/6
    14.67
    John deceased. His daus Rosamond Bailes and Anne Bailes in-
    herit land. 21 Jan 1660/1. 2.137
    John. M widow of Joseph Feilding. 21 Oct 1661. 2.148

Bailes, Jno. Dec'd. a/c of orphan's cattle submitted by Joseph
    Feilding. The orphans were Resamond Bailes, Anne Bailes
    and Elizabeth Bailes. 20 July 1663. 15.105
    John. (Bayles). Deed. 18 Jany 1705/6. of St. S. par. sells
        Tho. Gill of same par., planter, for 12000 lb tobo, 150
        acres. In Cupids Neck, being part of a pat. granted John
        Bailes grandfather of abvsd John. Adj land of Tho Webb,
        Dirty Branch, land of Mrs Spann and Wm Paine, land of Cha:
        Macgee, Stick Branch, Littleneck branch. Wit. by David
        Straughan and Patrick Quife. Ack by John Bayles and Angell
        his wife. Re-rec 17 Sept 1712 by Tho. Gill. 17.180
Bayles, Thomas. Appears to have been murdered. John Jones and John
    Richards to touch his corpse before jury. 20 Nov. 1669.
    3.41
Bales Creek. Adj land of And: Salsbury. 3 July 1701. 17.95
Baker, Mary. Depo. Age 32 or thabts. Exact date not shown but
    recorded latter part of 1664. 15.136
    Richard. Servant boy to Dan'l Suilevant. 29 Aug. 1704. 17.261
    Theodor. Assigned a cow by Capt Hen: Fleet. 15 Nov 1655.
        14.58
    Theodore. Son of Mrs Eliz Nichollas. 20 May 1670. 16.75
    Thomas.   "   "   "   "   "   "
    Thomas. Land adj Tho Brewer. 11 June 1697. 17.268
Ball, Mr. George. Re-rec Antho Haynie's will. 20 June 1711. 17.107
    Mr. George. Justice. 15 May 1717. 6.206
    Grace. Dau of Antho Haynie. 31 Jan 1709/10. 17.107
    Joseph. Guardian for Spencer Mottrom. 12 Mar. 1713/14. 6.22
    Joseph. Exor of Jno Coutanceau. 21 Jan 1718/19. 6.216
    Richard. Wit will of Antho Haynie. 31 Jan. 1709/10. 17.107
    Capt. Richd. Re-rec Antho Haynie's will. 20 June 1711. 17.107
Bancroft, Wm. Headright of Wm Presley. 21 Jan 1660/1. 2.136
Banks, Mrs Eliz. Inv. of P. Coutanceau dec'd at Cherry Point. 20 Apl.
    1709. 17.pages 216-221.
    Thomas. Left 100 acres to Tho. Williams "my son in Law" prior
        to 22 Feb 1705/6. 17.164
Bannister, Nicho: "that he privately fled and privately absented
    himselfe out of the Province of Maryland". May 1652.
    See Cornwalleys. 14.137
Bardon, see Burden, Burton, etc.
    John. Prob Quaker. see Tho Salisbury. 3 Mar 1656/7. 14.112
    John. Having departed this County without paying levies of
        5 persons, judgt agt his est for 350 lb tobo. 21 Nov. 1659.
        2.117
Barecroft, Tho. His wife Martha. To Williamsburg as witness. 30 May
    1715. 6.110
    Tho. Land adj Patrick Maley in main swamp of Mattaponi.
        7 July 1703. 17.127
Barnes, Edward. Deed. 21 Oct. 1702. of Cherry Point in N. Co.,
    planter, sells to Robt Reeves of N. Co. planter, 50 acres
    in Battyes Neck, adj land lately belonging to Tho: Tower,
    John Oldam. Wit by Saml Godwin and David Straughan.
    Re-rec 15 July 1713 by Robt Reeves. 17.200

Barnes, Edward and Anne his wife, one of the daus of Cath Auvelyne
dec'd, pet agst Henry Boggess admr of sd Cath for their
share of her estate. 20 Feb 1717/18. 6.258
   Thomas. of St S. par. Land adj that of Wm Wildey. Ref to
Barnes Bridge. 19 Nov. 1706. 17 pages 224-229
   William. 'of Sommersett County in the Province of Maryland'
submits a/c for taking up runaway servants. 22 Sept 1715
6.135

Barrett, Tho. Age 28 or th-abts. 4 Aug 1665. 15.162
   Tho and Dinna his wife. Sold 100 acres in Mattaponi to Tho
Helder. 1 May 1668. 17.232
   William. Buys 150 a from Andrew Salsbury. 3 July 1701.
17.95

Barton, William. Wit deed Towers to Colton. 8 Sept 1668. 16.38

Bashawe, Giles deceased. William Bashawe, one of his orphans to be
brought to Court by Abraham Joyce his guardian. 5 Sept
1660. 2.130
   William. An orphan bound to Ralph Horsley to be taught the
trade of a tailor. Horseley being dec'd, placed under the
guardianship of Mr James Hauley admr of Horsley. 20 Sept
1658. 2.92
   William. Claims his estate having attained to full age of
21. 20 May 1662. 2.158

Basye, Edmond. Wit will of Hen Mayes. 12 Apl 1702. 17.205
   Edmond. Wit deed Hill to Dunaway. 8 July 1702. 17.174
   Edmond. Uncle of Henry Mayes' daus Mary and Eliz. 10 Feb
1708/9. Re-rec Mayes' will 17 May 1711. 17.101
   Edmond. Re-rec deed Knight to Basie. 16 July 1712. 17.112
   Edmond, Junior. Buys 60 a from Jas Knight 20 Nov. 1705. 17.112
   Edmond, Junior. Land at head of G.W.River adj Jas Knight. 19th
June 1710. 17.198
   Edmond and Edmond Jr. Wit deed Benj Browne to Jno Dunaway 15th
July 1702. 17.75
   Edmond, Senior. Wit deed Jas Knight to Edmond Bazie Jr. 20th
Nov. 1705. 17.112
   Isaac. Wit deed Jas Knight to Edmond Bazie Jr. 20 Nov 1705.
17.112   Also this Isaac:
   Uncle of Henry Mayes' daus Mary and Eliz. 10 Feb 1708/9. 17.101
   Isaac. Wit Wm Howard's will late 1709 or early 1710. 17.236
   John.   "   "

Basknfeild, John. "A poor distempered man" complains agst Philip
Bustle, Edward Lewis and others who held him as a servt
under pretence of curing him. Discharged and told to
apply to Churchwardens of St S par for relief. 17 Mar.
1714/15. 6.107

Batten, William. Aged 36 or thereabouts. 20 Nov. 1655. 14.56

Bateman, Jane. To serve Mr Robt Jones 10 yrs. 8 Oct 1662. 2.163
        (Note: I am not positive as to whether this child would
be 8 or 11 years old. B.F.)

Bayly. Elinor. Entry mutilated. Possibly subject to correction. Christian Bayly widow of Paule Bayly decd, binds her child Elinor Bayly to Tho Dorrell in Virginia, planter, and Elinor his wife, or in case of their deaths to her daughter Anne Porter, for 17 years. 13 Aug 1663. 15.167
    Jacob, deceased. Saml Walker and Jane his wife, his admrs present inv of his est. 17 Feb 1714/15. 6.99
    Jacob, deceased. Jane his relict now wife of Saml Walker. 24 July 1714. 6.68
    Stephen. m widow of Wm Walker. Guardian of Wm Walker Junr. See entry Wm Jeffers. 21 May 1660. 2.124
Beach Branch. Fleet's Bay. N. Co. 14 Jan 1675/6. 17.244
Beardman, John. On jury to div land Saffin and Hull. 29 Nov.1669. 16.63
Bearemore, John. of Fairfield par. His will 20 Jan 1676/7. 21 March 1676/7. Wife Mary, Bro Thos. Sister Jeane. other bequests. 17.109
Beavan, Joseph. Headright of Wm Presley. 21 Jan 1660/1. 2.136
Beavin, Tho. Buys 300 a on S side G W River from Jno Bardon. 22 Jan 1656/7. 14.92
Bebe's Neck. Near land of Geo Dawking. 16 Dec 1707. 17.114
Beckley appears as Bickley in some entries.
Bedlam, William. Aged 35 or thabts. 20 Sept 1658. 15.10A
Bell, Eliza. Wit codicil Hancock Lee. 18 May 1709. 17.29
    Jeremiah. Wit deed Williams to Lattimore. 15 May 1705. 17.252
Bennett, Cuthbert. See entry Col Tho Brereton. In poss land 17 Sept 1714. 6. pp 83-86
    Cuthburd. Swears he wit will of Mary Norman decd. 21 Nov. 1716. 6.184
    Cuthbert. deceased. Wm Humphreys and Anne his wife next of kin swear he left no will. Admr granted. 20 Aug. 1718 6.276
    Edward. Wit Capt Tho Brereton's will. 23 Mar 1698/9. 17.189
    Edward and Grace Bennett (Bennitt) orphans of Cuthbert Bennett. Said Edwd 15 years old, bound to Tho Toulson to be taught shoemaking. 22 Aug 1718. 6.290
    John. Wit will of Tho Salisbury. 3 Mar 1656/7. 14.112
    John. Having m the sister of George Berry decd admr of his estate. 20 Jan 1658/9. 2.99
    John. His widow m Saml Man. 21 Oct 1661. 2.148
    John. Gives John son of Tho Prickett a calf. 18 Jan 1664/5. 15.144
    John. Will of Tho Berry ref to land formerly his. 15 Apl 1700. 17.106
Bennett, - . His widow m Jno Ingoe prior to 6 July 1695. 17. pp 76-78
Bennett's Swamp. Adj land of Benj Browne. 1695/6. 17.158
Bentley, Henry. Gives a cow to Thomas the child of Robt Crowder. 8 March 1663/4. 15.121
    John. Land adj Charles Ingram. Wit deed. 14 Oct 1707. 17.23
Berdon, Mr John. Land adj Capt Jno Whitty. See entry Wm Wildey. 15. May 1661. 17. pp 224-229

Berry, Geo. dec'd. His sister, wife of John Bennett, admr of estate. 20 Jan. 1658/9. 2.99
   George. Under 21. Youngest son of Tho. 15 Apl 1700. 17.106
   James " Son of Thos. " "
   John " " " "
   John. Wit deed Berry to Gill. 17 Feb 1708/9. 17.183
   Margaret. Wife of Tho. Sr. 15 Apl. 1700. 17.106
   Mary. Grand-dau of Mrs Eliz Bledsoe. 13 Feb 1707/8. 17.55
   Patience. Wife of Tho. 7 Apl. 1707. 17.116
   Thomas. Re-rec will d.1698 of Partin Hudnall. 4 Dec.1698. 17.117
   Thomas. Patience his wife. Land adj Mark Harding. 7 Apl 1707. 17.116
   Thomas. Deed 17 Feb 1708/9. of Wicco par, planter, sells Tho Gill of St.S par, cordwainer, for 4000 lb tobo, 1/2 part of land late in tenure of Tho Gill where he now liveth in St.S par, part of a patent granted to Roger Walters for 1000 acres which he in his will of 29 Dec 1669 bequeathed to "his sons Roger Walters and Francis the wife of Wm Smyth equally to be divided between them" The said Roger the son dieing without issue his part descended to Francis, which Francis and her husband Wm by deed dated 14 Feb 1682/3 sold to Tho Berry 300 acres, half the land thereof of this deed, to which Tho Berry, father of the Tho Berry party to these presents, by his will dated 15 April 1700, proved 17 July 1700, gave the said 300 acres to his 2 sons Tho and Wm Berry. The 300 acres adj a hickory near the church, Wildey's land, also adj 100 acres sold by Tho Berry the father in his life time to Nicho Parris out of the 300 acres.
Deed signed by Tho Berry. Witnessed by Wm Harcum, Jno Berry, Fra: McCormack. Ack by Tho Berry and Patience his wife by her atty Richd Lattemore.
Re-rec 17 Sept 1712 by Tho Gill.
   Thomas, Junior. Und 21. Son of Tho. 15 Apl.1700. 17.106
   Thomas, Senior. Will dated 15 April 1700. prob 17 July 1700. of St. S. par. 17.106
   William. Under 21. Son of Tho. 15 Apl.1700. 17.106
Betts, Charles. Grant from Prop of No Neck. 10 Nov 1694. 17.142
   Charles Jr. son of Charles Sr. 1 Oct 1709. 17.100
   Charles, Senior. Will dated 1 Oct 1709. Record of probate burned. of St.S par. Sick and weak. To sons Charles, Jonathan under 18, Royston under 17, William. To dau Mary. To wife Mary. "all my daughters" Mary the only one named. Signed Charles x Betts. Witnessed by Richard Wright, Edward Cole, Wm Tolson
Mary Betts re-recs the will 16 May 1711. Richard Wright swears he wrote the will and that rerecorded is a true copy. 17.100

19 N

Betts, Mary. Re-rec Pat d 10 Nov 1694 to Charles Betts. 19 Dec 1711.
   17.142
   Mary. Acks Deed of Gift for land to her son Wm Betts. 16th Dec
   1713. 6.9
   Mary. Deed of Gift to divers of her children presented to
   Court by Richard Smith who has married the sd Mary.
   18 March 1713/14. 6.25
   William. Land in Wicco River adj Jno Johnson. 4 June 1655.
   17.137
Bickley, Ralph Land adj Wm Wildey 13 Dec 1706. 17.24
   Ralph, planter. Name also appears in entry as Beckley.
   Agreement with Jno Ingram regarding boundry of land,
   100 a, purchased by his father Francis Bickley late
   of N. Co. decd, being part of a patent granted to
   John Motley decd. Adj land of James Allen, "the
   house called Emanuell Walkers"; land of Webb. dated
   2 July 1707. Signed Jno Ingram, Ralph Beckeley.
   Wit: Tho Gill, James Richardson, Lazarus Taylor Jr.
   17.24
Bishop's Neck. Adj land of Tho Brewer Sr. 21 Oct 1681. 17.204
Bisick, John. Will d 25 March 1706. p 19 March 1706/7. of St.S par.,
   planter. In my lifetime I pur of Capt Leond Howson
   gent, late of this Co dec'd, a mulatto woman named
   Eliza Winter commonly called Blassly, that she be
   free. She Extrx. To two daus Mary Tindall and Eliz
   Besick 5 s. to be div betw them. 17.173
   Witnessed by Tho Hayes, Jos Tipton and Timothy
   Swillevend. Re-rec 16 July 1712 by Tho Hobson at
   request of Nathan'l Walker. 17.173
Bixbe, Danl. Bought land from Mr Jas Hill and sold it to Wm Copedge
   Sr, dec'd prior to 18 May 1710. 17.50
Blackeby, Mary. Wit will of Mrs Jane Wildey. 11 Apl 1701. 17. 224-229
Blackman, Jno. Land adj Saml Churchill. 19 Dec. 1705. 17.161
Blackwell, Samll. Depo 18 July 1711. "Aged Thirty yeares or there-
   abouts" re Downing properties. 17.125
   Saml and Margery his wife, late Margery Hudnall exhib inv
   of est of Joseph Hudnall decd. 21 July 1714. 6.56
Blanch, Eliz. Presented for not going to church in Wicco par. 19 May
   1714. 6.35
Bledsoe, Abraham. Deed to John Burne. Part of land left by his father
   George Bledsoe, near to head of Dividing Creek in
   Wiccocomico Par. N. Co. Wit by Jno Grason, Susanna
   x Grason, James x Cox. Dated 12 Feb 1705/6. 17.17
   Elizabeth. Will d 13 Feb 1707/8. p 21 July 1708. Nuncupative.
   Will drawn, not signed. "being in good health of
   body and of perfect memory". To son Richd Lattimore.
   To grand-daus Mary Berry and Winifred Nelmes. To son
   in law Wm Nelmes and "my own daughter Elizabeth
   Nelmes wife of the said Wm Nelmes", they exors. Wit
   by Alexr Mulraine, Richd x Smith, Danl Dunaway.
   Re-rec by Wm Nelmes 22 March 1710/11. 17.55

Bledsoe, George. Will. d 23 Jany 1704/5. p 15 Aug 1705. To wife Eliz
all est she brought with her. To son John Bledsoe
land adj Mr Tho Damerone Sr. To son George. To son
William. To son Abraham land adj Mr John Nickless
and next the school house. To son Thos 3 yrs at
school, he und 21. Friends Mr James Waddy, Mr John
Nickless and James Richardson to divide est among
children. Exors sons Abraham and Wm. Signed George
Bledsoe. Wit Jas Richardson, John Nickles, Tho
Dameron Junr. Proved by oaths of Nickless and
Dameron Jr. Re-rec 22 Feb 1710/11 by Jno Burne.
17.16

Bletso, Jno. Presented for not going to church in Wicco par. 19 May
1714. 6.35

    John and Tho. Each fined for not going to church in Wicco par
21 Aug 1718. 6.279

Bledsoe, Wm. Deed to Jno Ingram. 14 July 1708. 17.22
Bledsoe's land adj Gaskins in Gr W River. 16 Jan 1710/11. 17.80
Bledsoe's Old Field. Ref to 14 July 1708. 17.22
Blount Point Court, Warwick Co. Va. Tho Kaye fined there 1620. 14.66
Blundle, Jno. Wit Jno Webb's will 5 Oct 1700. 17.265

    Jno. Wit Jno Robinson's will 13 Jan 1700/1. 17.108

    John. John Atkins orphan son of James Atkins chooses him as
guardian. 20 Feb 1717/18. 6.256

    Patience, now Patience Curtis wife of Geo Curtis ord to
answer suit of Churchwardens of St.S par for 581
lb tobo. The suit dated 18 Nov 1713. This order
dated 16 May 1717. 6.215

    William. his land adj that left Richd Robinson 13 Jan 1700/1.
17.108

Boaze; see Bowes, Bowers.
Boaze, John. Sold Jno Webb 150 a prior to 4 June 1709. 17.102
Boggess, Hen. Admr of est of Cath: Auveline 20 Feb 1717/18. 6.258
Boggis, Robt. His sons were John, Henry and Andrew. 30 Aug 1661.
15.93
Boharry, Wm. headright of Wm Wildey. 8 Sept 1662. 2.161
Boles, Wm. headright of Wm Presley. 21 Jan 1660/1. 2.136
Bond, Amy. Age 20 yrs or th-abts. 20 July 1658. 15.6

    Peter. For some time past an inhabitant of this Co. Certificate
for leaving the Colony. 4 May 1715. 6.358. Also
another certificate dated 30 May 1718. 6.359

Bonham, Saml. Wm Thomas, the fidler, owes him rent. 14 Nov 1660.
2.133

Bomum, Tho. Deed. 20 Sept 1709. Tho Bomum and Rebecca his wife dau and
sole heir of Wm Thomas late of N Co., sell Richard
Hudnall of Wicco par, for 16000 lb tobo, 200 acres
in Wicco par on S side of Wicco River, part of a
pat formerly granted Jno Shaw and by him granted
to abovesd Wm Thomas decd. Adj land of Saml Mahen
to a "great White Oake standing nigh the Church"
and Swanson's land. Wit by Geo Eskridge, Maurice
Jones. Re-rec 20 Aug 1712 by Richd Hudnall. 17.177

Booth, Adam. Sold land in Mattaponi to Phillip Drake 28 Mar 1680. Was deceased in 1703. 17,233

    Richard. Deed. 15 Sept 1703. of N Co planter. Sells David Straughan Gent of same Co, for 2500 lb tobo, 100 a in Mattapony Neck. As by deed 1 May 1668 in which Tho Barrett and Dinna his wife conveyed the land to Tho Helder, which he (Helder) by his atty Tho Matthews assigned the land on 11 Nov 1676 to Adam Booth, decd father of the sd Richd Booth. Wit by Richd Hews, Jno Claughton, Jas Kean. Re-rec 17th Mar 1716/17 by David Straughan. 17,232

    Richard. Next of kin to orphans of Hugh Salmon dec'd. Obtains letters of admr there being no will. 17 June 1714. 6,44

Boucher, Jno. dec'd. His admr Cath Boucher, by her son Tho Boucher, presents addl inv. 15 June 1715. 6,114

    Jno. dec'd. His dau Kath: wife of Jno Norman pets agt Kath: Boucher admr for her share of est. 19 Oct 1715. 6,140

Bound, Jno. Bought 300 a in G W par from James Pope 6 Jan 166-. Sold it to "one Bennett" prior 1695. 17. pp 76-78

Bouth, Robt. Wit agreemt Kaye to Higginson. 31 Oct 1636. 14,66

Bowen, Edwd. Pets for laying out the land in dower of his mother the wife of Richd Ruth. 19 Oct 1715. 6,141

Bowers, John the Elder. Will. d 29 Sept 1704. p 14 Nov 1704. of St.S par. To son John and dau Mary Bowers. To son Wm und 21. To son John Jr personal property "that came of his mother my former wife", he exor. To dau Mary land where Peter Russell now lives. To wife Jane, she extrx. To son John all "my Joyners and Coopers Tooles and Shoemakers Tools". Wit by Christopher Neale, Richd x Cross, Adham x Grenstead. Name also appears as Bows. Re-rec 19 June 1712 by Jane Bows extrx. 17,167 On p 169 Appraisal of Mary Bowes share of Jno Bowes decd. 17 Dec 1705. Amts to 3160 lb tobo. Signed Jno Webb, Robt Christopher, Robt Reeves, Vincent Garner.

Bowes, Jno. Signs Inv of Wm Sanders' est. 13 Oct 1704. 17,165

    Jno. Jr. Appraisal of his est. Name also spelled Boaze. That it is a true copy sworn to 19 Jan 1713/14 by Robert Reeves, Vincent Garner, James Oldham and Rod'm leale. Original burned, etc. 17,206

Bowler, Jno. Land formerly his in Somerset Co on Eastern Shore of Md. 11 Sept. 1702. Record Book 1706-1720 p.4

Bowles, Solomon. Dec'd. His will presented by Tho Gill the exor. 22nd Sept 1715. 6,134

Bowyer, Andrew. With Wm Thatcher, bought 500 acres in Wicco par from Tho Brewer. 24 Jan 1657/8. 17,255

    Andrew. Assigns land in Wicco par - - 1663 to Jno Essex. 17,255

    Andrew. Depo. Age 40 or th-abts. Exact date not shown but recorded latter part of 1664. 15,135

19 N

Boxberry, Saml. Serv't to Mr Nichos Jernew adj to be 15 yrs of age.
    26 Feb 1660/1. 2.137
Boy, Jno. Bequests from Henry Lambert Ests in Va and Md. 31 Mar 1670
    16.72
Boyd, Robert. Buys 150 a from Jno Pope. 1 Jan 1703/4. 17.194
Brable, Wm. decd. Dorothy his relict swears he left no will. Admr
    granted. 20 June 1716. 6.171
Bradley, Eliz. Sister of Robt Bradley. 4 Apl 1703. 17.12
    John. By testimony of John and Anne Taylor, Fraunces Burden,
        now deceased, desired that her son, John Bradley,
        might have tuition of her 2 little boys being own
        brothers of the sd John. Order that therefore he
        be guardian of his brothers Samuell and Richard
        Bradley. 21 Oct. 1658. 2.94
    Owen. Wit will of Wm Wildey. 1 Dec 1680. 17 pp 224-229
    Owen. Proves Wildey's will by Oath. 15 June 1681. 4.96
    Robert. Bro of Eliz Bradley. Son in law to Charles Dermott.
        4 April 1703. 17.12
    Robert. Lately occupied 100 a in Mattapony Neck. 16 Dec 1707.
        17. pp 130-135
    Robert. Land adj Jno Claughton in Mattapony Neck, St.S par.
        18 Jan 1707/8. 17.89
    Robert. Re-rec will of Charles Dermott. 22 Feb 1710/11. 17.12
    Robert. Re-rec Deed. 22 Feb 1710/11. 17.14
    Robert and Anne his wife. Sold land to Tho Evans prior to
        20 March 1702/3. 17.119 This Anne was dau of
        Robt Bradshaw. See next entries.
Bradshawe, Ann. Age 18 or th-abts. 20 March 1655/6. 14.71
    Anne. Dau of Robt Bradshaw. Married Robt Bradley prior to
        20 March 1702/3. 17.119
    Robert. Pat 400 a in Mattapony Neck. 18 Oct 1651. 17.130
    Robert. Aged 32 or th-abts. 6 Nov 1654. 14.60
    Robert. Wit will Nath Hickman. 26 Mar 1655. 14.98
    Robert. Aged 34 or th-abts. 20 March 1655/6. 14.71
    Robert. of Mattaponi, N.Co. Agrees to deliver to Temperance
        Bradshaw "where she now liveth" and also agrees
        to pay 1/2 of debts incurred in name of Jno Brad-
        shaw and Robt Bradshaw from 1640 to 1653.
        20 May 1656. 14.82
    Robert. Pat 345 a 20 Nov 1657. Sold it to Edw Williams - -.
        17.87
Brent. Geo. Wit deed Dunaway to Chilton. 3 Sept 1708. 17. 76

Brereton. The entries to follow, while they appear complicated check out perfectly and are simple enough if put upon a chart. It seems best to arrange them according to date here and follow the short items with an abstract of the long suit.

Brereton, Tho. Attests app of Lt Coll Saml Smith as sheriff. 26 March 1656. 14.78

Brereton, Tho. Clerk of the Council. James City. 20 March 1657/8. 14.143

Brereton, Tho. His servant Wm Vaughan 13 yrs old. 26 Feb 1660/1. 2.137

Brereton, Tho. Married Jane, daughter of Col. Wm Clayburne (see entry Wm Wildey) betw 10 Feb 1657/8 and 15 May 1661. 17 pp 224-229.

Brereton, Mr Tho. Pat 200 a 17 Oct 1660. Sold Saml Gouche 20 Jun 1663. Power of Atty from Jeffry Gouch 20 Dec 1666. 17.38

Brereton, Capt. Tho. Will 23 March 1698/9. 16 Aug 1699. of St. S. par Gent. To son Tho under 18. Wife Mary Brereton. To bro. Henry Brereton "his children if any". Neice Eliz Winder dau of my sister Eliz Winder. Plantation called Mulberry Fields 700 acres not to go over path from Fleets Point to Sweethall. Provision for unborn child. Son Thos to be put to school to be taught to read, write and cypher. If wife should marry before Tho is 18 then friends Capt Peter Hack, Mr Cuthbert Spann, Mr Tho Hobson and Geo Cooper exors. Wit by Geo Cooper, Edward Bennett and Mary Hill.
Re-recorded 18 July 1711. Produced in Court in trial "in the Ejectione Firma" brought by Robt Clay lesee of Tho Gaskins guardian and nearest friend of Eliza Brereton plt and Richd Kenner and Henry Brereton admitted Deft.

Brereton, Capt Tho. deceased. Agreement 2 July 1703. That Tho Brereton, gent, dec'd, late of St. S. par, N.Co., by will 23 March 1698/9 proved 16 Aug following, provided if his wife Mary marry before his son Thos was 18 that he appoint Capt. Peter Hack, Mr Cuthbert Spann, Tho Hobson and Geo Cooper exors. That the widow married Leonard Howson gent of this Co. That Tho Brereton the son of the testator died under 18. That a dau Elizabeth Brereton, born after her father's death, is an heiress. That Capt Hack refused to act as trustee. That Cuthbert Spann died shortly after assuming trusteeship.
Now Capt Tho Winder and Thos Brereton, son of Henry Brereton, demand delivery of a rateable part of the estate. That Elizabeth Brereton is now under 10 yrs of age.(actually abt 3). The agreement is signed by Henry Brereton and Tho Winder and wit by Wm Mason and Joseph Tipton. It was re-recorded 19 July 1717 by Tho Hobson.   17. pages 238-243

Brereton Entries (continued)

Brereton, Tho. Wit will Jno Cockerill Sr . 30 Dec 1695. 17.135
Brereton, Elizabeth. Legacy from Capt Leonard Howson. Ring with her
    grandfather Brereton's coat of arms. 13 Dec 1704.
    17.8
Brereton, Elizabeth. Her guardian Tho Gaskins sues Tho Hobson. 18th
    March 1713/14. 6.27
Brereton, Elizabeth. This day chooses Tho Pinkard her guardian. 18th
    Nov. 1714. 6.90
Brereton, Thomas the younger. Robt Jones and Elizabeth his wife pet
    for admr of his est. 18 June 1718. 6.266
Brereton, Thomas the younger. Robt Jones and Elizabeth his wife
    nearest of kin. 19 June 1718. 6.272

Brereton, Col. Thomas.
    Northumberland County, Virginia. Order Book No.6 pages 83 - 86.
Court of 17 Sept. 1714. Abstract. Suit of Ejectmt Robt Clay
agt Eliz Winder and Richd Kenner for lands in possession of
Cuthbert Bennett.
We of the jury find:
Wm Clayborne pat 5000 acres betw rivers of great and little
Wiccocomoco 5 Jan 1651/2. That sd Wm Clayborne and Wm Clayborne
Junr, by deed 16 Oct 1665, sold it to Tho Brereton of N. Co.
That Tho Brereton in his lifetime, 14 Nov 1670, conveyed by deed
2000 a. of above to his son Tho Brereton.
Mrs Sarah Dickinson sworn says "that sometime before Coll Tho.
Brereton went to the Susquehannah fort he came to their house
and delivered a bundle or pacquett of paper unto her then
husband Mr Thomas Hobson which said husband told her it was the
said Coll'o Breretons will".
"We also find by the oath of mr Tho. Hobson who being sworn
sayth That sometime after the Death of the aforesaid Collo Tho
Brereton that his father gave him a paper which he told him was
Collo Breretons will and bid him record it which he did a Copy
of which is with us the jury". Hobson says he knew Col Brereton's
hand well "as also he knew one Peter Platt x x an Evidence to
the said Instrument and that it was told him that Peter Platt
went to England betwixt the time of the Date of the said Instrument and the Death of Collo Brereton, as also one Jno Jennys
name was subscribed as an Evidence x x who he was not acquainted
with but know one of that name who was dead before Collo Brereton
dyed as he was informed, also the said Hobson being examined
how long it was from the making the said Instrument to the Death
of the said Brereton he sayeth seven years or thereabouts".
That the will was dated 11 Oct 1675. In it he devised the land
to his son Tho Brereton. The will states if the son Thomas die
before 21 that then his son Henry have the land. Also that Tho
was the Eldest son and that Henry "was by a second Venture".
That Thomas the father died about 1683.

Brereton Entries.

Brereton, Col. Thomas (continued)
Also that Tho the son, by deed 12 June 1688, sold 300 acres to Jno Downing, part of the land.
We also find that the son Tho had a son named Tho by his first wife and at his death "left his wife, being a second Venture privily with child – Elizabeth in the plaintiffs declaration mentioned". Also we find a will dated 23 March 1698/9 of Capt Tho Brereton, son of Col Tho Brereton. We find Mary relict of Tho the son married in 1701 Leond Howson and soon after the land and other property was div betw Leond in right of Mary and Geo Cooper and Tho Hobson in right of Tho the grandson. And Cooper and Hobson remained in possession till death of Tho the grandson, which was before he arrived at 10 yrs of age.
We also find that Henry Brereton, brother of the half blood to Tho the son had not any issue living at the time of the death of Tho the grandson, but we find likewise that some time after his death had issue living and yet hath issue living.
We find that Eliz Winder widow is the only sister of the whole blood to the said Tho Brereton the son, and that Elizabeth now the wife of Richard Kenner is the daughter of sd Eliz Winder and is the same Eliz in the will of the said Tho the son mentioned.
We find that Elizabeth the daughter of the aforesaid Tho the son, by a second venture, is the only issue of the said Thomas now living and is the Elizabeth in the plt's Declaration mentioned and in whose right the plt claims.

(end of Brereton entries)

Brewer, Jane. Wife and extrx of Tho. 11 June 1697. 17.268
John. Und 12 yrs. Son of Tho. 11 June 1697. 17.268
John. Orphan of Tho decd. His guardian Barth Scriver sues Jno Burn. 22 July 1714. 6.60
John. Son and heir of Tho Brewer decd pets agt Jno Burne. 19th Oct. 1715. 6.140
Sarah. Dau of Tho. 11 June 1697. 17.268
Thomas. Pat 1000 a in Wicco par 1st – 1656. 17.255
Thomas. Sold 500 a in Wicco par to Andrew Bowyer and William Thatcher. 24 Jan 1657/8. 17.255
Thomas. Married the relict of Dr Wm Adams. Admr of Adams' est to him. 21 Oct 1658 2.94
Thomas. His servant maid m Richd Peirce, carpenter, with his permission. 20 Jan 1661/2. 2.150
Thomas. That Rev David Lindsey, Isaac and Danl Foxcroft formerly lived at his house. Wm Forroughbush age 28 was his servant. 4 Aug 1665. 15.161

Brewer, Thomas Senior. Deed. 21 Oct 1681. of Wicco par, planter. Sells Richd Linsfield of Wicco par, for 3000 lb tobo, land on S side Dividing Creek, adj Bishops Neck and land formerly in poss of Lewis Shepeard. Signed Tho x Brewer, Sarah his wife. Wit by Tho Waddey, Tho Knight. Re-rec 18 Nov 1713 by Wm Dare atty of Mrs Mary Knight. 17.204

    Thomas. planter. Will d 11 June 1697. p 21 Feb 1699/00.17.268

    Tho. Jr. Und 12 yrs. Son of Tho. 11 June 1697. 17.268

Bridgman, Jno. Proves by oath as wit will of Peter Presly Jr. 19 Nov 1718. 6.296

    Rebecka. Wit P of A Price to Mortimer. 8 Nov 1701. 17.156

Briton. see LeBriton.

Britt, Winneyfred. Orphan of William Britt. Bound to Richd Vanlandingham till 18, she being 11 yrs old last July. 16 Sept 1719. 6.336

Brittaine, Francis. Son in law and heir to Richd Eaton. 13 Mar 1677/8. 17.158

Britton, Nicholas. Deposition of Tho Hopkins, age not shown dated 19 Jan 1664/5. Says abt 12 months since, being at Col Lee's house, Nich: Britton of this Co deceased told your depont "that he had a kinswoman newly come out of England into Peancitanck River", and requested your depon't to entertain this lady at his house until he could otherwise provide for her.

    Deposition of Jno Gustinge of the County of Gloster taken before Commrs of Northumberland Co 20th Jan 1664/5. "This Depon't sayeth that Tho Colles did marry Sarah Ropier who came into this Country about one yeare and a halfe agoe in the ship Wm and Mary Capt Sam: Groome commander and further sayeth not the mark of Jno Gustins".

    Deposition of Edw White of Co of Glos'ter. 20 Jan 1664/5. As above. The 3 entries 15.149

Broad Creek Swamp. Adj land of Jas Claughton and Jas Johnson. 8 Mar 1662/3. 17.87

Broad Creek. Adj land of Hugh Dermott. 20 Mar 1702/3. 17.119

Broad Creek. St.S. par. Adj land of Langley Conolin 21 July 1703. 17.96

Brodhurst, Walter. Mrs Anne B., his widow and admr, attaches 1200 lb tobo belonging to Jno Washington in hands of Isaac Foxcroft merchant. 20 July 1660. 2.127

Brodie, Alex. Wit deed of gift Waddington to Waddington. 20 Oct 1678. 17.118

Brooke, Michael. Drew papers for Wm Wildey. 28 Mar 1658. 15.14

Broughton, Mary. Will. d 2 Jan 1662/3. p 10 Feb 1662/3. Entry mutilated. Daughter Susanna Gardner and her husband Jno Gardner and their daughter my grandchild. Sons William, Thomas and Matthew Keene. Other bequests. 15.92

Broughton, Tho. Age 29 yrs or th-abts. 20 Sept 1652. 14.11

Broughton, Tho. Age 34 or th-abts. Says last March at Antho Lenton's house he heard Tho Shaw say among "other scandallous and opprobious termes" to Antho Lenton "thou ar a Runaway and didst runne away from Yorke". 20 May 1656. 14.77

    Tho. Formerly sold land to Laurence Dameron. 1 Aug 1708. 17.57

Browne, Anne. Wit deed Dunaway to Denny. 11 July 1706. 17.99

    Anne. Wife of Benj Sr. 16 Nov 1708. 17.158

    Benjamin. Wit will Chas Fallin dated 17 Dec 1700. Proved by his oath 16 Apl 1701. 17.159

    Benjamin. His corn field adj land of Jas Hill. Wit deed Hill to Dunaway. This land assigned to him by Dunaway same date. 8 July 1702. 17.174

    Benjamin. Wit deed Adams to Harrison. 2 Jan 1702/3. 17.161
        "   " Churchill to Harrison. 19 Dec 1705. 17.161
        "   " Harrison to Harrison. 19 Dec 1705. 17.162
        "   " Dunaway to Moon. 11 Mar 1705/6. 17.150
        "   " Dunaway to Denny. 11 July 1706. 17.99

    Benjamin. Bought land in G.W.par from Jno Ingoe after 6 July 1695 and sold it to Jno Dunaway 15 July 1702. Wit deed Dunaway to Chilton 3 Sept 1708. 17 pp 75-78

    Benjamin. Indenture. 16 Nov 1708. Benj Browne and Anne his wife of N Co of 1st part, George Murdock and Mary his wife of the 2nd part, Benja Browne son of afsd Benj Browne and Anne his wife of the 3rd part and Benj Murdock son of afsd Geo Murdock and Mary his wife of the last part.
That Mary wife of George Murdock is dau of Benj and Anne Browne.
That Benj Browne is son of Benj Browne and Anne B. and therefore bro of Mrs Mary Murdock.
That Benj Murdock is son of Geo and Mary Murdock.
Benja and Anne Browne make over 100 acres in N. Co adj Lancaster Co., being part of 300 acres pat by Jno Ingoe 6 July 1695 and conveyed by Ingoe and his wife to the afsd Benj Browne 15 Feb 1695/6. This 100 acres adj Bennetts Swamp, and to go to the Murdocks for life and then return to Benj Browne Jr. Signed Benjamin Browne, Anne x Browne. Wit by Robert x Marrall, Susanna Browne and Jno Dunaway. Re-rec 19 Mar 1711/12 by Geo Murdock. 17. 158

    Benjamin. Wit deed Knight to Knight. 19 June 1710. 17.198

    John. Wit deed 11 June 1680. 17.14

    John. Wit delivery of land Crosby to Purcell. 18 Oct 1705. 17.192

    John. Wit bond Tho Byram. 19 May 1708. 17.72

    John. Orph son of Tho dec'd. Barth Schriever, his guardian, sues Jno Burne and Eliz his wife. 18 March 1713/14 6.28

Brown, John. Jno Crawford orphan aged 9 bound to him to be taught trade of tailor. 18 June 1718. 6.269
Browne, Mary. Wit deed Dunaway to Denny. 11 July 1706. 17.99
    Phillip. Servant to Mr Rd Cole adj abt 16 yrs old. 21 Oct 1661 2.147
    Richard. Francis Little bound to him till 21. 22 July 1661. 2.144
    Richard. Married the widow of Wm Warder. 9 Sept 1661. 2.147
    Richard. Age 44 yrs or th-abts. 20 June 1663. 15.103
    Susanna. Wit deed Browne to Murdock. 16 Nov. 1708. 17.158
    Wm. Wit will Wm Coppage 4 June 1698. Proves 18 Sept 1700. 17.15
    Wm. Summoned for absenting himself from Church. 21 Jan 1713/14 6.15
Bryant, Anne. Deed of Gift to Robt Bryan her grandson admitted to record. 17 Oct 1716. 6.182
    Eliz. Wife of Henry. see entry Alex Cumins. 7 Apl 1707. 17.116
    Henry of Wicco par. " " "
    Henry. Wit deed Byram to Champion. 19 May 1708. 17.72
    John. Wit deed Loughman to Scott. 7 Sept 1702. 17.202
    John. "being a very ancient Inhabitant of the County and poor and incapable of much labour to support himselfe is excluded from paying any levy". 16 June 1714. 6.41
    John. Dec'd. Will presented by Ann Bryant extrx. Proved by oaths of Dennis Conway and Jno French witnesses. 16 May 1716. 6.156
    Mary. Deceased. Richd Swanson named exor refuses to act. John Swanson and Dennis Swanson appointed. 17 June 1714. 6.45
    Mary. Deed of Gift to her grandson Robert Bryant presented in Court by him. 17 July 1717. 6.221
    Mary. Left property to Chas and Mary Prichard. See entry Rd Swanson their guardian. 21 Aug 1718. 6.277
Budd, Mrs Eleanor. Accused of murdering her servant Tho Winn. Body dug up and she vindicated. 1 Jan 1655/6. 14.67
Budd, Capt Richd and Ellenor his wife. Richd Coring bound to them till 21. 11 March 1655/6. 14.73
    Capt Richd. His widow married Tho Williams. 8 Oct 1662. 2.163
Bunbury, Tho. His serv't Jos Headnett age 16. 10 Feb 1662/3. 2.168
Burbage, Col. Tho. Deceased. His widow m Capt Tho Streator prior to 17 March 1657. 15.4
Burberry, James. Guardian of Richd Nutt. 18 Nov 1719. 6.345
Burbury, Malachi. Wit P of A of Mrs Eliz Johnson. 18 Nov 1707. 17.40
    Mr Malachi. Now in poss of land bought by Mr Tho Burbery from Mr James Hill. 18 May 1710. 17.50
    Malachi. Assigns int in land of Wm Coppedge Sr dec'd to Wm Copedge Jr. 21 March 1710/11. 17.50
Burden. Also appears as Bardon, Barton, Berdon, Burton, etc.
Burden, Frances. Late deceased. See entry her son Jno Bradley. 21st Oct 1658. 2.94

Burden, John. Patent 1 July 1654. Richard Bennett to Martine Cole,
300 acres on S side G W River at head of a creek
div land of Mr Tho Salisbury and Henry Huste, S E
on land of Tho Kedby.
Cole sells above to John Bardon 20 Sept 1656. Wit
Peter Knight, Rice Maddocks. John Bardon assigns
the pat to Tho Hipkins and Tho Beavin 22 Jan 1656/7.
Hipkins sells the land to Jno Shaw 20 May 1657.
14.92

John. Wit agreement Sarah Kingwell and Jno Essex. 20 Nov 1655.
14.56

Burgin, Jane. Wife of John, binds her son Tho Hope to Capt Richard
Haynie till 21. 16 June 1714. 6.43

Burk, John. Wit deed Dameron to Dameron. 19 Feb 1705/6. 17.55
Wm. Deed from Peter Revoire and Ann his wife. 24 July 1714. 6.74
Wm. See entry Wm Howard. 20 March 1716/17. 17.236

Burkston, John. Wit P of A Mould to Eyes. 18 Feb 1669/70. 16.70

Burne, Jno. Deed from Abra: Bledsoe. 12 Feb 1705/6. 17.17
Jno. Wit Tho Knight's will 1 Oct 1706. Prov by his oath 15th
Feb 1709/10. 17.43
Jno. Re-rec will of Geo Bledsoe 22 Feb 1710/11. 17.16
Jno and Eliz his wife sued by Barth Scriever guardian of John
Brown an orphan. 18 March 1713/14. 6.28
Jno. Pet agt by Jno Brewer son of Tho Brewer decd. 19 Oct 1715
6.140
Jno. App Constable for lower limits of Wicco par. 16 May 1717
6.211
Jno. Will presented by Eliz Burn his exor. 18 Feb 1718/19.
6.298

Burrell, Robert. Chyrurgion. 1 Jan 1655/6. 14.67
Robert, Chirurgeon. Deed of Gift. 19 May 1670. To welbeloved
and only son John Burrell, all estate in Va. Friend
Tho Lane to act as atty. Wit by Daniell Lane and
John Russell. 16.75
Robert. Sold land 6 Dec 1669. Now, 7 Apl 1707, deceased. See
entry Alex Cumins et als. 17.116

Burrowes, Mathew. Wit will Robt Jones Sr. 14 Jan 1675/6. 17.244

Bussle, Phillip. Deed. 15 Sept 1703. Phillip Bussle and Jane his wife
of St.S. par planter sell David Straughan of same
par, for 6000 lb tobo, 75 acres land bequeathed to
them by will of Phillip Drake decd dated 9 April
1699 and proved 21 June 1699. The land in Mattapony
as shown by deed of Nathl Hickman to Edmond Elder.
And another tract bought by sd Phillip Drake from
Adam Booth decd by deed dated 28 March 1680 adj Tho
Hickman's Swamp. Wit Richd Hews, Tho x Millcr,
Jams Kean. Ro-rec 17 Mar 1716/7. 17.233
Philip. Fails to cure "a poor distempered man". 17 Mar 1714/15
6.107
Phillip. Jane his relict swears he died without a will. Admr
granted. 20 March 1716/17 6.200

Butler, Richd. Sued by Geo Gordon of Glasgow for debt. Broke out and
        escaped from prison. 20 Aug 1719. 6.335
Byram, Abra. Age 28 yrs or th-abts. 20 Jan 1655. 14.68
    Mrs. Sarah. Wife of Tho. 19 May 1708.
    Thomas. "who calls himself Thomas Clay als Byram" sells land
            to Jno Champion. 5 May 1670. 17.72
    Thomas. Pur 60 acres. 21 Mar 1693/4. 17.72
    Tho. Wit deed Wms to Champion. 2 Dec 1700. 17.70
    Tho. Land adj Tho Wms. 27 Mar 1703. 17.46
    Tho. "   "   15 Mar 1704/5. 17.67
    Tho. Wit P of A Champion to Lattimore. 15 May 1705. 17.71
    Tho. of W par. Deed to Jno Champion. 19 May 1708. 17.72

Callahan, Lawrence. Age 21 yrs or th-abts. 2 Nov 1704. Richmond Co
        Misc. Records. p.27
Callan, Eliz: "Eliza Callan orpht daughter of Hugh Callan decd seven
        years old the first day of July next" bound to Tho
        Harding till 18. 12 March 1713/14. 6.21
    Hugh. Wit will Partin Hudnall 4 Dec 1698. 17.117
    Hugh deceased. Inv of Est re-rec by John Lyon and Alexander
        Mulraine 20 June 1711. Original date of inv not shown
        it having been burned. 17.113
    Nicho: Orph son of Hugh Callan dec'd abt 12 yrs of age bound
        to Charles Moorhead till 21 to be taught the trade of
        cooper. 18 March 1713/14. 6.25
    Nicho: Orph son of Hugh Callan decd aged abt 13 yrs bound, by
        his request, to John Crump to learn trade of shoe-
        maker. 16 Mar 1714/15. 6.100
Calvert, Reuben. Summoned at suit of Danl Hornsby. 20 Feb 1718/19
        6.305
Campbell, Hugh. Bequest from Saml Griffin. 2 Feb 1702/3. 17.213
    John (Cammel) Murdered by Indians Feb last. 20 July 1659.
        2.110
    Saml. (Cammell) Wit deed Gaskins to Gaskins. 16 Jan 1710/11
        17.80
Canady, Timothy of Richmond Co. Deed from Wm Moore. 5 Sept 1707.
        Re-rec the deed 21 Mar 1710/11. 17.47
Cane, Tho. decd. His children: William his son, Thomas, Susana. Entry
        badly damaged. The name Mary Rayner appears. 3rd June
        1658. 15.2
Cannadie, Kath: Bequest from Tho Palmer of Maryland "to Katherine
        Cannadies Daughter Katherine Twenty shillings" 28th
        March 1709. 17.127
Caring, Tho: Gives his son Richard Caring "for many friendshipp and
        courtesies" to Capt Richard Budd and Ellenor Budd his
        wife, till 21. 17 March 1655/6. 14.73
Carnegie, Jno. Wit will of Jno Graham. 5 Mar 1705/6. 17.208
Carpenter, Cath: relict of Wm C. decd swears he made no will. Admr
        granted. 16 May 1716. 6.155
    Charles. Pat land later belonging to Wm Moore. 24 Nov 1670.
        17.47

Carpenter, Jno. Pat land later belonging to Wm Moore. 24 Nov 1670. 17.47
    Phillip. His dau Mary Carpenter has bequest from her godfather Francis Simmons. 16 Apl 1661. 15.93
    Sarah. Orph dau of Wm C, decd bound to Geo Chilton and Eliz his wife till 18. 17 Apl 1717. 6.205
    Wm. Orph son of Wm C. late of this Co dec'd, being 14 yrs of age or th-abts, with approbation and consent of his uncle Wm Cornish, offered to be bound apprentice to Saml Heath to be taught trade of cooper, etc. 16 May 1716. 6.156
Carter, John. Wit civil marriage Jno Merryday to Ann Nash. 11 Sept 1656. 14.90
Carpenter, Phill: In charge of Geo. orphan of Wm Metcalfe. Elizabeth Carpenter, bequest from Wm Metcalfe pd 2 yrs since. 18 April 1657. 14.105
Carter, Robt. Overseer of will Hancock Lee. 31 Dec 1709. 17.29
    Tho: App by Gov agt at Indian Storehouse in this Co. Hon Robt Carter security. 17 Nov 1714. 6.89
Carty, Sylvester. Serv't to Mr Charles Lee adj 12 yrs old. Indenture calls for 7 yrs service. 16 May 1717.
Catherall, Randle. Wit deed of gift Mrs Eliz Nichollas to her children 20 May 1670. 16.75
Cautanceau see Coutanceau.
Chackalate, Steph: His widow Eliz m Saml Webb. 21 Aug 1718. 6.278
Champion, John. Father of John Champion dec'd. 19 May 1708. Bought land 5 May 1670. 17.72
    Jno: Father of John. Confirms grant 22 Sept 1680. 17.72
    John. Assigns land to Saml Mahane 5 Feb 1704/5. 17.71
    John. Wit deed Mahane to Love. 21 Feb 1704/5. 17.51
    John. Formerly bought land of Tho Wms. 15 Mar 1704/5. 17.67
    John. Wit deed Cumins et als to Harding. 7 Apl 1707. 17.116
    John, Gent. of W par. Buys 60 a on S side G W River. 19th May 1708. 17.72
    John. Deed. 3 Dec 1709. of N Co, planter. Sells Pitts Curtis of N. Co planter, for 9000 lb tobo, 200 acres in G.W. par, remaining part of 300 acres bought by William Hartland of Cordery Ironmonger 5 Nov 1672 (after sale made by Wm Hartland to Jno Lance 9 Feb 1683/4) and by Wm Hartland sold to John Champion father of said John Champion 11 Feb 1685/6, and land sold by said John Champion to Pitts Curtis is part of 1000 acres granted to Thos Lane 26 July 1665. The land adjoins Dennis Creek. Wit: Jno Swanson, Samuel Lunsford, Wm Sutton. Ack 15 Feb 1709/10 by Jno Champion and Joshian his wife thru her atty Clement Lattimore. Re-rec 17 Sept 1712 by Pitts Curtis.
    P of A Mrs Joshian x Champion to Capt Tho Hobson or Mr Clement Lattimore to ack above. Wit: Tho Williams, Richd x Ruth. d 15 Feb 1709/10. 17.186

Champion, John. Re-rec deed 16 May 1711. 17.72
    Mrs Joshian. Wife of John. 5 Feb 1704/5. Also 16 May 1705. 17.71
Chandler, Danl. of Eliz City Co. Sells 700 a on Chickacoan River to Richd Smith. 22 Jan 1673/4. 17.120
Chandler's Patent. Ref to as belonging to Peter Coutanceau 20 April 1709. 17.20
Chauhady, Jno. Servant to Jno Forrester adj 8 yrs old. 18 Feb 1718/19 6.299
Cherry Point. See entry Saml Griffin. 2 Feb 1702/3. 17.213
    Peter Coutanceau dec'd had his quarter there. 20 Apl 1709. 17 pp 216-221
Chetwood, Mathias. Lately app constable for Newman's Neck and having departed out of this County, Sylvester Welsh is app in his place. 17 June 1714. 6.55
Chicacone branch. Adj land of Geo Dawking. 16 Dec 1707. 17.114
Chichester, Jno. Re-rec deed dated 1706 Wm Wildey to Richd Chichester. 15 Feb 1715/16. 17 pp 224-229
    Richd. of Lancaster Co. Deed 385 a from Wm Wildey. 19th Nov 1706. 17 pp 224-229
Chilton, Geo. Gent. of Lancaster Co. Son of Mr Stephen Chilton of Currotomen, Lancaster Co. Buys 200 acres from Saml Mahane Jr in G W par. 16 July 1705. 17.122
    Geo and Eliz his wife. Sarah Carpenter, orphan, bound to them. 17 Apl 1717. 6.205
    John and Mary his wife, of Christ Church par, Lancaster Co, buy, with Stephs Chilton Jr, 100 acres in G W par N Co from Jno Dunaway. 3 Sept 1708. 17. pp 76-78
    John and Mary his wife of G W par, buy with Stephn Chilton, land from Jas Hill. 15 June 1709. 17.78
    Stephen. of G W par. 15 June 1709. 17.78 Re-rec deed 100 a G W par 16 May 1711. 17. pp 76-78
Chockolate, Stephs see Chackalate.
Christmas, Frans Depo. Age 22 or th-abts. His wife Anne Christmas. Her child born dead on a/c of her being struck. She was a countrywoman of Robt Crowder. Exact date not shown but recorded latter part of 1664. 15.135
Christopher, Robt. Signed appraisal of Bowers est. 17 Dec 1705. 17.167
Church, Jno. Wit will of Richd Eaton 13 Mar 1677/8. 17.158
Church, St Stephens Parish. Near land of Tho Berry. 17 Feb 1708/9. 17.183
Church silver. See entry Rev Jno Farnefold. 3 July 1702. 17.234
Churchill, Anne. Signs deed with Saml Churchill 19 Dec 1705. 17.161
    Samuel. Will. d 4 June 1702. p 17 Feb 1702/3. To sons Saml and Joseph Churchill. To daus Sarah and Lydia Churchill. Witnesses Eliz Wooldridge, Chas Dermett, Anne Dermett, James Kean. 17.229
    Samuel. Sells Robt Harrison 207 a. 19 Dec 1705. 17.161
    Saml. Wit deed Harrison to Harrison. 19 Dec 1705. 17.162
    Saml. Wit deed Conolin to Hutson. 17 May 1708. 17.143

Civil Marriage. See entry Jno Merryday. 11 Sept 1656. 14.90

Clapham, Wm. Wit P of A Fleet to Stovens. 12 Sept 1657. 15.10A

Clare, Richd. Deed of Gift. For love and aff to Jno son of Charles Ashton, a calf. 20 May 1654. 14.61

    Richd. Exor of Wm Reynolds. 24 Sept 1656. 14.100

    Richd. In charge of Anne orphan of Wm Metcalf. With Anne Reynolds in chg of Kath Metcalfe. Both pd 2 yrs since 18 Apl 1657. 14.105

Clark, Ann. Aged 33 yrs or th-abts. Her former husband Wm Reynolds, now decd, wit an agreement dated 31 Oct 1636, betw Mr Kaye and Mr Humph: Higginson concerning Eliz Kaye. 20 Jan 1655/6. 14.67

Clarke, Geo. The path formerly called George Clarks adj land of Richd Nelmes Sr. 13 Apl 1706. 17.98

    Henery. Headright of Wm Wildey. 8 Sept 1662. ?.161

    Jno. carpenter, reg mark for cattle. 20 Jan 1656/7 14.98

    Jno. His wife Dennis in chg of Jane orphan of Wm Metcalfe. Pd 2 yrs since. 18 Apl 1657. 14.105

    Jno. His wife Dennis, now a servant to Danl Holland unable to continue as guardian of Jane Metcalfe. 22 July 1661. 2.144

    Jno. Acq of murdering Tho Hughes. 21 Apl 1662. 2.156

Claughton, Anne (Pemberton). Wife of Jno Claughton. 18 Jan 1707/8. 17.89

    Anne. Dau of Tho Hall Senr. Jas Claughton one of his exors. 10 Feb 1708/9 17.163

    James. Mary Lanman apprenticed to him till 21. 22 July 1661 2.144

    James. cooper. Wm Dawson bound to him. 22 July 1661. 2.144

    James. Pat 72 a on Broad Creek Swamp adj land he now ownes. 8 Mar 1662/3. 17.87

    James. Land adj Matthew Rodham. 17 Nov 1666. 16.22A

    James. Of Mataponi, cooper. Deed to Richd Pemberton. 17th Feb 1679/80. 17.87

    James. Land adj Jas Moore. 6 May 1679. 17.143

    James. Exor of Tho Hall Sr. 10 Feb 1708/9. 17.163

    James. See entry Wm Gradey. 17.152

    Joane. Wife of James. Also appears as Clayton. 17 Feb 1679/80. 17.87

    Jno. Wit deed Booth to Straughan. 15 Sept 1703. 17.232

    John. Deed of Gift. 18 Janry 1707/8. Jno Claughton of St S par, planter, and Anne his wife, for "Parental Love and good Will" give Pemberton Claughton, son of sd John and Anne, 249 acres in Mattapony Nook in St S par, known as Harry Hokin (?) Neck and adj land of Edward Wooldridge, Laurence Dameron, David Gill and Robert Bradley. Which land Richd Pemberton of the par and Co, chirurgeon, decd, died possessed in fee, and now by legal descent become the land of John Claughton and Anne his wife sole dau and heir of sd Richd Pemberton. Signed John Claughton, Ann x Claughton. Wit: David x Straughan, David x Gill, Marg'tt Hall. Re-rec by Mr Jno Claughton 16 May 1711. 17.89

Claughton, Jno. Re-rec deed David Jones of Westmorland Co to John Claughton for 40 a in N Co. 16 May 1711. 17.88

Jno. Re-rec deed dated 17 Feb 1679/80 James Claughton to Richd Pemberton. 16 May 1711. 17.87

Jno. Re-rec Inv of Est of Pemberton Claughton. 20 June 1711 17.112

Jno. Re-rec will of Tho Hall Sr. 19 March 1711/12. 17.163

Jno. Justice. His land adj Josiah Dameron. 17 March 1712/13 6. pp 78-81

John. App guardian of his grandson Pemberton Claughton, an infant, orph son of Pemberton Claughton decd. 24 July 1714. 6.68

John. Guardian of Pemberton Claughton pets agt Josiah Dameron who m the relict of Pemberton Claughton decd father of the orphan. 17 May 1716. 6.159

Mary. Widow of Pemberton Claughton. 15 Mar 1709/10. 17.112

Pemberton. Son of Jno And Anne (Pemberton) Claughton. 18th Jan 1707/8. 17/89

Pemberton. Inv of his est taken by Court order 15 March 1709/10. His relict Mary. Inv sworn before Capt John Cralle 12 May 1710. Re-rec by Jno Claughton 20 June 1711. 17.112

Clay, Francis. Admr of Wm Bacon. In dif with "Wm Thomas, Fidler" 21st July 1660. 2.128

Francis. Now m to Mrs Anne Temple. 5 Sept 1660. 2.130

Francis. Gentleman. Depo. Age abt 34 yrs. Says in 1649 when he first came into this country, etc. Regards mares belonging to Thompson orphans brought up from Kiquotan and disposed of by Col Jno Mottrom. 1 Oct 1660. 15.61

Francis. who m the widow of Mr Jno Temple. 8 Oct 1662. 2.164

Francis. Sold land to Richd Eaton prior 13 March 1677/8. 17.158

Robt. See entry Capt Tho Brereton. 18 July 1711. 17.189. Also 17 Sept 1714. 6.pp 83-86

Thomas. Tho Byram "who calls himself Thomas Clay als Byram" 5th May 1670. 17.72

Clayburne, Jane. Pat land (see entry Wm Wildey) 10 Feb 1657/8. 17.224

Jane. Dau of Col Wm Blayburne. Married Col Tho Brereton prior 15 May 1661. 17. pp 224-229

Thomas. An infant desires Capt Ashton be admitted his guardian to sue Lt Coll Smyth (Samll Smyth) for 3000 lb tobo, etc. 17 Dec 1660. 2.135

William. Secretary. 4 March 1656/7. 17.66

Col. Wm. Assigned pat to Capt Jno Whitty. 15 May 1661. 17. pp 224-229

Col. Wm of New Kent Co. Deeds of gift. Stock to sons Tho. and Leonard Claiborne. Rec 20 June 1663. 15.102

William Jr. and Sr. See entry Tho. Brereton. Pat 5000 acres 5 Jan 1651/2. Sold it to Brereton 16 Oct 1665. 6. pp 83-86

Capt Wm. Land adj Col Peter Aston 26 Sept 1668. 17.137

Clayton, Joane. Also as Claughton in same entry. 17 Feb 1679/80. 17.87
Clifford, Mrs Frances. Relict of Robt. Now wife of Jno Archbell. 18th March 1713/14. 6.24
 Frances. Sued by David and Ann Spense admrs of Nicho Edwards 17 June 1714
Coan Storehouse. On Coan River. Geo Eskridge app agt there. 17 Nov. 1714. 6.89
Cone Mill. Road to adj Jno Adams. 13 Feb 1701/2. 17.151
Cobbs Hall. To Charles Lee Jr. See entry Richd Lee. 17 Feb 1707/8. 17.60
Cock, Nicho. "an alien having long lived in this Country and truly behaved himself", order from Gov., Council and Burgesses that "said Cock be made a free Denizen of the Country of Virga". 20 Sept 1664. 16.37
Cocke, William. Surveyor. 20 Jan 1656/7. 14.98
Cockeram, Andr: On Jury to div land Saffin and Hull. 29 Nov 1669. 16.63
Cockrill, Andrew. Bequest for looking after Danl Neale in his sickness. 4 Nov. 1700. 17.249
Cockerill, Edwd. Son of Jno Sr. 30 Dec 1695. 17.135
 Edw. Wit Capt Leonard Howson's will 13 Dec 1704. 17.8
Cockrell, Edw. Fined for absenting himself from church in St.S par. 23 Sept 1715. 6.137. Also presented for ab from church in St.S par 15 May 1717. 6.202
 Elizabeth. Dau of Jno., neice of Danl Neale. 2 Nov 1700. 17.249
 Elizabeth. Wit will Saml Downing deed. Proves it by oath 19 Oct 1715. 6.141
 Elizabeth. Will presented by Cha Nelms exor. 20 May 1719. 6.316
 Mrs. Hannah. Wife of Jno Sr. 30 Dec 1695. 17.135
 Jno. 485 a from Col Peter Aston 20 Nov 1668. 17.137
 Jno. Wit Edw Neale's will in which Lucretia Cockrill rec bequest. See will of Danl Neale. 4 Nov 1700. 17.251
 John. deceased. Will presented by Elizabeth C. his extrx. 12 Mar 1713/14. 6.18
 Jno Jr. Son of Jno Sr. 30 Dec 1695. 17.135
 Jno. Jr. Eld son of Jno C of St S par deed. 19 Nov 1706. 19 Nov 1706. 17.138
 Jno Sr. Will d 30 Dec 1695. p 18 Nov 1704. 17.135
 Lucretia. Sister of Edw Neale. 4 Nov 1700. 17.251
 Richard. Son of Jno Sr. 30 Dec 1695. Re-rec his father's will 15 Aug 1711. 17.135
 Richard. Wit Capt L Howson's will 13 Dec 1704. 17.8
 Richd. Re-rec deed 1677 Wm Smyth to Rd Lugg. 15 Aug 1711 17.141
 Richd. Youngest son of Jno Sr decd whose will was d 30 Dec 1695. Deed from his bro Jno Jr 19 Nov 1706. Re-rec this 15 Aug 1711. 17.138
 Willoughby. Orphan of Eliz C. makes choice of Jno Cockrill as guardian. 20 May 1719. 6.316

Cocks, John. Bequest from Jno Eustace. 23 Dec 1701. 17.245
Coffy, Hugh (?) Wit deed Crosby to Purcell 18 Oct 1705. 17.192
Coggin, Tho. Above 60 yrs, exempt from levies. 22 July 1661. 2.143
Colclough, Geo: Wit marriage Jno Merryday to Ann Nash on 11 Sept 1656. 14.90
    Geo: and Ursula his wife guardians of Richard and Sarah Thompson. 29 Sept 1657. 15.8
    Geo: who married the relict of Col Jno Mottrom who was the relict of Mr Richd Thompson decd, app guardian to the children of the sd Thompson and admr of his estate. 20 Nov 1658. 2.95 Richd Wright admr of Col Mottrom objects. 2.96
    Geo: Attaches any est belonging to Lt Coll Henry Fleet in this Co. 20 Jan 1658/9. 2.100
    Major Geo: his widow Mrs Elizabeth C to admr his est. 8th Sept 1662. 2.160
    Major Geo: his widow m Isaac Allerton. 30 - 1664. 15.131
    Mrs Ursula. "Mr George Colclough in right of his wife the Relict of the said Coll Mottrom" 3 Jan 1656?7.14.124
    Mrs Ursula. "158 L. 2 s. 8 d was all the money I had when I married which my brother John paid my Brother Thomas Colclough's man for my husbands use" signed Ursula Colclough. 22 Sept 1657. 14.123
Coles, Edw: Sold land to Rich Spann prior to 4 Beb 1662/3. 17.177
Cole, Edwd. To carry Rev Jno Farnefold to his grave. 3 July 1702. 17.234
Coles, Edw: Jno Marston age 11 his serv't. 21 March 1716/17. 6.204
    Jno. Wit will Eliz Downing. Proves it by oath. 19 Oct 1715. 6.140
    Jno. His land on road to Sweet Hall. 22 Aug 1718. 6.292
    Martin. Pat 300 a on S side G W River. 1 July 1654. 14.92
    Martin and Alice his wife. Give a calf to Mary dau of Thomas Lampkin. 20 Sept 1658. 15.11
    Martin. Sold land on N side G W River to Mr Downing prior to 15 May 1661. 17 pp 224-229
Cole, Capt Richard. This day sworn Commissioner. 24 August 1658. 2.91
    Richd and Anna his wife of Salisbury Park, Northumberland Co. Mary Drury abt 7 yrs old assigned to them. 30 Aug. 1658. 15.11
    Mr Richd. The Court desires he be expelled as Commissioner for his misdemeanors. 24 Feb 1658/9. 2.102
    Richd. His serv't Phillip Browne age abt 16. 21 Oct 1661. 2.147
    Robert. Pets agt exor of Jno Garner decd for wages due. 17 Aug 1715. 6.129
    Saml, minister. see entry Jno Merrydeth. 14 July 1657. 14.111
    Thos and Edmond and also Simon White. Sons of Margritt Davis dec'd. 19 Feb 1717/18. 6.254
Colles, Tho. m Sarah Ropier abt June 1663. see entry Nicho Britton. 20 Jan 1664/5. 15.149
Colton, Tho. planter. buys 125 a on Morrattico path from Tho Towers. 8 Sept 1668. 16.38

Common, Henry. Orph son of Henry Common decd, aged abt 12 yrs, bound to Alice Nelmes till 21 she to have him taught trade of cooper or shoemaker. Ambrose Feilding Security. 15 May 1717. 6.209

Compton, Anne. Wit will of Edw Walker 2 Dec 1650. Proves it by oath 20 Sept 1656. 14.92
 John. Orphan. a/c of his cattle submitted by his mother Anne Hazelrigg. 20 July 1663. 15.105

Conner, Laurence. A serv't boy belonging to Jno Lewis adj to be 15 years old. 16 June 1714. 6.42
 Wm. Wit will of Tho Gill Sr. 10 Feb 1707/8. 17.97

Conaway see Conway.

Conolin, Laughly. of St S par. Also appears in same entry as Lockly Conolin. Deed to Teliffe Alverson. 21 July 1703. 17.96

 Laughly of St S par, planter and Sarah his wife. Deed. 17 May 1708. They sell Henry Hutson of same par, planter, for 6000 lb tobo, 100 a, being part of 400 a formerly sold by Antho Lynton on 22 Dec 1673 to James Moore, who by will devised it to his wife Sarah party to these parts and now wife of Laughly Conolin. The residue, not disposed of being the plantation where Jas Moore lived, 440 acres surveyed by Jas Gaylord surveyor late deceased. Survey made 6 May 1679. The land then adj James Claughton and Jas Johnson. This deed signed Loughly x Conolin, Sarah x Conolin. Wit: Jno x Alderson, Saml Churchill, Mary x Trussell. Re-rec 16 Jan 1711/12 by Henry Hutson. 17.143

 Loughly and Sarah his wife of St S par. Deed. 17 Apl 1700. They sell Henry Hutson, for 5500 lb tobo, 100 acres woodland in Mattapony Forest in St S par, late owned by Jas Moore decd. Adj land of Mr James Crane, Mr Geo Hutton, part of a greater tract pat by "old Mr Anthony Linton dec'ed" and by him sold to Jas Moore who left it to Sarah his wife now Sarah Conolin. Wit: by James Moor, Agnes Moor and James Crean. Re-rec 16 Jan 1711/12 by Henry Hutson. 17.146

 Laughly. Deed 21 May 1707. James Moor late of N. Co., now of Richmond Co, son of James Moor dec'd who by will d 17 Sept 1697 devised his land to his wife Sarah now Sarah Conolin, etc., confirms deed to Henry Hutson. Signed James Moor. Wit: Tho Conaway, Jno Garner, Tho Hobson. Delivery by turf and twigg wit by Diana x Jones, Agnes Moor. 21 May 1707. 17.148

 Laughly ..."Laughly Conolin haveing this Day in Court acknowledged his moveable Estate to Sarah Conolin and John Moore hir sone the same is admitted to record". Order Book No.5 p 256. A Court 21 July 1703.

19 N.

Conaway, Dennis. (Conway) His land. 11 Sept 1702. Record Book 1706-20 p.4
    Dennis. Wit will Richd Sutton. 1 Feb 1702/3. 17.172
    Dennis. Land adj Wm Moore. 5 Sept 1707. 17.47
    Dennis. Will. No date shown. Prob 15 June 1709, of St S par. To sons Dennis and Thomas "Long Neck. To sons John and Lazarus "Howard's Neck". To son Christopher other land. To son James, under 18, 2 yrs at school, etc. To daus Elizabeth and Winifred now unm. Wit: James Foulke, Danl McCarty, Thomas Thackrell. Re-rec by Capt Danl McCarty 22 Feb 1710/11. 17.19
    Dennis. Signs Inv of Simon Thompson 16 June 1714. 17.221
    Dennis. Swears he wit will of Jno Bryant decd. 16 May 1716. 6.156

Conway, Edwin. Re-rec deed Mahane to Geo Chilton. 18 July 1711. 17.122
    John. Signs Inv of Simon Thompson. 16 June 1714. 17.221
    John. Admr of Henry Dawson decd. 17 Mar 1714/15. 6.104
    John. Ownes land formerly Dennis Eyes. 22 Nov 1716. 6.186
    Tho. Wit deed Moor to Hutson. 21 May 1707. 17.146
    Tho. dec'd. Will presented by Jno Conway exor. 18 Sept 1717. 6.238

Cood, Mr James. Agreement for Mr Jas Waddy re boundry line. 14 Oct 1707. 17.23
    Patrick and Mary his wife. Fined for absenting themselves from Church. 21 Jan 1713/14. 6.15

Cooper, Geo: Gent. Surveyor. 22 Sept 1680. 17.72
    Geo: Exor of Capt Tho Brereton. 23 March 1698/99. 17.189
    Geo: Wit will Tho Berry Sr. 15 Apl 1700. 17.106
    Col Geo: Owes tobo to Rev Jno Farnefold. 3 July 1702. 17.234
    Geo: See entry Capt Tho Brereton. Party to agreement. 2 July 1703. 17 pp 238-243
    Geo: Surveyor. 15 Apl. 1706. 17.42
    Geo: Wit deed Wildey to Chichester. 19 Nov 1706. 17 pp 224-9
    Col Geo: Will d 18 Nov 1708. p -- of G W River in St S Par. To St S par all land "whereon I now live" for a Glebe. To Tho Hartt (or Harll) clothing. Bal of est to "Loveing friend" Mrs Elizabeth Robinson, she extrx. Wit by Charles Davis, Will x Dew. 18 July 1711 Richd Wright says he wrote Col Cooper's will and on motion of Saml Robinson the copy is Re-rec. 17. 123 Also Jno Copedge swears he wrote 1/2 of the will. 19 Dec 1711. 17.143 Also Saml Robinson and Eliz his wife exors of Geo Cooper decd. 18th Mar. 1713/14. 6.27
    Samuel. In his minority. Son of Sampson Cooper late deceased. 20 Feb 1659/60. 2.120
    Mr. Sampson. "late of Rippon in the County of York". Will d 12 Aug 1659. p 20 Feb 1659/60. Long will much damaged. Shows heirs. 15.33
    Wm. Nearest of kin to Matthew Garrett decd who d without will. 12 March 1713/14. 6.18 Also admr of Matthew Garrett. 22 Aug 1718. 6.293

Copedge, Charles. Son of Wm C. decd. Bro of Wm Jr. 18 May 1710. 17.50
　　Jane. widow. Land adj Tho Williams. 27 Mar 1703. 17.45
　　John. Surveyor of Northumberland Co. His land adj Wm and
　　　　Charles Copedge. 5 June 1710. 17.50
　　John. Re-recs will of Wm Coppage. 22 Feb 1710/11. 17.15
　　John. Says he wrote abt 1/2 of Coll Cooper's will which he
　　　　copied from the original. 19 Dec 1711. 17.143
　　John. Re-recs deed Knight to Basie for Edmond Basie. 16 July
　　　　1712. 17.112   Also re-recs will d 1702 of Peter
　　　　Knight. 16 July 1712. 17.175
　　John. Surveyor. See entry Josiah Dameron. 20 Feb 1712/13.
　　　　6. pp 78-81
　　John. Re-recs Henry Mayes' will. 18 Nov 1713. 17.205
　　John. His runaway servts ret by Wm Barnes of Md. 22 Sept 1715.
　　　　6.135
　　John. Justice. 18 July 1717. 6.222
　　John. Admr of Richd Ruth whose dau Mary Ruth chooses him as
　　　　guardian. 18 Mar 1718/19. 6.308
　　Mr. John. Justice. 21 Jan 1719/20. 6.353
　　William. Will. d 4 June 1698. p 18 Sept 1700. of N Co.,
　　　　planter. Sick and weak of body. To eldest son William
　　　　und 21. To sons John and James und 21. To Anne Copage.
　　　　To Charles Coppage youngest child. Body to be laid as
　　　　near my wife as possible. Dau Anne to have "what Close
　　　　shall be found of her Mothers att my Decease". Refers
　　　　to present wife Jane. Not clear but appears that former
　　　　wife now deceased was mother of dau Anne and possibly
　　　　other or all of the children. Son Wm exor. Signed Wm
　　　　x Coppage. Wit: John Howson, Wm Browne. Wm Howson.
　　　　Re-rec 22 Feb. 1710/11. 17.15
　　Wm. Land adj Jno Webb. 5 Oct 1700. 17.265
　　Wm. Re-recs land 21 Mar 1710/11. 17.50. Also Re-recs Inv
　　　　Capt Jno Graham's est. 17 Dec. 1712. 17.193
　　Wm. Chosen as guardian by Mayes Fletcher. 19 Dec 1717. 6.253
　　Wm Sr. Deed father of Wm Jr and Charles. 18 May 1710. 17.50
Corbell, Clement. He and Saml Nicholls buy 300 a in N Co on S side
　　　　Potomacke River 11 Feb 1652/3. Saml Nicholls who m
　　　　the relict of sd Corbell assigns land to Jno Haynie.
　　　　20 May 1656. 14.80
　　Clem't. His son Clem't Corbell given a calf by Wm Cornish.
　　　　20 Jan 1656/7. 14.100
Corbin, Henry. His serv't Jos Woodman age 14. 26 Feb 1660/1. 2.137
　　Henry. Atty of Capt Jno Whitty. 21 Jan 1664/5. 17. pp 224-9
Corbin, Esq. Land adj Saml Churchill. 19 Dec 1705. 17.161
Cornish, Wm. Gives a calf to Clem't Corbell Jr. 20 Jan 1656/7. 14.100
　　Wm. On Jury to div land Saffin and Hull. 29 Nov 1669. 16.63
　　Wm. Who m relict of Ralph Key. 6 June 1661. 2.141
　　Wm. Wit will Saml Griffin. 2 Feb 1702/3. 17.213
　　Wm. Uncle of Wm Carpenter orph son of Wm C. 16 May 1716.
　　　　6.156

Cornwaleys, Tho. Esq., Aged 53 yrs or th-abts. Says in May 1652 he trusted Nicho: Bannister with goods val at 481 lb tobo "that he privately fled or absented himselfe out of the Province of Maryland where the debt was made" etc. Dated 14 January 1657. Sworn before Philip Calvert. 14.137

Cotrell, Jno and Lucretia his wife. Sued by Robt Davis and Susanna his wife. 17 June 1714. 6.47

Coudre, Dennis. Wit Jos Palmore's will. 26 March 1703. 17.9

Coure, Dennis. Wit deed Knight to Basie. 20 Nov 1705. 17.112

Cousins, Mr Jno. Formerly gave land to God-son Maurice son of Robt Jones. 14 Jan 1675/6. 17.244

Coutanceau, John. Age 17 yrs or th-abts. 20 May 1653. 14.27

    John. Will presented by Mr Jos Ball his exor. 21 January 1718/9. 6.296 Also see entry Wm Gradey. 17.152

    Peter, Justice. 21 July 1703. 17.127

    Peter. Will. Sworn 20 Apl 1709. Prob. 20 Apl 1709. Nuncupative. of St S. par. To eldest son Jno home plantation. To son Peter plantation called Quarter which was Chandler's patent. Then follows oath of Tho Hobson describing making of will and death of Cautanceau. David Straughan and Mary Price swear to Hobson's stmt. Re-rec by Mrs Kath: Palmer 22 Feb 1710/11. 17.20 Also complete Inv of est. 17. pp 216-221

    Peter. One of the sons of Peter C. decd, by Kath Palmer his guardian and nearest friend complains agt John Coutanceau son and heir of sd Peter C decd. Ref to the time of death of Peter C as 10 Dec 1709. This entry dated 17 Feb 1714/5. 6.96

    Peter, son of Peter who d 10 Dec 1709. That his father possessed 13 slaves. They descended to Jno C as eldest son of dec'd who left only 3 children, John, a dau Ann and Peter. and his widow who died before any div of the slaves. Kath Palmer guardian of dau Ann, etc. 17th Feb 1714/15. 6.96

    William. Son of Sarah Coutanceau Sen'r. Reg mark for cattle. 20 Jan 1658/9. 15.15A

Cowpen Swamp. Adj land of Richd Nelmes. 13 Apl 1706. 17.98

Cox, Ann. Bequest from Danl Suilavant. 29 Aug 1704. 17.261

    Charnock and Mary his wife. See entry re her brother Capt Peter Presly. 21 Jan 1719/20. 6.353

    James. Wit deed Bledsoe to Burno. 12 Feb 1705/6. 17.17

    Mary. Extrx of Peter Presley Jr. 19 Nov 1718. 6.296

    Vincent. An heir of Danl Suilevant. 29 Aug 1704. 17.261

    Wm. of Wicco par. Fined for 2 mos ab from Church. Prob a Quaker. 23 Sept 1715. 6.138

    Winnefred. Bequest from Danl Suilevant. 29 Aug 1704. 17.261

Crab, Wm. Age 15 or th-abt. 4 Aug 1665. 15.165

Cralle, Hannah. Presents will of Jno Harris dec'd (does not say relict or widow). 20 May 1719. 6.316

    Capt. Jno. Justice of N Co. 12 May 1710. 17.112

    John. Bondsman for Geo Eskridge. 17 Nov 1714. 6.89

Cralle, Tho and Hannah. Exors of Jno Harris decd. 20 Aug 1719. 6.331
Crane, Mr James. Land adj Loughly Conolin in St S par. 17 Apl 1700. 17.146
Crean, James (Crane). Wit deed Conolin to Hutson. 17 Apl 1700. 17.146
Craven, Charles. Exor of Wm Percyfull. See entry Eliz Persyfull his mother. 18 June 1718. 6.269
Crawford, Eliz: wife of John. 15 June 1692. 17.212
    Jno. 100 a on Chicacone assigned from Robt Hobbs 6 Dec 1683. Sells it to Jno Legg 15 June 1692. 17.212
    John. Deed. 15 July 1706, of N Co. Sells Meredeth James of N Co, 80 a near head of G.W. River adj Richd Nelmes and Partin Hudnall, excepting 10 yards square "where my father and mother lies". Wit: Edward Kilpatrick, Partin Hudnall, Rd Nutt. 17.229
    John (Crafford). Deed of Lease to Wm Davis. 20 Dec 1706. 17.94
    John. Orph son of Jno C., 9 yrs old next Christmas, bound to Jno Brown to be taught trade of tailor. 18th June 1718. 6.269
    Richd. (Crafford) His land adj Jno Crafford 20 Dec 1706. 17.94
    Richd. of Wicco par. Fined for 2 mos ab from Church. Prob a Quaker. 23 Sept 1715. 6.138
Crosby, Dan'l. Father of Geo: C. Bought land from Richd Aylett. 30th July 1662. 17.192
    Danl. Land adj Jno Hudnall. 25 July 1665. 17.28
    George. Signs Inv Tho Shapleigh, decd. 29 Sept 1703. 17.11
    George. Deed. 18 Oct 1705, of N Co, planter. Sells Tobias Purcell of Lanc Co planter, for L 120., 316 1/2 acres in St S par where Crosby lives. Adj land of Edward Sanders, Wm Nutt, Christopher Newton and Geo Nicholls. Part of a pat first granted Roger Walters and by him sold to Richd Aylett 22 Apl 1659, and by Aylett assigned to Daniel Crosby father of sd Geo 30 July 1662. Wit: James Innis, Tho Routt, Tho Hooper. Delivery Wit: 20 Nov 1705 by Jno Brown, John Hart, Hugh Coffy, Peter Wood. Re-rec 17 Dec 1712 by Christo: Newton. 17.192
Crosse, James. Wit Edw Neale's will. 4 Nov. 1700. 17.251
Cross, Richd. Wit will Jno Bowers Sr. 29 Sept 1704. 17.167
Crowder, Ariskam. Orphan son of Tho Crowder decd bound to Mary Knight till 21 "he being seven years old on the first day of last August", to be taught the trade of a weaver. 20th Sept 1715. 6.130
    Robert. App guardian of Hannah Powlter. 21 Jan 1660/1. 2.137
    Robert. Age 36 or th-abts. Mrs Anne Christmas his countrywoman. Exact date not shown but recorded the latter part of 1664. 15.136
    Robert. Orphan of Tho Crowder, bound to Tho Dameron "complains of Hard usage". To remain with Jno Ingram until complaint is answered. 22 March 1715/16. 6.152 See next entry.

Crowder, Robert. Orpht son of Tho Crowder, complains through Wm Dare of his master Tho Dameron. 18 Apl 1716. 6.154

    Tho. A child, son of Robt Crowder given a cow by Henr: Bently. 8 March 1663/4. 15.121

    Tho. Sold a black mare to Tho Brewer prior to 11 June 1697. 17.268

    Tho. Deed 18 Sept 1705. Thos Crowder of G W par and Fearnot his wife sell to Barth: Schrever of same par, for L 45. Sterl, 199 a on main swamp on W side of Corotomen River adj Scotts branch and Webb's land. Wit: Danl Feilding, Jno Joy, Saml Heath. Re-rec 20 Feb 1711/12 by Barth Schrever. 17.155

Crump, Jno. yeoman, of Washington par, Westmorland Co buys 250 acres in "Yeocomoco" par N. Co. from Jno Wright. 18 Sept 1707. Re-recs deed 15 Aug 1711. 17.128

    Also Nicho Callan, orphan abt 13 yrs of age, bound to John Crump to be taught trade of shoemaking. 16 March 1714/15. 6.100

Culpeper, Alex. Esq. One of the Propr No Neck. 10 Nov. 1694. 17.142

    Also Margaret, Lady Culpeper. Same entry.

Cultsalley, Andrew. Servant to Capt Maurice Jones adj to be 14 years old. 20 Aug 1718. 6.275

Cumins, Alexr et als. Deed 7 April 1707.
    Alexander Cumming and Sarah his wife)
    Henry Robinson and Mary his wife)
    Henry Bryan and Elizabeth his wife)
All of Wicco par, sell to Mark Harding of same par, for 5000 lb tobo, 50 acres. This land: whereas Robt Burrell late of N Co decd sold on 6 Dec 1669 to Valentine Munslow and Paul Littlefield, a neck of land in sd par, adj land where Burrell lived, which sd Munslow sold 11 Feb 1678/9 to Paul Littlefield, who assigned it on 19th of sd Feb to John Lyinum (this name may possibly be Lenham or Lynum) who with his wife Jane the 9th Feb 1685/6 sold it to John Multon (prob. John Muttoone) late of N co decd, and the sd John dieing without will and leaving no male heirs, the land descended to his daughters Sarah Cumings, Mary Robinson and Elizabeth Bryan. The land adj that of Tho Berry and Patience his wife. Deed signed by 6 parties. Wit: Timothy Higgins, John Champion. Re-rec 20 June 1711 by Mark Harding. 17.116

Cunningham, Thos. Wit deed Byram to Champion. 19 May 1708. 17.72

Cupid's Creek. Adj land of Jeffery Gooch. 21 March 1658/9. 15.18

    Also ref to as being in Wicco par 19 Nov 1707. 17.38

Cupid's Neck. Land of Jno Bayles. 18 Jan 1705/6. 17.180

Curtis, George. His wife formerly Patience Blundle. 16 May 1717. 6.215

    Pitts. Wit assignment Champion to Mahane. 5 Feb 1704/5. 17.71

Curtis, Pitts. Buys 200 a in G W par from Jno Champion. 3 Dec. 1709. Re-rec deed 17 Sept 1712. 17,186
    Pitts. Wit deed White to Smith. 17 Dec 1713. 19.3
Cussion, Richd. Servt to Mrs Eliz Kenner adj 13 yrs of age. 21 Dec. 1698. 4,848
Cussin, David. To have chg of Tho Salisbury's orphans. 3 March 1656/7 14,112
    David. Persecuted. His property sold. See entry Quakers. 26th June 1660. 2,128
    Fran: also Mary Cussons. As wit prove will of Dan Holland. 17 April 1672. 3,145
    John. Bequest of 50 shillings for a ring from Tho Steed. Also overseer of will. 2 Apl 1670. 16,149

Dabbs, Jno. Wit deed Bledsoe to Ingram. 14 July 1708. 17,22
Daingerfield, Jno. Aged 70 or th-abt. 28 Apl 1701. Essex Co Va Records. No. 10, p.84
Dameron, And: Presented for not going to church in Wicco par. 19 May 1714. 6,35
    Barth: Will d 1 Aug 1708. p 17 Nov 1708. Mentions son Barth Dameron Jr., son Christo:, son Josiah, son John und 21. Dau Eliz:, dau Sarah. Wife Eliz:, his bro John overseer of will. 17,57
    Bartholomew. Wit will Tho Ingram 12 Oct 1700. Prov by his oath 21 May 1707. 17,21
    Barth: Uncle to Tho Dameron Jr. Prob dec'd. 19 Feb 1705/6. 17, 55
    Barth: Buys land from Tho Dawson Jr 19 Feb 1705/6. 17,55
    Barth: Re. his runaway servts. 21 Aug 1673. 4,4
    Barth: To div est of Robt Jones. 21 Aug 1673. 4,2
    Charles. Presented for not going to church in Wicco par. 19 May 1714. 6,35
    George. To be pd for having a horse pressed. 16 Oct 1678. 4,7
    George. Deceased. Son of Laurence Dameron dec'd. Father of Thos Dameron Jr. 19 Feb 1705/6. 17,55
    George. Wit will Barth: Dameron. 8 Aug 1708. 17,57
    George. Wit will of Isaac Gaskins. 22 Oct 1709. 17,167
    George. Permitted to bring Dennis Tignor orph son of Phillip Tignor decd to next Court for examination (Dennis got a little out of hand) 19 Sept 1716. 6,182
    George. Phillip Tignor, orphan, bound to him. Robt Jones security. 16 Jan 1716/17. 6,187
    Josiah. Complained agt Jam: Johnson and Eliz Wooldridge on 4 Oct 1710 for trespass in St S par. They pleaded 21 Aug 1712, Not Guilty. On 8 Sept following a jury met with Mr Jno Copedge surveyor and reported 20 Feb 1712/13, that Copedge swore before Mr John Claughton, Justice, delivered a patent for 342 a. granted Laurence Dameron, decd, 10 Oct.1665. Report states land adj Dr Pemberton dec'd. Mattapony River, Henry Hutson, Jno Evans, Mr Jno Claughton, James Johnson. Dated 17 March 1712/13. 6 pp 78 to 81

Dameron, Josias. Re-rec deed Tho Dameron Jr to Barth Dameron, 21 Mar 1710/11. 17.55 Also re-rec will Barth Dameron 22 March 1710/11, 17. • 57
Josiah, m relict of Pemberton Claughton. See entry Jno Claughton. 17 May 1716. 6.159
Josiah, Chosen guardian by Sarah Dawson. 21 Jan 1718/9.6.297
Mrs Kath: wife of Thos. D. Jr. 19 Feb 1705/6. 17.55
Laurence. Claims 450 a for importation of 9 persons, incl himself and wife. 21 Feb 1658/9. 2.102
Laurence. Dorothy Dameron relict of Lew Dameron decd and Bartholomew Dameron his eldest son and Eliz his wife, give for love and affection "unto our Loving Brother Lawrence Dameron" all int in 324 a in Yeocomico par. 20 Nov. 1669. 16.145
Laurence. Grant from Sir Wm Berkeley Knt etc, 18 March 1662/3 342 a. in N Co, adj head of Yeocomoco River. This land formerly granted to sd Laurence 10 Oct 1655, now renewed. Re-rec 20 June 1711. Does not show who did. 17. 112
Laurence. Dec'd. Father of Geo. Gr-father of Tho.Jr. 19 Feb. 1705/6. 17.55
Laurence. Land adj Jno Claughton in Mattapony Neck, St. S.par. 18 Jan 1707/8. 17.89
Laurence. Father of Barth: 1 Aug 1708. 17.57
Laurence. Son of Barth:, Gr-son of Laurence. Formerly bought a mare from Coxe. 1 Aug 1708. 17.57
Laurence and Jane his wife circa 1713. See entry Steph Kean. 16 May 1717. 6.213
Thomas. Presented for being drunk on the Sabbath day about the month of August last past; by information of Lazarus Dameron. 16 Nov 1715. 6.143
Tho. An orphan bound to him, Robt Crowder "complains of hard usage", 22 March 1715/16. 6.152. Also reported as cruel to an orphan 18 Apl 1716. 6.154
Tho. Estate of Edwin Feilding orphan deliv to Jno Hill his guardian. 18 June 1719. 6.324
Tho. Junr. Wit will of Geo Bledsoe. 23 Jan 1704/5. 17.16
Tho. Junr. Son and heir to Geo D. decd. Deed to Barth Dameron 19 Feb 1705/6. 17.55
Tho. Junr. Complained agt by Jno Kean guardian of Steph Kean. 16 May 1717. 6.213
Mr. Thos. Senior. His land. 23 Jan 1704/5. 17.16
Dameron's land adj Gaskins in Gr. Wicco River. 16 Jan 1710/11. 17.80
Daniell, Tho. Wit deed Eyes to Fallon and Atkins. 26 Oct 1671.16.201
Tho. Wit deed Gibble to Price 16 Jan 1671/2. 17.156
Dare, Jeremiah. Servt to Jas Gardner adj 12 yrs of age. 18 Mar 1718/9. 6.309
William. P of A from Rd Chichester of Lancaster Co. 20 Nov 1706. 17 pp 224-229.
Mr. Wm. Re-rec will Joseph Hudnall 22 Mar 1710/11. 17.58
Wm. Re-recs deed Richd Robinson to his bro Saml R. 18 May 1711. 17. 105.

Dare, Wm. Re-recs will d 1677/8 of Richd Eaton on 19 Feb 1711/12. 17.158
    Wm. Atty for Wm Copedge. 17 Dec 1712. 17.193
    Wm. Re-recs deed d 1681 Brewer to Linsfield as atty for Mrs Mary Knight. 18 Nov 1713. 17.204
    Wm. Atty for Mrs Goodlove Jones. 18 Nov 1713. -6.2
    Wm. for Qu-Atornay 1000 lb tobo. 30 Dec 1713. 6.11
    Wm. Atty for Robt Crowder, orphan. 22 March 1715/16. 6.152
    Wm. Complains of Tho Dameron being cruel to an orphan. 18 April 1716. 6.154
Darling, Richd. headright of Capt Gyles Brent. 21 Jan 1651/2. 1.70
Darrell, Tho. decd. Admr of his estate to Edw Coles who m Elinor the widow. 15 Jan 1678/9. 4.18
Dasheild, Jas. His servt Jno Thomas age 13. 20 Apl 1860. 2.112
Daukes, Jno. decd. His est to be sold at outcry according to his will. 15 July 1696. 4.732
Davey, Walter. Headright of Wm Sheares. 21 Aug 1678. 4.4
Davis, Charles. Wit Col Geo Cooper's will. 18 Nov 1708. 17.123
    Hen: Wit P of A Theriatt to Maddison. 9 May 1665. 16.19
    Henry. Servt to Tho Downing adj 14 yrs of age. 21 Dec 1698. 4.847
Davies, James. Servt to Maj Brereton adj 17 yrs of age. 19 Jan 1675/6. 3.249
Davis, John. Land adj Jas Loughman. 7 Sept 1702.
    John. An orphan child now 14 yrs old chooses Richard Smith as guardian with Richd Smith Jr as security. 16th June 1714. 6.40
    Margary. Age 27 or th-abts. Exact date not shown but entry recorded latter part of 1664. 15.136
    Margritt. deceased. Thos and Edmond Cole and Simon White sons of Margritt Davis dec'd swear she left no will. Admr granted. 19 Feb 1717/18. 6.254
    Mary. Re-recs deed Salsbury to Barrett. 16 May 1711. 17.94
    Also re-recs deed Jno Crafford to Wm Davis. 16 May 1711. 17.94
    Mary. Isaac Swalmie an orphan aged 3 bound to her till 21. 12 March 1713/14. 6.18
    Reg: Reported for striking fish contrary to recent law. 22nd June 1669. 3.65
    Richd. Summoned to ans complaint of Richd Smith guardian of Jno Davis an orphan. 16 June 1714. 6.40
    Robert. Deed from Richd Orland and Margarett his wife. 16 Dec 1696. 4.752
    Robt and Susanna his wife. Mary Sharp bound to them. 16 June 1714. 6.42
    Robt and Susannah his wife against Jno Cotrell and Lucretia his wife to next Court. 17 June 1714. 6.47
    Robert. His land adj that sold by Josias White to Richd Smith. 17 Dec 1718. 19.3

Davis, Thomas and Mary his wife sell land to Wm Coppidge. Deed wit by Geo Chattell, Elis: De La briere, Jno Dennis and Rd Hardwood. 1 Oct. 1670. 16.165

Thomas. Bought land from Mr Jas Hill and sold it to Wm Coppege dec'd prior to 18 May 1710. 17.50

William. In charge of Henry orphan of Wm Metcalf. Also Susan Davis, her bequest from Wm Metcalfe pd 2 yrs since. 18 April 1657. 14.105

Wm. of N. Co., blacksmith. Deed of lease from Jno Crafford. 20 Dec 1706. 17.94

Dawes, Tho. Servt to Col Rd Lee adj 14 yrs of age. 7 March 1680/1. 2.139

Dawkins, Geo. 200 acres assigned from Jas White 4 Sept 1680. 17.120

Dawking, Geo. Buys land from Mary Roberts and Tho Timmons. See entry Mary Roberts. 16 Dec 1707. Re-recs deed 20 June 1711. 17. 114

Dawkins, Geo. Re-rec assignment d 4 Sept 1680, 200 acres from James White. 18 July 1711. 17.120

Geo. land assigned from Jas Nipper in Fairfield per 19 Oct 1700. Re-records it 18 July 1711. 17.120

Geo. Junr. App admr of Wm Warrick dec'd. 21 Mar 1716/17 6.202

Wm. wit deed Roberts and Timmons to Geo Dawking. 16 Dec 1707. 17.114

Dawson, Fra: Wit P of A Mrs Mary Gooch to Ro Nash. 15 Apl 1706. 17.195

Fra: wit deed Garner to Reeves 18 June 1706. 17.201. Also wit deed Garner to Grinstead. 18 June 1706. 17.202.

Hen: admr of Henry Dawson dec'd. 17 March 1714/15. 6.104

Hen: deceased. Cath: his widow now wife of Wm Wiltshire. 16 Nov. 1715. 6.144

Henry. Deed of Gift dated 13 Aug 1703. Gives Elizabeth Dawson grand-dau of sd Henry, and dau of Sarah Dawson, land where sd Sarah now lives. Wit names omitted. Re-rec by John Foushee on 19 Feb 1718. 17.249

Sarah, deceased. Elizabeth Foushee exhibits addl inventory. 21 Jan 1718/19. 6.297

Sarah. Orphan of Sarah Dawson, makes choice of Josiah Dameron as guardian. 21 Jan 1718/19. 6.297

William. Son of John Dawson, bound to James Claughton to be taught trade of cooper. To be free 20 April 1664. Entry dated 22 July 1661. 2.144

Wm. To be pd for taking care of Tho Quick now dec'd. 18 Mar 1684/5 4.257

Deacon, Mr Geo: Sues Henry Moseley for 323 lb tobo. 21 Jan 1668/9. 3.52

Deane, James Jr. Wit will of Tho Hall Sr. 10 Feb 1708/9. 17.163

Deawy, William. Servt to Jno Howson adj 14 yrs of age. 21 Dec 1698. 4.847

De Conti, Michaell. P of A to Jas Gaylard. Wit: Wm Wildey and John Sanson. 20 July 1671. 16.194

Deeds Quarter. In Wicco par. Was property of P Coutanceau dec'd.
20 Apl 1709. 17 pp 216-221
Delabriere, Andrew of G W par. Will. d 24 June 1670. p 20 July 1670.
Wife Elizabeth. Son Andrew. Dau Katherine. Trustees
Jno Taylor and Henry Mayes. Wit: John Taylor, Ric:
Sweetland, Geo Chattell. 16.137
Elizabeth. Wit deed Davis to Coppidge. 1 Oct 1670. 16.165
Delahay, Jno. Appr est of Ro Seagrave decd. 20 March 1649/50. 1.48
Tho. (prob a Quaker). Bequest of 10 shillings from Thomas
Steed. 2 April 1670. 16.149
Delaware. Ref to as "Deloway" in depo of Wm Dowdane. Recorded - Jan
1666/7. 16.9
Demeratt, Luke. Headright of Capt Jno Haynie. 15 July 1696. 4.733
Dennis, Barbary. widow. Gives her dau Mary Dennis 4 cows. 26 Dec 1664.
15. 139
John. Land adj Tho Gascoyne. 15 Sept 1649. 17.80
John. Signs oath to Commonwealth of England. 13 April 1652.
1. pp 72-73
John.(Account of cattle belonging to his children in hands of
(David Spiller:
(Richd Dennis   2 cows 1 heifer
(Paschall Dennis   "   "
(13 April 1657. 14.105
John. Wit deed Davis to Coppidge 1 Oct 1670. 16.165
John. Age 11 yrs. 21 Aug 1678. 4.1
Richard, Pasco and John. Ref to as "my sonnes" in David
Spiller's will. 21 Oct 1658. 15.11
Richd. Next of kin to Jno Nipper decd. 18 June 1718. 6.270
Walt: Values est of Jno Hull decd. 11 Jan 1668/9. 3.51
Walt. On jury Presly vs Mathew. 21 Jan 1668/9. 3.53
Dennis Creek. G W parish. adj land of Tho Williams. 26 Sept 1702.
17. pp 252-254. Also adj land of Jno Champion 3rd
Dec 1709. 17.186
Denny, David. Swears he wit will of Tho Haydon decd. 21 March 1716/17
Denns (Denny) Edmond of St S par. Deed from Jno Dunaway. Land at
head of G W River. 11 July 1706. Re-recs this deed
16 May 1711. 17.99
Denny, Fanwell. Orphan daughter of Edmd Denny dec'd being more than
12 yrs of age chooses Ambrose Feilding as guardian.
20 June 1716. 6.171
John. Court order that Ann Haydon, admr of Edmond Denny, pay
him a child's part of the estate. 18 Feb 1718/19.
6.300
Richd. Fined for absenting himself from church. 21 Jan 1713/14
6.16
Dermott, Mrs Anne. Wife of Charles Dermott. Mother of Elizabeth and
Robert Bradley. 4 April 1703. 17.12
Charles. Wit deed Jones to Claughton. 16 Nov 1699. 17.88
Cha: and also Anne Dermett. Wit will Saml Churchill. 4 June
1702. 17.229

Dermott, Charles, planter, deed from Wm Short. 1 Oct 1702. 17.13
    Charles. Will. d 4 Apl 1703. p. 17 May 1703. To son in law Robert Bradley land bought of Wm Short. To his sister Elizabeth Bradley. Wife Anne Dermott. All estate to wife and step children. Wit: Eliz Pemberton, Elizabeth Woodbridge and David Straughan who prove will. Re-rec by Robt Bradley 22 Feb 1710/11. 17.12
    Hugh of Cherry Point. Son of Owen Dermott (prob dec'd) 20th March 1702/3. 17.119
    Owen. Dorothy Waters a wit in suit agt David Gill. 16 May 1717. 6.215
Dew, Wm. Wit will Col Geo Cooper 18 Nov. 1708. 17.123
Dewell, Joane. Would assume this name phonetic or spelled wrong. That it is Dowlin. Wit codicil Jno Hull 16 Apl 1668. See P of A Hull to Hull same date (16.36) 16.60
Dewey see Deawy
Dickinson, Mrs Sarah. Formerly wife of Tho Hobson betw 1675 - 1683. See entry Col Tho Brereton. 6 pp 83-86
    Sarah. Sister of Jno Webb. 4 June 1709. 17.102
    Sarah. With Edw Sanders and Tho Webb exors of Jno Webb deed. 17 Feb 1714/15. 6.99 Also as extrx of Jno Webb acts for his dau Sarah Webb. 15 June 1715. 6.114
    Tho. Wit will of Steph Wells 31 Oct 1712. 19.12
Dickey, David. Wit Tho Knight's will. 1 Oct 1706. 17.43
Diggs, Edw. Patent to Coll R. Lee. 4 Mar 1656/7. 17.66
Dinnie, Walter. His servt Jeremiah Thomas adj 17 yrs of age. 19 Jan 1675/6. 3.249
Dirty Branch. Adj land of Jno Bayles in Cupids Neck. 18 Jan 1705/6. 17.180
Dividing Creek. Adj land Col Richd Lee and land of Tho Wilson marriner. 21 May 1651. 17.65
Dobbins, Ellener. daughter of James Dobbins. 3 June 1658. 15.3
Dodman, John. Wit deed Dodson to Ball. 16 May 1654. Westmorland Co. 1653 - 9. p 24
Dodson, Gervase of Westmorland Co. Sells 200 a in W Co to Geo Ball. Wit: Jno Dodman, Peter Knight. Westmorland Co 1653-9 p.24
    Gervase, surveyor, sells 1600 acres in Westmorland Co to John Dodman. 22 Aug 1654. Westmorland Co 1653-9 p.24
    Gervase (the following entries are all of Northumberland Co) Age 34 or th-abts. 20 Aug 1655. 14.52
    Ger: Sworn statement re his survey of Indian lands. Shows boundries, etc. 25 Feb 1655. 16.72
    Gervase. Gives a calf to John son of John Hulett. 20 May 1659. 15.21
    Gervase. Given 20 lashes for being a Quaker. See entry Quakers. 26 June 1660. 2.122
    Gervase. Will. Entry so mutilated as to be illegible. Tho will d. 7 Jan 1660/1. p. 6 June 1661. Isabel Dodson relict and extrx. 15.58

Dodson, Gervase. His widow Isabel in dif with Saml Man who m the widow of Jno Bennett. 21 Oct 1661. 2.148
 Gervase. His widow m Andrew Pettigrew. 8 Oct 1662. 2.163
 Jervas. Land adj Jno Hudnall. 25 July 1665. 17.28
 Jervise. Surveyor. Abra Joyce ran a chain for him 14 or 15 yrs ago for surveying land for Glebe. 23 Aug 1669. 16.93
 Gervase, gent, dec'd. Formerly gave Hen Boggus 100 acres, now sold to Eliz Hughlett. 24 Feb 1670/1. 16.162
 Mr Gervise, dec'd pat 750 a in G W par 27 Apl 1658 which devolved to Isabel the widow, now wife of Andrew Pettigrow. 17 May 1671. 16.223
 Thomas. Gave land to Jervas Dodson. 2 Oct 1660. 3.64
Doggitt, Benj: Wit will Robt Jones Sr. 14 Jan 1675/6. 17.244
Doharte, Jervas. Wit tfr land Leechman to Smith. 8 Feb 1708/9. 17.91
Doherty see Odohoty.
Domibielle, Simon. His admr, Jno Ayres, ord to pay debt of 496 lb tobo to Seth Foster. Also pay 450 lb "sweete well salted venison" to Humfry Tabb. Also 590 lb tobo to Rice Maddox. 10 Jan 1650/1. 1.46
Donaldson, Jno. Div 300 acres with Claudius Tulles. 20 July 1687. 17.127
 Mrs Mary. Wife of John Donaldson who was living 1687. She had been wife of Clement Arledge. 7 July 1703. 17.127
Doniphan, Alex. Wit P of A LeBreton to Mathew. 3 Apl 1671. 16.192
Donoway, John. His hogs stolen. 6 Apl 1669. 3.62
Donnoway, Jno. Reg mark for cattle. Also Frances Donnoway dau of sd John D. regs her mark. No date but Summer 1669. 16.87
Dorgan, Thaddeus and Joan his wife, servants of Timothy Greenham, agree to serve 1 yr above indentures in consideration he would keep them together. 18 Nov 1719. 6.345
Dorhoty, Neale. Servt to Jas Naper adj 15 yrs of age. 19 Jan 1675/6. 3.249
Dorrell, Tho and Elinor his wife in Virginia, planter. Elinor Bayly bound to them for 17 yrs. 13 Aug 1663. 15.167
Douglas, Jno. Wit deed Lambert to Myars. 16 Dec 1707. 17. pp 130-135
Douiouville, Saml. Wit will Geo Leasure. 17 Nov 1708. 17.59
Dovell, Rich. Headright of Jno Vaughan. 20 Nov 1651. 1.67
Dowlen, Joseph. Wit codicil to will of Jno Hull of Fairfield par. 16 April 1668. 16.97
Dowlin, Joseph. Also Joan Dowl:. Wit P of A Hull to Hull. 16 April 1668. 16.36
 Joseph. Wit codicil Jno Hull. 16 April 1668. 16.60
Downeman, Tho. His servt Danl Mackarty adj 15 yrs of age. 19 January 1675/6. 3.249
Downham, Jno. with Tho Gilbert buys 100 a from Jno Gibson. 3rd Dec 1666. 16.3

Dowlane, Wm. aged 19 or th-abts. Servt to James Phillips. Depo re Tho Barratt's urging him to steal clothes from his master and offer to convey him over the Potomac river and thence to "Deloway". No date but recorded January 1666/7. 16.9

Downing, Mr. Bought land from Martin Cole adj Capt Jno Whitty. 15 May 1661. 17. pp 224-229

Downing, Mr. Land adj Antho and Tho Robinson. 13 Jan 1700/1. 17.108

Downinge, Mrs. Land adj Jas Loughman at head of Wicco River. 7 Sept 1702. 17.202

   Elizabeth. decd. Will presented by Tho Hughlet, gent, exor. Proved by oaths of Jno Cole and Jame White, Witnesses. 19 Oct 1715. 6.140

   Mrs. Eliz: Conf judgt to Mr Jos Tipton. 17 July 1717. 6.221

Downing, George. His boundry line. 26 March 1703. 17.9

   Jno. Chosen for guardian by Jno Cockrell son of Adr Cockrell decd. 19 Oct 1681. 4.105

   Mr. Jno. Churchwarden of Fairfield parish. 4 June 1684. 4.233

   John. Security for Jno Houghton and Dorothy his wife when Wm Powell, age 3 1/2, is bound to them. 5 Oct 1687. 4.404

   John. Atty of Sam Tipton. Sues Richd Rout. 6 Oct 1687. 4.407

   John. Bought 300 acres from Capt Tho Brereton. 12 June 1688. 6. pp 83-86

   John. See affidavit of Tho Hobson. 17.110

   John. Justice. 21 Sept 1692. 4.599

   Mr. John. Justice 19 Apl 1693. 4.619

   John. Jno Dunaway Jr his witness agt Jno Dunaway decd. 21 May 1696. 4.725

   Mr John. Justice. 16 July 1696. 4.734.

   Mr. John. Justice 18 Dec 1696. 4.755

   Margarett. Wit assignmt 200 a from White to Dawkins. 4 Sept 1680. 17.120

   Mrs Patience. Now wife of Danl Neale. 21 May 1696. 4.726

   Peter. See affidavit Tho Hobson. 17.110

   Saml. decd. Will presented by Eliz Downing Extrx and proved by oaths of Joseph Tipton and Eliz Cockrell wits. 19 Oct 1715. 6.141

   Thomas. His servt Henry Davis adj 14 yrs of age. 21 Dec 1698. 4.847

   Thos. Re his boundry line. Exor of Jos Palmore. 26 Mar 1703. 17.9

   Tho. Div land betw Capt Jno Howson and orphan of Capt Wm. Howson. 15 April 1706. 17.42

   Wm. Selected guardian by Jno Hudnall. 28 Jan 1661/2. 2.151

   Wm. His servt Christo: Little age 13. 26 Feb 1660/1. 2.137

   Wm. Gives a colt to his son John Downing. 15 Apl 1671. 16.166

Downing, William. His servt Cornelius Valey adj 15 yrs of age. 17th
    April 1672. 3.144
    Mr Wm. Security on bond of Mrs Mary Thomas admr Wm Thomas
        for 70000 lb tobo. 16 Oct. 1678. 4.6
    Wm. Wit assignmt 200 acres White to Dawkins. 4 Sept 1680.
        17.120
    Wm. See affidavit Tho Hobson. 17.110
    Wm. Jr. His servt Dav Mag-gone adj 12 yrs of age. 19 Jan
        1675/6. 3.249
    Wm. Jr. and Wm. Sr. to appraise est of Jno Lee decd. 16 Oct
        1676. 4.6
    Wm. Jr. to app est of Wm Perriman. 16 Oct 1678. 4.7
    Mr Wm. Jr. Bondsman 30000 lb tobo for Sarah Lee admr of Jno
        Lee decd. 17 Oct 1678. 4.8
    Wm. Jr. His servt Susan Hall adj 9 yrs of age. 15 Jan 1678/9
        4.18
    Will: Sr. His servt Danl Hall adj 8 yrs of age. 15th Jany
        1678/9. 4.18
Drake, Phillip. Wit deed Howes to Hill. 15 Nov 1671. 16.204
    Phillip. Bought land in Mattaponi from Adam Booth. 28 March
        1680. 17.233
    Phil. Oath re Mrs Mary Barnes' child held by Rd Cox. 19 Oct
        1681. 4.106
    Phillip. Dec'd. Will d 9 Apl 1699 leaves land to Philip Bussle
        and Jane his wife. The will prob 21 June 1699.
        17.233
Draper, Jos. On jury Saffin vs Thompson. 6 Apl 1669. 3.63
    Josias. Pat land in G W par prior to 1670. 17. pp 76-78
Drapers Branch. Adj land of Jas Hill. 15 June 1709. 17.78
Drew, Victor. To take charge of hands (laborers) of Mr Xpher Neale.
    Agreemt unsatisfactory. 17 Oct 1678. 4.10
Driscoll, Florence. Wit agreemt Parker and Wood. 10 Mar 1669/70.
    16.165 Also wit will Hen Lambert 31 March 1670. 16.72
Drury, Mary, an Irish girl abt 7 yrs old assigned to Mrs Anna Cole
    wife of Richd Cole. 30 Aug 1658. 15.11
Dryer, Alice. Servt to Tho Williams having runaway 10 weeks and 3
    days ord to serve extra time. 6 Apl 1669. 3.62
Ducket, Jno. To serve Rd Nelmes 4 yrs. 8 Oct 1662. 2.163
Dudson, Sym: Depo in Ashton-Lindsay scandle. 4 Aug 1665. 15.163
    Symon. Age 30. 4 Aug 1665. 15.166
    Symon. Values est of Jno Hull decd. 11 Jan 1668/9. 3.51
    Sym: to pay arrears in levies from est of Capt Wm Nutt decd.
        11 Jan 1668/9. 3.50
Duke, Tho. headright of Wm Sheares. 21 Aug 1678. 4.4
Dunaway, Danl. Wit will Eliz Bledsoe 13 Feb 1707/8. 17.55
    Danl. His wife Jane formerly wife of Jno Wall decd. 18 Mar
        1713/14. 6.29
    James. As wit proves will of Patrick Keeve. 18 June 1718.
        6.268

Dunaway, Jno. Dennis Eyes gives him his home plantation. Refs to him as "my very good friend and Son Law John Dunaway" 20 May 1667. 16.17
    Jno. "and Margrett my now wife" buy land from Jas Hill and assign it to Benj Brown same date. 8 July 1702. 17.174
    Jno. deceased. His est indebted to Kath: Dunaway his widow for funeral and other expenses. 21 May 1696. 4.725
    Jno. Sells Benj Browne land in G W par. 15 July 1702. 17.75
    Jno. (Donoway) of G W par, planter. Deed to Edmond Denne (Denny). 11 July 1706. 17.99
    Jno. of G W par, planter, sells 100 a to Steph: Chilton and John Chilton and Mary his wife. 3 Sept 1708. 17.76
    Jno. Wit deed Browne to Murdock. 16 Nov 1708. 17.158
    Jno. lately lived on land sold by Jas Hill to Chiltons. 15 June 1709. 17.78
    Jno. Suit agt him and Enoch Hill by Exors of Jno Webb dismissed. 17 Feb 1714/15. 6.99
    Jno. Fined for ab from church in St S par. 23 Sept 1715. 6.138
    John, Junior. Having attended 14 days as an evidence in behalf of Mr Jno Downing agt John Dunaway dec'd to have 40 lb tobo per day. 21 May 1696. 4.725
    Margaret. Wife of Jno. Dau of James Hill. 16 July 1706. 17.99 Also wife of Jno. 17 Nov 1708. 17.76-8
Dunaway, various. Deed. 11 March 1705/6. Kath:, Abraham and Daniel Dunaway of N Co, sell Tho Moon land at head of G W, adj land of Richd Russell, Mr Hughlett's branch, the main road called the Rowling Road. Likewise it is alleged that Jno., Saml and Joseph Dunaway have a small title to the land, they therefore join in the deed. Wit: Benj Browne, Jno Lansdell. Re-rec 16 Jan 1711/12 by Elenour the widdo of Tho Moon decd. 17.150
Dunkinton, Tho. who m widow of Robt Lord app admr of his est. 10 Mar 1661/2. 2.154
Dunne, Walter. Gives a heifer to Mary Cornish dau of Wm Cornish. 20 Dec 1671. 16.214
Durant, Geo. Age 25 yrs or th-abts. 20 July 1658. 15.7
Dyer, Hannah. Her mistress Mrs Rachel Phillpot acquitted of her murder. 14 Nov. 1660. 2.134
    Thomas. buys land from Tho Towers. 18 Oct 1670. 16.201
Dyne, Luke. Signs oath to Commonwealth of England. 13 Apl 1652. 1. 72-3
    Luke. Age 27 or th-abts. 21 July 1656. 14.86

Earle, Mary the younger. Given a calf by James Willis. 22 Jan 1651/2. 1.71
East, Wm. headright of Wm Sheares. 21 Aug 1678. 4.4
Eaton, Richd. Owes by bill, 200 lb tobo to John Pearse. 17 Feb. 1663. 16.37
 Richd. Long deposition. Age not shown, but much family detail. See entry Adam Yarratt. 22 Oct 1667. 16.25
 Richd. Will. d 13 Mar 1677/8. p 20 March 1677/8. To son Richd land bought of Mr Jno Haynie and Mr Jno Hughlett. To Francis Brittain land bought of Mr Francis Clay. To Debora Allinson. Son Richd to stay with his brother in law Francis Brittain till 21. Wit: Jno Church and Jno Hamond. Re-rec by Mr Wm Dare 19 Feb 1711/12. 17.158
Edmonds, Geo. Servt to Jno Williams adj 13 yrs of age. 21 Jan 1660/1 2.136
 Joseph. P of A to Rob Sech. 17 Feb 1664/5. 16.13 Also see entry Wm Gradey. 17.152
Edwards, Charles. Son of Nicholas Edwards decd. David and Ann Spence ord to answer his petition. 16 Sept 1719. 6.337
 Isaac. Bought land from Richd Gibble prior to 16 Jan 1671/2. 17. 156
 Isaac. Wit Smith to Nelmes. 16 Dec. 1710
 Isaac. Chosen guardian by Joshua Nelms. 21 Mar 1716/17. 6.201
 John. Sold land on N side G W river to Mr Downing prior to 15 May 1661. 17. pp 224-229
 Nicho: Appraisal of estate. 2 1/3 pages. No date shown but rerecorded 18 June 1712. Peter Presly, one of the appraisers says this was a rough copy. 17. pp 169-71
 Nicho: David Spence and Ann his wife admrs. 17 June 1714. 6.47
 Thomas. P of A re tfr of land to Jas Robinson. 18 February 1669/70. 16.70
 Thomas. Will 9 March 1669/70. To friend Dennis Eys 100 acres bought of Jas Robinson. To Tho Aldwell a castor. To Davi Jennis a great coat. Bal of est to Tho Mould. Wit: Tho Aldwell. Chas: Valon. 16.71
Eeale, Humphrey. Servt to Phill Shaply adj 13 yrs of age. 19 January 1675/6. 3.249
Elder, Edmond. Bought land in Mattaponi from Nathl Hickman prior to 1699. Appears to be abt 1680. This mentioned 15 Sept 1703. 17.233
Elliott, Edw. Wit deed Holland to Warner. 20 Feb 1671/2. 16.230
 Edw. Sues Joane, admr of Jno Rogers Jr., for bal due from April 1679 on 1302 lb tobo. 20 Apl 1681. 4.92
 Edw. deceased. Prob of his will to Saml Sanford who m Eliz his extrx. 16 Sept 1685. 4.291. Also same date and page his extrx Eliz Keen m Saml Sanford.
Ellistone, Geo. Age 21 yrs. No date but recorded Jan 1666/7. 16.9
 Geo. See entry Jno Saffin. 21 Aug 1669. 16.62

Ellstone, Garvis. Petitions regarding Jno Reed a poor orphan child.
21 March 1716/17. 6.201
Ellistone, Jarvass. Wit will of Jno Harris. 20 Sept 1718. 19.44
Embry, Jno. Land assigned to him by Hen Robinson. 28 July 1704. 17.153
English, Alice. Deposition but age not shown. 4 Aug 1665. 15.166
 Geo. His servt Robt Stiles age betw 16 and 17. 14 Nov 1660.
  2.134 Also ref to his servt Jno Serves 21 Jan
  1660/1. 2.136
 Tho: Wit will Rd Sutton 1 Feb 1702/3. 17.172
Ennis, Jas. Exor of Jno Eustace. 23 Dec 1701. 17.245
Ennis see Innis.
Erwin, Mr Jones. For some time past an inhabitant of this Co. Certificate for leaving the Colony. 1 Apl 1723. 6.359
 John. Wit deed Pope to Boyd. 1 Jan 1703/4. 17.194
Eskridge, George. Wit deed Loughman to Scott 7 Sept 1702. 17.202
 P of A from Rd Chichester 20 Nov 1706. 17.224-9
 Wit deed Lee to Lee. 15 Feb 1707/8. 17.60
 Wit will Geo Leasure 17 Nov 1708. 17.59
 Wit deed Bomum to Hudnall 20 Sept 1709. 17.177
 Re-rec will Geo Leasure 22 Mar 1710/11. 17.59
 App by Gov. agt at Coan Storehouse on Coan River
 his bondsman Jno Cralle. 17 Nov 1714. 6.89
 Atty for Peter Hamond's orphans 16 Feb 1715/16
 6.150
 Atty for Wm Pickering 17 May 1716. 6.163
 App guardian of Allen Hunter 20 Sept 1717. 6.249
Essex, Bridget Junior. "wee Jno Essex and Wm Flower for our naturall affection that wee beare unto Bridget Essex Junior" give a 3 yr old heifer. 17 Apl 1672. 16.229
 John. In legal dif agt Tho Rice. 20 Feb 1651/2. 1.50-
 John. Signs oath to Commonwealth of England. 13 Apl 1652.
  1. 72-3
 John. Tho Kingwell bound to him till 21. 20 Nov 1655. 14.56
 John. Aged 36 or th-abts. Says he heard Jno Gresham had changed a cow with his dau Mary, etc. Also ref to Martha dau of Jno Gresham. 20 May 1656. 14.77
 Jno. 500 acres assigned from Andrew Bowyer 1663. Essex sells it to Tho Lane 8 Feb 1668/9. 17.255
 Jno. of Rappa Co. P of A to Saml Bayly of G W. Wit Tho Wilson, David Kuffin. 9 Feb 1671/2. 16.225
Eustace, Mr John and Mr Wm Jones ask release from admr bond on est of Mr Erasmus Withers decd, Mr Jno Curtis having m the admr. 20 July 1687. 4.400
 Jno. Owed 400 lb tobo by Jno Guy who he has arrested. 20th Sept 1696. Lancaster Co Records. No.22 p 2.
 John of N. Co. Will. d 23 Dec 1701. p 15 Apl 1702. A ring to Maurice Jones. To Tho Pinchard and Margt his wife. To Jno Steptoe. To John Husk. Other legatees illegible - Wm W-wn and Eliz his wife (?) - Maurice Linenah (?) on day of his freedom. To John Cooks. To son Wm Eustace und 18. To Geo Wale. Mentions wife but does not give her name. Exors Tho Pinkard, Jas Ennis, Jno Steptoe. 17.245

Eustace, John of N. Co. His widow Elizabeth now wife of Jno Steptoe.
  16 Nov 1719. 19.73
    John. His will prob 15 Apl 1702 re-rec by Richd Lee. 21st
      Jan 1718/9. 17.245
Evans, Elizabeth. Servt to Mrs Grace Hopkins ran away with Isaac
      Hudson. To be punished by Sheriff and both ret'd
      to their mistress. 21 Jan 1668/9. 3.51
Evans, Mrs Eliz:, widow, requests her dower rights. Robt Sech, Thomas
      Adams, Richd Flynt and Peter Flynt to meet at her
      plantation "and Assort her said Dower". 6th Oct
      1687. 4.407
    John. Has been owed 450 lb tobo by Roger Williams since 28th
      Nov 1867, etc. 11 Jan 1668/9. 3.50
    John. Owed 372 lb tobo by Walt: Prior. 21 Jan 1668/9. 3.55
    John. Sues Wm Wathen. 23 June 1669. 3.68
Eveins, Jno. Buys land from Miles Goreham and Alice his wife. 18 Jan
      1671/2. 16.225
Evans, Jno. Appointed Constable Upper Great Wicco: 18 May 1687. 4.394
    Jno. Land adj Josiah Dameron 17 March 1712/13. 6. pp 78-81
    Philip. Wit P of A Edmonds to Sech. 17 Feb 1664/5. 16.13
    Phillip. Land adj Hugh Harris. 20 Apl 1681. 17.251
    Thos. Land he bought from Robt Bradley to be surveyed. James
      Claughton complains of his falling timber on his
      land. 16 Oct 1678. 4.7
Eve, Eves, Ize see Eyes.
Everett, Tho. Two orphans Wm and Matthew Garratt bound to him. He to
      teach them shoemaking. 12 Mar 1713/14. 6.21
    Tho. Security for Mrs Sarah Haynie. 19 May 1714. 6.33
Everitt, Tho. Exor of Wm Persyfull. See entry Eliz Percyfull, his
      mother. 18 June 1718. 6.269
Eyes, Mr. having sold pistols etc to Dennis Conaway. 15 June 1709.
      17.19
    Dennis (Ize). Deed of Gift. Land whereon I now live to "my very
      good friend and Son Law John Dunaway". 20th May
      1667. 16.17
    Dennis. P of A from Tho Mould to ack tfr of land. 18 February
      1669/70. 16.70
    Dennis (Eys) Bequest from Tho Edwards. 9 Mar 1669/70. 16.71
    Dennis. Sells Charles Fallon and Joshua Atkins 370 acres. His
      wife Hannah Eyes agrees. Wit: Tho Daniell and
      Tho Aldwell. 26 Oct 1671. 16.201
    Dennis. Wit deed Gibble to Price. 16 Jan 1671/2. 17.156
    Dennis (Eyse). His servt Samll Cammell adj 12 yrs of age. 19th
      Jan. 1675/6. 3.249
Eves, Graves. Withholds will of Jno Jones decd. 18 Nov 1713. 6.2
    Graves. Son in law to Goodlove Matthews. 12 March 1713/14. 6.23
Eyes, Mary, formerly wife of Dennis Eyes decd, by Richd Haynie her
      attorney, claims dower rights in land now in poss.
      of Jno Conway. 22 Nov. 1716. 6.186
Eves, Tho. Chain Carrier on survey. 5 June 1710. 17.50

Eve, Tho. His house robbed. See entry Roger Moor. 15 Aug 1716. 6,171
Eves, Tho. Wit deed White to Smith. 17 Dec 1718. 19,3
    William. Arrested in debt of 2115 lb tobo due Maj Jno West.
        Failed to appear. 17 Oct 1676. 4,9
Exeter Lodge. See entry Jno Saffin. 21 Aug 1669. 16,62

Fagan, Jno. Servt to Phill Norgate adj 12 yrs of age. 28 Dec 1687.
    4,416
Fairfax, Ferdinando. Age 19 yrs or th=abts. That in 1655 he was on
    the ship "Golden Fortune" etc. 22 Feb 1655/6.
    14,70
Fairefeilds. Bought by Wm Wildey from Capt Jno Whitty. 21 Jan 1664/5
    17. pp 224-229
Fairfield. Church in F. par. "To the Church wardens for Nayles, Tymber
    carying in the tymbor of the Church, and takeing the
    sap of the boards. . . 4425 lb tobo" Listed under
    Fairfield par in County charges 5 Nov 1668. 3,47
Faizell, Francisco. Wit will of Antho Haynie. 31 Jan 1709/10. 17,107
Fallon, Charles. He and Joshua Atkins buy 370 a from Dennis Eyes. 26
    Oct 1671. 16,201
    Charles. (Fallons) Will. d 17 Dec 1700. p 16 Apl 1701. Sick
    and weak in body. To son Dennis Fallon land adj Saml
    Webb's spring branch. To sons Charles and William.
    Wife Jane, she sole extrx. Wit Bonja: Browne, Else x
    Fallin, Jno Hogan. Provod by oaths of Browne and
    Hogan. Re-rec 19 March 1711/12 by Wm Fallin. 17,159
Fallin, Dennis. Wit " deed Locchman to Tho Jones 8 Feb 1708/9. Also
    wit tfr 18 July 1709. 17,91
    Dennis. Re-rec will Wm Tignor. 19 Mar 1711/12. 17,160
    Dennis. Adm'r Wm Godwyn. 12 March 1713/14. 6,20
Fallon, Jane. Presented for not going to church in Wicco: par. 19th
    May 1714. 6,35
Fallin, Dennis. Guardian of Philip Tignor. 20 Jan 1719/20. 6,352
Fantleroy, Mr Griffin. Justice. 17 Feb 1713/14. 6,17
Farguson, Andrew. Servt to Charles Mooreland adj 11 yrs of age. 16th
    Nov. 1698. 4,482
Farlowe, Wm. Adjudged 12 yrs of age. 9 May 1660. 2,122
Farnefold, Mr Jno., minister of Great Wickocomicoe. P of A from John
    Browne of Bristoll, mercht, to collect accounts.
    30 Aug. 1670. " " : " 16,143
    John. Wit deed of gift Mary Mottly to Jno Mottley. 23 Oct
    1671. 16,198
    Mr Jno. Presided at Vestry meeting Chicacone par. 20 March
    1671/2. 16,158
    Mr. Jno. His servt Edw Killpatrick adj 12 yrs of age. 19th
    Jan 1675/6. 3,249
    John of Chiccacone par., Gent., buys 300 acres on S side
    Wicco: River. See entry Peter Knight. 19 April 1676.
    17,230

Farnefold, Rev. John. 600 lb tobo is pd him for funeral sermon for Mr Charles Morgan. 15 June 1681. 4.97
    Rev. Jno. Wit will Hen: Franklin 11 Nov 1698. 17.124
    John. Will. d 3 July 1702. p 16 Sept 1702. Of St S par., minister. To be bur 'by my wife Mary' in the garden. To dau in law Eliz: Tarpley. To son in law Richd Nutt and to Anne his wife. To Farnefold Nutt his son. To my 'cozen' Rawleigh Travers' wife. To Rebecca Travers my wife's picture. To each church in this par a chalice of silver for communion, price L 5. each, to have this inscription on them: "Ex:do:Johannis Farnefold". And "that my Executors provide two Grave Stones about a yd long for my selfe and my wife Mary on her Grave Stone this Inscription here lyes the body of Mary Farnefold the wife of John Farnefold the daughter of Mr George Rookes mercht in London and on the other this Inscription here lyes the body of John Farnefold minister the Son of Sir Thomas Farnefold of Gatewickes in Stayning in the County of Sussex Knight". Gives 100 acres of land "where I now live" for a free school and to be called Winchester School for 4 or 5 poor children. That Mr Tarpley, Mr Leon'd Howson, Rich'd Nutt and Edward Cole carry him to his grave. Ref to a bill for tobo owed by Coll Geo Cooper. Ref to Farnefold Nutt son of Richd Nutt. Exors Major Rod'm Kenner, Capt Hack, Mr Christopher Neale, Mr John Haynie and Mr Tho Hobson. Wit: Chas: x Nelmes, Wm x Nelmes, Simon Thompson. Re-rec 19 Sept 1716 by Tho Hobson. 17. 234

Farrar, John. Servt to Jno Motley adj 13 yrs of age. 19 Jan 1675/6. 3.249
Fauntleroy, Griffin. Gr-son of Saml Griffin and son of Wm Fauntleroy. 2 Feb 1702/3. 17.213 Also he re-recs will Saml Griffin 15 Sept 1714. 17.215
    Griffin. As Churchwarden of St S par he sues George and Patience Curtis. 16 May 1717. 6.215
    Moore. See entry Saml Griffin. 2 Feb 1702/3. 17.213
    William   "   "   "   "
Fausitt, Jno. Wit deed Saffell to Hudnall. 20 Nov 1655. 14.59
Faver, Mary decd. Bequests to her children, not individually named in the will of her father Steph: Wells, 31st Oct 1712. 19.12
Feild, John. Wit. See entry Jno Ingram. 29 Apl 1670. 16.76
Feilding, Ambrose. On jury to try Jno Saffin. 21 Jan 1668/9. 3.53
    Ambrose. Atty of Mr Edw Feilding ord to pay Jno Symmons a feather bed and other goods which "the sd Mr Edw Feilding did not send in". 6 April 1669. 3.62

Feilding, Mr Ambr: This day sworn Justice. 22 June 1669. 3.64
Ambrose, deceased. His est to be appraised. 17 Mar 1674/5 3.114
Mr. Ambros. Wit div of land betw Wm and Charles Copedge. 5th June 1710. 17.50
Ambrose. Security for Alice Nelms. 15 May 1717. 6.209
Ambrose. Chosen guardian by Fanwell Denny. 20 June 1716. 6.171
Danl. Wit will Jno Lewis. 4 July 1702. 17.223 Also wit deed Crowder to Schrever. 18 Sept 1705. 17.155 Also wit codicil to Hancock Lee's will 18 May 1709 and proved it 20 July 1709. 17.29
Edward. Arrests Jno Harris. See entry his name. 19 Febry 1678/9. 4.26
Mr. Edw. 2718 lb tobo owed him by Capt Peter Knight. 16th Oct 1678. 4.5
Mr. Edw. Jno Hudnall atty of Jno Palmer conf judgt to him for 6000 lb tobo. 17 Oct 1678. 4.8
Edw. As exor of Mr Tho Jones decd is sued by Danl Neale for 400 lb tobo. 21 May 1696. 4.726
Edwin. a minor. His est in hands of Tho Dameron del to Jno Hill his guardian. 18 June 1719. 6.324
John. On jury to div land betw Saffin and Hull. 29 Nov 1669. 16.63
John, decd. See entry Owen Jones and Rachel his wife. 19th Sept 1716. 6.182
John, decd. His dau Rachel now wife of Owen Jones. 10 Oct. 1718. 19.8
Joseph. Wit deed Gibble to Smyth. 4 March 1657/8. 16.13
Joseph who m the widow of Jno Bailes. 21 Oct 1661. 2.148
Joseph. Guardian of Rosamond, Anne and Eliz Bailes orphans of Jno Bailes. 20 July 1663. 15.105
Joseph. Wit deed of gift Island to Gregory. 20 June 1666. 16.3
Joseph Jr son of Joseph Feilding given a heifer by Richard Island. 20 June 1666. 16.15
Joseph. 400 acres assigned to him by Wm Ballingall. 20 Jan 1666/7. 16.4
Joseph. On jury Evans vs Wathen. 23 June 1669. 3.68
Joseph. Submits a/c of cattle of Eliz Bayles orphan of John Bayles. 22 Aug 1670.
Richard. Will. d 16 July 1666. p 8 Apl 1667. To bro Mr Robt Feilding of Gloucestershire. To sister Eliz: Gwyn of Horton in Gloucestershire. To "Bro:law" Giles Monning and his now wife. To Francis Monning eldest son of Giles Monning. To "Bro:law" Francis Monning and his now wife, if they have a son or if they have a dau. To sister Margaret Fryer, her husband Walter Fryer to have nothing to do with the bequest (L 20.) the money to be paid by the executors to Jno Cooke
(continued next page)

Feilding, Richard. His will (continued) of Bristol and by him to her.
To brother Ambrose Feilding land in Great Wicco:
and all on it, he following orders from "my brother
Mr Edw Feilding" and at his death to Richard Feild-
ing the son of Ambrose.
To brother Edward Feilding in Bristol all part in
ship Phoenix and cargo on board, he exor.
Wit: Tho Brereton, Wm Brereton, Wm Morgan, John
Salter. 16.12

Feilding, Richd. His nuncupative will presented by Ambrose Feilding.
Admr granted. 20 Sept 1717. 6.248

Fell, Owen. Servt to Tho Williams adj to be 9 yrs of age. 10th Mar 1661/2. 2.153

Fenner, Richd. headright of Lau: Dameron. 21 Feb 1658/9. 2.102

Ferebee, Jno. P of A from Cornelius Johnson. 16 Oct 1667. 16.24

Ferne, Tho: to clear the roads from Scotland Mill to Doggetts hole.
20 Nov 1696. 4.750

Tho: Prob of his will granted Martha Ferne. 21 Dec 1698. 4.846

Ferry Point. Adj land of And: Salsbury. 3 July 1701. 17.95

Field, Jno. Wit receipt Ingram to Harris. 29 Apl 1670. 16.128

Fighting Creek Swamp or Howson' Creek, adj land of Wm and Charles
Copedge. 18 May 1710. 17.50

Finch, Jno. Signs oath to Commonwealth of England. 13 Apl 1652. 1.72

Fish - Law agt striking with harping irons, fish gigs etc. 6 Apl 1669.
3.63

Fisher, Fran: Arrested at suit of Saml Bradley who failed to appear.
Nonsuit to Fisher. 20 Nov 1668. 3.48

William. 335 lb tobo in his hands belonging to Jno Fountayne
attached by Mrs Eliz Tyngey. 21 Jan 1668/9. 3.54

Wm. his land adj Hugh Dermott. 20 Mar 1702/3. 17.119

Fishing Creek. Land of Capt Leond Howson decd there. 15 Apl 1706.
17.42 Also adj land of Malachi Burbery, William
and Charles Copedge. 10 May 1710. 17.50

Fitzhugh, Mr Wm. See entry Hen: Fleet. 19 Nov 1685. 4.313 Also Agent
for Prop: No. Neck. 10 Nov 1694. 17.142

Fleet, Mrs Elizabeth. Wife of Henry Fleet and dau of Wm and Jane
Wildey. 11 Apl 1701. 17 pp 224-229

Capt Henry. Jno Ingram of N Co sells Henry Fleet gent of
Lancaster Co a cow. Wit Peter Knight. 29 Jan 1653.
14.58

Capt Hen: Assigns a cow to Theodor Baker. Wit Jno Grisham,
Samman x Scott. 15 Nov 1655

Lt Coll Henry. P of A to Jno Stevens to collect debts. Wit Wm
Clapham, Tho Mansoy. 12 Sept 1657. 15.10

Capt Henry. Bill to him from Mr Thomas Reade for 2000 lb tobo
dated 20 March 1654/5. Wit Teague Floyne. Recorded
21 Nov 1657. 14.127

Lt Coll Henry. "liveing out of this county" attachment to Geo
Cololough 460 lb tobo agt any est to be found in
this Co. 20 Jan 1658/9. 2.100

Fleet, Mr Hen: Arrested Pet: Comodo and not appearing, nonsuit to
    Comodo. 16 Aug 1682. 4,142
  Mrs. Eliz: She and her mother Mrs Jane Wildey fined for not
    appearing as evidence in dif betw Xphr Kirk and Eliz
    Williams. 18 July 1683. 4,190
  Mr Henry. By bill dated 13 Dec 1684 is indebted to Capt Thos
    Jones, the assignee of Mr Wm Fitzhugh L 5. Sterl.
    Judgt to Jones agt him. 19 Nov 1685. 4,513
  Henry. Arrested at suit of Tho Hobson for 10000 lb tobo and
    cask and not appearing. judgt to Hobson. 6 Oct 1687.
    4. 409
  Henry. His wife Eliz dau of Wm and Jane Wildey. 11 April 1701.
    17. pp 224-9
  Capt Henry. Prob will of James Wildey, decd., he Exor. 19th
    Nov. 1701. 5,180
  John (Fleete). headright of Capt Gyles Brent. 21 Jan 1651/2.
    1,70
Fleet's Bay. in Northumberland Co. See will Robt Jones Sr. 14th Jan
    1675/6. 17,244
Fleet's Point. Adj Mulberry Fields belonging to Capt Tho Brereston.
    23 March 1698/99. 17,189 Also Robt Jones surveyor
    of highway to: 22 Aug 1718. 6,292
Fleming, Alexr. Wit P of A Salisbury to Salisbury. 21 Jan 1670/1.
    16,147
  Alex: "being ancient person" excluded from levy. 19 April
    1693. 4,619
Fletcher, Lt Coll Geo: Justice. 28 May 1652. 1,76
  Issabella. Wit will Tho Webb. 11 Sept 1702. 17,5
  John. Signs oath to Commonwealth of England 13 Apl 1652.
    1, 72-3
  Laurence. Presented for not going to Church in St S par.
    19 May 1714. 6,35 (Rev Jno Span minister 1712-22)
  Laurence. Presented for absence from Church in St S. par
    15 May 1717. 6,202
  Laurence. Grandjury's presentment. "a poor lame man for not
    goeing to Church". Dismissed. 18 July 1717. 6,223
  Mary. Ref to as "my white girl" by Mrs Elinor Oliver in her
    will. 4 Sept 1719. 19,56
  Mayes. Orph son of Wm F. chooses Mr Wm Copedge as guardian.
    19 Dec 1717. 6,253
  Wm. Wit assig'mt Mayes to Innis. 15 Apl 1702. 17,255
  Wm. (Fleeker) Wit deed Williams to Lattimore. 26 Sept
    1702. 17,252-54
  William, decd. His land adj'd that sold by Josias White to
    Rd Smith. 17 Dec 1718. 19,3
Flower, Geo: Wit P of A Theriatt to Maddison. 9 May 1665. 16,19
  John. His land adj And: Salsbury. 3 July 1701. 17,95
  William. P of A from Bennett Madring. 1 Dec 1566. 16,24
  Wm. Conf judgt 846 lb tobo to Jno Hainie admr of Jno Shaw.
    11 Jan 1668/9. 3,50

Flowers, Wm. In dif with Summer Adams. 21 Jan 1668/9. 3.55
 Wm. Wit deed of gift Price to Price. 17 Jan 1671/2. 16.215
 Wm. His wife Mary Flowers. 21 Feb 1671/2. 16.227
 Wm. With Jno Essex gives a heifer to Bridget Essex Jr. 17th Apl 1672. 16.229
 Wm. To appraise cattle at the quarter of Wm Thomas decd. 16 Oct 1676. 4.6
 Wm. Ord to deliver a maid servant to Roger Thomas. 21 Nov. 1677. 4.2
 Wm. Trustee for the children of Dr Edw Sanders decd. Pets agst est of Mr Wm Thomas decd for his ward's cattle. 17 Oct 1678. 4.10
 Wm. dec'd. Admr to his son John Flowers. 20 May 1685. 4.270
Floyne, Teago. Wit bill Tho Reade to Hen Fleet. 20 Mar 1654/5. 14.127
Fluker, David. Orph son of David Fluker decd chooses Alex Love to be his guardian. 22 July 1714. 6.59 Also David Fluker orph son of David Fluker late of this Co decd, aged abt 17, bound to Alexander Love to be taught "Trade mystery or Occupation of a Taylor". 24 July 1714. 6.66
Flynt, Peter. Wit deed Rice to Hobbs. 19 Dec 1681. 17.212
 Peter. The orphans of Edwd Algood, John and Richd Algood, bound to him. Richd Flynt, security. 5 Oct 1687. 4.403
 Ri: Signs oath to Commonwealth of England 13 Apl 1652. 1.72-3
 Richard. Deed of Gift. A heifer to Anne Gamblin dau of John Gamblin. 2 July 1659. 15.27
 Richd. of Cherry Point, and Martha his wife, she being dau. of John Gresham decd, late of G W par, sell Jno Harris of of G W par, 520 acres, granted on 5th May 1652 and renowed 10 June 1664, to and by sd Gresham. 24 January 1670/1. 16.168
 Richd. Deed. 11 March 1677/8, of Chiccacone par. Sells Richd Kenner, for 11000 lb tobo, 200 acres in C par adj the road to Rappa. Martha wife of Richd Flynt gives consent. Re-rec 21 Sept 1715 by Capt Fra: Kenner. 17.224
 Richd and Peter. To 'assort' dower for Mrs Eliz Evans, widow. 6 Oct 1687. 4.407
 Tho: Land of. 10 Oct 1702. 17.13
 Thos. decd. His sons Tho and Peter Flynt pet for appraisal of estate. 16 May 1717. 6.214
 Tho: His relict, Elen Flynt, swears he left no will, Admr granted. 16 Sept 1719. 3.336
Flynts Mill. St S. par. Mattapony Neck. 21 July 1703. 17.96
Flyntts Pond. in St S par. Adj land of Capt Philip Shapleigh. 11th Sept 1703. 17.104
Focke, Wm, who wit Edw Elliott's will now deceased. 16 Sept 1685. 4.291
Foord, Abra: Wit deed. 11 June 1680. 17.14
Forest, Jno. Wit deed Brower to Bleeker. 15 Apl 1672. 16.229
Forrester, Jno. His servt Jno Chauhady 8 yrs of age. 18 Feb 1718/19. 6.299

Foster, Isaac. His land adj that sold by Josias White to Rd Smith. 17 Dec 1718. 19.3
    Seth. Jno Ayres admr Est of Simon Domibielle ord to pay him 496 lb tobo. 10 Jan 1650/1. 1.46
    Thomas. headright of Capt Gyles Brent. 21 Jan 1651/2. 1.70
Fouch, Hugh. Deed of gift to Hugh Magregor the son of Jas Magrigor, a calf. 20 Sept 1659. 15.27
    Hugh. His house on N side Little Wicco adj 135 acres sold by Wm Wildey to Tho Hobson. 8 Nov 1664. 16.1664
    Hugh. Pd from Co levy 100 lb tobo for shooting a wolf. 5 Nov 1668. 3.47
    Hugh. Certif for 150 acres for Imp 3 persons. 22 June 1669. 3.65
    Hugh. Submits a/c of cattle of James White orphan of Richard White. 22 Aug 1670. 16.144
    Rosamond. Wife of Hugh Fouch consents to sale of land. 27th Aug 1669. 16.98
Foulke, James. Wit Dennis Conaway's will. 15 June 1709. 17.19
Fountaine, Jno. Wit will Richd Wright. 18 Aug 1663. 15.114
Fountayne, Jno. Age 28. 4th Aug 1665. 15.166 Also judgt agt him awarded Mrs Eliz Tyngey. 20 Dec 1667. 3.54
Fourobush, Wm. Age 28 yrs or th-abts. Was serv't of Tho Brewer. Says that Mr David Lindsay lived there and Isaac and Danl Foxcroft at the same time. 4 Aug 1665. 15.161
Foushee, Eliz: Exhibits ad'd: inv of est of Sarah Dawson, decd. 21st Jan 1718/19. 6.297
    John. Re-recs deed of gift dated 13 Aug 1703 Dawson to Dawson. 19 Feb 1718/19. 17.249
Fowke, Col Gerard. Appears as Justice 20 May 1662. 2.156
Fowne, Thos. His servt Teague Hogan adj age 10. 21 Aug 1678. 4.1
Foxcroft, Isaac. Merchant. 1200 lb tobo in his hands belonging to Jno Washington, attached, by Mrs Anne Brodhurst. 20 July 1660. 2.127
    Isaac and Danl. Formerly lived at Tho Brewer's house. 4th August 1665. 15.161
Foxcroft's line. Adj land of Malachi Burbery, Wm and Charles Copedge. 18 May 1710. 17.50
Francis, Robt. Will. d 22 Oct 1671. p 15 Nov 1671. "my Countryman Robt Hughes shall have all that I have in this world" except paying Dr Glover, 150 lb tobo to Alice Huff, a calf to Mary Jones "and this Wastcoat and breeches which I now have upon my back and my two old shirts to Hughes and Susan his wife," and 10 lb tobo "to Thomas Gaskins wives son for an hankerchiefe". Wit: Wm Kitt, Jno Hale. 16.204
Franklin, Edw: Aged 30 yrs or th-abts. No date but recorded January 1666/7. 16.11
    Edw: planter. Overseer of Jno Webber's will. 12 Feb 1670/1. 16.166
    Hannah. Wife of Henry. 11 Nov 1698. 17.124

Franklin, Henry. To be Constable in G W par in place of John Southerland. 20 Apl 1681. 4.92

Henry. Will. d 11 Nov 1698. p 21 Feb 1700/1. "my now loveing wife Hannah" est for life. After her death the land to Richard and Henry White the sons of Joseph White of Newmans Neck. Wit: John Farnifold, John Langsdell, Anne x Langsell. Proved by oaths of John Langsdell and Anne his wife. Re-rec 19 July 1711 by Thomas Smyth. 17.124

Freake, Wm. A bill of Mr Hallowes was passed him by Wm Thomas, 21st Oct. 1654. Westmorland County Records. 1653-9 p 28

Freeman, John. Will of Danl Holland refers to land leased to him. No date. Recorded 17 Apl 1672. 16.232

John. Nicho Rhodes, a poor child age 3 next October, bound to him till 21 with his mother's consent. 15 July 1685. 4.274

Freemans Ford. In pat to Col Rd Lee 4 March 1656/7. 17.66

French, Jno. Swears he wit will of Jno Bryant decd. 16 May 1716. 6.156

Freshwater, Tho. Sold 4031 a to Danl Sullevant prior to 29 Aug 1704. 17. 261

Frost, Jno. Servt to Peter Maxwell adj 12 yrs of age. 21 Jan 1684/5. 4.252

Franco, John, tailor. Danl Maley orphan bound to him. 15 May 1717. 6.209

Fryer, Margaret and her husband Walter Fryer. Bequest from Richard Feilding. 16 July 1666. 16/12

Fulkes, Jas. Wit Gradey to Shirley. 12 Mar 1705/6. 17 152

Fulks, James and Sarah his wife. She one of the daus and legatees of Sarah Tullos late of this Co deceased. Richd Tullos exor having refused they apply for admr. 12 March 1713/14. 6.19 Also Jas Fulkes and Sarah his wife admr of Sarah Tullos decd. With will annexed. 17 March 1714/15. 6.104

Fulks, Jem. Presented for absence from Church in St S par. 15th May 1717. 6.202

Fulk, Rebecca. An orphan. Continually runs away from Jno Thomas. 16th March 1714/15. 6.100

Fuller, Jane. Headright of Wm Wildey. 8 Sept 1662. 2.161

Furnett, Lucy. Com of admr of est of Richd Cox decd. 20 July 1687. 4.397

Gaither see Guyther.

Galloway, Alice. Binds her son William to Mr Charles Lee. 17 June 1719. 6.321 Also Alice Galloway binds her son Moses Galloway to Tho Hubbard. He being 5 yrs old last May, to be taught trade of shoemaker. 19 Aug 1719. 6.326

Gallway, James. Servt to Den Conaway adj 17 yrs of age. 19 Jan 1675/6 3.249

Gallaway, Wm. Swears he wit will d 18 May 1709 of Christo Garlington. 19 May 1714. 17.210

Gamblin, Anne. Dau of Jno. G. Gift from Richd Flynt. 2 July 1659. 15.27

    John. Tho Gaskins gives a heifer to "my Cozen Elizabeth daughter of Jno Gamlin". 19 July 1657. 14.113

Game Law. 6 April 1669. 3.63

Garner appears as Gardiner in the same entry. 12 Feb 1718/19. 19.29

Gardner, Jas. His servt Jere: Dare adj 12 yrs of age. 18 Mar 1718/19 6.309

    John. His wife Susanna dau of Mrs Mary Broughton formerly Mrs Mary Keene. 2 Jan 1662/3. 15.92

    John. (Garner). Son of Jno Garner of Cherry Point Neck registers mark of cattle. 20 June 1663. 15.100

    John. (Garner). Age 30 or th-abts. 4 Aug 1665. 15.162

Garner, Jno. Assigned 200 acres by Tho Watson. 14 Feb 1667/8. 16.42

    Jno. Assigned land by Ralph Stevens. 1 Apl 1667. 16.15

    Jno. Owed 982 lb of tobo by Jas Robinson. 20 Nov 1668. 3.48

    Jno. Wit deed V. Garner to Reeves. 18 June 1706. 17.201

    Jno. Wit deed Garner to Grinstead. 18 June 1706. 17.202

    Jno. Wit deed Moor to Hutson. 21 May 1707. 17.148

Gardoner, Nath: To serve Rd Nelmes 6 yrs. 8 Oct 1662. 2.163

Garner, Parish. Inv of P Contanceau at Cherry Point. 20 Apl 1709. 17. pp 216-221

    Parish. Will. d 12 Feb 1718/19. p 18 Mar 1718/19. 4 sons, Geo. Parish, Wm., Saml. Wife Elizabeth. 19.29

    Parish. Will presented by Jas Gardner and Wm Metcalf exors. 18 March 1718/19. 6.308

    Tho. Wit P of A Gradey to Vanlandingham. 8 Oct 1705. 17.152

    Tho. Wit Gradey to Shirley. 12 Mar 1705/6. 17.152

Gardner, Thos. Serv't boy belonging to Tho Smith adj 11 yrs old. 20th Feb 1717/18. 6.258

Garner, Vincent. Signs Inv of Wm Sanders est. 13 Oct. 1704. 17.165

    Vincent. Signs appraisal of Bowers est. 17 Dec 1705. 17.167

    Vincent. Deed. 18 June 1706. Of Northumberland Co., planter. Sells Wm Gimstead of N Co., smith, 50 acres in Bettys Neck adj land of Wm Taylor and that of Robt. Reeves. Signed by Vincent Garner, Martha Garner. Wit: Fra: Dawson, Jno Garner. Re-rec by Wm Grinstead 15 July 1713. 17.202

    Vincent. Deed. 18 June 1706. of N co. planter. Sells Robert Reeves of same Co, planter, 50 acres in Bettys Neck, land where Garner now lives, adj main road to Rice's Bridge, Jno Ward's land. Wit Jno Garner, Fra Dawson. Signed by Vincent Garner and Martha Garner his wife. Re-rec 15 July 1713 by Robt Reeves. 17.201

    Vincent. Wit deed Wright to Crump. 16 Sept 1707. 17.128

    Vincent. Swears to inv of Jno Bowes Jr. 12 Jan 1713/14. 17.206

Garner, Wm. Bought land near Chisacone branch from Richd Rice prior to 9 Oct 1674. 17.114

    Wm. Exor of Jno Garner decd. 15 June 1715. 6.113 Also as exor of Jno. G. is petitioned agt by Robt Cole for wages due. 17 Aug 1715. 6.128

Garlington, Christo: His serv't Sarah Oventon 13 yrs old. 20 May 1662. 2.157

Garlington, Mr. 5 years since Patrick Morphew and Jno Taylor were his servants. 1664. 15.136

    Xphor: To be paid for a horse and equip prest for service. 16 Oct 1676. 4.7

    Mrs Joane. Relict of Christopher Garlington pets the est be div betw the children and herself. 21 August 1678. 4.2

    Xp'her. His serv't Edw Chilton ran away from 13th May to 14th June. 21 Aug 1678. 4.4

    Xpfer. Heavily fined for abusing Lt Coll Smith, breaking his collar bone, etc. 2 March 1680/1. 4.85

    Christo: Gent of N. Co., deed to Maurice Jones. 18 June 1706. 17.1

    Margarett, wife of Christo: 18 June 1706. 17.3

    Christo: Will. dated 18 May 1709. probate date missing. of Wicoc: par. To sons Christo, Saml and Wm. Refs to land adj Maurice Jones. Wife Margaret. Dau Frances. Dau Sarah Jones. Exors "my Bro Maurice Jones", wife Margaret, son Christopher and friend Tho Gaskins. Maurice Jones swears he wrote the will. Wm Gallaway and Tho Hill swear they wit it. No dates for these depos but would be recorded 19 May 1714. 17.210

    Christo: His serv't Tho Welsh 15 yrs old. 20 Mar 1716/17 6.201

Garnett, Will. Deposition. Age not shown. 20 July 1670. 16.76

Garrard, Tho. Pat 300 acres 24 Oct 1655. Sold it to Danl Neale 1st Dec 1656. 17.91

    Tho. Exempt from levies on a/c of age. 21 Oct 1661. 2.147

Garrett, Graves. Son of Thos G. decd, asks indenture to serve Clemt Aldridge to learn trade of joiner. 21 Aug 1678. 4.1

    Mary. Orph dau of Matthew Garratt decd chooses Saml Smith guardian. Wm Wildey security. 17 June 1714. 6.46 Also complains that Wm Cooper, her father's admr has not pd her share of the est. 22 Aug 1718. 6.293

    Matthew. late deceased. Wm Cooper nearest of kin. 12 March 1713/14. 6.18

    Rebecca. Orph dau of Matthew Garrett, late of this Co. bound to Mrs Sarah Haynie till 18. Tho Everett security. 19 May 1714. 6.33

    Tho. Buys 300 a from Tho Watts of Nansemond Co, now dec'd. Sale confirmed by Tho Adderson admr. 11 Dec 1654. 14.79

    Tho: Land adj Wm Nutt 4 Feb 1662/3. 17.177

Garratt, William. "Wm Garratt orpht son of Matthew Garratt late of this County dec'd twelve years old and Matthew Garratt other son of the said dec'd seven years old the fifth day of next April" bound to Thomas Everett till 21 to be taught the trade of shoemaker. 12th March 1713/14. 6.21

Garrison, R —. 4 letters illegible. Wit bond of Tho Byram. 19th May 1708. 17.72

Gaylord, James. Wit deed Wildey to Hobson 8 Nov 1664. 16.125
   P of A from Wm Wildey 21 Dec 1666. 16.5
   Appointment as Surveyor of this Co. 25 Apl 1668. 16.47
   Atty of Mr Jno Motley. 11 Jan 1668/9. 3.50
   P of A from Michael DeConti 20 July 1671. 16.194
   Informs the Court "that the Honr'ble the Secretary is dead". 16 Oct 1676. 4.6
   Surveyor. 6 May 1679. 17.143
   Wit will Wm Wildey. 1 Dec 1680. 17 pp 224-9
   Wit will of Wm Wildey but dead before it was proved on 15 June 1681. 4.96
   Surveyed land for Jno Adams prior 2 Jan 1702/3. (that being prior to his death) 17.161

Gascoyne see Gaskins.

Gaskins, Dorothy. Married Onocephorus Harvey, a Quaker, some time before 18 Nov 1713. 6.5

   Isaac. Will d 22 Oct 1709. p 18 June 1712. To 2 sons Isaac and Saml. Wife extrx. To my wife's son Thomas a colt. Daus Sarah, Elizabeth and Hannah. Brothers Thomas Gaskins and Barth: Schrever overseers. Wit: George Dameron, Charles Ingram and Saml Heath. On 18th June 1712 Saml Heath swears he wrote the will. Re-recorded on motion of Barth: Schrever for Elizabeth Gaskins the extrx. 17.167

   Jonas. deceased. Father of Tho. 19 May 1714. 6.35

   Laurence. Presented for not going to Church in Wicco Par. (prob a Quaker) 19 May 1714. 6.35 Also fined for 2 mos absence from Church. 23 Sept 1715. 6.138

   Martha. Wife of Tho: 16 May 1711. 17.80

   Thomas. (Gascoyne). Patent. 15 Sept 1649. 250 acres in Great Wiccocomoco River, being a neck of land bounded on the N by a branch parting it from the land of John Dennis and on S by land of Peter Knight. 17.80
   Also: Indenture. 16 Jan 1710/11. Josias Gaskins of one part and Tho Gaskins of the other. Whereas Tho. Gaskins decd by will d 20 June 1663 gave his son Josias Gaskins ~~party to these presents~~, the father of the said Josias Gaskins party to these presents, the Plantation whereon the testator lived, being 250 acres granted 15 Sept 1649, now Josias the devisee being dead, and Thomas party to these presents conceiving by the words of the said devisee that he, the

Gaskins, Thomas (continued) devisee, had but an Estate for life in sd land, which terminated at his death and reverted to Tho Gaskins party to these presents, the son of Tho Gaskins Elder Brother of Josias Gaskins the said devisee and Eldest Son of the said devisor, brought a Writ of Ejectment in Gen'l Court to oust the said Josias party to these presents who was in possession of the land. But in friendly settlement, Thomas dropped the suit, and there was an agreement betw them to pass deeds to each other, which they ack in Northumberland Court 21 Dec 1709. But the records being burned, Josias Gaskins conveys to Thos the 250 acres, and Thos conveys to Josias 100 acres part of the 250 acres. The indenture is signed by Josias Gaskins. Wit by Sammell x Carnell, Thomas x Shears, Thomas x Laurencett. It was acknowledged by Josias Gaskins and Elizabeth his wife on 16 May 1711. These entries Vol.17. p 80 plus.

Also: On 14th January 1710/11. deed. Thomas To Josias Gascoyne, 100 acres, part of 250 acres. Ref to the land, 250 acres being patented 15 Sept 1649 by Thos Gaskins grandfather to the said parties, who by will devised the land to his son Josias, father of said Josias party to this. The 100 acres adjoines the land of Doneron, Harris, Bledsoe and Nickless (Nicholas). Acknowledged by Tho Gaskins and Martha his wife 16 May 1711. 17 pp 80-87

Note: This is a long and involved entry. A number of pages. I can only hope I've made it perfectly clear. If the numerous Gaskins descendants and their genealogists are not satisfied, then may I modestly remark that their ancestors selected 3 witnesses for the transaction. None of them could read or write. Just put me in the class with the associates of the Colonial Gaskins. That's good enough for me.
B.F.

And further: did anyone ever bother to look up the complimentary notation made by the diarist Saml Pepys concerning the high Court standing of Gascoyne Camy King James would not have liked the next entry very much.
B.F.

Gaskins, Thomas. Signs oath to Commonwealth of England. 13th April 1652. 1. 72-3 Also: note that there are two signatures on this oath, one Tho Gaskins, the other Thomas Gaskines. See next page.

Tho: Gives a heifer to "my Cozen Elizabeth daughter of Jno Ganlin". 19 July 1657. 14.113

Tho. Aged 57 or th-abts. Says about 7 yrs ago, going to Fleets bay, etc. 20 May 1658. 14.141

Gaskins, Tho. (Gaskin) Wit David Spiller's will. Prob 21 Oct 1658. 15.11

    Tho: Will d 20 June 1663. p 20 Nov 1665. Sons Josias and Henry. 15.171

Gascoyne, Tho. Aged 53 yrs. Date not shown but recorded 1664. 15.136

Gaskins, Tho: Robt Francis leaves 10 lb tobo "to Thomas Gaskins wives son for an hankerchiefe". 22 Oct 1677. 16.204

    Mr. Tho. His servt Charles Mulloy adj 14 yrs of age. 16 Nov 1698. 4.842

Gascoyne, Tho: lately bought land in G W per from Tho Williams. 26th Sept 1702. 17. pp 252-4

    Tho: Deed from Tho Williams 27 March 1703. Re-recs this deed 21 March 1710/11. 17.45 Also deed from same 18 Dec 1699. 17.44

Gaskins, Tho. Wit will Barth: Damaron 8 Aug 1708. 17.57

    Tho. Friend and exor of Christo Garlington. 18 May 1709. 17.210

    Tho. Guardian of Eliz Brereton. 18 July 1711. 17.189

    Tho. Suit as guardian of Eliz Brereton agt Tho Hobson in Chancery to next Court. 13 March 1713/14. 6.27

    Thomas son of Josias Gaskins decd. Presented for not going to Church in Wicco par. 19 May 1714. 6.35

    Tho. Presented to Grand Jury for being drunk on Sunday "which was committed on Easter day last past" in St. S. par. 16 June 1715. 6.116 (Rev Jno Span minister St S par 1712-1722)

    Tho. of St S par fined for being drunk on the Sabath day. 23 Sept 1715. 6.138

    Tho. Guardian of Sarah Hull. 18 Nov 1719. 6.345

    Tho. Jr. App Constable S side Dennis Creek. 22 July 1661. 2.143

    Tho. Jr. Godson of Isaac Weaver who leaves him his estate. 13 Jan 1663/4. 15.116

    Tho. Senr. Above 60 yrs of age. Exempt from levy. 22 July 1661. 2.143

Genn, Jas. decd. Ann his relict swears he left no will. Admr granted. 19 Aug 1719. 6.327

Genesis, Ezekiell. On jury Saffin vs Thompson. 6 Apl 1669. 3.63

    Ezekel. Wit will Jno Muttoone Sr of G W par. 26 Sept 1678. 17.260

    Ezekiell. Ordered to settle Mrs Frances Lewis' rights in Jno Muttoone's est. 21 Apl 1681. 4.93

    Ezekiell. dec'd. Prob to Alice Hudnall his Extrx. 4 June 1684. 4.228

George, Saml and Jeffery. Wit will of Nicho Morris. 21 Nov 1660. 15.140

Gerrard, Saml. dec'd. His admrx Elizabeth Gerrard arrests Gilbert Harrold for debt. 15 July 1685. 4.279

Gesse, James. Servt to Saml Mahon adj 13 yrs of age. 21 Aug 1678. 4.1

Gibble, Richard (Entry damaged). Deed. 4 March 1657/8. to Richard
    Smyth. 30 acres. adj Wm Nutt. Wit: Wm Thomas, Joseph
    Feilding. 15.13
    James. Headright of Lau: Dameron. 21 Feb 1658/9. 2.102
    Richard. His dau Ann given a cow by Richd Span. 20 May 1667.
    16.17
    Richard. Deed. 16 Jan 1671/2. of G W River. planter. Sells
    Jno Price 50 acres. Adj land he (Gibble) sold to
    Isaac Edwards. Adjs Taylor's land. Wit Dennis Eyes,
    Thomas Daniel. Re-rec 20 Feb 1711/12 "by the wife
    of Neal Odohoty on his behalf". 17.156.
    On 8 Nov 1701 Flora x Price asks sale of this land
    to Neal Odohoty. 17.157
    Richd. 100 acres formerly belonging to him sold by Daniel
    Holland to Jno Warner and Prue his wife. 20 Febry
    1671/2. 16.230
Gibbons, Steph: Attachmt to Mr Richd Smith agt him for 5 pair shoes
    due by bill dated 4 Jan 1695/6. This entry 15 July
    1696. 4.732
Gibson, John, with consent of his wife Eliz, assigns 100 acres to Jno
    Downham and Tho Gilbert. Wit Richd Tipton, Dennis
    Ize. 3 Dec 1666. 16.3
Gilbard, Tho: His hogs stolen. 6 Apl 1669. 3.62
Gilhampton, Francis. Attachmt 400 lb tobo agst his estate to William
    Harcom. served on Mr Richd Kenner atty of Mr Wm
    Bodely marcht "the Imployer of the said Gilhampton.
    16 Oct 1676. 4.7
Gill, David of Mattapony. Buys land from Hugh Dermott. 20 Mar 1702/3.
    17.119 Re-recs this deed 18 July 1711. 17.119
    David. Land adj Jno Claughton in Mattapony Neck. St S par. He
    is wit in deed Claughton to Claughton. 18 Jan 1707/8
    17.89
    David "a poor Ancient man" exempt from levy. 16 May 1717. 6.214
    David. When he is sued by Owen Dermott, Dorothy Waters appears
    as witness. 16 May 1717. 6.215
    Dinah. Dau of Tho Gill Senr. 10 Feb 1707/8. 17.97
    Mary. Re-recs will of Tho Gill Senr. 16 May 1711. 17.97
    Thomas. Tho Algrove age 8 bound to him till 21. 19 Nov 1696.
    4.749
    Tho: His serv't Francis Macarnuet adj 13 yrs of age. 21st Dec
    1698. 4.848
    Tho. Signs inv of Tho Shapleigh deed. 29 Sept 1703. 17.11
    Tho. of St S par. Deed from Jno Bayles 18 Jany 1705/6. Re-recs
    it 17 Sept 1712. 17.180
    Tho. Wit agreemt Bickley and Ingram. 2 July 1707. 17.24
    Tho. Senr. Mentioned but not individually named as grand-
    children in his will. 10 Feb 1707/8. 17.97
    Tho. As witness proved will of Wm Harcum. 15 March 1709/10.
    17.111 (see next entry)

Gill, Tho. Deposition. 20 June 1711. "aged thirty nine yeares or
        thereabouts". Says he wrote the will of Mr William
        Harcum and was a witness thereto. The will was prob
        15 March 1709/10. Estate devised to Harcom's wife
        and children to his best rememberance thus: To son
        James 5 s. To each of sons John, William and Thos.
        a bed. To wife Hannah Harcum a silver bowl, etc.
        Ref to land adj Staynie's Nook. To daughters Hannah,
        Mary and Elizabeth. To son Samuel. That the wit were
        Jno Way, Wm Godwyn and Tho Gill. 17.111
    Tho. of St S par, Cordwainer. Buys land from Tho Berry 17 Feb
        1708/9. Re-recs the deed 17 Sept 1712. 17.183
    Tho. Re-recs will of Tho Berry Sr 20 June 1711. 17.106
    Tho. His two servants adj to be 8 and 10 yrs old. 18 Nov 1713.
        6.3
    Tho. Exor of Solomon Bowles decd. Presents his will. 22 Sept
        1715. 6.134
    Tho. Security for Robt Vaulx. 21 Nov 1716. 6.185
    Thomas, Senior. Will. d 10 Feb 1707/8. p 21 Jan 1708/9. of
        St S par. "sick and weak". To son William Gill 100
        acres "bought of my Cosen John Jones" in St S par
        adj land "I now live on", it being formerly given
        to sd Jno Jones by his Grandfather Roger Walters.
        To dau Dinah Gill. Sheep to be div betw "all my
        grandchildren". Son Tho Gill exor. Dau Susanna
        Robinson. Daughter Frances Waddington. Signed Thomas
        x Gill. Wit: Richard Wright, Wm x Conner. Re-rec 16
        May 1711 by Mary Gill. 17.97
Gilman, John. Signs oath to Commonwealth of England. 13 Apl 1652.
        1 pp 72-3
Gilpin, Jane. Headright of Capt Gyles Brent. 21 Jan 1651/2. 1.70
Gilbert, Tho. With Jno Downham buys 100 a from Jno Gibson. 3 Dec.
        1666. 16.3
    Tho. See entry Adam Yarratt. 22 Oct 1667. 16.25
    Wm. Wit Jno Bearemore's will 20 Jan 1676/7. 17.109
Glebe, the. Rented by Mrs Joan Winlow prior to 1667. See entry Adam
        Yarratt. 22 Oct 1667. 16.25
Glebe. St Stephens Parish. Land left by Col Geo Cooper 18 Nov 1708.
        17.123
Glover, Tho. Chyrurion. Summoned "to view and search the Corps of
        Lewis Jones and one of - Williams his servt that was
        drowned". To be pd 200 lb tobo. 20 May 1671. 3.121
    Doctor. To be paid. See will Robt Francis. 22 Oct 1671.
        16.204
Goddard, Tho. His wife Anne has been in bad company. 20 Apl 1681.
        4.92
Godwin, Saml. Wit deed Barnes to Reeves. 21 Oct 1702. 17.200
    Saml. Bequest from his kinsman Saml Griffin. 2 Feb 1702/3.
        17.213
    William. Wit will of Wm Harcum which he proved by oath 15th
        March 1709/10. 17.111

Godwyn, William. Dec'd. Dennis Fallon admr. 12 Mar 1713/14. 6.20
Gelson, Benj. Dec'd. Jno Million pets his est be appraised. 19 Nov. 1696. 4.743
Gooch. Appears as Goche, Gouch, etc.
Goche, Mrs Ann. Was widow 10 Nov 1683. Now wife of Pet. Byram. 17th Sept 1684. 4.240
Gooch, Jeoffrey. Pat land on S side G W River. 30 Jan 1650. 17.195
Gouche, Jeoffry. Pat 500 a 30 Jan 1651/2. Conveyed to Saml Gouch by deed 21 March 1658/9. Sold 1/2 to Jeoffry Johnson 20 Dec 1666. 17.38
Goche, Jaffery, of G.W. par. Deed of Gift. 21 Mar 1658/9. Gives for love and affection, land on Cupids Creek, to Saml Goche, the son of his brother John and Katherine Goche. 15.18
Gouch, John. Son and heir of Saml Gouch decd. Sued by Jno Harris admr of David Whitford. Refs to deft's mother, extrx of Saml G. decd, now the wife of Peter Byram, etc. 21 May 1696. 4.724
Gouche, Jno. Son and heir of Saml Gouche, Sues Jeoffry Johnson in Gen'l Court 22 Oct 1690. Amicable settlement 20th Jan. 1696/7. 17.38
Gouch, John. Deed 7 April 1706, of G W par, planter. Sells Richard Neale of same par, Gent, for L 80. Sterl. 130 acres in G W par on S side of G W River. Adjs Vulcans Creek, land of Jeoffry Johnson, the road that goes to the Church, the land of Mr Richd Hudnall, etc. This land pat by Jeoffrey Gooch uncle to said John on 30 Jan 1650. 17.195 This deed wit by David Straughan, Richd Hull, Fra Kenner. Acknowledged 16 April 1706 by Jno Gouch and Mary his wife by her atty Robt Nash. The delivery wit 11 Oct 1706 by Tho Stretton and Rodham Neale. Re-rec 20 May 1713 by Mr Richd Neale.
P of A 15 Apl 1706 Mary Gouch to Ro: Nash wit by Fra: Dawson. 17.195
Gouché, John. Appears as a witness 28 Nov 1707. 17.40
Goche, Sam: of G W par gives to Jeffery Johnson son of Jno Johnson of G W par 1/2 of plantation he now ownes and rec'd by deed of gift from his uncle Jeffery Goche. With the provision that Jno Johnson and Anne his wife, father and mother of the said Jeffery Johnson have the use of the plantation. Dated 14 Dec 1663. Recorded 20 Dec 1666. Wit by Geo Spe and Jeffery Goche. 16. 2
Goche, Sam. Wit deed Lane to Whitford. 18 Jan 1669/70. 16.154
Goche, Sam. As overseer probates will of Henry Wicker decd. 22 June 1669. 3.65
Gouch, Sam. Atty of Da- Whitford. 3 July 1677. 17.255
Goche, Saml. Settles dif betw Tho Hobson and Tho Tope. 24 Aug 1678. 4.5

Goehe, Saml. Requested by the Court to make inquiry concerning the settlement of Jno Mottoone's estate. 21 Apl 1681. 4.93

Goehe, Sam: Deceased. Prob of will to Anne the widow. 4 June 1684. 4.228

Goodrich — see entry Capt Peter Knight. 21 Aug 1678. 4.4

Gordon, Geo: of Glasgow, sues Richd Butler. (Note: Butler arrested for debt, broke prison and escaped) 20 Aug 1719. 6.335

   Robert. Wit will of Tho Wms. 11 Mar 1706/7. Proved it by oath 23 May 1707. 17.72

Gorham, Miles. Confesses present paymt 960 lb tobo to Wm Rust. 20th Nov 1668. 3.49

   Miles. Wit deed Howes to Hill. 15 Nov 1671. 16.204

   Miles and Alice his wife sell land to Jno Eveins. 18 Janry 1671/2. 16.225

   Miles. Petitions that his child be returned to him "who he pretends was bound to Capt John Rogers in the absence of him the said Gorham". This referred to the next Court. 21 Aug 1678. 4.3

Goreham, Miles. Order to Capt John Rogers to deliver Goreham's son to him, the child having been bound out in his father's absence. 17 October 1678. 4.8

Govley, Tho: His servt Jno Hine age 14. 21 Jan 1660/1. 2.136. Now what sort of phonetic spelling is this ? — what can this name be ? I presume any good Englishman would know. B.F.

Grace, William and James. Orphan sons of John Grace. Wm 12 yrs old in Oct next. James 8 yrs old in August next. The boys bound to Wm Tynan to be taught trade of shoemakers. 20 May 1719. 6.316

Gradey, Wm of Stafford Co. Decd. 12 March 1705/6. Sells Jno Shirly of N Co, for 4000 lb tobo, 1/2 of 100 acres, which was "first appropriated" by Col Jno Trussell Decd, and by him assigned to James Claughton, and by him to Robt Look and Jno Cautanceau. The 100 acres then div and 50 a sold by Cautanceau sold to Henry Moseley, and by him sold to Jos Edmunds, and by Mr L'strange Mordant atty of Edmunds sold to John Oliver. Oliver dying without heirs, the land escheated and was bought by Robert Wilson who married the relict of Oliver, and by him sold to Walter Greadey Dec'd from whom the land descended "to me the said Wm Gradey". The land in Kings Creek (?) in St S par. Deed wit by James Fulkes, Richd Tulloc, Thos Garner. Ack 20th March 1705 by Frn Vallandeghm (Vanlandingham) atty for Grady. Re-rec by Jno Shirley 20 Feb 1711/12. P of A Grady to Vanlandingham 8 Oct 1705. Wit by Richd Proverb, Tho Garner. 17.152

Graham, John. On jury to div land Saffin and Hull. 29 Nov 1669. 16.63

   Jno. Signs Inv. Tho Shapleigh decd. 29 Sept 1703. 17.11

Graham, Jno. Will. 2 Mar 1705/6. 20 Nov 1706. Of N. Co. To son John he under 18. To dau not yet christened but to be called Mary. Wife Patience. Wit Jno Carnegie, John Hull, Thos Hobson. Re-rec 18 March 1713/14 by Mr Richd. Hull. 17.208

 Capt John. Appraisal of estate. No exact date shown. Taken by Richd Hull. Includes "To 2 years service of a white hand named Daniel James", "To a servt by nam Matthew Simonds about five years to serve". Re-rec 17 Dec 1712 on motion of Wm Copedge by his atty Wm Dare. Mr Richd Hull swears he appraised the estate. 17.193

 John. Chooses Mr Saml Span his guardian. 21 Mar 1716/17. 6.202

 John. His land adj Owen Jones. 10 Oct 1718. 19.8

 Mary. Deed of Gift from her mother Mrs Patience Graham. 18th March 1713/14. 6.26

Gralesse, John. Late of N Co. Father of Mrs Eliz Leechman. 8 Febry 1708/9. 17.91

Grason, John. Wit deed Bledsoe to Burne. 12 Feb 1705/6. 17.17
 Susanna. " " "

Gray. Francis. App est of Jno Hampton dec'd. 7 Mar 1649/50. 1.49
 Francis. App est of Ro Seagrave dec'd. 20 Mar 1649/50. 1.48
 Francis. Gives his wife Alice Gray a cow. 30 Dec 1651. 1.70
 Francis. Submits a/c of Wm Butler's cattle. 9 Sept 1654. Records of Westmorland Co. Va. 1653-1659. p 28
 John. See entry Capt Giles Russell. 18 Nov 1719. 6.346

Great Pond. On Potomac River. Adj land of Saml Smith. 11 Sept 1703. 17.104

Green Branch. Adj land of Wm and Chas Copedge. 5 June 1710. 17.50

Green, Robt. To serve Col Rd Lee 6 yrs. 8 Oct 1662. 2.163

Greenham, Timothy. That Thaddeus Dorgan and Joan his wife are his servants. 18 Nov 1719. 6.345

Greenstone, Anne. Dau of Jno Greenstone, being 9 yrs of age, with consent of her father to serve Wm Yarratt and Jane his wife till 17. 18 March 1684/5. 4.256

Gregory, Esau. Given a cow by Rd Island. 20 June 1666. 16.3

Gremlett, Jno. Wit will of Partin Hudnall. 4 Dec 1698. 17.117

Gresham, John. Signs oath to Commonwealth of England. 13 April 1652. 1 pp 72-3

Grisham, John. Wit deed Fleet to Baker. 15 Nov 1655. 14.58

Gresham, John. His daughters Mary and Martha. He is incensed with Mary concerning the trade of a cow. 20 May 1656. 14.77

 John. Deceased. John Waddy guardian for his dau Martha claims land belonging to her. 22 July 1661. 2.145

 John. Deceased. Had pat 520 acres 5 May 1652. His daughter Martha, wife of Richd Flint, sells it to Jno Harris. 24 Jan 1670/1. 16.168

Griffin, Alex: of G W par. Buys 100 acres from Corderoy Ironmonger. 20 Dec 1667. 16.32

Griffin, Alex: Tfrs int in bill of sale to Angell Jacobus. 17 April 1672. 16.231
    Michall. Servt to Wm Keyne adj 18 yrs of age. 17 Mar 1674/5. 3.224
    Mrs Priscilla. Age 78 yrs or th-abts. Exact date not shown but recorded latter part of 1664. 15.135
    Colo Saml and his wife Sarah. Their dau Kath: (who later m David Gwyn) born 31 Dec 1692. From Tayloe Family Bible, "Mt. Airy", Richmond Co., Virginia.
    Lt Coll Saml. Justice 19 Apl 1693. 4.619
    " 18 Dec 1696. 4.755
    " 16 Nov 1698 4.841
    Lieut Coll Saml. Will. 2 Feb 1702/3. 5 Sept 1703. of N. Co. Gentleman. To Gr-son Griffin Fauntleroy the son of Wm Fauntleroy decd all land in Cherry Point Neck. To Gr-son Wm Fauntleroy another son of Wm Fauntleroy decd land called Quintenneke in Richmond Co. To Gr-son Moore Fauntleroy.
    To Gr-daus Elizabeth Gwyn and Sarah Gwyn, daus of "my son in law" David Gwyn.
    To "my Grandson in Law Thos Griffin and my Granddaughter in Law Winnifred Presley" son and dau of "my Son in Law" Leroy Griffin decd.
    To dau Kath: Gwyn now wife of David Gwyn.
    To my dau in law Winnifred Griffin widow, late wife of Leroy Griffin decd.
    To bro in law John Hobbs of London and my dear sister Elizabeth his wife. To my cozen Tho: Hewett son of my sister Mrs Eliz Hobbs. Also to Mrs Hobbs' son Jno Hewett.
    To Kath: dau of my sister Kath: Sprigg decd. Ref to Mrs S having other children but does not name them.
    To kinsman Coll Wm Tayloe.
    To Hugh Campbell and Mary Thompson who were my servants.
    To my kinsman Saml Godwin.
    Overseers: Col Wm Tayloe and Mr Saml Godwin in Va and my coz Tho Hewett in England.
    Wit: Wm Cornish, Wm Medcalfe, Hen Medcalfe, who by oaths prove the will 5 Sept 1703.
    Re-recorded 15 Sept 1714 by Mr Griffin Fauntleroy. 17. pp 213-215
Griffin, Wm. Wit will of Jno Hull of Fairfield par. 4 May 1667. 16.97
    Wm. Excluded from levy "in respect of his age" 6 April 1669. 3.60
Grimsted, John and William. Bequest of 500 acres from Jno Parse who refers to them as sons in law. No date but the will is recorded 20 May 1667. 16.16

Grimstead, Thomas age 7 and John Grimstead age 4, with consent of their father Wm Grimstead, to serve Wm Taylor till they are 21. 18 March 1684/5. 4,256
Grenstead, Adham. Wit will Jno Bowers Sr. 29 Sept 1704. 17,167
Grimstead, Tho. with Wm Moulton next of kin to Jas Lockman dec'd. 18 June 1718. 6,269
 Tho: Kath Lowry bound to him. 17 Sept 1719. 6,340
Grinsted, Wm. Aged 21 or th-abts. 20 Aug 1655. 14,52
 Wm. 2 children born to him and Eliz Kaye prior to 20 Jam 1655/6. 14,67
Greensted, William. "These are to Certifie whome it may concerne that Willm Greensted and Elizabeth Key intends to be joyned together in the Holy Estate of Matrimony If anyone can shew any Lawfull cause why they may not be joyned together lett them speake or ever after hold their tongues
Signum Wm Greensted Signum Elizabeth Key
21 July 1656 this Certificate was Published in open Court and is Recorded". 14,65
 Wm. His wife, formerly Elizabeth Key a maid servant in the Mottrom estate. 21 July 1659. 15,27
 Wm. Deposition. Age 29 or th-abts (sic). Re mares belonging to the orphans of Richd Thompson decd. Eliz Grinsted, aged abt 28 yrs, refers to her former master Col Jno Mottrom decd, etc. 1 Oct 1660. 15,61
 Wm. Buys 50 acres from Vincent Garner. 16 June 1706. Re-rec the deed 15 July 1713. 17,202
Grimstead, Wm. Security for Wm Lewis. 21 Mar 1716/17. 6,204
Groome, Capt Saml. of the ship Wm and Mary. In Va abt June 1663. 15,149
Groves, Geo: as marrying the admr of James Seabury sues Mr Richard Rogers for 550 lb tobo. 20 Nov 1696. 4,751
 Geo: Wit deed Conolin to Alverson. 21 July 1703. 17,96
Grymes, Richard. Aged 34 yrs or th-abts. 22 Feb 1655/6. 14,70
"Guillian an Irish wench servt to Mr Mathew Rhoden" adj 14 yrs of age. 22 June 1669. 3,65
Gulpey, Maudlin (Magdalene) Headright of Tho Lane. 23 June 1669. 3,66
Gustinge, Jno. of Gloucester Co. See entry Nicho: Britton. 20th Jan 1664/5. 15,149
Guyther, Geo: Wit Tho Palmer's will 28 March 1709. 17,127
Gwyn, David, Katherine, Sarah and Elizabeth. See entry Saml Griffin. 2 Feb 1702/3. 17,213
 Elizabeth of Horton in Gloucestershire. Sister of Rd Feilding. 16 July 1666. 16,12
Gwyn, Mrs Kath: "Katherine Gwyn Daughter of Collo Sam'll Griffin and Sarah his wife was born 16th day of March 1664". "Elizabeth Gwyn her Daughter borne the 31 December 1692 and dyed the 28th Janry 1745". Tayloe Family Bible. "Mt Airy", Richmond Co., Virginia.

Hack, Eliz: ref to as "my cousin" in will of Jno Coutanceau. 17 Dec 1718. 19.10
    Capt Peter. Justice. 16 July 1696. 4.734
       " 18 Dec 1696. 4.755
       " 16 Nov 1698. 4.841
    Capt. Peter. Exor of Capt Tho Brereton. 23 Mar 1698/9. 17.189
       Exor of Rev Jno Farnefold. 3 July 1702. 17.234
       Signs paper as official. 14 Dec 1702. 17.8
    Coll. Peter. His land adj Antho Haynie. 31 Jan 1709/10. 17.107
    Coll. Peter. Sworn Commissioner. 16 March 1714/15. 6.100
    Nicholas. Wit div of land betw Antho and Tho Robinson. 12 Aug 1703. 17.108
    Capt Nicho: His will presented by Jno Hack his exor. 18 June 1718. 6.266
Hackne, Mr Richd. Wit div land betw Wm and Charles Copedge. 5 June 1710. 17.50
Hackney, Richd. Exor of Richd Ruth. 26 Jan 1718/9. 19.31
    Rich: Re-recs deed dated 20 Apl 1681 Hugh Harris to John Sowell. 20 Jan 1719/20
Haddaway, Rowland. Fined 200 lb tobo for beating Robt Lambdon. 20th Feb 1651/2. 1.50
Hadwell, James. Headright of Hugh Fouch. 22 June 1669. 3.65
    James. A poor impotent person freed from the levy. 20 May 1685. 4.269
    John. Wit deed Wildey to Ingram. 17.24
    Jno. of St S par. Fined for absenting himself from Church. 18 Nov 1713
Hailes, Geo: Sells 300 acres to Tho Mallett. 21 Feb 1651/2. 14.94
Hale, Geo: Above 60 yrs, exempt from levy. 22 July 1661. 2.143
    John. Wit Robt Francis' will. 22 Oct 1671. 16.204
    Mr Nich: Wants satisfaction of Walter Price for entertaining his runaway servant. 11 Jan 1668/9. 3.50
    Thomas. Aged 50 yrs or th-abts. 17 Jan 1651/2. 1.70
Haile, Tho. Signs oath to Commonwealth of England. 13 April 1652. 1 pp 72-3
Hales, Tho. Signs oath to Commonwealth of England. 13 April 1652. 1 pp 72-3 (Note preceeding entry - appears there were two of the name who signed. Possibly father and son)
Haile, Tho. Wit will of Nath: Hickman. 26 Mar 1655. 14.98
Hayles, Thos. Age 50 yrs or th-abts. Says upwards of 7 years ago he had 100 acres surveyed by Wm Cooke, surveyor, for Phillip Silvester, the land where Mr Nicho Jernew now liveth. The land adj Wm Reynolds, etc. 20th Jan 1656. 14.98
Hales, Tho. Will. dated 3 Sept 1658. prob 23 Nov 1658. Whole estate to wife Anne. 15.15
Haler, Henry. Age 34 or th-abt. Deposition re Geo Thompson. 20th Feb 1650/1. 1.58
Hall, Danl. Servt to Will Downing Sr adj 8 yrs of age. 15 Jan 1678/9. 4.18

Hall, Daniel. Note the entry on the preceeding page concerning this
            child. Then refer to the entry Susan Hall below.
            The two entries are side by each in the original
            record book. Looks very much as though they were
            brother and sister.
Hall, Marg'tt. Wit deed Claughton to Claughton. 18 Jan 1707/8. 17.89
Hall, Peter, of St S par. Presented for "prophaine swearing three
            prophane oathes". 16 May 1716. 6.157
Hall, Susan. Servant to Wm Downing Jr adjudged 9 yrs of age. 15 Jan
            1678/9. 4.18 (see entry Danl Hall)
Hall, Thos Senr. Wit deed Jones to Rogers. 19 Aug 1707. 17.153
Hall, Thos Senr. Will. d 10 Feb 1708/9. p 15 June 1709. of St S par.
            To son Stephen Hall 50 acres where he now lives.
            To sons Thomas, Peter, John, James.
            To daughters Martha, Anne Claughton, Margaret,
            Elizabeth, Hannah, Mary.
            Exors: son Thos Hall and James Claughton.
            Wit: Phillip Rogers, James Deane Junr, David
            Straughn.
            Re-rec by John Claughton 19 March 1711/12. 17.163
Hallowes, John. Gives a cow and calf to James Baldridge Junior 10th
            May 1648. Confirmed and recorded 12 Jan 1650/1.
            1.48
    John. Justice 24 Aug 1650. 1.41
    John. Signs oath to Commonwealth of England. 13 Apl 1652.
            1. pp 72-3
    Mr Jno. Justice. 20 July 1652. 1.76
    Mr. Pd 1800 lb tobo by Wm Thomas. 21 Oct 1654. Records of
            Westmorland Co. Va. 1653 - 1659. p 28
Hally, Tho. Presented for swearing 21 oaths. 21 Jan 1713/14. 6.15
Hamilton, George. Who married Elizabeth the heir of Hannah Bridgeman
            "enteres a Caviate that noe will might be proved
            whereby she might be presudual in his wifes right
            to her inheritance". 21 Aug 1678. 4.1
Hamilton, Geo and Jno Holland to be Surveyors in place of Adam Yarrat
            and James Nepper. 15 Oct 1679. 4.47
Hamilton, Jno. Tobo shipped by John Harris in that name. 23 May 1669.
            4.26
Hampton, John deceased. Robt Matthews owes his estate 100 lb tobo.
            7 March 1649/50. 1.49
Hamond, John. Wit will of Richd Eaton. 13 March 1677/8. 17.158
Hamonds, John. George Eskridge, atty for John, James and Thomas
            Hamonds, orphan sons of Peter Hamonds deceased,
            complains against Charles Hamonds exor of the
            dec'd. 16 Feb 1715/16. 6.150
Ham't, Thos who married Mary, extrx of Wm Cornish late of this Co
            deed, granted admr of Cornish's estate. 5th Oct
            1687. 4.402
Hampton, Jno. dec'd. His inv appraised by Francis Gray, Thomas Peake
            and Peter Phispound. 7 March 1649/50. 1.49

Hancock, William. Wit deed Tho Brewer to Jno Nickles. 13 Dec 1671. 16.226
Hanley, John. Signs oath to Commonwealth of England. 13 April 1652. 1. pp 72-73
Hanson, Wm. For some time past an inhabitant of this County. Certificate for leaving the Colony. 21 Apl 1714. 6.358
Harcum, Elizabeth, Hannah, James, John, Mary, Saml, William Jr and Sr. See deposition of Tho Gill. 15 March 1709/10. 17.111
Harcum, William. Attachmt agt est of Mr Frances Gilhampton 400 lb tobacco. 16 Oct 1676. 4.7
 Mr Wm. His servt Matthew Welch adj 15 yrs old. 21 Dec 1698. 8.847
 William. Wit will of Tho Berry. 15 Apl 1700. 17.106
 William. Wit will of Rodham Kenner. 26 July 1706. 17.126
 William. His land adj Tho Leechman. 8 Feb 1708/9. 17.91
 Wm. Wit deed Berry to Gill. 17 Feb 1708/9. 17.183
 William and Thomas. Sons of Hannah Harcum dec'd. Swear she left no will. Admr granted. 18 Feb 1718/9. 6.298
Harden, Tho and Anne. (apparently brother and sister). "Cosens" of John Mosely. Bequests from him. 18 May 1668. 16.126
Hardinge, George of London. Power of Attorney dated 22 Sept 1664. Geo Hardinge, citizen and grocer of London, and Mary Hardinge his wife, dau of Tho Orley of London and Anne his wife deceased and sister of . . (torn away) . . Orley late of Cherry Poynt in Potomack dec'd to . . (torn away) . . to demand from Rebecca Orley late wife and extrx of the will of the said Thomas Orley of Cherry Pt dec'd, and from Wm Jollins of Cherry Point her now husband, planter, money, etc. Further, and this part of the entry is not at all clear but it seems that somebody was told to "go search the Register Church Booke of the Parish churge of St Mary White Chappell did find that the above declared Mary Orley daughter of Tho and Anne Orley was Babtized on the 25th of April 1622". This dated London, 29 Sept 1664. 15. pp 144-5
This remarkable entry is to be considered. The Parish of St Mary White Chapel was just over the line in Lancaster County. The Rev. Wm White was minister there prior to 1658. There were instances where entries in the Virginia registers were dated far back. But naturally one would assume that this would refer to an English parish. Not Virginia. B.F.
Harding, Henry. Wit deed Leechman to Tho Smith. 8 Feb 1708/9. 17.91
 John and Jane his wife, late Jane Trussell relict of John Trussell, swear he left no will. Admr of his estate granted. 18 Sept 1717. 6.241
 Mark. of Wicoco par, carpenter. See entry Alex Cumins et als. 7 Apl 1707. He re-recs deed 20 June 1711. 17.116

Harden, Mark. His runaway servant ret'd by Wm Barnes of Maryland. 22 Sept 1715. 6.135

Harding, Thos: His eldest boy (name not shown) has bequest from John Tyngey. 1 Aug 1667. 16.30
    Thos: On jury Presly vs Mathew. 21 Jan 1668/9. 3.53
    Thos: Chosen by Wm Moseley as guardian. 6 Apl 1669. 3.61
    Thos: Member of Vestry Chicacone par. 20 Mar 1671/2. 16.158
    Thos: Orphan of Tho Harding sr. His guardian, Capt Jno Haynie sues Luke Rowland who m Anne the admr of Thomas Harding deceased. 22 May 1696. 4.728
    Thos: An orphan, Eliza Callan, bound to him. 12 Mar 1713/14. 6.21
    Thos: Ref to by Wm Humphreyes and Ann his wife as "their son". 24 July 1714. 6.73
    Thos: Orphan son of Jno Harding decd makes choice of his 'cosin' Tho Harding as guardian. 21 Aug 1717. 6.234

Hardwood, Richd. Wit deed Davis to Coppedge. 1 Oct 1670. 16.165
Harley, Tho. Headright of Capt Jno Haynie. 15 July 1696. 4.733
Harman, Eliz: Servant of Mrs Joane Henley. 26 Dec 1663. 15.150
Harris's Neck Creek. In St S par. Adj land of Saml Smith. 19 Dec. 1709. 17.53
Harrington, Joseph. Headright of Wm Wildey. 8 Sept 1662. 2.161
Harris - Land adj Gaskins in G W River. 16 Jan 1710/11. 17.80
Harris, George. Servt to Sym: Richardson adj 17 yrs of age. 24 Aug 1669. 3.69
    Mrs Grace (als Hopkins). See entry Tho Ingram. 29 Apl 1670. 16.128
    Mrs Hannah. Relict of Richd Hull exhib Inv of his est. 18th Feb 1718/19. 6.299
    Henry. "a poor cripled young man" exempt from levy. 16 May 1716. 6.155
    Hugh. As wit proves will of Wm Shorter. 21 Aug 1678. 4.1
    Hugh. Deed. 20 Apl 1681. Sells Jno Sowell 100 acres adj the land of Phillip Evans, etc. Wit by Richd Haynie and John Hughlett Junr. Ack by Hugh Harris and Ann his wife. Re-rec on motion of Richard Hackney on 20 Jan 1719. "Capt Richard Haynie came into Court and swore he wrote the Deed and was an Evidence thereto". 17.251
    Jon. Wit deed Nash to Howson. 17 Jan 1671/2. 16.219
    Jno. of G W par. Buys 520 acres from Rd Flint and Martha his wife. 24 Jan 1670/1. 16.168
    Mr Jno. Petitions his land be surveyed to fix boundries. 21st Aug. 1678. 4.3
    Mr Jno. Judgt for 1200 lb tobo confessed to him by Jno Hudnall atty of Jno Palmer. 21 Aug 1678. 4.2
    Mr Jno: Swears Tho Marshall owes him 908 lb tobo. 17 Oct 1678. 4.8

Harris, John. Arrested at suit of Edw Feilding for 8640 lb tobo by
    obligation dated 23 May 1677. Harris produced a
    B/L signed by Mr John Teague, master of the ship
    Phenix of Bristol, dated 14 Feb 1669/70, that "said
    Harris did by the name of John Hamilton" consign
    to Feilding 9 hhd tobo for which he had rec'd no
    credit. 19 Feb 1678/9. 4.26
  John. Arrests Mrs Jane Wildey for debt but does not appear.
    Nonsuit to Mrs Wildey. 16 Aug 1682. 4.141
  Jno. Servant to Robt Bryery adj 14 yrs of age. 18 Apl 1683.
    4.176
  Jno. Admr of David Whitford brings action agt Jno Gouch son
    and heir of Saml Gouch decd. Ref to deft's mother,
    extrx of Saml Gouch decd as being then married to
    Peter Byram, etc. 21 May 1696. 4.724
  Mr Jno. Certificate for 250 acres for importing 5 persons. 15
    July 1696. 4.733
  Mr. John. Justice. 16 Nov 1698. 4.841
  John. Wit will of Patrick Pollick. 4 Dec 1702. 17.235
  John. Foreclosed mortgage on Tho Evans and sold the land to
    Owen Dermott prior to 20 March 1702/3. 17.119
  Jno. Wit will of Tho Ingram 12 Oct 1700. His oath 21 May 1707.
    17.21
  Jno. Wit Hancock Lee's codicil. 20 May 1709. 17. pp 29-32
  Jno. Father of Sarah the wife of Antho: Haynie. 31 Janry
    1709/10. 17.107
  Jno. Wit will of Antho Haynie. 31 Jan 1709/10. 17.107
  Jno of St S par. Will. d 20 Sept 1718. p 20 Mar 1719/20.
    "Legacy left me by my Uncle William Harris Esq'r
    of haynie (or Laynie) in the parish of Stow Ford
    in the County of Devon .. (L 300. Sterl.) in
    the hands of Christopher Harris Esqr in the Parrish
    of Padstow and County of Devon". "Unto my Dear
    Father Joseph Harris". Bros Christopher and Willm.
    Harris. To sisters Margritt Pengelty and Jane Kitt.
    Wife Hannah, she extrx. Wit Tho Hobson, Jarvass
    Ellistone. 19.43
    Tho Cralle and Hannah Cralle exhib inv of est of
    Jno Harris decd. No date, entry follows will. 19.44
  Jno. dec'd. Will presented by Hannah Cralle, late Hannah
    Harris. 20 May 1719. 6.316
  Jno. His excors are Tho and Hannah Cralle. 20 Aug 1719. 6.331
  Tho. Headright of Mr Edw Sanders. 22 June 1669. 3.65
Harrison. Mr Charles and Tho Harwood to be overseers of the highways
    on Newmans Neck. 20 Nov 1696. 4.749
  Geo. Land formerly sold to him adj Jno Wright in Wicco par.
    16 Sept 1707. 17.128
  Geo. Wit will of Geo Leasure. 17 Nov 1708. 17.59
  Nicholas. Bought land from Wm Newman and Jno Meeks long
    prior to 19 Aug 1707. 17.153

Harrison, Richd. Headright of Richd Flint. 10 Mar 1661/2. 2.154
　　Robt. Buys 241 acres from Jno Adams. 2 Jan 1702/3. 17.161
　　Robt. of N. Co., planter. Deed. 19 Dec 1705. Assigns land
　　　bought of Jno Adams to his dau Mary Harrison. Also
　　　land to his dau Alice Harrison. Refs to Eliz his wife.
　　　Wit Benj Browne, Saml Churchill, Wm Hill. Re-rec by
　　　Robt Harrison 19 March 1711/12. 17.162
　　Robt. Buys 207 acres from Saml Churchill 19 Dec 1705. 17.161
　　Tho. and Mary his wife. She formerly wife of Wm Sanders.
　　　File addl inv of Sanders est. 18 Jan 1704/5. 17.165
　　Tho: Lives on 150 a belonging to Jno Webb. 4 June 1709.
　　　17.102
Harrold, Gilbert. Arrested at suit of Eliz Gerrard admrx of Samuel
　　　Gerrard. 15 July 1685. 4.279
　　Gilbert and his wife Joan. To appear in Williamsburg as
　　　witnesses. 30 May 1715. 6.110
Harry, Charles. Servt to Wm Tignall adj 12 yrs of age. 6 Apl 1669.
　　3.60
Hart, Jno. Wit del of land Crosby to Purcell. 18 Oct 1705. 17.192
Hartt, Tho. Left clothing by Col Geo Cooper. Wit Cooper's will. 18th
　　Nov 1708. 17.123
Hartington, Wm. Servt to Tho Williams adj 16 yrs of age. 21 Jan 1660.
　　2.136
Hartland, Wm. Aged 44 yrs or th-abts. "in March last or thereabouts
　　　being at Mr Neales house". Depo regarding witchcraft.
　　　20 May 1671. 16.180
　　Wm. Aged 30 or th-abts. 20 May 1671. 16.180
　　Wm. Sold land to John Lunce. 9 Feb 1683/4. 17.186
　　Wm. Buys 300 acres from Corderoy Ironmonger 5 Nov 1672. Sold
　　　it to Jno Champion 11 Feb 1685/6. 17.186
　　Wm. The Vestry of Wiccomocoe par complain he agreed, 3 July
　　　1678, to finish the Church. He has not done so. Ord to
　　　finish the work by Christmas. 16 July 1685. 4.289
Hartley, Henry. Age 26 yrs or th-abts. Says in Apl 1665 being in Mary-
　　　land on business of his master. etc. No date but rec
　　　Jan 1666/7. 16.10
Hartly, Henry. Land adj Wm Moore 5 Sept 1707. 17.47
Harvey, Mrs Dorothy. married Onecephorus Harvey some time before 18th
　　　Nov 1713. 6.5
Harvie, Jno. Wit will of Jno Webb 4 June 1709. 17.102
　　Jno. of Wicco par. Presented for swearing. 15 May 1717. 6.207
Harvey, Onecephorus. Wit deed Mahane to Chilton. 16 July 1705. 17.122
　　Onecephorus. The Grandjury having presented Dorothy Gaskins
　　　for having a bastard child and Onecephorus Harvey
　　　coming into Court affirmed that tho said Dorothy is
　　　and for some time before the child was borne (for
　　　which she was presented) was his wife, and that they
　　　were marryed according to the Rule of the Quakers whose
　　　Religion they profess And having here in Court proved
　　　such their marryage the said Presentment is therefore
　　　dismissed the said Harvie paying Costs. 18 Nov. 1713.
　　　6.5

Harvie, Onecepherus. Presented for not going to Church in Wicco par
              18 Nov 1714. 6.91 (Quaker)
Harvey, Onecephorus. Wit will of Patrick Pollick. 4 Dec 1702. Re-rec
              this will 16 Jan 1716/17. 17.235
         Onecep: Presented for not going to Church in Wicco par. 15th
              May 1717. 6.208
Harwood, Tho. with Mr Chas: Harrison overseer of highways in Newmans
              Neck. 20 Nov 1696. 4.749
Haskins, Mr. Ref to his ship being at Mr Griffin's. - Jan 1664. 16.10
         Richard of Bristol, marriner. 18 Nov 1666. 16.21
         Richd. Wit P of A Lyndsey to Bridges. 6 Apl 1667. 16.13
         Tho: His servt boy Boaz Hollis adj 14 yrs of age. 8 Sept.
              1662. 2.161
Hatfield, Gervase. Swears to nuncupative will of Erasmus Withers
              dated 1 Nov 1680. Oath on 15 June 1681. 4.94
Hawley see Orley.
Hauley, Ann. Aged 40 yrs or th-abts 20 Nov 1655. 14.62
         Mr Jas. Land in Wicco River adj Jno Johnson. 4 June 1655.
              17.137
Hauley, Jas. Wit agreement Kingwell and Essex. 20 Nov 1655. 14.56
         Jas. Transfers guardianship of Eliz Perry to Abraham Joyce
              who m her sister. 20 Sept 1658. 2.94
         Jas. Admr of Ralph Horsley, tailor, decd. 20 Sept 1658. 2.92
         Jas. Gift to grandchild Elizabeth Knight.15 Feb 1660/1.15.56
         Mr James and his son Edward live out of the County. Mr Peter
              Knight to take their depositions. 8 Oct 1662. 2.164
Hawley - See entry Geo: Hardinge of London. 8 Feb 1708/9. 17.91
Hawkins, Fran: Age 30 yrs or th-abts. His wife Elizabeth Hawkins.
              Depositions re witchcraft. 20 May 1671. 16.180
         Richd. Certif for land for importing himself, Kath Willowbye,
              Samuel Challenge, Edmud Larkin. 20 Feb 1651/2. 1.50
         Tho: Kept store at Mr Mottrom's house. 17 Jan 1651/2. 1.70
Hayden, Tho: Wit will Jno Lewis 4 July 1702. 17.223.
Haydon, Ann. Admr of Edmond Denny ord to pay Jno Denny a child's part
              of the est. 18 Feb 1718/19. 6.300
Hayes, Jno. Servt to Jno Cockrell adj 14 yrs of age. 21 Dec 1698.
              4.847
Haynie, Antho: Wit will of Patrick Pollick. 4 Dec 1702. 17.235
         Antho: Wit assignmt Innis to Horton. 26 June 1704. 17.255
         Antho: Wit deed Johnson to Howson. 19 Nov 1707. 17.40
         Antho: Wit will Tho Ingram 12 Oct 1700. His oath 21 May 1707.
              17.21
         Antho: Will dated 31 Jan 1709/10. Re-rec 20 June 1711 by Mr
              Geo Ball, Capt Richd Ball and Hancock Nickless.
              17.107
Haney, Jane. Daughter of Nicho: Morris. Her children Martha, Eliz and
              Richd Haney. 21 Nov 1660. 15.140
Haynie, Jno: Signs oath to Commonwealth of England 13 April 1652.
              1. pp 72-3
         Jno. Buys 300 a from Saml Nicholls. 20 May 1656. 14.80

Haynie, Jno. Wit will Tho Salisbury. 3 Mar 1656/7. 14.112.
Jno: See entry Wm Presley. 13 Apl 1659. 15.21
Jno. Deed of Gift. To his two daughters Martha and Elizabeth, and "my daughter in Law Susanna Warr". Cattle. 20th May 1659. 15.22
Mr. Jno. 1002 lb tobo owed him by Jno Salisbury. 20 Nov 1668. 3.48
Hainie, Jno. Admr of Jno Shaw. Wm Flowers owes the est 846 lb tobo. 11 Jan 1668/9. 3.50
Jno. Probates, as overseer, will of Henry Wicker decd. 22nd June 1669. 3.65
Jno. P of A from Tho Chetwood. 18 Dec 1671. 16.213
Haynie, Jno. Sold land to Richd Eaton prior to Mar 1677/8. 17.158
Jno. Proves will of Hannah Bridgman by oath as witness. 21st August 1678. 4.1
Mr Jno. Liberty to set up and keep ordinary near new Court House with Mr Phill Shapleigh. 15 June 1681. 4.97
Capt Jno. Justice. 18 Aug 1681. 4.101
Capt "for enterteyning the Justices 600 lb tobo". 2 Nov 1681. 4.681
Capt Jno. Justice. 18 Apl 1683. 4.176
Capt Jno. To div land betw Tho Hughes and his bro Jno Hughes. 19 March 1684/5. 4.262
Capt Jno. Justice. 16 Sept 1685. 4.291
Capt. Jno. Guardian of Tho Harding orph of Tho Harding Sr agt Luke Rowland who m Anne the admr of Tho Harding decd, ref to next Court. 22 May 1696. 4.728
Mr Jno. (Hayne) His servt Ebenezer Ram adj 11 yrs of age. 16 Nov. 1698. 4.842
Jno. Exor of Rev Jno Farnefold. 3 July 1702. 17.234
Jno. Brother of Antho Haynie. 31 Jan 1709/10. 17.107
Jno. of St S par. Fined for ab of 2 mos from Church. 23 Sept 1715. 6.138
Jno and Hanah his wife. She relict and admr of Tho Shapleigh decd. Sued by Jno S. guardian of Eliz S dau of said Tho. 19 Oct 1715. 6.141
Jno Junr. Sub poena agt him and Hannah his wife to answer suit of Jno Shapleigh guardian of Eliz Shapleigh. 19 May 1714. 6.36
Martha and Elizabeth. Gifts from Mrs Eliz Newman. 13 April 1659. 15.21
Richd. As Atty for Danl Webb "a molatto" obtains in peaceful agreement, his freedom from the est of Major John Mottrom dec'd. 5 Oct 1687. 4.405
Rd. Security for Alex and Jane Wetherstone when Rebecca Maudley, aged 2, is bound to them. 6 Oct 1687. 4.407
Richd. Certif for 200 acres for imp. 4 persons. 15 July 1696. 4.733
Richd. Wit deed Robinson to Robinson 14 July 1702. 17.105

Haynie, Capt Richd. Fined for absenting himself from Church. 21 Jan 1713. 6.15
    Capt. Richd. Tho Hope bound to him till 21. 16 Jun 1714. 6.43
    Capt. Richd. Fined for ab from Church in St S par. 25 Septr 1715. 6.137
    Richd. Attorney of Mrs Mary Eyes. 22 Nov 1716. 6.186
    Capt Richard. Wit deed dated 20 April 1681 Harris to Sowell. "Capt Richard Haynie came into Court and swore he wrote the Deed and was an Evidence thereto" 20th Jan 1719/20. 17.251
    Rd Jr. As wit proves will of Peter Presly Jr. 19 Nov 1718. 6.296
    Sarah. Wit will of Patrick Pollick. 4 Dec 1702. 17.235
    Sarah. Wife of Antho: Haynie who says she is "the Daughter of my Father in Law John Harris". 31 Jan 1709/10. 17.107
    Mrs. Sarah. An orphan, Rebecca Garratt, bound to her. Thos Everett security. 19 May 1714. 6.33
Hayward, Jno. Signs oath to Commonwealth of England. 13 April 1652. 1. pp 72-3
Hayler, Hen. To take inv of est of his friend Edw Walker. 2 Dec 1650. Proves will by oath 20 Sept 1656. 14.92
    Henry. Gives a cow to Jno son of Richd Holden. 19 July 1656. 14.87
    Henry. Aged 37 or th-abts. 21 July 1656. 14.86
    Henry. His widow Charity Hayler (Haylor) left with children, petitions for personal items from his estate. 21st Oct 1661. 2.148
Hayes, Tho. Wit will of Jno Bisick. 25 March 1706. 17.173
    Tho. Will presented by Sarah Hayes his extrx. 20 March 1716/17. 6.198
Haydon, Tho. His will presented by Anne Haydon his relict. Proved by oaths of Mutton Lewis and David Denny, wits. 21st March 1716/17. 6.205
Haynes, Tho. Ref to in will of Robt Jones Sr. 14 Jan 1675/6. 17.244
Hays, Richd. His land adj Jas Hill. 15 June 1709. 17.78
Hazelrigg, Mrs Anne. Mother of Jno Compton who is under age. 20 July 1663. 15.105
Head, Jane. Wit will of Robt Walton, Gent. 14 Jan 1669/70. 16.188
Headnett, Jos. Servt to Tho Bunbury to serve 5 yrs. 10 Feb 1662/3. 2.168
Heale, Ellnor. Age 50 or th-abts. 4 Aug 1665. 15.163
Healle, Francis. See entry Jas Jones. Bought land from Wm Newman and Jno Meeke long prior to 19 Aug 1707. 17.153
Heard, Henry. Under age. Deed of Gift from his mother Mrs Elizabeth Niccolas. 20 May 1670. 16.127
    Walter, deceased. Elizabeth his relict. 19 Feb 1678/9. 4.23
Heath, Ann. Phillip Thompson 11 yrs old bound to her. 18 Nov 1719. 6.345
    Saml. Wit deed Crowder to Schrover. 18 Sept 1705. 17.155

Heath, Saml. Wit will of Isaac Gaskins 22 Oct 1709. Swears he wrote
   the will for Gaskins. 18 June 1712. 17.167
   Saml. Appointed Sub-Sheriff. 16 June 1714. 6.42 Also sworn
      Sub-Sheriff. 15 June 1715. 6.113
   Saml. An orphan, Wm Carpenter age 14, bound to him to learn
      the trade of cooper. 16 May 1716. 6.156
   Saml. See entry Jno Nipper decd. 18 June 1718. 6.270
   Saml. Has property of Charles and Mary Prichard. See entry
      Rd Swanson their guardian. 21 Aug 1718. 6.277
   Saml. Margaret Pine his servant. 20 Aug 1719. 6.334
   Saml. Re-recs Tho Brewer's will. 15 Jan 1723/4. 17.268
   Tho: Son in law of Mrs Sarah Jones who bequeaths about half
      of her est to him. 26 Jan 1719/20. 19.98
   Wm. Re-recs deed dated 1703/4 Pope to Boyd. 18 Feb 1712/13.
      17.194
   Wm. His relict Ann swears he left no will. Admr granted. 20th
      May 1719. 6.316
Holder, Edmund. Wit will of Richd Wright. 16 Aug 1663. 15.114
   Edmond. Bequest from Simon Kirby. Also wit his will. 22 Mar
      1666/7. 16.13
   Edm. Buys 75 acres from Nath Hickman 1 May 1668. 16.45 Also
      buys 100 acres from Dinah the wife of Tho Barratt
      dau of Nath: Hickman decd. 1 May 1668. 16.44
   Edm. 409 lb tobo owed him by Jno Bryan. Also 818 lb tobo owed
      him by Robt Hitchock. 21 Jan 1668/9. 3.52
   Dr. Edmd. Buys crop from Saml Leverton. Pmt made to Richard
      Todwell for Leverton's use. 25 Oct 1671. 16.201
   Tho: Bought 100 acres in Mattaponi from Tho Barrett and Dinna
      his wife. 1 May 1668. 17.232
   Tho. Sold 100 acres in Mattaponi Neck, by Tho Matthews his
      atty, to Adam Booth. 11 Nov 1676. 17.232
Hele, Geo: Signs oath to Commonwealth of England. 13 Apl 1652. 1.72-3
Henly, Edw: "   "   "   "   "   "
   Edw. With Phill Carpenter buys 200 acres from Rd Walker. 10th
      June 1652. 1.76
   Edw. Deceased. His dau Sarah Henly given a cow by Robt
      Hitchock. 7 Mar 1667/8. 16.42
   Edw. His widow Joane also widow of Henry Willoughby and widow
      of Robt Hitchock. 17 Mar 1674/5. 3.224
   Edw. Deceased. Prob to his widow and extrx Mrs Eliz Henly.
      19 Nov 1696. 4.747
   Joane. of Cherry Point, widow. Gives her children Anne,
      Susanna, Sarah and Edward Henly 2 servants named
      Richd Jones and Eliz Harman. 26 Dec 1663. 15.150
   Mary. Bequest from her godfather Jno Tyngey. 1 Aug 1667. 16.30
Hergill, Christo: Wit will of Robt Walton, Gent. 14 Jan 1669/70.
      16.188
Hesler, Valentine. His relict, Mary, swears he left no will. Admr
      granted. 15 May 1717. 6.210
Hester, Isaac. Wit P of A Pascall to Pascall. 14 Feb 1671/2. 16.225

Hewett, Clayton. Wit P of A LeBreton to Matthew. 3 Apl 1671. 16.192
John. Deceased. Inventory of estate. 20 July 1658. 15.7
Olliver. Wit will of Jno Cookerill Sr on 30 Dec 1695. He had died prior to 18 Nov 1704. 17.135
Thomas and John. See entry Saml Griffin. 2 Feb 1702/3. 17.213

Hickley, James. Servt to Geo Clark adj 14 yrs of age. 22 June 1669. 3.65

Hickman, the Widdow. Jam: Parker said "he must give the Widdow Hickman a spell of work for 3 small pigs about 2 dayes old which were brought up by and fed with a spoon". Recorded - Jan 1666/7. 16.9 Also in the County expenses for the year she was pd 500 lb tobo. Does not show what for. 5 Nov 1668. 3.47

Dinah, now wife of Tho Barratt, sells Edmd Helder 100 acres in N Co. Adj another parcel Helder bought of Nath: Hickman. Part of 450 acres granted Nath: Hickman decd, father of said Dinah Barrat and left her in his will. 1 May 1668. 16.44

Hickman, Fra: Clerk of the Council. 10 Oct 1655. 17.112
Nath: Signs oath to Commonwealth of England. 13 Apl 1652. 1. 72-3
Nath: Will. d 26 March 1655. p 20 Jan 1656/7. Sons Thomas and Nathaniel. Dau Diana. "Nathaniel Hickman the younger". "The mother the 4 children". (Note: this will looks as though there were two sons named Nathaniel). Wit: Robt Bradshaw. Tho Haile. 14.98
Nath: Age 17 yrs. 4 Aug 1665. 15.162
Nath: His daughter married Wm Lyndsey. Then ranaway with Tho Barrett, considered a loose fellow in the neighborhood, and was said to have married him in Rappahannock. Jan 1666/7. 16.10 (Note-she did'ent run very far, for Rappahannock was right over yonder beyond the blackberry bushes. She did marry him. See entry above. What about Lyndsey we do not know.
Nath: Sells Edm Helder 75 acres inherited from his father Nath: Hickman decd. 1 May 1668. 16.45
Nath: P of A from Dinah Barret to ack sale of land to Edmd Helder. Wit Jno Dunslow. Pet Michaell. 13 June 1668 16.44
Nath: Accused of hog stealing. 6 Apl. 1669. 3.62
Robert. See entry Jno Saffin. 21 Aug 1669. 16.62
Tho: Aged 29 yrs or th abts. Says abt 5 yrs ago Tho Barrett enticed Diana Lyndsey wife of Wm Lyndsey to runaway or forsake her husband which he "was both an eye and eare witnesse of seeinge them on their Journey towards Rappahannock". That Barratt did jugling tricks that people said could not be done without aid of the Devil. No exact date of this deposition but recorded Jan 1666/7. 16.11
Tho: Age 27 yrs. His wife Mary Hickman. 17 Feb 1667/8.16.39

Hickman, Tho: 440 lb tobo in his hands belonging to Jno Fountayne attached by Mrs Eliz Tyngey. 21 Jan 1668/9. 3.54

Tho. His swamp in Mattaponi mentioned 15 Sept 1703. Prob ref to a deed dated 28 Mar 1680. 17.233

Hickory Neck. See Richd Lee. 15 Feb 1707. 17.60

Higgins, Tho. Servt to Jno Hull adj 17 yrs of age. 18 Mar 1684/5. 4.256

Timothy. Wit deed Cumins et als to Harding. 7 Apl 1707. 17.116

Higginson, Jno. Who m the relict of James Pope has much impaired the children's estate. 19 Feb 1678/9. 4.21

Hill, Eliz: wife of Jno Hill of Rappa Co. His land 1691. 17.47

Enock. Suit agt him and Jno Dunaway by exors of Jno Webb dismissed. 17 Feb 1714/15. 6.99

Enock. Francis his relict swears he left no will. She and Ezekial Hill app admrs. 18 Nov 1719. 6.346

Mr. Jas. Pat 350 acres now in G W par. 10 May 1661. 17.50

Jas. His wife Jone consents to sale of land. - Jan 1662. 15.91

Jas. Assigns int in land to Jno Taylor. 10 Aug 1667. 16.70

Jas. His servt Eliz Burke adj 15 yrs of age. 16 Nov 1698. 4.842

James. Decd. 8 July 1702. planter. Sells Jno Dunaway land adj Matchotigues Path, Benj Browne's corn field. Wit Edmd Bazie. Benj Browne. Re-rec 16 July 1710 by Benj Browne.

Jno Dunaway "and Margarett my now wife" assign the land to Benj Browne 8 July 1702. 17.174

Jas. "my Loveing Father James Hill" atty for Marg'tt Dunaway to ack a deed. 16 July 1706. 17.99

Jas. planter of G W par. Sells land where Jno Dunaway lately dwelt to John Chilton and Mary his wife and Steph: Chilton. 15 June 1709. 17.78

Mr. Jas Hill. Sold land to Tho Davis and Danl Bixbe prior to 18 May 1710. 17.50 Also sold land to Mr Tho Burbury prior to 18 May 1710. 17.50

James. Decd. Will proved by Joan Hill extrx. 17 May 1716. 6.159

Jno. of Rappa Co. Wife Eliz. His land 1691 later belonged to Wm Moore. 17.47

Jno. Wit deed Byram to Champion. 19 May 1708. 17.72

Jno. App guardian of Edwin Feilding a minor. His est in hands of Tho Dameron to be del to Hill. 18 June 1719. 6.324

Mabel. Dau of Wm Tignor. 28 Nov 1698. 17.160

Margaret. Dau of Jas Hill now m to Jno Dunaway. 16 July 1706. 17.99

Mary. Wit Capt Tho Brereton's will. 23 Mar 1698/99. 17.189

Rich. His servt Jane Macklaughn adj 14 yrs of age. 19 Jan 1675/6 3.249

Tho. Swears he wit will dated 18 May 1709 of Christo Garlington. 19 May 1714. 17.210

Hill, William. Aged 20 yrs or tha-abts. Says that the day Jonathan
          Parker was buried about the middle of Jan 1664, etc.
          No date for entry. Recorded Jan 1666/7. 16.10
     Wm. 589 acres assigned him by Jonathan Howes. 15 Nov 1671.
          16.204
     Wm. To val buildings put on land to be ret'd by Geo Hutton to
          Antho: Lynton. 16 Oct 1676. 4.7
     Wm. deceased. Prob of his will to Anne Hill the widow. Proved
          by oathes of wit Richd Pemberton, Geo Hutton and
          James Moor. 20 May 1685. 4.269
     Wm. To be constable of Mattapony. 19 Apl 1693. 4. 620
     Wm. Wit deed Churchill to Harrison. 19 Dec 1705. 17.161
     Wm. Nearest of kin to George Hill dec'd. Swears he made no will.
          Admr granted. 21 Aug 1717. 6.234
Hillier, Jno. P of A from Abra Palmer of New England to collect a/cs.
          26 Feb 1649/50. 1.69
Hiller, Jno. Gent. Aged 50 yrs or th-abts. 20 July 1658. 15.7
Hinderson, Herman. Servt to Mr Robt Jones adj to be 3 yrs old last
          Christmas. 20 Aug 1718. 6.274 (Note: Observe that
          far instance. This child doubtless brought from
          Great Britain, and of nobody knows what high or low
          family, a servant at 3. B.F.)
Hine, Jno. Servt to Mr Tho Govley adj 14 yrs of age. 21 Jan 1660/1.
          2.136
Hipkins, Tho. Buys 300 acres on S side G W River from Jno Bardon 22
          Jan 1656/7. Sells it to Jno Shaw 20 May 1657. 14.92
Hitchcok, Joane. Age 40 or th-abts. 4 Aug 1665. 15.162
Hitchcock, Jno. Adj 12 yrs of age. 9 May 1660. 2.122
          Robt. Aged 50 yrs or th-abts. His oath in agreement with
          Richd Rice. 21 July 1660. 2.127
Hitchcock, Robt. Gives a cow to Sarah Henly dau of Edw Henly decd.
          7 March 1667/8. 16.42
Hitchcock, Robt. His dau Mary given a cow by Robt Sech. 7 Mar 1667/8.
          16.42
Hitchcock, Robt. Owes Edm Helder 818 lb tobo. 21 Jan 1668/9. 3.52
          Robt. Deceased. His widow Joane also widow of Hen: Willough-
          bey and widow of Edw Henly. 17 Mar 1674/5. 3.224
Hoback, Jas. Attachmt agt est of Jno Raven 2020 lb tobo. 6 Apl 1669.
          3.62
Hobbs, Anne. Wife of Robt. 6 Dec 1683. 17.212
Hobbs, John of London and Elizabeth his wife. See entry Saml Griffin.
          2 Feb 1702/3. 17.213
     Robt. Deed 100 acres on Chicacone from Richd Rice Sr. 19 Dec
          1681. 17.212
Hobson, Clark. Wit div of land betw Antho and Tho Robinson. 12 August
          1703. 17.108
     Mrs Clark. Wit Deed of Gift Norman to Norman. 27 Aug 1705.
          17.223
     Clark. Wit Deed of Gift Webb to Wornum. 16 May 1707. 17.209

Hobson, Mrs Clerk. "widdow and relict" of Capt Tho Hobson decd, late
    Clerk of this Court. Ordered to deliver records to Mr
    Richd Lee now Clerk. 21 March 1716/17. 6.202
Mr Tho: Buys 135 acres on N side Little Wicco: from William
    Wildey. 9 Nov 1664. 16.125
Tho: Buys 135 acres on N side Little Wicco: from Wm Wildey.
    9 Nov 1664. 16.74
Tho: Age 30. 4 Aug 1665. 15.163
Tho: P of A from Thaddeus Riddan of Lynn in "Newengland".
    5 Apl 1667. 16.21
Tho and Sarah. Wit Deed of Gift Robinson to Robinson. 20 July
    1668. 16.36
Tho: Deed of Gift by "Henry Watts to my Grandson in lawe
    Thomas Hobson son of Thomas Hobson" property known as
    "little Wiccocomico mill house". 9 Jan 1668/9. 16.72
    This Handsome gift again brings up the question as to
    whether the name Wyatt was pronounced 'Watt' at this
    period. B.F.
Tho: His servt Wm Sparks to serve extra time for running away.
    10 Mar 1668/9. 3.58
Tho: As wit proves will of Wm Anderson. 6 Apl 1669. 3.61
Tho. Wit will of Robt Walton Gent. 14 Jan 1669/70. 16.188
Tho. Gives a colt to Tho, son of John Waddy. 20 May 1670.
    16.126
Tho: Age 35 yrs or th-abts. Deposition re witchcraft. "hee
    and his wife being sometime the last autumne at the
    house of Mr Edward Coles". No date shown, but actually
    it is 20 May 1671. 16.181.
Tho. Security for Barbara Salesbury admrx of Jno Jones decd.
    19 Jan 1675/6. 3.250
Tho: Wit deed Knight to Farnefold. 19 Apl 1676. 17.230
Mr. Tho. Commission to continue as "Clarke if this Court".
    16 Oct 1676. 4.6
Tho: Bondsman for Jno Atkins admr est of Wm Perriman. 5000 lb
    tobo. 16 Oct 1676. 4.7
Thos. In dif with Tho Tope (Tap and Tapp) his overseer. Order-
    ed to pay him. 24 Aug 1678. 4.5
Tho. Judgt agt est of Mrs Marth Jones decd 5192 lb tobo. 20
    Nov. 1678 . . (Note: Here] Here [- this is my own
    family washing a little dirty linen in public. B.F.)
Tho. High Sheriff in 1684. 16 July 1685. 4.290.
Tho. Sr. Justice. 16 Sept 1685. 4.291
Tho: Judgt agt Henry Fleet for 10000 lb tobo. 6 Oct 1687.
    4.409 (Note: I wish our family would NOT do this kind
    of thing - but they always have, and I presume we
    always will. Property rights being so much more im-
    portant than common humanity, etc., etc, forever. B.F.
Tho: Exor of Capt Tho Brereton. 23 Mar 1698/99. 17 189.
Tho: P of A. from Alice wife of Tho Williams. 18 Dec 1699.
    17.44

Hobson, Tho: Wit Jno Robinson's will. 13 Jan 1700/1. 17.108.
Tho: Wit deed Robinson to Robinson. 14 July 1702. 17.105
Tho. Wit deed Loughman to Scott. 7 Sept 1702. 17.202
Tho. Nephew and overseer of will of Tho Webb. Also witness. 11 Sept 1702. 17.5
Tho. Wit div of land betw Antho and Tho Robinson. 12 Aug 1703 17.108
Tho. Wit deed Smith to Sims. 11 Sept 1703. 17.104
Tho. Clerk of Court. 18 June 1706. 17.3
Tho. Wit deed Wildey to Chichester. 19 Nov 1706. 17. 224-9
Tho. Wit deed Cookrill to Cookrill. 19 Nov 1706. 17.138
Tho. of St S par. Land adj Wm Wildey. 19 Nov 1706. 17. 224-9
Tho. Wit deed Wildey to Ingram. 13 Dec 1706. 17.24
Tho. To ack sale of land Tho Williams to Saml Mahane. 11 Mar 1706/7. 17.72
Tho. Wit deed Moor to Hutson. 21 May 1707. 17.148
Tho. Atty of Mr Hancock Lee. 9 Sept 1707. 17.65
Tho. Wit deed Johnson to Hawson. 19 Nov 1707. 17.40
Tho. Wit deed Byram to Champion. 19 May 1708. 17.72
Tho. Makes will for P Coutanceau. 20 Apl 1709. 17.20
Tho. Affidavit. "aged Forty Five Yeares of Age or thereabouts" Says having perused his Father's a/c book of Clerk's Fees 1675 to 1682, finds Mr Peter Downing charged for drawing or writing or recording his father's deed and also for drawing or writing or recording his brother's deed. And this deponent well remembers that on a Book of Records belonging to this County, now burnt, containing Records, Wills, Conveyances and other Instruments of writing between 1675 - 1682, the record of a deed for 150 acres from Mr Wm Downing to his son John Downing, the same land where John Howson now lives. Also recorded in the book another deed for 300 acres (part of 600 acres, from Wm Downing to his two sons Wm and John Downing) from Wm Downing the younger to John Downing, this 300 a being part of land where John Downing now lives. That he, Hobson, has collected Quit rents and accounted with John Downing the father of the John Downing now in possession of the land. Signed Tho Hobson. Sworn 20 June 1711. 17.110
Tho. See entry Capt Tho Brereton. 17. pp 238-243
Tho. Re-recs Jno Beareman's will 1676/7 in which he is left land. 20 June 1711. 17.109
Tho. Sued by Tho Gaskins Guardian of Eliz Brereton. 18 Mar 1713/14. 6.27
Tho. Indenture that Jno and Mary Seward children of William Seward serve him. 22 July 1714. 6.60
Tho. Bondsman for Richd Neale. 17 Nov 1714. 6.88
Tho. As admr of Wm Winder decd sues Rainsford Smith. 17 Mar 1714/15. 6.107
Tho. Re-recs will d. 1702 of Jno Lewis. 17 June 1715. 17.223

Hobson, Tho. Sworn Deputy Clerk. 20 March 1716/17. 6.198
    Tho. Dec'd. Will presented by Clerk Hobson his Exor. 20 March 1716/17. 6.199
    Tho. Arrests Wm Wildey in debt of 440 lb tobo. 18 May 1716. 6.169
    Tho. Exor of Rev Jno Farnefold 3 July 1702. Re-recs his will 19 Sept 1716. 17.234
    Tho. Swears he wit Phillip Shapleigh's will. 15 May 1717. 6.208
    Tho. Wit will Jno Harris. 20 Sept 1718. 19.44
    Tho. Jr. Son of Tho Sr. 20 Jan 1676/7. 17.109
    Tho Jr and Sr. See entry Col Tho Brereton circa 1675-83. 6. pp 83-6
Hogan, Jno. Wit will Charles Fallin. 17 Dec 1700. Proves it by oath 16 Apl 1701. 17.159
    Teage. Servt to Tho Fownn adj 10 yrs of age. 21 Aug 1678. 4.1
Holdbrooke, Jno. Wit Deed of Gift Island to Feilding. 20 June 1666. 16.15
Holbrooke, Tho. Attachmt agt Benj Pride 595 lb tobo. 20 Nov 1668. 3.49
    Tho. Appointed Constable for Cone. 22 June 1669. 3.64
Holden, Grace. Wit will Edw Walker. 2 Dec 1650. 14.92
    Jno. Son of Richd Holden. Given a cow by Henry Haylor. 19th July 1656. 14.67
    Rich: Signs oath to Commonwealth of England. 13 April 1652. 1. 73-2
    Richd. Assigns a cow to Frances Roberts and Edwd Roberts Jr children of Edward Roberts. 21 Sept 1658. 15.11
Holland, Daniel. Dennis the wife of Jno Clarke now his servant. 22nd July 1661. 2.144
    Danl. Acquitted of murdering Tho Hughes. 21 Apl 1662. 2.156
    Danll. Sells Jno Warner and his wife Prue Warner 100 acres formerly owned by Richd Gibble. 20 Feb 1671/2. 16.230
    Dan: Deceased. Admr of his est to his widow Mrs Joyce Holland. Will proved by oaths of wit: Jeremiah Robins, Fran Cussons, Paul Winborough and Mary Cussons. 17th April 1672. 3.145
    Danl. Will. Half destroyed. Date gone but recorded 17 April 1672. To wife Joyce Holland. Daughter Elizabeth. Ref to land leased to Jno Freeman. 16.232
    Jno. Servt to Jonathan Parker adj 13 yrs of age. 6 June 1661 2.142
    Joice. Her servt Cornelius Mohohory adj 17 yrs of age. 17th Apl 1673. 3.144
    Mrs Joyce. Her servant Mich Waterland has runaway, etc. 17th Apl. 1672. 3.145
    Mrs Joyce. Registers mark of cattle. 18 June 1672. 16.235
    Symon. Servt to Mr Jas Waddy adj 14 yrs of age. 16 Nov 1698. 4.847
Holling, Nathl: Submits appraisal of David Spiller's est. Prob his bro or bro-in-law. 21 Oct 1658. 15.11 See next entry.

Holling, Susanna. Ref to as "my Brothers childe" in David Spiller's will. Prob 21 Oct 1658. 15.11
Hollis, Boaz. Servt to Tho Haskins to serve 7 yrs from next Nov. 8th Sept 1662. 2.161
Hollise Old Field. Owned by Wm Tignor. 28 Nov 1698. 17.160
Hollum, Jno. Appointed Surveyor. 15 Oct 1679. 4.47
Holly Branch. In G W par adj Jno Dunaway. 3 Sept 1708. 17. 76-8
Holsworth, Eliz. For some time past an inhabitant of this County. Certificate for leaving the Colony. 1 July 1714. 6.358
Homes, Robt. Servt to Nicholas Lancaster acks indenture for 6 years. 21 March 1716/17. 6.201
Hood, Wm. Adjudged 14 yrs old. 9 May 1660. 2.122
Hooper, Tho. Wit deed Crosby to Purcell. 18 Oct 1705. 17.192
Hope, Tho. Headright of Capt Jno Hatnic. 15 July 1696. 4.733
    Tho. 9 yrs old, with consent of his mother, Jane the wife of Jno Burgin, bound to Capt Richd Haynie till 21. 16 June 1714. 6.43
Hopkins, Mrs Grace. Widow of Mr Tho Hopkins to have inventory taken of his est. 11 Jan 1668/9. 3.51
    Mrs Grace. Her servts Eliz Evans and Isaac Hudson having run away, the sheriff ordered to take them "and give them 20 stripes a pece on their backes untill the blood come" and deliver them to their mistress' house. 21 Jan 1668/9. 3.51
    Mrs. Grace. See entry Tho Ingram. 29 Apl 1670. 16.128
    Mrs Mary. Relict of Henry Hopkins. 16 June 1714. 6.39
    Mary. Extrx of Hen: Hopkins, ordered to pay Maurice Jones a judgt obt agt sd Hen: on 20 Aug 1712 in his lifetime for L 6. 8. 6. 21 July 1714. 6.57
    Matthew. Age 28 or th-abts. 4 Aug 1665. 15.165
    Mr Tho. Justice. 24 Aug 1658. 2.91
    Tho. See entry Nicho: Britton. 19 Jan 1664/5. 15.149
    Tho. Request from Jno Ingram that Tho Hopkins' will not be proved untill he is notified. 11 Jan 1668/9. 3.51
    Mr Tho. Deceased. Inv of est appraised 19 Feb 1668/9. 16.89
    Tho. His relict Mrs Grace Hopkins is one of the overseers of the will of Jno Ingram decd. 22 June 1669. 3.65
    Tho. Decd. His widow Grace. In life he gave Joanna, orphan of Jnc Meredith decd, a mare. Order that Dorothy widow of sd Jno Meredith be secured by bond. 20th Nov 1669. 3.40
    Tho. See entry Jno Ingram. 29 Apl 1670. 16.76
Hopwood, Richd. hatter. Jno Melton orphan bound to him. 18 Sept 1717. 6.238
Hornsby, Danl. Has Reuben Calvert summoned at his suit. 20 Feb 1718/9 6.305
    Mary. Judith Short age 7 bound to her. Jos Knight security. 21 July 1714. 6.56
Horse Head Branch. In G W par. adj Geo Chilton and Saml Mahane Jr. 16 July 1705. 17.122

Horsley, Jos. Promises not to trouble his mother or any part of her estate. 20 July 1656. 14.100
   Jos. Age 22 years or th-abts. 20 July 1658. 15.5
   Ralph. Signs oath to Commonwealth of England. 13 April 1652. 1. 72-3
   Ralph. Age 42 years or th-abts. 20 Sept 1652. 14.11
   Ralph. Buys 300 acres in Westmorland County from Rice Maddox. 8 Feb 1654/5. Westmorland Co records.1653-9. p 23
   Ralph. Deceased. His relict Jane Horsley confirms personal property to her son Joseph Horsley. 21 July 1656. 14. 84
   Ralph. tailor. deceased. James Hauley admr. 20 Sept 1658. 2.92

Houghton, Jno. Wit P of A Johnson to Ferebee. 16 Oct 1667. 16.24
   John and Dorothy his wife. Wm Powell age 3 1/2, son of Edmd Powell, bound to them with his father's consent. Jno Downing sec. 5 Oct 1687. 4.404

Hoult, Joseph. of St S par. adj land of Wm Wildey. 19 Nov 1706. 17. pp 224-9

Hoult, Joseph. Land formerly his adj Owen Jones. 10 Oct 1718. 19.8

How, Joise. Headright of Hugh Fouch. 22 June 1669. 3.65

Howard, Hen: Servant to Tho Webb to be free. Says Indenture from Bristol states that he serve 4 yrs after his arrival in this country and he "hath fully served the said terme". 16 Oct 1676. 4.6

Howard, William. Will. Late 1709 or early 1710. Deposition 20 March 1716/7. Geo Murdock aged 40 yrs or th-abts, says Wm Howard on his death bed late 1709 or early 1710 desired that he make his will. As best he can remember: To Godson Taylor. Does not remember his Christian name but he is a son of Mr John Taylor, the first horse colt. The mare to George Murdock after the death of his wife. To wife Sarah all other property, she extrx. The will was signed in presence of Isaac Basie and Jno Basie witnesses called for that purpose. Deposition presented by Wm Burke on behalf of Sarah Howard. 17.236

Howe, Robt. Adj betw 15 and 16 yrs of age. 4 May 1660. 2.122

Howell, John. planter of N. Co. Pre-nuptial contract with Joan Phillpott of N Co widow. 30 Dec 1649. 1.40

Howes, Jonathan. planter of Mattapony. Assigns int in 589 acres pat by him 8 Oct 1668 to Wm Hill. 15 Nov 1671. 16.204

Howett, John. Age 48 or th-abts. 21 July 1656. 14.86

Howson, Ann. Left all estate by Ann Webb. Jno Howson exor. 21st Sept 1710. 19.89
   Elizabeth. Will presented by Francis Kenner, Charles Lee and Richd Wright her exors and proved by oath of Matthew Kenner a witness. 16 March 1714/5. 6.101

Howson, Hannah. Dau to Capt Leonard Howson and neice of Jno Howson. 13 Dec 1704. 17.8
    John. His servt Wm Deawy adj 14 yrs of age. 21 Dec 1698. 4.847
    John. Wit will Wm Coppage. 4 June 1698. Proves it 18 Sept 1700. 17.15
    John. Wit assignmt Innes to Howson. 26 Jun 1704. 17.255
    John. Bro and exor to Capt Leonard Howson. 13 Dec 1704. 17.8
    Capt Jno. Ack agreemt Lee to Lee. 17 Sept 1707. 17.65
    Jno. Gent of Wicco: par. Deed from Jeoffrey Johnson. 19 Nov. 1707. 17.38
    Capt Jno. "cozen" of Hancock Lee. 31 Dec 1709. 17.29
    Capt Jno. Land devised him by Capt Leonard Howson surveyed. Re-recs it 21 Mar 1710/11. 17.42
    Capt. Jno. Re-rec Hancock Lee's will 21 March 1710/11. 17.29
    Jno. Land he lives on formerly owned by Wm then Jno Downing. 20 June 1711. 17.110
    Howson spelled "Howton" in ref to Jno Howson's land. 18 July 1711. 17.125
    John. Deceased. His will prob by Eliz Howson and Francis Konner exors. 17 Sept 1714. 6.87
    Capt John. Francis Konner, Charles Lee and Richd Wright exors. Eliz: the relict. Swear to inventory. 17 Aug 1715. 6.128
    Leond. Sold land to Tho Bayles. 19 Feb 1665/6. 19.3
    Leonard. Wit deed Hill to Taylor. 10 Aug 1667. 16.70
    Mr Leond: His servt Mary Levistone adj 17 yrs old. 20 Oct 1668. 3.44
    Mr Leond: Justice. 20 Nov 1668. 3.48
    Leond. Buys 2 servants, Lewis Jenkin and Nicholas Allgrone, from Georg Courtnell. Wit: Jam: Gaylord and John Rotheram. 27 Jan 1668/9. 16.69
    Leond. Wit P of A Mould to Eyes. 18 Feb 1669/70. 16.70
    Leond: Buys 3000 acres from Tho Nash of Rappa: Co. 17 Janry 1671/2. 16.219
    Capt Leonard. Mrs Martha Jones gives him a bill for 4000 lb tobo 10 Aug 1677. Part pd. Judgt agt her for bal. 21 Aug 1678. 4.3
    Capt Leonard. He and Mr Jno Pinckard ord to div estate of Christo Garlington betw widow and the children. 21 Aug 1678. 4.2
    Capt Leonard. Justice. 20 July 1687. 4.397
              " 16 Novr 1687. 4.410
    Leond. Married Mary widow of Capt Tho Brereton. See entry Colonel Tho Brereton. 1701. 6, pp 83-6
    Mr Leond. To carry Rev Jno Farnefold to his grave. 3 July 1702. 17.234
    Leonard, Gent. His wife Mary widow of Capt Tho Brereton. 2nd July 1703. 17, pp 238-243
    Leonard. Buys 147 acres from Jas Innis in Wicco par. 19 July 1704. 17.255

Howson, Capt Leonard. of St S par. Will. d 13 Dec 1704. p 21 Febry
1704/5. Re-rec 22 Feb 1710/11 by Richard Wright
Daughter in law Mary Nutt to be pd her portion left
by her Father and Mother.
    Mrs Anne Webb to keep my child Hannah Howson now a
minor. Brother John Howson, he exor. To Elizabeth
Brereton 2 gold rings, one with a small seal with
her Grandfather Brereton's coat of arms. To David
Williams, my overseer, clothing. To Richd Wright a
ring, he exor, Land lately bought of James Innis.
To Cozen Leonard Howson son of bro John Howson.
Wit: Richd Cockerill, Edwd Cockerill, David
Williams. Proved by 3 wit 21 Feb 1704/5. 17,8

    Leond. decd. Sold mulato woman to Jno Bisick prior to 25 Mar
1706. 1.7.173

    Capt Leonard. 15 Apl 1706. John Taylor, Tho Taylor, Richard
Lattimore, Tho Downing and Geo Cooper surveyor, to
survey land formerly belonging to Capt Leon: Howson
decd and div betw Capt Jno Howson and the orphan
(name not shown) of his brother Capt Wm Howson. The
land at Fishing Creek. Re-rec by Capt Jno Howson
21 March 1710/11. 17,42

    Leond. Judgt to Richd Wright Gent Exor of Leond Howson decd
agt John Tarpleigh Gent of Richmond Co surviving
admr of Mary Nutt decd for 2918 lb tobo. 18 June
1719. 6,325

    Mrs Mary. Wife of Leonard. Widow of Capt Tho Brereton. 2 July
1703. 17, pp 238-243

    William. Wit will of Wm Coppage. 4 June 1698. Proves it 18
Sept 1700. 17.15

Howson's Creek or Fighting Creek. Adj land of Wm and Charles Copedge.
18 May 1710. 17,50

Hubball, Richd. Signs oath to Commonwealth of England. 13 April 1652.
1. pp 72-3

Hubbard, Tho. Moses Galloway age 5 yrs bound to him to be taught
trade of shoemaker. 19 Aug 1719. 6,326

Hudnall, Alice. Wife of John Hudnall. 5 June 1677. 17,28

    Alice. Prob of Ezekiel Genesis' will to her. She extrx. 4th
June 1684. 4,228

    John. of Isle of Wight Co. Buys 500 acres in Northumberland
Co from Tho Saffell of New England. 20 Nov 1655.
14.59

    Jno. His widow has married Edw Sanders. 18 Sept 1660. 2,132

    John. Son of John Hudnall decd. In his minority. Petitions
that Wm Downing be his guardian. 20 Jan 1661/2.
2,151

    John. Father of John. Put land 14 Aug 1658. Decd prior 25th
July 1665. 17,28

    John. Age 20. 4 Aug 1665. 15,166

Hudnall, John. Grant from Sir Wm Berkeley. 25 July 1665. 250 acres on S side Wiccocomoco River. Adj land of Mr Nicholas Morris, land of Danl Crosby, land of Wm Thomas, land of Jarvas Dodson "Said Land being formerly granted unto John Hudnall decd by Pattent dated the 14th of Aug't 1658 and now become due unto John Hudnall aforesaid son and heire to the said John Hudnall decd".
: 5 June 1677. John Hudnall and Alice his wife sold the above to Joseph Palmer, cooper, except a small parcel which "I sold to my Brother Partin Hudnall which he sold to John Palmer". Wit Henry Mayes, Jas Montgomerie Re-rec by Alice Palmer 15 March 1710/11. 17,28

John. Registers mark for cattle. 20 Jan 1666/7. 16,7

Jno. His wife Margaret joins in deed to Partin Hudnall. 25th Jan 1670/1. 16,151

Jno. To appraise est of Jno Lee decd. 16 Oct 1676. 4,6

Jno. Atty of Jno Palmer. 21 Aug 1678. 4,2 Also as Atty of Jno Palmer conf judgt to Edw Feilding 6000 lb tobo. 17 Oct 1678. 4,8

Jno. His land adj Partin Hudnall and Jno Crafford. 20 Dec 1706. 17,94

John. Son of Joseph Hudnall. 9 July 1709. 17,58

Joseph. His servt Richd Nornitt adj 11 yrs of age. 21 Dec 1698. 4,847

Joseph. Will dated 9 July 1709. prob 18 Aug 1709. 17,58

Joseph. Margery his widow now wife of Saml Blackwell. 21st July 1714. 6,56

Joseph Jr. Son of Joseph Hudnall. 9 July 1709 17,58

Mrs Margery. Wife and extrx of Joseph. 9 July 1709. 17,58

Mary. Dau of Joseph. 9 July 1709. 17,58

Partin. Son of John and bro of Jno Jr. Sold land prior to 5 June 1677. 17,28

Partin. Land adj Jno Crawford. Wit deed Crawford to James. 15 July 1706. 17,229

Parton. Will. d 4 Dec 1698. p 16 Feb 1703/4. To "my Cozen Partin Hudnall son of Henry Hudnall" 1/2 of land. He exor. To Patience dau of Alice Nelmes. To "my Cozen Anne Hudnall daughter to Henry Hudnall" a cow. Wit: Hugh Callan, John Gremlett, Richard x Smith. Re-rec 18 July 1711 by Tho Barry. 17,117

Partin. Presented for being drunk. 15 May 1717. 6,207

Mr Richd. Land adj Richd Neale. 7 April 1706. 17,195

Richd. As witness 28 Nov 1707. 17,40

Richd. Buys 200 acres in Wicco Par from Tho and Rebecca Bomum. 20 Sept 1709. Re-rec decd 20 Aug 1712. 17,177

Richd. Presented "for drinking and singing on the Saboth day". 21 Jan 1713/14. 6,17

Richd. His servt Roger Moor accused of house breaking. (long entries) 15 Aug 1716. 6,171

Hudson, Edw. Signs oath to Commonwealth of England. 13 April 1652. 1, 72-3
 Henry, Land adj Laughly Conolin. 21 July 1703. 17,96
 Isaac. Servt to Mrs Grace Hopkins. See entry her name. 21st Jan 1668/9. 3,51
 Mary. Wit deed Ingram to Winter. 29 Dec 1671. 16,216
Huff, Alice. Bequest 150 lb tobo from Robt Francis. 22 Oct 1671. 16,204
Huggall, Michael. Of Rappa. P of A to Jno Rotheram of N Co. 25 Oct 1668. 16,55
Hughes. Also as Hugh:, Hews, Hues, etc.
Hughs, Cath: Petitions agt Telelife Alverson that she was bound to serve him till 18, which time is expired. 17 Sept 1714. 6,87
Hows, Richd. Wit deed Booth to Straughan. 15 Sept 1703. 17,232.
Hews, Richd. Wit deed Jones to Rogers. 19 Aug 1707. 17,153
Hues, Richd. Decd. Mary Hues his extrx obtains probate. 17 Feb 1713/4. 6,17
Hughes, Robt. (his wife Susan) Countryman of Robt Francis. See his will. 22 Oct 1671. 16,204
Hues, Robt. Ref to as "my cozen Robt Hues" by Robert Jones in his will. 14 Jan 1675/6. 17,244
Hughes, Thos. Danl Holland and Jno Clark acquitted of murdering him. 21 April 1662. 2,156
Hughes, Tho. "he being at age" petitions that land left him by will of his father be div botw him and his brother John Hughes. Capt Jno Haynie ord to div the land. 19th March 1684/5. 4,262
Hughlett, Alice. Wife of John. 12 Feb 1667/8. 16,36
 Elizabeth. Daughter of John Hughlett and Alice his wife of Fairfield par, buys 100 acres in Wiccocimocco or Lee par. from Hen Boggus and Kath his wife formerly given him by Gervase Dodson gent decd. 24 February 1670/1. 16,162
 Ephriam. Wit will of Jos Hudnall. 9 July 1709. 17,58
 Jno. Bequest from Tho Salisbury to his dau Eliz Hulett. 3 March 1656/7. 14,112
 Jno. Robt Jones says he is "very dangerously ill". 8 Sept 1662. 2,162
 Jno. Judgt passed agt him for 1,000 lb tobo for concealing a tithable. "the said Hughlett made oath that his sonn John who was the person Concealed was then a housekeeper", Judgt cancelled. 21 Aug 1678. 4,4
 Jno. His servt Jno Williams adj 9 yrs of age. 15 Jan 1678/9. 4,18
 John. Sold land to Rd Exton prior to 13 Mar 1677/8. 17,153
 Mr Jno. "for fower Acres of Land where the new Court house now stands 1000 lb tobo". 2 Nov 1681. 4,681
 Jno. Wit deed Rice to Hobbs. 19 Dec 1681. 17,212
 Jno. Wit deed Benj Browne to Jno Dunnway. 15 July 1702. 17,75

19 N

Hughlett, Jno. Will 19 Oct 1704. prob 18 Jan 1718/19. To son John land "I had with his mother" on Totoskey Creek in Richmond Co. To sons Ephraim, William and Yarratt. To 2 daus Winnefred and Elizabeth, both under 18. 19.50
    John Jr. Wit deed Harris to Sowell. 20 Apl 1686. 17.251
    Mary. Wife of Tho: Hughlett. Daughter of Wm Tignor. 28 Nov. 1698. 17.160
    Tho: and Mary his wife. Jno Algrove 5 yrs old bound to them till 21. with consent of his mother. 19 Nov 1696. 4.748
    Mr Tho. "to build a prison such as the former and to find all things". 2000 lb tobo. 19 Nov 1696. 4.748
    Tho: Wit deed of gift Oldam to Oldam. 15 Jan 1700/1. 17.185
    Tho. Atty for Mrs Alice Smith. 11 Sept 1703. 17.104
    Tho. Signs inv Peter Coutanceau. 20 Apl 1709. 17. 216-231
    Tho. Justice. 17 Feb 1713/14. 6.17
    Tho. Signs inv of Simon Thompson. 16 June 1714. 17.221
    Tho. Exor of Eliz Downing decd. Presents her will. 19 Oct 1715. 6.141
    Mr Tho. Justice. 18 Apl 1716. 6.153
        Justice. 21 Nov 1716. 6.183
    Tho: and Mary his wife. Elizabeth Tignor orphan abt 9 yrs old bound to them. 21 Nov 1716. 6.184
    Mr Tho. Justice. 15 May 1717. 6.206
        Justice. 21 Jan 1719/20 6.353
    William. Chosen guardian by Francis Webb. 17 Jan 1716/17 6.191
    William. Decd. Will presented by Yarratt Hughlett exor. 17 July 1717. 6.222
    Yarratt. Chosen guardian by Francis Webb. 19 June 1717. 6.219
Hughletts branch. Adj land of Dunaway at head of G W. 11 Mar 1705/6. 17.150
Hughson, Wm. Servt to Col Rd Lee adj 14 yrs of age. 20 Jan 1661/2. 2.149
Hulett, Jno. Son of Jno Hulett. Gift from Gervase Dodson. 20 May 1659 15.21
Hull, John of Fairfields par. Will. dated 4 May 1667. date of probate not shown here, but see next entry. Dau Maryam Hull. Dau Anne Hull. Son Thos Hull under 17. Wife Anne Hull. "my two sons" Richd and John Hull. Wit: Wm Griffin. Robt Webb.
    Codicil. 16 Apl 1668. His son John is dead. Wife with child. Wit: Joseph Dowlen, Joane Dewell. 16.97
    Mr John. deceased. His will prob by oaths of witnesses. 11 Jan 1668/9. 3.50
    John. See entry Jno Saffin. 21 Aug 1669. 16.62

Hull, John. Age 58 or th-abts. Deposition re Sam: Nichols. Agrees
            with Robt Island's depo. Also says he heard Hamp-
            shire men call Nichols countryman and that he was
            born in 'Garnsey'. 20 Dec 1667. 16.32
    John of Chicacone, planter. P of A to his son Richd and his wife
            Anne Hull to transact all business. Wit Jos Dowlin,
            Joan Dowe. 16 Apl 1668. 16.36
    Jno. deceased. His est to be appraised by Sym Dudson, Sam
            Nichols, Walt: Dennis and Andr Cockerill and divid-
            ed. Richard Hull to have his full share of the crop
            before division. 11 Jan 1668/9. 3.51
    John. His widow m Rd Smith. See entry Jno Saffin. 29 Nov 1669.
            16.62
    Jno. His servt Tho Higgins adj 17 yrs of age. 18 Mar 1684/5.
            4.256
    John. Wit will of Jno Graham. 5 Mar 1705/6. 17.208
    John. Decd. Will presented by Ann Hull Extrx. 16 March 1714/15
            6.100
    Rich: His servt Arthur Oneale adj 15 yrs of age. 19 Jan 1675/6.
            3.249
    Richd. Owed 2900 lb tobo by Tho Morris. 21 Aug 1678. 4.5
    Richd. Wit deed Williams to Maurice Jones. 22 Feb 1705/6.
            17.164
    Richd. Wit deed Gooch to Neale. 7 Apl 1706. 17.195
    Richd. Took inv of Capt Jno Graham's est. Date missing. Swears
            he did 17 Dec 1712. 17.193
    Richd and Hannah his wife late Hannah Kenner, one of the daus
            and legatees of Rodham Kenner, gentleman, decd.
            20 Jan 1713/14. 6.14
    Mr Richd. Justice. 17 Feb 1713/14. 6.17
    Richd. Re-recs will dated 1705/6 of Jno Graham. 18 Mar 1713/14.
            17. 208
    Mr Richd. Produces Deed of Gift Mrs Patience Graham to her dau
            Mary Graham. 18 Mar 1713/14. 6.26
    Richd and Hannah his wife one of the daus of Rodham Kenner decd.
            To have recd bequest of L 100. Sterl, and 10000 lb
            tobo at 18. That she brought suit for it in Jan
            Court 1713, etc. That Elizabeth the elder dau was
            paid, etc. 15 Feb 1715/16. 6.148
    Richd. decd. Mrs Hannah Hull his relict swears he left no will.
            Admr granted. 18 Dec 1717. 6.251
    Richd. His widow, now Mrs Hannah Hurris exhibits inv of his est.
            18 Feb 1718/19. 6.299
    Richd. Son of Richd Hull decd. Inv of his share of the est sub
            mitted by Mrs Hannah Cralle formerly Hannah Hull.
            18 May 1720. 19.105
    Sarah. Orphan of Mr Richd Hull chooses Thos Gaskins as guardian.
            18 Nov 1719. 6.345
Hulls Creek. Adj land of Danl Neale. 4 Nov 1700. 17.249 Also: in
            St S par. Adj Wm Wildey's land. 19 Nov 1706.
            17. pp 224-9

Humphreyes, Jno. "An ancient feeble poor man" excused from paying
    levy. 16 June 1714. 6.39
  Joseph. Judgt agt him to Mrs Jane Wildey for bill dated
    6 July 1691 for 850 lb tobo. 15 June 1692. 4.594
  Jos. His servt Jas Bourne adj 14 yrs of age. 16 Nov 1698.
    4.842
  Jos. His servt Wm Tully adg 11 yrs of age. 20 May 1719.
    6.316
  Wm. Wit deed Williams to Lattimore. 26 Sept 1706. 17.252
  Wm and Ann his wife on behalf of 'their son' Tho Harding,
    bind him to Grant Jewsbury. 24 July 1714. 6.73
  Wm and Anne his wife next of kin to Cuthbert Bennett decd
    20 Aug 1718. 6.276
Humpston, Edw. His servt Jne Smyth age 15. 10 Feb 1662/3. 2.168
Hunter, Allen. His mother, Mary Hunter, requests Capt Geo Eskridge
    be app his guardian. 20 Sept 1717. 6.249
  Mary. Relict of Allen Hunter decd swears he died without a
    will. Admr granted. 20 Sept 1715. 6.130
  Robt. In prison for having "unseemingly kept Company with
    Anne Goddard wife of Thomas Goddard". 20 April
    1681. 4.92
Hurst, Henry. Gives "for my good will and affection" a heifer to Anne
    Abbott. Wit Willm Cooke. 24 May 1650. 1.40
  Henry. Signs oath to Commonwealth of England. 13 April 1652.
    1. 72-3
  Henry. Concerning John Place:"The Body of the said Place is to
    be under the tuition of Henry Hurst of Wiccomoco
    till hee bee of age to make choice of his
    Guardian". 22 May 1656. 14.83
Husbands, Mr Edward, chirurgeon. Pd 200 lb tobo for medicines adm to
    Mr Charles Morgan decd. 15 June 1681. 4.97
Husk, Jno. Also appears as Hust. Bequest from Jno Eustace. 23rd Dec
    1701. 17.245
Huste, Hen. His land on S side G W River adj Martin Cole. 1 July 1654.
    14.92
Hutson, Henry. planter of St S par. Buys land from Loughly Conalin.
    17 May 1708. 17.143
  Hen: Land adj Josiah Dameron. 17 Mar 1712/13. 6. pp 78-81
  Henry. This entry is not clear to me. It includes "To Robert
    Hutson Wm Trussell (admr) and Tho Hutson sons of
    Henry Hutson and Eliza his wife". 16 Jan 1716/17.
    6.188
Hutton, Geo. Wit Deed of Gift Lenton to Lenton. 26 Jan 1668/9. 16.67
  Geo: Age 30 yrs or th-abts. 28 Apl 1671. 16.185
  Geo: Buildings to be valued that he put upon land to be retd
    to Antho: Lynton. 16 Oct 1676. 4.7
  Geo: Married the relict of Henry Lynton the son of Antho:
    Lynton. Protests order of 17th April 1678 to
    vacate land. Ref to next Court. 21 Aug 1678. 4.5

19 N

Hutton, Geo: Appointed Constable of Mattapony. 7 Oct 1683. 4,198
 Geo. As wit proves will of Wm Hill. 20 May 1685. 4,269
 Geo. His land adj Loughly Conclin. 17 Apl 1700. 17,146
 Geo. Under 21. Heir of Danl Suilevant who refs to him as "Coz'n". 29 Aug 1704. 17,261
 Rebecca. Heiress of Danl Suilevant who refs to her as "Coz'n" 29 Aug 1704. 17,261

Iles, Christ: Wit P of A Johnson to Farebee. 16 Oct 1667. 16,24
Indian Lands. Surveyed by Ger Dodson. Boundries shown in entry. 25th Feb 1655/6. 16,72
Indian Storehouse. Jno Carter appointed agent there. 17 Nov 1714. 6,89
Ingoe, Jno. Married widow of Bennett prior 6 July 1695. Pat land this date and sold it to Benj Browne. 17, pp 76-8
Ingram, Abra: One of two youngest sons of Tho. 12 Oct 1700. 17,21
 Abra: Wit Deed of Partition Jno Ingram to Chas Ingram. 14th Oct 1707. 17,23
 Abra: Re-rec will of Patrick Pollick. 16 Jan 1716/7. 17,235
 Mrs Anne. Wife of Thos. 12 Oct 1700. 17,21
 Charles. Father of Thos. This entry prob in error. It states that Charles is under age 11 June 1680. I believe it actually means that Thomas Ingram, son of Charles, was under age 11 June 1680. 17,14 Or it may be that the names of the father and son are reversed.
 Charles. One of two youngest sons of Tho. 12 Oct 1700. 17,21
 Charles. Deed of Partition from Jno Ingram. 14 Oct 1707. 17,23
 Charles. Wit deed Wm Bledsoe to Jno Ingram. 14 July 1708. 17,22
 Charles. Wit will Isaac Gaskins. 22 Oct 1709. 17,167
 Charles. Re-rec deed dated 1680. 23 Feb 1710/11 17,14
Ingerom, Jno. Signs oath to Commonwealth of England. 13 April 1652. 1, 72-3
Ingram, Jno. Sells a cow to Capt Hen Fleet of Lanc Co. 29 Jan 1653. 14,58
 Jno. Requests that will of Tho Hopkins not be proved until he is notified. 11 Jan 1668/9. 3,51
 Jno. Receipt for payment for 9 horses. To Mrs Grace Harris, als Hopkins, and by her order from Robt Jones of Fleets Bay. Refers to a breed of horses formerly belonging to his late father Jno Ingram decd or to Mr Thom Hopkins decd consigned to Robt Jones. Wit: Tho Morrill, John Feild. Dated 29 Apl 1678. 16,76
 Jno. Bought 6000 acres. The names of Wm Vincent, Tho Nash and Mr Leond Howson appear as former owners or part owners. 17 Jan 1671/2. 16,219
 Jno. Eldest son of Thos. 12 Oct 1700. Re-recs his father's will. 22 Feb 1710/11. Also Re-rec deed from Wm Wildey d 18 Dec 1706. 22 Feb 1710/11. 21,24

Ingram, Jno. Agreement with Ralph Bickley re boundry. 2 July 1707. 17.24
    Jno. Deed from Wm Bledsoe dated 14 July 1708. Re-rec 22 Feb 1710/11. 17.22
    Jno. Wit will Barth Dameron. 8 Aug 1708. 17.57
    Jno. Signs Inventory of Hancock Lee. Date destroyed. Re-rec 21 March 1710/11. 17.38
    Jno. Bondsman for Wm Jones as Sheriff. 16 June 1714. 6.42
    Jno. To keep and protect Robt Crowder an orphan until his case is settled. 22 March 1715/16. 6.152
    Mr Jno. Justice. 18 Apl 1716. 6.153
    Jno. Takes an orphan who has been cruelly treated. 18 April 1716. 6.154
    Jno. Justice. See entry Roger Moor. 15 Aug 1716. 6.171
    Jno. Re-rec will of Patrick Pollick. 16 Jan 1716/17. 17.235
    Jno. Sworn Sheriff this day. 18 June 1718. 6.285
    Tho. Claims property under will of Jno Ingram his deceased father. Refs to Mrs Grace Hopkins relict and admr of Mr Tho Hopkins one of the overseers of the will, etc. 22 June 1669. 3.65
    Tho. Receipt to Mrs Grace Harris als Hopkins. Ref to a breed of horses belonging either to "Jno Ingram my late father decd or to Mr Thom: Hopkins decd". Wit: Tho Morriss, Jno Feild. 29 Apl 1670. 16.128
    Thos. Deed. Makes over property to Thos Winter marcht for his wife Kath: Ingram. Wit: Robt Jones, Mary Hudson. 29th Dec. 1671. 16.216
    Tho. and Kath: his wife. Sell Mr Tho Winter of Rappahannock 600 acres. Acknowledged in Court unto John Ingram and given by him, in his will, "unto mee Tho Ingram his onely sonne". Wit: Wm Barry, Tho Williams. 16 April 1672. 16.231
    Thos. Youngest son of Charles. Gift from Tho Winter. 11 June 1680. 17.14
    Thos. Will. d 12 Oct 1700. p 21 May 1707. John Ingram and Anne his wife. He eldest son and exer. Charles Ingram and Abraham Ingram 2 youngest sons. Dau Thomasine Parker. Wit: John Harris, Batt Dameron. (Bartholomew Dameron), Antho Haynie. Proved by oaths of 3 wit. Re-rec by John Ingram 22 Feb 1710/11. 17.21
    Thos. Wit will Hancock Lee. 31 Dec 1706. 17.29
Ingram entries. Note: I am not at all satisfied with these items concerning this good old Virginia family that have done so much to create, protect and enforce our laws. Of course this represents only about 1/4 of the data in Northumberland Records of the period. But in this case I fear I've missed the essential entries. B.F.
Innis, Dr James. Henry Mayes refs to land sold him adj Tho Mayes. 12 April 1702. 17.203
    James. of Lancaster Co. Gent. Sells Leonard Howson 147 acres in Wicco par. 19 July 1704. 17.255

Innis, James. Lately sold land to Capt Leonard Howson. 13 Dec 1704. 17.8
    Jas. Wit deed Crosby to Purcell. 18 Oct 1705. 17.192
    Mrs Kath: wife of James. 17 July 1704. 17.255
Ironmonger, Corderoy of Great Wiccocomoco par. Sells Alex Griffin of same par 100 acres. Adj land of Jno Swanson, etc. Wit: Tho Peirce, Kendall Cotterall. 20 Dec 1667. 16.32
    Corderoy. Owes Tho Lane bal of 1797 lb tobo on a bill d 18 May 1667 for 4597 lb tobo for a parcel of land. 21 Jan 1668/9. 3.54
    Corderoy. To ask Col St Ledger Codd's forgiveness in open Court for spreading scandle in regard to ill treating and murdering his servants. 17 Apl 1672. 3.146
    Cordery. Sold 300 acres in G W par to Wm Hartland. 5 Nov 1672. 17.186
    Wm. Deed of Gift. Gives a heifer "to my Nephew and God sonne Wm Jones the son of my Br in Law Robt Jones". In case of his death before marriage or 21 to be div among his bros and sisters. 7 Apl 1668. 16.42
Iland, Richd. Deed of Gift. A cow to Sarah Smyth dau of Lt Col Saml Smyth. 21 July 1656. 14.85
Island, Richd. Deed of Gift. A cow to Esau Gregory. Wit Tho Ashley, Jos: Feilding. 20 June 1666. 16.3
Island, Rich. Gives a heifer to Jos Feilding Jr son of Jos Feilding. Wit: — Ashley, Jno Holdbrooke. 20 June 1666. 16.15
Island, Robt. Age 56 or th=abts. Says Sam Nichols living 2 yrs at Kings Creek at his first coming out of Barbadoes to Va in York River, but only 6 weeks in James River before he came thither. He heard people calling him Countryman that were born in Isle of Wight and some that were born in Jersey, saying Sam Nichols was born in Garnsey. 20 Dec 1667. 16.32
Island Creek. Adj land of Wm Nutt. 4 Feb 1662/3. 17.177
Ize – See Eyes.
Ize, Dennis. Wit deed Gibson to Downham and Gilbert. 3 Dec 1666. 16.3
    Dennis. See entry Adam Yarratt. 22 Oct 1667. 16.25
Izzard, Nich: As witness proves will of Wm Anderson. 6 Apl 1669. 3.61

Jackland, Sam. Wit P of A Chetwood to Hayney. 18 Dec 1671. 16.213
Jackson, Charles. Swears to nuncupative will of Augustine Rhodes, bro of Mrs Rachell Yarratt. The will declared void. 17th April 1678. 4.8
    Richd. Servt to Mr Wm Wildey adj 14 yrs old. 21 Jan 1660/1. 2.136
    Richd. Headright of Wm Wildey. 8 Sept 1662. 2.161
Jacob, Edw. Headright of Mr Edw Sanders. 22 June 1669. 3.65
Jacobus, Angell. Alex Griffin tfrs int in bill of sale to him. 17 Apl 1672. 16.231
James, Anne. Re-recs deed d 15 July 1706 Crawford to James. 18 April 1716. 17.229

James, Danl. Servt to Capt Jno Graham prior to 17 Dec 1712. 17.193
    Meredith. Deed from Jno Crawford. 15 July 1706. 17.229 Also as Meredy James shown as having formerly bought land, adj that of Wm Davis, from Jno Crafford. 20 Dec 1706. 17.94
    Moulder. Jane his relict swears he left no will. Admr granted. 21 Nov 1716. 6.183
    Tho. His will presented by Margt James his extrx. 16 May 1716. 6.155
    Tho. His land adj that sold by Josias White to Rd Smith. 17th Dec 1718. 19.3
    William. Adj 15 yrs old. 20 Dec 1669. 3.42
    William. Left a cow when he is free. 20 Jan 1676/7. 17.109
Janna, Wm. Wit deed Innis to Howson. 19 July 1704. 17.255
Jeffes, Wm. Age 30 or th-abts. 20 Mar 1655/6. 14.72
Jeffers, William. Pre-nuptial agreement with Elizabeth Austin. States they intend to be married and is in regard to two cows belonging to her. The entry is headed "Elizab Austin his nowe wife" which is sufficient to show they were already married when the agreement was recorded. We can only hope his sister Mrs Walker gave them a handsome wedding gift sans a good moral lecture. 7 July 1656. 14.89
Jeffars, Wm. Age 31 or th-abts. 21 July 1656. 14.86
Jeffers, Wm. His sister, now wife of Wm Walker, insulted him last November at a funeral. See entry Mary Laud. 21st July 1656. 14.86
    William. Petitions that Stephen Bailey, who married the relict of Wm Walker decd, has in tuition his (Jeffers') wife's brother. Which orphan, Wm Walker, he "doth much abuse". The orphan ordered to remain with Jeffers. 21 May 1660. 2.124
    William. In dif with Steph Bailey. Order that Wm Walker the son of Wm Walker decd, remain with Bailey who m the relict of Walker. Both parties ordered to cease "Lybigious vexations and turbulent suits" 21 July 1660. 2.128
Jeffery, Eliz. Headright of Geo Cololough. 21 Jan 1651/2. 1.71
Jammison, Jno. His wife Eliz mother of Mary Sharp. 16 June 1714. 6.42
Jenkin, Lewis. A servant sold by Geo Courtnall to Leond Howson. 27th Jan 1668/9. 16.69
Jenkins, Morris. Headright of Wm Thomas. This is an error. He was a headright of Wm Shoares or Sheares. 21 Aug 1678. 4.4
Jenking, Walter. Servt to Jno Cockrell adj to be 10 yrs of age. 6th April 1669. 3.60
Jennings, Edw. Headright of Mr Robt King. 10 March 1661/2. 2.154
    Edw. Servt to Mr Tho Phillpott to serve 5 yrs from Nov next. 8 Sept 1662. 2.161

Jennis, Davi. Bequest from Tho Edwards. 9 March 1669/70. 16.71
Jennys, Jno. Wit Col Tho Brereton's will 11 Oct 1675. Died prior 1683 6. pp 83-6
Jenney, Mr Jne who wit Col Tho Brereton's will is now dead. 4 June 1684. 4.231
Jepsen, Jos. Headright of Lau Dameron. 21 Feb 1658/9. 2.102
    Jos: Lewis Sheapard owes him 650 lb tobo. 21 Jan 1668/9. 3.54
Jermin, Eliz: Headright of Mr Edw Sanders.
Jetts, Wm. Servt to Wm Shear adj 13 yrs of age. 10 Mar 1668/9. 3.58
Jewsbury, Grant. Tho Harding bound to him. 24 July 1714. 6.73
Jinkins, Walter. Left Charles Lee 500 acres prior to 13 July 1700. 17.248
Johnson, Abraham. "An ancient poor person" excluded from levy. 19th Apl 1693. 4.619
    Benj. Age 23 or th=abts. Servt to David Lindsey. 4 Aug 1665. 15.162 Also deposition in Ashton - Lindsey case. Does not show age. 4 Aug 1665. 15.165
    Cornelius. P of A to John Ferebee. Wit: Christ: Iles, John Houghton. 16 Oct 1667. 16.24
    Elizabeth. Wife of Jeoffrey. 19 Nov 1707. 17.40
    Jas. Land adj patent to Jas Claughton on Broad Creek Swamp. 8 March 1662/3. 17.87
    James. His wife Anne. 19 Aug 1665. 15.169
    James. Aged abt 32 yrs. No exact date in entry but recorded Jan 1666/7. 16.11
    James. Wit deed Rice to Saffin. 16 Apl 166-. Recorded 20 Jan 1666/7. 16.7
    James. His house, etc. See long entry Adam Yarratt. 22 Oct 1667. 16.25
    Jas. To lay out land left by Henry Roach to Mrs Eliz Tyngey. 21 Jan 1668/9. 3.55
    Jam. Vestryman Chicacone par. 20 Mar 1671/2. 16.158
    James. To value buildings put on land to be retd by George Hutton to Antho Lynton. 16 Oct 1676. 4.7
    Jas. Proves will of Wm Shorter by oath as witness. 21 Aug 1678. 4.1
    Jas. His land adjs Jas Moore. 6 May 1679. 17.143
    Jam: He and Eliz Wooldridge complained agt for trespass by Josiah Dameron whose land adj theirs. 17 Mar 1712/13 6. pp 78-81
    Jas. "an antient Feeble and declining person" excused from any levy. 19 May 1714. 6.32
    Jas. Will presented by Mary Johnson and Lewis ap Lewis, Exors. 20 Feb 1717/18. 6.258. (Note: for those who may not know 'ap' means son of, and is still used rather than 'Jr.' by certain old Virginia families. B.F.)
    Jeffery. Son of Jno and Anne Johnson given a plantation by Sam Gocho. 14 Dec 1663. 16.2

Johnson, Jeffery. Brother of Peter Byram's wife. Was asked to stay at their home but abused them to their sorrow, etc. 16 July 1685. 4,287
    Jeoffrey. His land adj that patented in 1650 by Jeoffrey Gooch and inherited by his nephew Jno Gooch. 7th April 1706. 17,195
    Jeoffry of Wicco par, planter. Deed to Jno Howson Gent 19 Nov 1707. This land bought 20 Dec 1666 from Jeoffry Gouche. There was a suit concerning it brought by John, son and heir of Saml Gooche in the General Court at James City 22 Oct 1690. This was settled amicably 20 Jan 1696/7. 17,38
    John. Patented 85 acres 4 June 1655. 17,137
    John. Owned 50 acres adj Tho Garrard 1 Dec 1656. Sold it to Wm Thomas in April 1660. 17,91
    John. Pd 48 lb tobo from Co levy. Does not state what for. 5 Nov 1668. 3,47
    John. Wit deed Lane to Whitford. 18 Jan 1669/70. 16,154
    Jno. Presented for not going to Church in Wicco par. 19 May 1714. 6,35
Jolland, Wm. who m widow of Tho Orley. Admr of Orley's est. 8 Oct 1662. 2,163
Jollins, Wm of Cherry Point, planter. Married Robecca widow of Thos Orley. See entry Geo Hardinge of London. 22 Sept 1664. 15,144
Jallon, Wm. Appointed Constable for Cherry Point. 22 June 1669. 3,64
Jolland, Wm. Submits a/c of cattle belonging to Hen Medcalf orphan of Wm Medcalfe. 22 Aug 1670. 16,144
Jones, David and Diana, of Westmorland Co, planter. Deed to John Claughton of Northumberland Co. 40 acres in N Co. 16 Nov 1699. 17,88
    David. "a poor Ancient man" exempt from levy. 16 May 1717. 6,212
    Diana. Wit tfr Moor to Hutson. 21 May 1707. 17,148
    Edw. Appointed Constable for little Wicco. 22 June 1669. 3,64
    Francis. Summoned at suit of Clement Lattimore for 500 lb tobo. 20 Feb 1718/19. 6,306
    Goodlove. On motion of Goodlove Jones, by her atty Wm Dare, order that Graves Eves produce the will of John Jones at the next Court. 16 Nov 1713. 6,2
    James. See entry Dennis Odie. 8 Oct 1662. 2,166
    Jas. Deed. 19 Aug 1707. of St S par, planter. Sells Phillip Rogers of St S par, for 7440 lb tobo, 124 acres in St S par. Part of a pat granted Wm Newman and Jno Meeke 6 May 1651 for 1000 acres. Also part of 400 (part of the 1000 acres) which became thus conveyed to James Jones, to Wit: 200 acres part of the 400 acres sold by afsd patentees to Nicholas Harrison and from him by several descents and conveyances came to Clement Spelman. The other 200 acres residue of the 400 sold by the Patentees to Francis

Jones, James (continued) Healle and by several conveyances come to
    Clement Spelman, which 400 acres the sd Clement by
    his will proved in Westmorland Co Court gave to Ralph
    Spelman, who sold it to James Jones. Which 124 acres
    is on S side of Wicco River, adj road to Mundays
    Point. Wit Richd Hews, Thos x Hall senr, David
    Straughan. Ack 20 Aug 1707 by James Jones and Elia:
    his wife. Re-rec by Mr Jno Opie who has purchased the
    land 20 Feb 1711/12. 17.153
James. His will being burned, Henry Metcalfe and John Turner
    who married Phoebe and Priscilla Shippey, the legatees
    of sd Jones, produced depositions of Robt Phillips
    and Barth Leasure relating to the will. Accepted for
    record 17 Feb 1714. 6.96
Joanes. Headright of Laur Dameron. 21 Feb 1658/9. 2.102
John. Suspected, with Jno Richards, of murder. Ordered to touch
    the corpse of Tho Rolph and that of Tho Bayles before
    a jury. 20 Nov 1669. 3.41
John. Son of Hugh Jones, tailor. Bequest of land from Roger
    Walters. 29 Dec 1669. 16.115
Jno. Ref to in will of Robt Jones sr as "my Cosen Jno Jones"
    14 Jan 1675/6. 17.244
Jno. decd. Barbara Salisbury app to admr est. Tho Hobson, sec.
    19 Jan 1675/6. 3.256
Jno. a "Very Lame weake and Impotent person" freed from levy.
    21 Aug 1678. 4.3
Jno. Will of Tho Gill Sr ref to 100 acres "bought of my Cosen
    John Jones" in St S par, given him by his Grandfather
    Roger Walters. 10 Feb 1707/8. 17.97
Jno. late dec'd. Heir demands will from Graves Eves. 18 Novr
    1713. 6.2
Mrs Leeanna. See entry Richd Lee. 15 Feb 1707/8. 17.60
Mrs Leeanna. Wife of Wm Jones. Deed from Charles Lee. 19 May
    1714. 6.34
Lewis. Dr Tho Glover summoned to view his corpse and that of
    his servt - Williams, they being drowned. 20th May
    1671. 3.121
Mrs Martha. Wife of Robt Sr and his extrx. 14 Jan 1675/6.
    17.244
Mrs Martha. Gives bill to Capt Leonard Howson for 4000 lb tobo.
    10 Aug 1677. Part pd. Judgt agt her for bal 21 Aug
    1678. 4.3
Mrs. Martha. At time of her decease owed Tho Hobson 5192 lb
    tobo. Judgt agst her est. 20 Nov 1678. 4.12
Mrs Martha. deceased, widow of Robt Jones decd. Her son Mr Wm
    Jones exor. 19 Feb 1678/9. 4.22
Mrs Martha. Obtained judgt agt Charles Morgan for 16 bu salt
    22 Nov 1677. Now renewed agt his admr. 20 Oct 1681.
    4.107
Mary. Bequest. Asalf from Robt Francis. 22 Oct 1671. 16.204

Jones, Maurice. Now under age. Has land given him by his Godfather, Mr Jno Cousins. 14 Jan 1675/6. 17,244
    Maurice. Exor of Mr Jno Eustace. Bequest from him. 23 Dec 1701. 17,245
    Maurice. Buys 100 acres from Tho Williams. 22 Feb 1705/6. 17,154
    Maurice. Of Northumberland Co, Gent. Deed from C Garlington. 18 June 1706. 17,1
    Maurice. Land adj that of Christo: Garlington. 16 May 1709. 17,210
    Maurice. Wit deed Bonum to Hudnall. 20 Sept 1709. 17,177
    Capt Maurice. Records deed. 22 Feb 1710/11. 17,3
    Maurice. Signs inventory of Hancock Lee. Date missing but Recres 21 Mar 1710/11. 17,38
    Maurice. Exor of Christo Garlington, who refers to him as "my Brother Maurice Jones" in his will dated 18 May 1709. Swears he wrote the will 19 May 1714. 17,210
    Maurice. Mary Hopkins extrx of Hen: Hopkins ordered to pay a judgt to him. 21 July 1714. 6,57
    Capt Maurice. His servt Andr: Cultcally age 14. 20 Aug 1718. 6,275
    Maurice. Wit in entry regarding Wm Tapptico, King of the Wiccocomoco Indians. 31 Dec 1718. 19,95
    Owen and Rachel his wife. She late Rachel Feilding the dau and sole heir of Jno Feilding decd. They complain agst Wm Payne who married Susanna relict of the sd Jno, for due proportion of her father's estate. 19 Sept 1716. 6,182
    Owen and Rachel his wife. She dau and heir of Jno Feilding decd. They sell Nickolas Lancaster 50 acres, adj the land of Mr Sam: Span, land of Jno Graham and land formerly Joseph Hoult's. Wit Samuel Span. Abner Neale. 10 Oct 1718. 19,6
    Richd. Servt of Mrs Joane Henly. 26 Dec 1663. 15,150.
    Richd. Deceased. Jno Walters his exor to have prob of will. 15 July 1685. 4,275
    Mr Robert, on behalf of Exors of Hon Samuel Mathews Esqr, late Governor, appeals to the Quarterly Court at James City concerning Mathews' title to land near the Wiccocomoco Indians. 21 May 1660. 2,124
    Robert. Says Jno Hughlet is "very dangerously ill". Requests all cases re him be postponed. 8 Sept 1662. 2,162
    Robt. Justice. 8 Sept 1662. 2,160
    Robt. His servt Jane Bateman to serve 10 yrs. 8 Oct 1662. 2,163
    Robt. Deed of Gift a heifer to John the son of "my Bro Maurice Jones. 7 Apl 1668. 16,41
    Robt. His son William Jones given a heifer by his uncle Wm Ironmonger. See entry his name. 7 Apl 1668. 16,42

Jones, Mr Robt. Justice. 20 Oct 1668. 3,44
   Justice. 11 Jan 1668/9. 3,50
  Mr. Robt. Sues Wm Brudenall. 21 Jan 1668/9. 3,52
  Mr Robt. Justice. 10 Mar 1668/9. 3,58
  Robert. Complains that his house has been broken into by the Wecocomoco Indians. Mr Peter Knight and Edm Lyster ordered to punish them. 6 April 1669. 3,61
  Robt. Justice. 24 Aug 1669. 3,35
  Robt. of Fleet's Bay. Entry concerns a breed of horses in his possession. 29 Apl 1670. 16,76
  Robt. Wit deed Ingram to Winter. 29 Dec 1671. 16,216
  Robert. Will. dated 14 Jan 1675/6. probated 1 March 1675/6.
   Robert Jones of Fleet's Bay in Northumberland Co.
   To son Wm Jones land from Beach branch to "the plumb tree swamp".
   To son Saml Jones land from afsd Beach branch to the ditch east about the glade adj the swamp by the house "of my Cozen Robert Hues".
   To son Robert Jones land as far as the Mill Path up the Hill, all the glade that is ditched in and the old plantation whereon I now live.
   Son Maurice Jones having a competent seat of land given him by his Godfather Mr John Cousins, etc.
   The 3 eldest sons under age. Also Maurice Jones under age.
   To "my Cozen Jno Jones" stock.
   Wife Martha Jones. She extrx.
   Overseers: Mr Tho: Haynes and Mr Geo —. (Both of these names opor to question)
   Wit: Benja Doggitt, Mathew Burrowes.
   Re-recorded by — — on 19 Nov 1718. 17,244
  Robert, deceased. His estate owes Capt John Mottrom 4425 lb tobo for levies and Sheriff's fees. 21 Aug 1678. 4,3
  Robert, deceased. Mr Erasmus Withers, Tho Winter and Barth Dameron to divide the estate betw Robt Jones' dau Mary who married Geo Wale and the other heirs. 21 August 1678. 4,2
  Robert. Wit Tho Knight's will. 1 Oct 1706. 17,43
  Robert. Swears he wit will of Mary Norman decd. 21 Nov 1716. 6,184
  Mr Robt. Security for Geo Dameron. 16 Jan 1716/17. 6,187
  Robt. "Mr Robert Jones and Eliza his wife Petition about administration on Tho Brereton the youngers Estate Posponed till tomorrow". 18 June 1718. 6,266
  Robert and Elizabeth his wife, next of kin to Tho Brereton the younger decd swear he left no will so far as they know. Admr granted. 19 June 1718. 6,273
  Robt. His servant Herman Hinderson adj 3 yrs old last Christmas. 20 Aug 1718. 6,274

Jones, Robt. Appointed Surveyor of Highways from Mr Jno Coles to
    Sweet Hall and from - Coles to Fleets Point. 22 Aug
    1718. 6.292
Robert and Elizabeth. Sue Wm Williams for 7200 lb tobo. 20th
    Feb 1718/19. 6.306
Robt. Judgt 330 lb tobo agt Saml Hoath atty of Geo Gordon
    mercht. 17 June 1719. 6.321
Robert, Jr. Under age. Son of Robt. Sr. 14 Jan 1675/6. 17.244
Roger. Wit Jno Webb's will. 5 Oct 1700. 17.265
Saml. His estate attached by Mrs Jane Wildey for 800 lb tobo.
    18 Nov 1685. 4.308
Sarah. Will. dated 26 Jan 1719/20, prob 18 May 1720. To Son in
    law Tho Heath land formerly belonging to Thomas
    Salisbury. To son Morris Jones. The estate to be
    equally divided betw them. Wit Barth Schrever Junr.
    Saml Mahain Jr. 19.98
Capt Tho. As witness swears to will of Tho Williamson Jr decd.
    18 Apl 1683. 4.176
Capt. Tho. Obtains judgt on a bill L 5. Sterl dated 13 Decr
    1684 of Mr Henry Fleet assigned to him by Mr William
    Fitzhugh. 19 Nov 1685. 4.313
Capt Tho. Coroner. Pd 532 lb tobo for 11 inquests. 16 Nov 1687.
    4.411
Tho. Wit deed Leechman to Tho Jones. 8 Feb 1708/9. 17.91
William. Swears to nuncupative will of Erasmus Withers dated
    1 Nov 1680 when proved on 15 June 1681. 4.94
William. With Mr Jno Eustace brought action agst Mr Jno
    Curtis who married the admr of Mr Erasmus Withers
    late deceased asking to be released from bond for
    admr of Withers' estate. 20 July 1687. 4.400
Capt Wm. Justice. 21 Sept 1692. 4.599
Wm. His servt Benj Soape adj 17 yrs of age. 16 Sept 1696. 4.740
William. Wit deed Dermott to Gill. 20 March 1702/3. 17.119
Wm. Jr. Wit Hancock Lee's codicil. 20 May 1709. Proved 20 July
    1709. 17.29
William. Re-rec deed Lee to Lee. 16 May 1711. 17.66
William. Son of Wm Jones decd late of this Co who signed a
    bond 2 Apl 1707, etc. This is a long entry. 18 Mar
    1713/14. 6.29
Wm. Gent. Sworn Sheriff. Saml Heath his sub-sheriff. Bondsmen
    Richd Lee and Jno Ingrum. 16 June 1714. 6.42
Wm. Sworn High Sheriff. Saml Heath and Clemt Lattemore sub-
    sheriffs. 15 June 1715. 6.113
William. Admr of Wm Jones decd. Presents addl inventory. 15th
    May 1717. 6.208
Jey, Jno. Wit deed Crowder to Schrever. 18 Sept 1705. 17.155
Joyce, Abra: Appointed guardian of Eliz Perry, he having married her
    sister. 20 Sept 1658. 2.94

Joyce, Abraham. Who married one of the orphans of Giles Bashawe decd claims tobo due from her father's estate. 21st July 1660. 2.129
    Abra: Guardian of Wm Bashawe. 5 Sept 1660. 2.130
    Abra: His servt Jno Shenton 15 yrs old. 21 Apl 1662. 2.156
    Abra. Deposition in Aston - Linfsey scandle. Age not shown. 4 Aug 1665. 15.162
    Abra. Says 14 or 15 yrs ago he ran a chain for surveying land for a Globe. Jervise Dodson being surveyor. 23rd Aug 1669. 16.93
    Abra. On vestry Chicacone par. 20 Mar 1671/2. 16.158

Julian, Mr Jno. decd. Prob of will to Mr Nich: Owen. 18 Mar 1684/5. 4.255

Jurnew, Mr Nicholas. Age 53 yrs or th-abts. 20 Jan 1655/6. 14.66
    Nicho. Land where he now lives adj Wm Reynolds. 20 Jan 1656/7 14.98
    Nicho: His servt Saml Boxberry age 15. 26 Feb 1660/1. 2.137
    Nicho. His servt Hen: Pickerell to serve 9 yrs. His servt Adam Kinge to serve 6 yrs. 8 Oct 1662. 2.163

Kanhady, Jno (Chauhady ?) Servt to Jno Forrester adj 8 yrs old. 18 Feb 1718/19. 6.299

Kaye, Eliz: Age 25. Natural dau of Mr Tho Kaye. 19 Jan 1655. 14.67
    Eliz: 19 years since was a servant to Mr Humph Higginson. Then abt 6 yrs old. 20 Jan 1655. 14.66 Also Natural dau of Mr Tho Kaye. She a servt in estate of Col Jno Mottrom decd. 20 Jan 1655/6. 14.66
    Eliz. Certificate of Freedom from Jas. City. 20 Mar 1655/6. 14.85 Also: Certificate of marriage to William Greensted. 21 July 1656. 14.85 Also: Maid servt in Mottrom estate. She m Wm Grenstead. 21 July 1659. 15.27

Kaye, Jno. Son of Tho Kay decd. Acks Eliz Kay (natural dau of his father) as his 1/2 sister. 20 Jan 1655. 14.67

Kaye, Tho. Fined at Blount Point Court, Warwick Co. for having an illigitimate child (Elizabeth Kay). - 1630. 14.66
    Tho. Agreement with Humph: Higginson prior to leaving for England (but he died at Kecotan before he left) regarding. 31 Oct 1636. 14.66

Kedby, Tho. Land on S side G W river adj Martin Cole. 1 July 1654. 14.92
    Tho. Gives a heifer to Peter Presley, now eldest son of Wm. Presley. 15 May 1658. 14.143

Keene see Cane.

Keen, Eliz. Extrx Edw Elliott. She had married Saml Sanford. 16 Sept 1685. 4.291

Kean, James. Wit will Saml Churchill. 4 June 1702. 17.229
    James. Wit deed Booth to Straughan. 15 Sept 1703. 17.232
    Jams: Wit deed Bussle to Straughan. 15 Sept 1703. 17.233

Keene, Jno. Wit Jno Webber's will. 12 Feb 1670/1. 16,166
Kean, Jno. Wit will Danl Suilevant. 29 Aug 1704. 17,261
    Jno. Nearest of kin to Maurice Westherstone decd. Says he made no will. Granted administration. 17 Mar 1714/15 6,106
Keen, Jno and Eliz: with Ellinor Oliver exors of Ignatious Oliver. 22 Nov 1716. 6,136 Also Jno Keen and Eliz his wife. She dau of Mrs Elinor Oliver. See her will. 4 Sept 1719. 19,56
Keen, Mr Jno. Justice. 21 Jan 1719/20. 6,353
Keene, Mrs Mary. Now Mrs Mary Broughton. Her sons Wm, Tho and Matthew Keene. 2 Jan 1662/3. 15,92
Kean, Stephen. A long entry. By John Kean his guardian and nearest friend, complains agt Tho Dameron Junr. Concerns a copper still and pewter worm of L 50. Sterling value. That the still was set under an apple tree near the house of Laurence Dameron at the time of the death of his wife Jane Dameron, etc. Appears to have been abt 1713. 16 May 1717. 6,213
Keen, Tho. Oath to Commonwealth of England. 13 Apl 1652. 1, 72-3
Keene, Tho. Orphan of Tho Keene (Cane). "one steere of Thomas Keenes given for two yeares schooleing". 10 Oct 1659. 15,30
Keene, Tho dec'd. The name appears in the same entry as Cane. An a/c of the cattle belonging to his orphans Wm, Thos and Mathew Keene. 10 Oct 1659. 15,30
    Tho. His son Tho Keene has bequest from his Godfather Francis Simmons. 16 Apl 1661. 15,93
Keane, Tho. Godson and heir to Jno Lewis. 4 July 1702. 17,223
Keen, Wm. Pd 100 lb tobo from Co levy "for a wolf shott". 5th Novr 1668. 3,47
Keyne, Wm. His servt Michall Griffin adj 18 yrs of age. 17 March 1674/5. 3,224
Keyne, Wm. Aged 38 or th-abt. 2 March 1680/1. 4,85
Keen, Wm. Decd. Prob of his will to Mrs Eliz Keen his widow. 20 May 1685. 4,268
Keeve, Patrick. His will presented by James Magoone and Jno Poer exors. Proved by oaths of wits: Tho Abicins, Jas Dunaway, Jno Reilly, 18 June 1718. 6,268
Keire, Lawrence. Servt to Phill Shaply adj 13 yrs old. 19 Jan 1675/6. 3,249
Kellins, Nath. "Nathaniell Killins Branch" ref to 18 June 1706. 17,1
Kelly, Jno. Servt to Capt Edm Lyster adj 13 yrs of age. 17 Apl 1672. 3,144
Kelsey, Jacob. Servant to Jas Symmons adj 15 yrs of age. 16 Nov 1698. 4,842
Kemmys, Jno. Swears he wit will of Edw Woolridge decd. 16 Mar 1714/5. 6,100
Kendall, Margaret. Headright of Capt Gyles Brent. 21 Jan 1651/2. 1,70

Kennedy, Richd. Servt boy to Eliz Million adj 12 yrs old. 18 Dec 1717. 6,251
Kennedy see Cannadie.
Kenner, Mrs Eliz: Her servt Richd Cussion adj 13 yrs of age. 21 Dec 1698. 4,848
 Fra: Wit deed Gooch to Neale. 7 Apl 1706. 17,195
 Francis. Signs inventory Peter Coutanceau. 2o Apl 1709. 17, pp 216-221.
 Francis. Exor of Jno Howson. Prob his will. 17 Sept 1714. 6,87
 Francis. Exor of Eliz Howson decd. 16 Mar 1714/15. 6,101
 Francis. Churchwarden St S par. 16 Mar 1714/15. 6,102
 Francis. Guardian of Richd Kenner. 16 June 1715. 6,116
 Francis. Exor of Capt Jno Howson decd. 17 Aug 1715. 6,128
 Capt Fra. Re-recs deed dated 11 Mar 1677/8 Flynt to Kenner. 21 Sept 1715. 17,224
 Francis. See entry Richd Kenner his ward. 16 Aug 1716. 6,177
 Fra: Sued by exors of Ignatious Oliver. 22 Nov 1716. 6,186
 Matthew. Swears he wit will of Eliz Howson decd. 16 Mar 1714/5 6,101
 Matt: Wit will Mrs Elinor Oliver. 4 Sept 1719. 19,56
 Matthew. Guardian of Jno Wooldridge. 20 Jan 1719/20. 6,351
 Richd. Wit deed of gift Rodham to Neale. 17 Nov 1666. 16,22
 Richd. On Jury to settle dif betw Mr Peter Presly and Mr Tho Mathew. 21 Jan 1668/9. 3,53
 Rd. Wit deed Knight to Farnefold. 19 Apl 1676. 17,230
 Mr Richd. Attorney of Mr Wm Bodely mercht, employer of Mr Francis Gilhampton. 16 Oct 1676. 4,7
 Richd. Deed. 200 acres in Chicacone par from Richd Flynt. 11 Mar 1677/8. 17,224
 Richd. Justice. 18 Aug 1681. 4,101
  Justice. 18 Apl 1683. 4,176
  Justice. 16 Sep 1685. 4,291
  Justice. 18 May 1687. 4,493
  Justice. 20 July 1687. 4,397
  Justice. 16 Nov 1687. 4,410
 Mr Richd. Sues Danll Swillivant for 20 shillings wages due his son Rhodon Kenner. Tried before Jury and wins. 18 Nov 1687. 4,414
 Richd. Deft with Henry Brereton in suit of ejectment. 18 July 1711. 17,189
 Richd. Petitions for liberty to make choice of a guardian. Now under wardship of Francis Kenner and Christo: Neale. 16 June 1715. 6,116
 Richd. Danl McCarty says Rodham Kenner at first decided to leave his son Richd Kenner out of will, but then changed. 16 Aug 1716. 6,177
 Richd. Son and heir of Rodham Kenner gent decd. Petitions that he is of age to choose a guardian. Whereat Christo: Neale gent, one of the exors, objected that according to the will he was ward to Francis Kenner gent

Kenner, Richd (continued). and him the said Neale "and he the said
   Kenner the petr being but nineteen years of age".
   Danl McCarty aged 25 yrs swears he wrote the will
   for Rodham Kenner decd, which affidavit was sworn 20
   Nov 1705 and now produced. Richd Kenner's petition
   denied by the Court. 16 Aug 1716. 6.177
  Richd. By order of the General Court Robert Vaulx appointed
   his guardian. Thos Gill and Wm Metcalf Securities.
   21 Nov 1716. 6.185
  Richd. Married Elizabeth Winder. See entry Col Tho Brereton.
   6. pp 85-6
  Capt Rodham. Justice. 16 July 1696. 4.734
  Capt Rodham. Pd 11060 lb tobo Burgess charges for 2 Assemblies.
   19 Nov 1696. 4.748
  Capt. Rodham. Justice. 16 Dec 1696. 4.755
     Justice. 16 Nov 1698. 4.841
  Major Rod'm. Exor Rev Jno Farnefold. 3 July 1702. 17.234
  Rodham. Will. d 26 July 1706. p 21 Aug 1706. of St S par Gent.
   To dau Elizabeth land in Westmorland Co betw Lower
   Machotig River and Nomaine River in the Neck called
   Matchotig Neck. She under 18.
   To dau Hannah. She under 18.
   Brother Capt Francis Kenner and "Cozen" Christopher
   Neale, exors.
   To Brother John Kenner. To Brother Matthew Kenner.
   To son Richd Kenner.
   Wits: Wm Harcum. Danl McCarty. Elizabeth Kenner, Hanah
   Neale.
   Proved by Mr Danll McCarty, Mrs Eliz Kenner and Mrs
   Hannah Neale.
   Re-rec by Capt Christo: Neale and Capt Francis
   Kenner, exers. 15 Aug 1711. 17.125
  Rodham. Deceased. His daughter Hannah new wife of Richd Hull.
   20 Jan 1712/3. 6.14
Kent, Jo. Signs oath to Commonwealth of England. 13 April 1652. 1.72-3
  Pha'be. Wife and attorney of Jno Kent, carpenter, of Northumber-
   land Co. 10 March 1664/5. 15.146
Key, Mary. Says she is great with child and expects to be delivered
   any day. The Court orders Wm Cornish to deliver to
   her, her bed and any other estate he holds belonging
   to Ralph Key her husband. 21 July 1660. 2.129
  Peter. Wit P of A Fra: Clay to his wife Ann Clay. 24 Apl 1666.
   16.5
  Ralph. His widow married Wm Cornish. 6 June 1661. 2.141
Key see Kaye.
Kiffin, David. Land adj Peter Knight. 26 Nov 1651. 17.179
Killpatrick, Edw. Servt to Mr Jno Farnefold adj 12 yrs of age. 19 Jan
   1675/6. 3.249
Kilpatrick, Edw. Wit deed Crawford to James. 15 July 1706. 17.229

Kinge, Adam. To serve Nicho Jurnew 6 yrs. 8 Oct 1662. 2,163
    Francis. Headright of Capt Gyles Brent. 21 Jan 1651/2. 1,70
King, Rich: Headright of Jno Vaughan. 20 Nov 1651. 1,67
King, Mr Robert. Certificate for 400 acres for transportation of 8 persons: Robert King Senr, Hannah King, Robert King Junr, Daniell Nibbs, Richard King, Edward Jennings, Thomas Stowe and Eve a maid servant. 10 March 1661/2. 2,154
Kings Creek. Adj Hugh Lee's land prior to 17 Nov 1666. 16,22 Also in St S par adj land of Jno Oldham Sr. 15 Jan 1700/1. 17,185
Kingwell, Sarah. Bestows her son Tho Kingwell unto Jno Essex till 21. Wit: James Hauley, Jno Burdon. 20 Nov 1655. 14,56
    Tho. Signs oath to Commonwealth of England. 13 Apl 1652. 1, 72-3
Kirby, Simon. Will. 22 March 1666/7. prob 8 Apl 1667.
    To my landlady Mrs Ann Owen "my silver tooth picker"
    To Mr Nicho Owen "my silver buttons"
    To Mrs Ann Reynolds "my Ring and Davids repentance"
    To Wm Reynolds "my practice of piety"
    To Peter Ch–
    To Edmond Holder.
    Bal of est to friend David Miles, he sending what it pleaseth him to my Bros.
    Wit: Jno Tingey, Nicho Owen, Edm Holder. 16,13
Kirk, Xphr. In legal dif with Eliz Williams. 18 May 1683. 4,190
    John. (Kyrke) Sues Mr Shapleigh. 21 Aug 1678. 4,4
Kirkman, Fra. Clerk of the Council. Signs patent. 8 Mar 1662/3. 17,87
Kitt, Jane. Bequest from her bro Jno Harris of St S par. 20 Sept 1718. 19,44
    Wm. Wit Robt Francis will. 22 Oct 1671. 15,204
Knight, Eliz. Gift from her grandfather James Hawley. 15 Feb 1660/1. 15,56
    James. Deed. 20 Nov 1705, of N Co, planter, sells to Edmond Bazie Junr, 50 acres. Part of patent formerly granted to Capt Peter Knight 1 Nov 1661. Adj land of Leon'd Knight which land is now land of Wm Short, Mr Mayes plantation, etc. Wit: Edmond Basie Senr, Isaac Baysie, Dennis Coure.
    Re-rec by Jno Copadge for Edmond Baysie. 16 July 1712. 17,112
    James. Deed. 19 June 1710, of G W par, planter, Sells to Jos. Knight of same par, for 3000 lb tobo, 50 acres land "formerly my Father Peter Knights". Adj head of G. W River, land of Edmond Basie Junr. Wit Benja Browne, Martha Knight, John x Smith.
    Re-rec by Joseph Knight. 19 June 1713. 17,198

Knight, Jas. Re-recs grant 1651 to Peter Knight. 21 Aug 1712. 17.179
Joseph. Security for Mary Hornsby. 21 July 1714. 6.56
Jos. An orphan, Anne Lowry, bound to him. 19 Sept 1717. 6.246
Leond. His land formerly adj Jas Knight. 20 Nov 1705. 17.112
Mary. Wit will Hancock Lee 31 Dec 1706. Proves it by oath 20 July 1709. 17.29
Mrs Mary. Re-recs deed dated 1681 Brewer to Linsfield. 18 Nov 1713. 17/204
Mary. Ariskam Crowder orphan son of Tho Crowder, bound to her to be taught trade of weaver. 20 Sept 1715. 6.130
Peter. His land adj Tho Gascoyne. 15 Sept 1649. 17.80
Peter. Signs oath to Commonwealth of England. 13 Apl 1652. 1. 72-3
Peter. Wit deed Dodson to Ball. 16 May 1652. Westmorland Co Va records. 1653-9. p 24
Peter. Wit deed Ingram to Fleet. 29 Jan 1653. 14.58
Peter. Wit deed Martin Cole to Jno Bardon. 20 Sept 1656. 14.92
Peter. Pat land 1 Nov 1661. 17.112
Peter. To take depositions of James and Edw Hawly who live out of the County. 8 Oct 1662. 2.164
Mr Pet. His servt Sam Ortland adj 18 yrs of age. 5 Nov 1668. 3.46
Mr Pet: Ordered to collect County Levies, Public Short Charges and Parish Charges. 5 Nov 1668. 3.46
Mr Peter. Order to punish Wicocomoco Indians who broke into Mr Robt Jones' house. 6 Apl 1669. 3.61
Peter. Wit P of A Chetwood to Hatnoy. 18 Dec 1671. 16.213
Peter. Deed. 19 Apl 1676, of Wicco par Gent. Sells John Farnefold of Chicacoone par in N Co Gent, 300 acres on S side Wicco River adj land of Mr Richd Nutt. To be ack by wife Anne Knight. Wit Tho Hobson. Richd Kenner. On 20 Nov 1679 John Farnefold assigns this land to "my son in law Richd Nutt Junr". Recorded 20 Apl 1681. Re-rec by Mrs Anne Nutt 18 Apl 1716. 17.230
Capt Peter. Suit agt him by Mr Tho Wilks to next Court. 16th Oct 1676. 4.7
Capt. Pet: Justice. 21 Aug 1678. 4.1
Capt Pet. "Whereas a Trumpitt belonging to Capt Peter Knight was press by Capt Yowell when the soldiars went agt Goodrich and spoyled", he to be allowed 650 lb tobo from the levy. 21 Aug 1678. 4.4
Capt Peter. Justice. 16 Oct 1678. 4.5
Capt Pet. Owes Mr Edw Feilding 2718 lb tobo. 16 Oct 1678. 4.5
Capt Peter. Justice. 20 Nov 1678. 4.12
Justice. 18 Aug 1681. 4.101
Pet. Wm Bescuth als Woodamore is his servt. 16 July 1685. 4.287
Mr Peter. Justice. 20 July 1687. 4.397

Knight, Mr Peter. Will. d 28 Nov 1702. p 18 July 1705. of Wicoe: par
Gent. To son Leon'd Knight land near Mr Mayes path,
adj Richd Nutt, Mr Peter Preslyes. To son James, he
exor. Daus Eliz and Mary. Wit: Robt Nash, Patrick
Maley, Joan Maley. Re-rec by Jno Coppedge 16 July
1712. 17.175

Capt Peter. Formerly sold land to Laurence Dameron. 19 Feby
1705/6. 17.55

Tho: Age 28. 4 Aug 1665. 15.166

Tho. Wit deed Brewer to Linsfield. 21 Oct 1681. 17.204

Tho. Will. d 1 Oct 1706. p 15 Feb 1709/10. of N Co, planter.
Wife Mary and HER 3 children, viz: Linsfield, Jno
and Mary Sharp. Mary Sharp under age. Overseer
good friend Mr Hancock Lee. To Linsefeild Sharp
600 acres in Richmond Co part of 1250 acres pat.
by me. To John Sharp the other half. Wife sole exor.
Wit Robt Jones, Jno Burn, David Dickey. Proved by
oath of Burn. 17.43

Tho. Wit will of Hancock Lee 31 Dec 1709. Proves it 20 July
1709. 17.29

Knott, Geo. Gift from his mother Mrs Eliz Man. Personal property. 20
May 1667. 16.17

Geo. Forced off Kent Isle, etc. See entry Mrs Eliz Sheares
formerly his widow. 22 June 1669. 16.153

Geo. Name does not appear in Wm Claiborne's a/cs 1631 - 1637.
See Va Col. Abstracts. Vol 18, Appendix.

Geo. Seated on Glebe land 21 or 22 years since, after he fled
from Kent Isle. 22 June 1669. 16.152

Jane. Orphan of John Knott having an estate and now qualified
to secure it. 20 Nov 1696. 4.752

John. Age 37 yrs or th-abts. Westmorland Co Va Records 1653-9
p 32

Wm. Appointed Constable of Mattapony. 18 May 1687. 4.394

Kuffin, David. Wit P of A Essex to Bayly. 9 Feb 1671/2. 16.226

Lambert, Mrs Anne. Wife of Wm. Daughter of Robt Bradshaw decd. 16th
Dec 1707. 17. pp 130-5

Hen. Mercht, deceased, late of Chippenham in the County of
Wilts. Inv of estate. Signed by Jno Boye. 26 Apl
1670. 16.124

Henry. Will. dated last day of March 1670. prob 20 Apl 1670.
To son Henry a ring. To daughters Sarah and
Abigall rings. Bal of est in Va and Md to "my
servt John Boy", he exor. Wit Dan Neale, Florence
Driscoll. 16.72 Also will as foregoing with
statement by wit of 20 Apl 1670 referring to his
brother Elias Lambert of London and his brother's
wife and children. 16.119

Lambert, Wm. of North Farnham par, Richmond Co, and Anne his wife sell Matthew Myars 100 acres in Mattaponie Neck, N Co. 17 Dec 1707. 17. pp 130-5

Lambdon, Robt. A fine of 200 lb tobo agst Rowland Haddaway for fighting with him. 20 Feb 1651/2. 1.50

    Robt. Persecuted. See entry Quakers. 26 June 1660. 2.126

Lambdon's Creek. Adj land of Wm Nutt. 4 Feb 1662/3. 17.177

Lampkin, Tho. His daughter Mary Lampkin receives gift from Martin Cole and Alice his wife. 20 Sept 1658. 15.11

Lancaster, Jno. Re-recs Deed of Gift dated 20 Oct 1678 Waddington to Waddington. 18 July 1711. 17.118

Lankester, Jno. Of nearest kin to Richd L. decd. 18 Nov 1713. 6.2

Lancaster, Jno. Chosen guardian by Eliz Million. 19 Jun 1717. 6.218

Lankester, Nicho: Of nearest kin to Richd L. decd. 18 Nov 1713. 6.2

Lancaster, Nicho: and Marg't his wife ack deed. 19 Sep 1716. 6.180

    Nicho. Robt Homes to serve him 6 yrs. 21 Mar 1716/7.6.201

    Nicho: Chosen guardian by Tho Lucas. 19 Dec 1717. 6.253

    Nicholas. Buys 60 acres from Owen Jones and Rachell his wife. 10 Oct 1718. 19.8

    Richd. Wit tfr land Burbury to Copedge. 21 Mar 1710/1.17.50

Lankester, Richd. decd. Jno Lankester, Nicholas Lankester and John Million nearest kindred (during the minority of his children). They swear he left no will. They to have letters of admr. 18 Nov 1713. 6.2

    Richd. Orphan son of Richd Lankester adj to be 8 yrs old, bound to Nicholas Lankester till 21 to be taught the trade of cooper. 16 Dec 1713. 6.10

    Richd. Orphan of Richd L., bound to Wm Pickering till 21 to learn the trade of shoemaker. He 14 yrs old Apl next. 16 Sept 1719. 6.336

Landman, Jno. Bequest from Jno Tyngey. 1 Aug 1667. 16.30

    John Senr. Gives cattle to his sons Jno Landman Jr and Wm Landman. 20 May 1658. 14.144

Lanman, Mary. Dau of Jno Lanman decd. Apprenticed to Jas Claughton till 18. 22 July 1661. 2.144

Landman, Steph: Son of Jno L. decd. chooses Jno Aires his guardian. 21 Jan 1660/1. 2.137

Lane, Danl. Wit Deed of Gift Burrell to Burrell. 19 May 1670. 16.75

    John and Roger. Headrights of Wm Presley. 21 Jan 1660/1. 2.136

    John. Age 22. 4 Aug 1665. 15.165

    Tho. Pat 1000 acres adj Dennis Creek. See entry Jno Champion. 26 July 1665. 17.186

    Tho. Is owed bal of 1797 lb tobo by Corderoy Ironmonger on bill dated 18 May 1667 of 4597 lb tobo for land. 21 Jan 1668/9. 3.54

    Tho. On Jury Saffin vs Thompson. 6 Apl 1669. 3.63

    Tho. Certif for 100 acres for imp of Rog: Thomas and Maudlin Gulpey. 23 June 1669. 3.66

    Tho. of G W par, tailor, with consent of wife Martha, sells to David Whitford mercht of Edinburgh Scotland, half int in water mill on Dameron's Creek. 18 Jan 1669/70. 16.154

Laud, Mary. (continued) said shee is a whore and I will prove it, and further this depon't sayeth not. Signum Mary Laud. 21th July 1656. Jurat in Cur". 14.86

    Robt. Aged 50 yrs or th-abts. 20 Nov 1655. 14.57

Laurense, Jno. Signed bill 18 Apl 1677 to Phillip Shapleigh for 1452 lb tobo. Judgt agst him 17 Oct 1678. 4.9

    Jno. Wit deed Dermott to Gill. 20 Mar 1702/3. 17.119

    Tho. of Wisco par. Fined for 2 mos ab from Church. Prob a Quaker. 23 Sept 1715. 6.138

    Wm. Servt to Barth Dameron. Ran away from 13th May to 14th June. To serve 18 mos after time. 21 Aug 1678. 4.4

Laurencett, Tho. Wit deed Gaskins to Gaskins. 16 Jan 1710/1. 17.80

Leasure, Barth. Statement re James Jones' will which was burned. 17th Feb 1714. 6.98

    George. Will. dated 17 Nov 1708. prob 20 Apl 1709. To dau Hannah land pur of Edw Minty in Westmorland Co. To dau Elinor land pur of Will Short in Westmorland Co. To dau Eliz: The 3 daus all under 10 yrs of age. The child my wife goes with. Wife Hannah, she and his brother Barthol: Leasure exors. Wit: G: Eskridge, Sam'll Douiouville, George Harryson. Re-rec by Capt Geo Eskridge 22 March 1710/11. 17.59

Le Briton see Briton.

Le Breton, Edw. of the Island of Jersey, mercht. P of A to Thomas Matthew of Cherry Point in Northumberland Co to transact business in Va and Md.
"Whereas my dear Brother Mr John Le Breton of the Island of Jersey" merchant, did in 1664 place certain bills and a/cs in the hands of Coll Peter Ashton (and by P of A dated 24 May 1664) for collection. He did remit some, but the sd Edw coming into Va found him deceased, and there was involved in much trouble in law with Major Isaac Allerton and Major Tho Breroton the exors. The sd Edw now about to depart this country, etc. Wit: Christopher Neale, Alex: Doniphan, Clayton Hewett, John Rock, Rich Pemberton. 16.192

Le Breton, Edw. Reference to the arrival of his ship from Barbadoes. Statement re Edw Cole, who told him of Mrs Neale who bewitched his wife. Some other dirty detail of Cole's gossip. Heard him relate it all not 10 days since at the house of John Cockrell. 11 April 1671. 16.186

Le Briton, John. Letter to Capt Peter Aston, 24 May 1664. "Whereas I am Bound a long Voyage and leave heare in this Colony of Virginia and Province of Maryland a considerable quantity of Tobacco" - entry mutilated, appears to be if not heard from by next Febry the property to go to Edward Le Breton in Jersey. 15.146

Lee, Mr Charles. Justice. 16 Sept 1685. 4,291
Justice. 16 Novr 1687. 4,410
Mr Chas to assist in settlement of The Brewer's est. 11 June 1697. 17,268
Charles. Will. d 13 July 1700. p 17 Dec 1701. To son Thos. land "had by my wife" also 500 acres left me by Walter Jinkins. To son Charles 600 acres whereon I now am. To dau Lee Hannah Lee 200 acres had out of brother Hancock's tract.
To dau Elizabeth slaves, cattle and other personal property.
Wife Elizabeth extrx. Wit not shown. Jno Turberville acts for Mrs Eliz Lee in having will probated. 17,248.
Charles. Ack deeds of Lease and Release to Barth Schriever atty of Mrs Leeanna Jones wife of Wm Jones. 19 May 1714. 6,34
Charles. Exor of Eliz Howson, dec'd. 16 Mar 1714/15. 6,101
Charles. Exor of Capt Jno Howson dec'd. 17 Aug 1715. 6,128
Charles. His servt Sylvester Carty adj 12 yrs old. 16 May 1717. 6,213
Charles. William son of Alice Galloway bound to him. 17 June 1719. 6,321
Charles. Justice. 16 Sept 1719. 6,335
Charles. Swears Wm McEldoe dec'd left no will. Admr granted. 19 Nov 1719. 6,349
Mr Charles. Justice. 21 Jan 1719/20. 6,353
Francis. States that Jno Squire has served full time to estate of Col. Richd Lee and himself. 5 Jan 1670/1. 16,149
Mr Hancock. Justice. 18 May 1687. 4,393
Justice. 6 Oct 1687. 4,406
Justice. 16 Nov 1687. 4,410
Hancock. Overseer Tho Knight's will. 1 Oct 1706. 17,43
Hancock. "his corner red oak". 18 June 1706. 17,1
Hancock. Will. d 31 Dec 1706. p 20 July 1709. To dau Mrs Anne Armsteed. To son Richd Lee bulk of estate. The greater part of the Foundation of my Estate came by his Mother. Will be 18 in 1709. He to be exor.
Wife receives bequests, her name not shown.
Overseers Robt Carter, Bro Richd Lee Esq and 'Cozen' Captn Jno Howson. Wit: Thos Knight, Thos x Ingram, Mary x Knight. Proved by oaths of Tho and Mary Knight.
Codicil. 1 Jan 1706/7. To son Isaac Lee land above Falls on Rappa River. Same wit.
Codicil. 18 May 1709. To son John Lee land. "my wife is now with child". Wit Danl Feilding, Robt Spencer. Proved by oaths of Feilding and Spencer.
Codicil. 20 May 1709. Communion plate to Church. Mr Bartholomew Schreever L 3. rec'd of his "from a Gentlewoman in Maryland". To Rev Mr Joseph --- to

Lee, Hancock. His will (continued) preach funeral sermon in Wiccocomoco Church L 3.
: Wit: Jno Harris, Wm Jones Jr. Proved by oaths of both. Re-rec by Capt Jno Howson 21 March 1710/11. 17.29-32

Hancock. Deceased. Inv of Est. 5 pages double columns. Many items exceedingly handsome. Silver, books, etc. Signed by Jno Stepto, Maurice Jones, Jno Ingram. Date torn away. Re-rec by Capt Jno Howson. 21 Mar 1710/11. 17. 33-8

Mrs Hanah. Gives a cow to Mathew Rhoden for use of his dau Hanah Rhoden. 8 Nov 1651. 1.69

Hugh. Signs oath to Commonwealth of England. 13 Apl 1652. 1.72-3

Hugh. His wife (Mrs Hannah Lee) seen at Flushing (Holland) by Richd Wright, etc. See entry Capt Wm Whittington. 14th May 1653. 14.145

Mr Hugh. Justice. 26 May 1656. 14.84

Hugh. Deceased. His widow Mrs Hannah Lee etc. 8 Sept 1662. 2.161

Hugh. Formerly owned 393 acres now owned by Matthew Rodham. 17th Nov 1666. 16.22

John, tailor. His wife Sarah Lee. Sells land to Edr Phillips. 19 Feb 1671/2. 16.218

Jno. dec'd. His est to be appraised. 16 Oct 1676. 4.6

Richd. Wit P of A Henry Corbin to Capt Peter Aston. 29 Aug 1663. 17. 224-9

Col. Richd. Lease and Release. 15-17 Feb 1707. Richd Lee of Westmorland Co Esq sells to Hancock Lee of N. Co Gent, 800 acres, provided Leeanna Jones use and occupy 200 acres of this land called Hickory Neck during her natural life. The 800 acres adj Dividing Creek, the land of Mr Thos Willson marriner and the land of Col Richd Lee. Refers to will of "his good Father Coll'o Richd Lee deced". That lands left his brothers Hancock Lee and Charles Lee are in Law but an Estate for life. Therefore gives Hancock Lee 600 acres and the balance of 200 acres to Charles the youngest son of Charles Lee his brother. He failing in heirs to Tho Lee eldest son of sd Charles Lee. That Leeanna Jones dau of sd Charles Lee enjoy the 200 acres known as Hickory Neck during life, on S side of Dividing Creek in Lee par., Northumberland Co. Wit: Da: McCarty, G Eskridge. Re-rec by Tho Stretton 16 May 1711. 17.60 plus.
P of A. 17 Feb 1707/8. Richd Lee to Mr Tho Stretton to ack deed to bro Hancock Lee for 800 acres, also deed to Charles Lee youngest son of Charles Lee Gent for 600 acres known as Cobbs Hall. 17. 60 plus
Patent. 21 May 1651. Sir Wm Berkeley to "Collo Richd Lee Esqr Secretary of State for this Colony", 800 acres in Northumberland Co on S side Dividing Creek, adj land of Mr Thos Wilson marriner, for transportation of 15 persons. 17.65

(continued)

Lee, Richd. Deed. 9 Sept 1707. Richard Lee of Lower Matchotigues,
  Cople par, Westmorland Co. Repeats terms of Lease and
  Release 15-17 Feb 1707. No witnesses shown. Ack 17 Sep
  1707 by Capt Jno Howson atty for Col Richd Lee to Thos
  Hobson atty of Mr Hancock Lee. Re-rec by Tho Stretton
  16 May 1711. 17.66
  Patent. 4 March 1656/7. Edward Diggs Esqr to Col Richd
  Lee 600 acres in N Co on S side Divi Creek, adj other
  land of sd Lee, Andrewes Creek, a Creek called Free-
  mans Ford. Due for transportation of 12 persons. On 9
  Sept 1707 Col R. Lee assigns above to "my Cozen Charles
  Lee". Assignmt ack by Capt Jno Howson atty of Col R
  Lee to Tho Hobson atty of Mr Hancock Lee guardian of
  Mr Charles Lee. Re-rec by Mr Wm Jones 16 May 1711. 17.66

Lee, Richd. Bondsman for Wm Jones as Sheriff. 16 June 1714. 6.42
  Richd. This day sworn Clerk of this County. Tho Hobson sworn
    deputy. 20 March 1716/17. 6.198
  Rd. 1st appearance in Vol.17 as clerk. 20 March 1716/17. 17.236
  Rd. Clerk of N Co. 21 Jan 1718/19. 19.2 He re-rec Jno Eustace's
    will 21 Jan 1718/9. 17.245. He re-rec will d 1700 of
    Edw Neale and also will of Danl. Neale. 16 September
    1719. 17.251. He re-rec deed d 1705 Williams to
    Lattimore. 18 Feb 1719/20. 17.252-4
  Mrs Sarah. Relict of Jno Lee. Admr to her. 16 Oct 1676. 4.6
    Also gives bond 30000 lb tobo. Wm Downing and John
    Robinson go security. 16 Oct 1676. 4.7
  Tho. Judgt agt estate of John Lee decd 300 lb tobo "for his
    coffin and winding sheet". 20 Nov 1696. 4.750
  Mr Wm. Appointed High Sheriff by Governor. Mr Jno Sharpe Sub-
    Sheriff. 26 Apl 1687. 4.394
  Capt Wm. Land adj Tho Brewer. 11 June 1697. 17.268
  Capt Wm. decd. Barth Schreever and Mary his wife exors. 18 Novr
    1698. 4.845

Lee's Neck. Adj land of Geo Chilton and Saml Mahane Jr. 16 July 1705.
  17.122

Lee Parish. Ref to as Wiccocimocce or Lee. 24 Feb 1670/1. 16.162

Leechman, Eliz. Wife of Tho. Dau and sole heir of Jno Gralesse late
  of N Co. 8 Feb 1708/9. Acks deed 20 July 1709. 17.91

Leachman, Tho. Age 40 yrs or th-abts. 20 May 1656. 14.76

Leechman, Tho. of Stafford Co. Deed to Tho Smith 100 acres in St S
  par, 8 Feb 1708/9. Acks deed 20 July 1709. 17.91

Legg, Andrew. Age 30 yrs or th-abts. 22 Feb 1655/6. 14/70
  Jno. 100 acres on Chicacone assigned from Jno Crawford. 15 June
    1692. 17.212

Le'Hugh, Nich: Deceased. Mary Le'Hugh relict and Peter Le'Hugh son of
  dec'd swear he left no will. Admr granted. 18 Feb
  1718/19. 6.298

Lempriere, Clement. Deposition re witchcraft. He evidently came in
  ship with LeBriton. 11 Apl 1671. 16.186

Lenham see Lyinum. 17.116

Lenton see Lynton.

Levistone, Mary. Servt to Mr Leond Howson adj 17 yrs old. 20 Oct 1668. 3,44

Leverton, Saml. Sells his crop to Dr Edmd Helder. Paymt made to Richd Todwell for Leverton. 25 Oct 1671. 16,201

Lewis, Edwd and Tho. Land adj Saml Churchill. 19 Dec 1705. 17,161

    Edward. Fails to cure "a poor distempered man". 17 Mar 1714/15. 6,107

    Jno. Servt to Capt Peter Aston adj 11 yrs old. 20 Jan 1661/2. 2,149

    Jno. Bro in Law to Jno Mottoone Jr. 26 Sep 1678. 17,260

    John. "who Married Frances the daughter of John Mottoone deceased" complains that Jno Mottoon by will left legacies to the rest of his children but nothing to his wife. Order that Mr Tho Williams, Saml Goohe, Ezekiell Genesis and Clement Lattimore make inquiry into est given sd Frances by her father at the time of her marriage and make equal portions with the rest of the daughters out of the whole. 21 Apl 1681. 4,93

    Jno. Prob of will of Tho Tapp deed to him. 18 May 1687. 4,394

    Jno. His servt Laurence Conner age 15. 16 June 1714. 6,42

    Jno. Will. d 4 July 1702. p 17 Mar 1702/3. To Godson Thomas Keane bulk of est, he under 21. To Jno Shaw. Wife Elloner, she to care for Godson till 21. Wit Tho Hayden, Danl Feilding, Edwd Weston, Jno Steptoe. Re-rec by Tho Hobson 17 June 1715. 17,223

    Jno. Wit will of Mrs Elinor Oliver. 4 Sept 1719. 19,56

Lewis ap Lewis. Exor of Jas Johnson. 20 Feb 1717/18. 6,258

Lewis, Mutton. Swears he wit Tho Haydon's will. 21 Mar 1716/17. 6,205

    William of Va. See entry Danl Roberts in England. 1649. 14,89

    William. An orphan, Geo Warrick, bound to him to be taught bricklaying. Jno Lewis and Wm Grimstead Securities. 21 Mar 1716/17. 6,204

Lightfoot, Phil. Signs patent to Tho Gascoyne. 15 Sept 1649. 17,80

Limekill, (Creek). In St S par. Adj land of Richd and Saml Robinson. 14 July 1702. 17,105

Lindsey see Lyndsey.

Linen. Bonus for. Mr Jno Taylor makes claim. 16 Mar 1683/4. 4,226

    "Ignatius Oliver the best peece of Cloth the last yeare 600 lb tobo Wm Beane the worst peece last yeare 400 lb tobo". 19 Nov 1696. 4,748

Linenah, Maurice. Bequest from Jno Eustace, 2 cows on day he is free. 23 Dec 1701. 17,245

Linsfeild, Richd. of Wicco par. Buys land on S side Dividing Creek from Tho Brewer Senr. 21 Oct 1681. 17,204

Linton see Lynton.

Little, Christo: Servt to Wm Downinge adj 13 yrs old. 26 Feb 1660/1. 2,137

Little, Francis. Son of Wm Little decd bound to Mr Richd Browne till 21. 22 July 1661. 2.144
    Wm. Aged 43 yrs or th-abts. 21 July 1656. 14.86
Littlefield, Paul. Living 6 Dec 1669. See entry Alex Cum'ins et als dated 7 Apl 1707. 17.116
Littleneck branch. Adj land of Jno Bayles in Cupids Neck. 18 Jan 1705/6. 17.180
Liversage, Wm. Being sick freed from levy this year. 17 Sep 1685. 4.298
Lock, Jno. Wit deed Williams to Champion. 2 Dec 1700. 17.70
    Jno and Sarry. Wit deed Williams to Gascoyne. 27 Mar 1703. 17.45
    Jno. His land adj Tho Williams. 25 Nov 1706. 17.67
    Jno. Wit deed Williams to Mahane. 25 Nov 1706. 17.67
    Robt. See entry Wm Gradey. 17.152
Lockman, Jas. Presented for being drunk. 15 May 1717. 6.207
    James. Deceased. Wm Moulton and Tho Grimstead next of kin swear he left no will. Admr granted. 18 Jun 1718. 6.269
Long, Josias. Wit deed Crawford to Legg. 15 June 1692. 17.212
    Jos. Deceased. Timothy Sacheverill his nearest relation. 18th Nov 1719. 6.345
Longdale, Tho. Age 24 yrs or th-abts. 2 Nov 1704. Richmond Co Va. Misc. Records. page 26
Lord, Jno. of "Harfort in New England mercht". 12 Jan 1656/7. 14.101
    Robt. Will. d 1 Dec 166-. p. 10 March 1661/2. To wife Mary. To 2 sons Alexander and Jno Lord. To servant Mary Pargater. Other bequests. 15.71
    Robt. His widow m Tho Dunkinton. 10 March 1661/2. 2.154
Loughman, James. Deed. 7 Sept 1702. of N Co, planter, and Margrett his wife, soll Jno Scott of N Co, cooper, for 2000 lb tobo, 50 acres in Wicoo par, where he now lives, adj head of Wicoo River, the land of Mrs Downinge, Jno Davis and land lately owned by Capt Edw Sauders. Wit Tho Hobson, Geo Eskridge, Jno x Bryant. On 16 Jan 1702/3 John Scott sells, for 3000 lb tobo, the land to Jno Rose. Wit: Jas Richardson, Richd Robinson, Tho Hobson. Ack on 17 Feb 1702/3 by Jno Scott and Anne his wife. Re-rec 16 Sept 1713 by Jno Rose. 17.202
Love, Alex. Wit assignmt Champion to Mahane. 5 Feb 1704/5. 17.71
    Alex: of G W par. Buys 50 acres from Saml Mahane. 21 Feb 1704/5. Re-rcos it 22 March 1710/11. 17.51
    Alex: Chosen by David Fluker an orphan as guardian. 22 July 1714. 6.59
    Alex: a tailor. 24 July 1714. 6.66
Lowrey, Anne. Orphan dau of Elias Lowrey decd, 8 yrs old last March, bound to Joseph Knight till 18. 19 Sept 1717. 6.246
    Elias. of Wicoo par. Fined for absenting himself from Church. 19 Nov 1713. 6.7
    Kath: Orphan of Elias Lowrey bound to Tho Grinstead till 18. 17 Sept 1719. 6.340

Lucas, Ann. Orphan of Thos Lucas chooses Abner Neale as guardian. 18 Feb 1718/19. 6.299

 Charles. Thos Lucas next of kin says he died without will. Admr granted. 19 Feb 1717/18. 6.255

 Thomas. Orphan son of Tho Lucas makes choice of Nicho: Lancaster for guardian. Also whereas Charles Lucas another son of Tho dec'd was made exor, Thos Lucas presents the will and obtains admr, etc. 19 Dec 1717. 6.253

Ludwell, Hon Phillip. Agt and atty of the Rt Hon the Proprietors of the No N of Va. 23 July 1691. 17.72

 Hon Phillip. Issues patent 250 acres to Jno Wright. 7th Sept 1691. 17.128

Lugg, Richd. Buys 1/2 of Wm Smyth's land in G W par. 18 Nov 1677. 17.141

Luke, Mr Geo. Given a bill dated 29 Oct 1683 by Maj Jno Mottrom now deed for 692 lb tobo. Judgt to him agt Mottrom's est. 5 Oct 1687. 4.406

Lunsford, Saml. Wit deed Champion to Curtis, 3 Dec 1709. 17.186

Lunte, Jne. His servt Jacob Kelsey adj 15 yrs old. 16 Nov 1698. 4.842

Lyinum, Jne and Jane his wife. (Lenham ? Lynum ?) Living 19 February 1678/9 and on 9 February 1685/6. See entry Alex: Cumins et als dated 7 Apl 1707. 17.116

Lylisse. Thos. Servt to Capt Edm Lyster adj 14 yrs of age. 17 April 1672. 3.144

Lyn, James. Servt to Maj Brereton adj 13 yrs of age. 19 Jan 1675/6. 3.249

Lyndsay, David, minister. Fined 10000 lb tobo for marrying Richard Peirce, carpenter, servant to Col Richd Lee, to a woman servant belonging to Tho Brewer, without permission from Col Lee. Rev Lyndsay appeals to next Quarter Court at James City. 20 Jan 1661/2. 2.150

 Rev. David. Acquitted of 10000 lb tobo fine. 8 Oct 1662. 2.167

 Rev. David and Susanna his wife. In dif with Charles and Isabel Ashton. Very scandalous. 4 Aug 1665. 15.158-66

 David "minister of God's word in Virginia". Will. d 2 April 1667. p 8 April 1667. All estate to daughter Helen Lyndsey, she exor. Wit: Jas Clayton, Clemt Arlidge, George Reason. 16.12

 Mr Dav. decd. Prob of will to his dau Mrs Helena Lyndsay. 8 April 1667. 3.11

 Mr David. Capt Tho Brereton atty of Wm Wathen (this name may well be Walker) Exor of Mr David Lyndsey petitions for 1178 lb tobo due from Charles Ashton. 21st Jan 1668/9. 3.55

 Mr David. Joane Willioughby widow assigns her thirds in land belonging to Mr Tho Opie formerly in possession of Mr David Lyndsay. 17 Mar 1674/5. 3.224

 David. Wit deed Hobbs to Crawford. 6 Dec 1683. 17.212

Lyndsey, Helen. P of A to Anthony Bridges of Westmorland Co. Refers to her deceased father Mr David Lyndsey. Wit: Richd Haskins, Wm Wathen. 6 Apl 1667. 16.13

Robt. Age 24 yrs or th-abts. 4 Aug 1665. 15.162 also p 165

Wm. His wife Diana, dau of Nath Hickman, enticed to runaway with Tho Barrett to Rappahannock. Sam Perry says he was informed she married him there.(She did) - Jan 1666/7. 16. pp 10. 11

Lynton as Lenton, Linton.

Linton, Antho: Age 41 or th-abts. Says "that about 19 years past this depon't was a servant to Mr Humphrey Higginson". 20 Jan 1655/6. 14.66

Lenton, Antho: Accused in "scandallous and opprobious termes" by Tho Shaw as being a Run-away from York. 20 May 1656. 14.77

Linton, Antho: His wife Jane Linton. 8 Sept 1668. 16.55

Lenton, Antho. Deed of Gift, a heifer to "my Cosen William Lonton" Wit: Cuthbert Witham, Geo Hutton. 26 Jan 1668/9. 16.67

Lenton, Anth: On vestry Chicacone parish. 20 Mar 1671/2. 16.158

Lynton, Antho. Sold 400 acres to Jas Moore. 22 Dec 1673. 17.145

Lynton, Antho: To have land claimed by Geo Hutton. 16 Oct 1676. 4.7

Lynton, Antho: At a Court 17 Apl 1678 it was ordered that Antho Lynton have possession of land on which his son Henry lived. Geo Hutton who married the relict of Henry Lynton protests. All ref to next Court. 21 Aug 1678. 4.5

Linton, Mrs Jane. Pd 600 lb tobo from Co levy for "Two wolves in a Pitt". 19 Nov 1696. 4.748

Linton, Antho: "old Mr Anthony Linton dec'ed" formerly sold land to Jas Moore. 17 Apl 1700. 17.146

Lyon, Jno. Re-rec Inv of est of Hugh Callan, decd. 20 June 1711. 17.113

Lyster, Capt Edm. Justice. 5 Nov 1668. 3.46

Capt Edm. Ordered to punish Wiccocomoco Indians that broke into Mr Robt Jones' house. 6 Apl 1669. 3.61

Capt Edm. His servt Tho Lylisse adj 14 yrs of age. 17 April 1672. 3.144

APPENDIX

Genealogists.

As the key states, only about one in five items appear in this collection. For benefit of those who desire more, this list, of 15th August 1943, is added. Like the Abstracts, not commercial. Not advertising. No one asked to be included. Merely personal friends who have assisted me.
                                                                Beverley Fleet.

Miss Estelle Bass, 5306 Dorchester Road, Richmond, Va. Is senior member of the staff in Archives Division, Va. State Library. Helps willingly any who seek aid there.

Mrs. William Dabney Duke, Genealogist, 3606 Seminary Ave., Richmond, Va. Is also a writer and critic of discrimination.

Mrs. Augusta B. Fothergill, 1011 West Grace St., Richmond, Va. This lady is actually the Dean of Virginia genealogists. We all agree that we are never with her but that she gives the solution of some difficult problem. Her library and files are remarkably complete.

Mrs. Edward L. Gibbon, 1420 Nottoway Ave., Richmond, Va. Works hard. Much too generous and conscientious for her own profit. Her reports, usually books for permanent family record are beautifully done.

Mrs. L. W. Glazebrook, 3005 Patterson Ave., Richmond, Va. Keen and far seeing. Her 'Virginia Migrations' to come out later is a very fine work.

Mrs. James Claiborne Pollard, 1610 Confederate Ave., Richmond, Va. I could never have prepared these 19 volumes had it not been for her kind and continued assistance in the Archives Division. Has the most remarkable memory for minute detail in the Virginia records. I never knew anything to equal it. As a guide to Virginia source material there is no one so astute as this kindly lady.

Miss Anne Waller Reddy, 1005 East Marshall St., Richmond, Va. My good and constant friend. Works more steadily than any other genealogist in the Archives Division. Authoritive on any Virginia lines. Very fine on Revolutionary Services. The best, so far as Virginia is concerned, in the country for that. Is prompt. Honest. Has distinguished clientele and following. Much of the data, difficult items, in Virginia Colonial Abstracts, was generously given me by Miss Reddy from her notes.

And of course it would be folly to attempt to prepare any 17th century genealogy of Virginia without consulting 'Cavaliers and Pioneers' by Mrs. Nell M. Nugent, 2902 Monument Ave., Richmond, Va.

The prevailing rates among professional genealogists are ten dollars a day, eight hours, more or less according to individual agreement.

Errata.

That good friend of Virginia genealogy, Major John Bailey Calvert Nicklin of Chattanooga, was kind enough to assist in sending me promptly the following corrections for Vol. 19.

Vol.19   page 3.   The last item, Bailes Feilding. Omit. The names are reversed.

"   page 63.   Griffin, Col. Saml and his wife Sarah. The birth of their daughter Katherine was 16 March 1664/5, not 1692 as shown. See page 64.

"   page 108.   Lansdale, Wharton and Ursula his wife. Regardless of how this looks in the original the name is Ransdall or Ransdell. Westmorland County records prove that. The Northumberland County scribe omitted the tail on the R making a perfect 17th Century L. He meant it for an R just the same. There are other examples of this in his work but not quite so aggrevated.

NORTHUMBRIA COLLECTANEA
M to Z

Macarnuot, Francis. Serv't to Tho Gill adj 13 yrs of age. 21 Dec 1698.
    4.848

MaCarty, Neal. Headright of Mr Jno Harris. 15 July 1696. 4.733

Mac-gaaino, Owen. Headright of Mrs. Jane Wildey. 19 Oct 1681. 4.105

Macgee, Cha: His land adj Jno Bayles in Cupid's Neck. 18 Janry 1705/6
    17.180

Macgill, Jno. Headright of Capt Jno Haynie. 15 July 1696. 4.733

Macgreggor, James. Signs oath to Commonwealth of England. 13 Apl 1652.
    1. pp 72-3

Mackarty, Danl. Serv't to Tho Downeman adj 15 yrs of age. 19 Jan 1675/6
    3.249

Mackreger, James. Gift to his son Hugh Mackreger. 21 Apl 1662. 15.71

Macklaughn, Jane. Serv't to Rd Hill adj 14 yrs of age. 19 Jan 1675/6.
    3.249

    Mommey, Serv't to Tho Sadler adj 13 yrs of age. 19 Janry
        1675/6. 3.249

Macksfield, Peter. Wit Jno Bearemore's will. 20 Jan 1676/7. 17.109

Macktire, Wm. Serv't to Wm Coutanceau adj 14 yrs of age. 19th Janry
    1675/6. 3.249

Mc Carty see entry Sylvester Carty. 16 May 1717. 6.213

McCarty, Danl. Age 25. Says he wrote Rodham Kenner's will for him.
    20 Nov 1705. 6.177

    Danl. wit will Rodham Kenner. 26 July 1706. 17.126

McCarty, Danl. Atty for Rd Chichester of Lancaster Co. See entry Wm.
    Wildey. 20 Nov 1706. 17. pp 224-9
    Wit deed Lee to Lee. 15 Feb 1707/8. 17.60
    Wit Dennis Conaway's will. 15 June 1709. 17.19

McCarty, Capt Danl. Rerecords Dennis Conaway's will. 22 Feb 1710/11.
    17. 19

    Danl. See entries Richd Kenner. 16 Aug 1716. 6.177
    Danl. Atty for Mr Wharton Ransdale and Mr Charnock Cox. See
        entry Capt Peter Presly. 21 Jan 1719/20. 6.353
    Danl. Rerecords Danl Suilevants will. 21 March 1721/22.
        17.261

McClane, Jno. For some time past an inhabitant of this Co. Certificate
    for leaving the Colony. 1 Aug 1715. 6.358

McCormack, Fra: Wit deed Barry to Gill. 17 Feb 1708/9. 17.183

McDaniell, Duke. His relict Eliz McDaniell swears he left no will. Admr
    granted to her. 21 Aug 1718. 6.278

McDonnell appears as McDaniel.

McEldoe, Wm. dec'd. Charles Loe admr. 19 Nov 1719. 6.349

McGoone, James. App overseer of highways from Cone to the Court House.
    15 May 1717. 6.207

M'nall, Wm. One of the sons of Jas M'nall dec'd late of this Co. Swears
    he died without will, etc. 17 Aug 1715. 6.128

    Wm and Jno. Apply for admr of their dec'd father's est now in
        hands of Wm Payne. 15 June 1715. 6.113

Madison see Medison.

Maddison, Jno. Complains he bound himself to Henry Tapscott 6 yrs in consideration he was to be taught "trades of a cooper Carpenter and Joyner" which he has not done, etc. 18 May 1715. 6.109

    Tho. P of A from Dominick Theriatt to sue Rd Pearce in Northumberland Court. 9 May 1665. 16.19

Maddox, Rice. Order that the admr of est of Simon Domibiell pay him debt of 590 lb tobo. 10 Jan 1650/1. 1.46

    Rice. Sued by Robt Newman. 10 Jan 1650/1. 1.47

    Rice. Certificate for 200 acres for importing Tho Cockrill, Tho: Tillitt, Susan Cale, Rice Maddox. 10 Jan 1650/1. 1.47

    Rice of Westmorland Co. Sells 300 acres in Westmorland Co to Ralph Horsley. 8 Feb 1654/5. Westmorland Co Records. 1653-9. p.23

Maddocke, Rice. "Doctor of Phisick in the County of Westmorland". 21st June 1656. 14.88

    Rice. Wit deed Martin Cole to Jno Bardon. 20 Sept 1656. 14.92

    Rice of Nominy, Chirurgeon, Assigns an Irish girl named Mary Drury abt 7 yrs old to Mrs Anna Cole, wife of Richd Cole of Salisbury Park, Northumberland Co., merchant. 30 August 1658. 15.11

Maddox als Nelms. See entries Trip and Trape. 1684. 4.235 and 242.

Madring, Bennett of Northumberland Co "being shortly bound on a Voyage to sea", P of A to Wm Flowers to complete a transaction of 3 Nov 1666 with Arthur Steevens. 1st Dec 1666. 16.24

    Bennett. In difficulties with his servants. 22 Oct 1667. 16.27

Mag-gone, Dav. Serv't to Wm Downing Jr adj 12 yrs of age. 19 Jan 1675/6 3.249

Magoune, Jas. Wit will Edw Singer of St S par. 6 Jan 1711/12. 18.261

Magoone, Jas. Exor of Patrick Keeve. 18 June 1718. 6.268

    Jas. and Mary his wife preve by oaths nuncupitive will of Jno Thomas. 19 June 1718. 6.272

    Jas. As witness, proves by oath, will of Peter Presly Jr. 19 Nov 1718. 6.296

Magow, Jas. of St S, par. See entry Anne Wiggins. 3 July 1708. 17.204

Magray, Edmund. Serv't to Jno Dennis adj 11 yrs of age. 21 August 1673 4.1

Magreger, Hugh. Son of James, Gift from Hugh Fouch. 20 Sept 1659. 15. 27 A

Magregory, Jas. Bequest from David Spiller. 21 Oct 1658. 15.11

Magregar, Jas. Formerly sold Mr Richd Span 600 acres. See entry John Read. 30 Jan 1670/1. 16.159

Maguire, Cornelius. Serv't to Mr Edw Coles adj to be 15 yrs of age. 4 Apl 1672. 3.144

Mahan see Mehone.

Mahane, Dorothy. Wife of Saml Jr. 16 July 1705. 17.122

    Dorothy. Wife of Saml. 21 Feb 1704/5. 17.51

Mahan, Saml. See entry Edw Potees. 1675. 18.158
Mahan, Saml. Bought land from David Whitford. 5 Aug 1675. 18.27
Mahane, Mr Saml. 1967 acres surveyed for him. 8 Jan 1710/11. 18.166
    Mr Saml. His land adj that of Ebenezer Sanders dec'd. 2 April 1711. 18.57
    Saml of Wicco par sells Jno Brown of same par 80 acres on S side G W River. Dorothy Mahan wife of Saml relinq her dower rights. 8 July 1712. 18.199
Mahons, Meredith. Presented for not going to Church in Wicco par. 19 May 1714. 6.35
Mahens, Meredith. of Wicco par, fined for 2 months absence from Church. 23 Sept 1715. 6.138
Mahon, Sam. Age 33. 1665. Day and month not shown. 15.172
Mahon, Saml. To appraise cattle at quarter of Wm Thomas dec'd. 16 Oct 1676. 4.6
Mahon, Saml. His serv't Jas Gesse aged 13 yrs. 21 Aug 1678. 4.1
    Saml. Suit vs Rd Wells to next Court. Oliver Cotanco to give evidence for him. 17 Oct 1678. 4.8
Mahaines, Saml. His land adj Jno Webb. 5 Oct 1700. 17.265
Mahane, Saml. Land assigned to him by Jno Champion. 5 Feb 1704/5. 17.71
Mahane, Saml. of G Wicco par. sells 50 acres to Alex Love. 21 Feb 1704/5 17.51
Mahan, Saml. Deed from Tho Williams. 15 Mar 1704/5. 17.67
Mahane, Saml Jr. Sells Geo Chilton 200 acres in G W par. 16 July 1705 17.122
Mahan, Saml. Witness. 18 June 1706. 17.3
Mahane, Saml. Gent of Northumberland Co. Deed from Tho Williams. 25th Nov. 1706. 17.67
Mahen, Saml. His land adj Tho Bonum in Wicco par near the Church. 20th Sept 1709. 17.177
Mahane, Saml. Re-rec deed from Champion. 16 May 1711. 17.71
    Re-rec deed from Tho Williams. 16 May 1711. 17.67
    Re-rec " " " " 16 May 1711. 17.72
Mahain, Saml Jr. Wit will Mrs Sarah Jones. 26 Jan 1719/20. 19.98
Mahane, Saml Sr. Father of Saml Jr. Patented 766 acres in G W par on 17 May 1692. His will proved in Northumberland Co 1697. 17.122
Mahoon, Mary. See entry Capt Giles Russell. 18 Nov 1719. 6.346
Maley, Danl. Orphan son of Patrick Maley dec'd, age 14 yrs, bound to Jno Franco till 21 to be taught the trade of tailor. 15 May 1717. 6.209
    Jean, with Patrick Maley, wit will of Peter Knight. 28 Nov 1702. 17.175
    Patrick. Deed from Clement Arledge. 7 July 1703. Rerecords it 15 Aug 1711. 17.127
    Patrick. Wit deed Conolin to Alverson. 21 July 1703. 17.96
Maley, Patrick Senr of St S par, planter. Will d 25 Oct 1712. p. 20th May 1713. To 2 sons "John Mealy and Patrick Maley" (sic) Wife Joan Mealey. "all my children John Mealey, Patrick Mealey, Elizabeth Booth, Elinor Hall, Hannah Mealey and Daniel Mealey". 18.290

M20

Mallett. Mrs Ann Mash als Mallett. Now married to Jno Merryday. 11 Sept 1659. 14.90
    Tho. Buys 300 acres from Geo Hailes. 21 Feb 1651/2. 14.94
Malin, Wm. Age 18 or th-abts. Date not shown but recorded 1664. 15.136
Malim, Will. Aged 23 yrs or th-abts. 5 Oct 1669. 16.58A Also 16.94
Mallin, Patrick. Servt to Mr Tho Matthew adj 5 yrs of age. 21 Aug 1678. 4.2
Mallory, Phillip, Clerk. Guardian of Tho Oldis vs Capt Tho Streator who married the relict of Col Tho Burbage, etc. To Sheriffs of Nansemum, Elizabeth City, Northumberland and Lancaster Counties. 17 March 1657. 15.4
Maloy, Charles. Wit deed Williams to Mahane. 25 Nov 1706. 17.67
Malpus, Edwd. Owes est of Tho Crowder 500 lb tobo. 20 June 1711. 18.62
Man, Elizabeth. Deed of Gift to "my Loving Son George Knott", personal property, various. 20 May 1667. 16.17
    Elizabeth, widow. Now Mrs Eliz Tyngey. 21 Jan 1668/9. 3.55
    Saml. married widow of Jno Bennett. 21 Oct 1661. 2.148
    Samuel. Will. dated 1 Jan 1664/5. prob 21 Nov 1665. To dau Mary Man, she under 15. Wife Elizabeth. Land etc to Geo Nott and to Jno Nott. 15.170
Manning, Tho. Wit Tho Palmer's will. 28 March 1709. 17.127
Mansoy, Tho. Wit P of A Fleet to Stevens. 12 Sept 1657. 15.10A
Marrall, Robt. Wit deed Brown to Murdock. 16 Nov 1708. 17.158
Marsh, Arter (sic). Signs appraisal of est of Arther Bridgeman dec'd. 29 Aug 1711. 18.101
    John. Presented for not going to Church in Wicco par. 19 May 1714. 6.35
Marshall, John. Servt to Barth Dameron ran away from 13th May to 14th June. To serve 18 months after time. 21 Aug 1678. 4.4
    Tho. Mr Jno Harris swears Marshall owes him 908 lb tobo. 17 Oct 1678. 4.8
Marson, Jno. Servt to Mr Edwd Coles adj 11 yrs old. Was sold to Coles by Nath'l Watson for 8 yrs. 21 March 1716/17. 6.204
Masey, David. Wit bond Tho Hubbard of Christ Church par, Lancaster Co., to Jno Wright of same par re property. 9 March 1712/13. 18.287
Mash, Arthur dec'd. His will presented by Richd Mash his exor. 15 May 1717. 6.211
    Geo: Wit will of Jno Harris. 23 Feb 1709/10. 18.318
    Jno. Wit will of Peter Hammond. 18 Jan 1711/12. 18.151
    Jno. Wit deed Embry to Tapscott. 19 Feb 1711/12. 18.150
Mask, Geo. Wit deed Embry to Tapscott. 19 Feb 1711/12. 18.150
Mash, John dec'd. Lylia his relict swears he left no will. Admr to her. 16 Oct 1717. 6.250
    Tho. Headright of Wm Wildey. 8 Sept 1662. 2.161
    Wm. Wit deed Adams to Shirley. 13 Feb 1701/2. 17.151
Mason of Maryland. See Spence entry. 27 May 1712. 18. 320 plus.

Mason, Jno. Views P Coutanceau's inventory at Deeds Quarter. 20 April 1709. 17, pp 216-221

Jno. His widow Sarah m James Moon. Richd Smith desires part of est to pay orphans. 19 July 1718. 6,271

Matthew. Wit will of Tho Palmer. 28 Mar 1709. 17,127

Sarah. Relict of Jno. Swears he left no will. Admr granted her. 18 Apl 1716. 6,153

Wm. Wit agreement Brereton et als. 2 July 1703. 17, pp 238-243

Wm. Wit deed Downing to Palmer. 16 Jan 1710/11. 18,6

Wm. Security for Jno Taylor, blacksmith, fined for absence from Church. 23 Sept 1715. 6,138

Mathes, Wm. Wit deed Adams to Harrison. 2 Jan 1702/3. 17,161

Matchotigues Path. Adj land of Jas Hill. 8 July 1702. 17,174

Matchohotique Path. In G W par, adj Jno Dunaway. 3 Sept 1708. 17,76-8

Machotique Path. Adj land of Jas Hill. 15 June 1709. 17,78

Mattapony River. Adj land of Hugh Dermott. 20 Mar 1702/3. 17,119

Matthewes, Goodlove. Ack deed of gift to her son in law Graves Eves. 12 Mar 1713/14. 6,23

Mathew, Mrs Rebecca. Mrs Welthian Bonas left her dau Eliz to her till of age. 20 Aug 1684. 4,236

Matthewes, Robt. Owes est of Jno Hampton decd 100 lb tobo. 7th March 1649/50. 1,49

Matthews, Hon Saml late Governor decd. Robt Jones represents his est regarding land near Wicocomoco Indians. 21st May 1660. 2,124

Matthew, Tho. His servt Jno Rumley adj 16 yrs of age. 22 June 1669. 3,64

Matthew, Tho and Frisis his wife (sic). Ref to as his bro and sister in will of Robt Walton, gent. 14 Jan 1669/70. 16,188

Tho. Buys 67 acres from Wm Shears and Eliz his wife. She was relict of Jno Tingey. 22 Feb 1670/71. 16,164

Tho. of Cherry Point. P of A from Edw LeBreton to collect a/cs. 3 Apl 1671. 16,192

Mr. Tho. His servts Ignatus Oliver adj 10 yrs of age and Danll Thomas adj 9 yrs of age. 17 Mar 1674/5. 3,224

Mr. Tho. Justice. 16 Oct 1676. 4,7

Mr. Tho. To see that Benj Adington is punished for killing a hog belonging to Mr Nicho Owen and running away. 16 Oct 1676. 4,6

Tho. Atty of Tho Helder in sale of land. 11 Nov 1676. 17,232

Mr. Tho. Justice. 21 Aug 1678. 4,1

Mr. Tho. 3346 lb tobo due him for public services. 21st Aug 1678. 4,4

Mr. Tho. His servt Patrick Mallin adj 5 yrs of age. 21st Aug 1678. 4,2

Mr. Tho. Ordered to deliver bills of Tho Morris dec'd, now pd, to Jno Turine. 21 Aug 1678. 4,1

Mr. Tho. Justice. 16 Oct 1678. 4,5

Capt Tho. To be pd 2840 lb tobo for the 40 men "to the Garrison". 2 Nov 1681. 4,681

Mathew, Capt Tho. An a/c to the Assembly, for 980 lb tobo "for his charge in enterteyning the Secretary of Maryland and his Company sent over by the Lord Baltimore to his honor the Governor on publique concernes" 2 Nov 1681. 4.681

Matthew, Capt Tho. Justice. 18 Apl 1683. 4.176

Matthew, Thos. Will of Tho Matthew, formerly of Cherry Point, N. Co., merchant. Dated 6 May 1703. Prob in London.
To 3 children John, Thomas and Anna Matthew land in Cherry Point. To "my Brother in Law Capt Jno Cralle and my old and faithfull servants Mr James Genn and Mary his wife", etc. 18.217

Mattocks als Nelms. See entries Trip and Trape. 1684. 4.235 and 242

Maudly, Mary of St S par, gives her Godson Richd Hull all her personal estate, he to maintain her for life. 10 Oct 1710. 18.22

Maudley, Rebecca, daughter of Edmund Maudley being abt 2 yrs old, bound, with consent of her father, to Alex Wetherstone and Jane his now wife till 21. Rd Haynie Security. 6th Oct 1687. 4.407

Maukin, Robt. Wit deed Wiggin to Tulles. 8 July 1708. 17.204

Maxwell, Peter. His servt Jno Frost adj 12 yrs of age. 21 Jan 1684/5. 4.252

Peter, deed. Prob to Mary Maxwell the widow. 19 May 1686. 4.339

Mayes, Christopher. Wit assignmt Mayes to Innis. 15 Apl 1702. 17.255
Eliz. Dau of Henry. 10 Feb 1708/9. 17.101
Hen: Trustee of will of Andrew Delabriere. 24 June 1670. 16.137
Henry. Wit deed Hudnall to Palmer. 5 June 1677. 17.28
Henry. Bought 1000 acres on N side of a branch of Dennis Creek on 26 Oct 1680 from Jno Pinkard and bequeathed part of this tract to Christopher Mayes. 18.27

Mayes, Henry. Will 12 April 1702. 18 June 1702. To wife Elitia. To sons Henry, Josias and Christopher Mayes. Dau Elizabeth. Refers to land sold to Dr James Innis, it adj land of Tho: Mayes. Exors son Henry and wife. 17.205
Wit: Edmond Basye, Jos Palmer, Richd Smith.
Rerecorded by Jno Copedge 18 Nov 1713. 17.205

Mayes, Hen. Bought 500 acres in Wicco par 26 Oct 1680 from Jno Pinkard and sold it to James Innis 15 Apl 1702. 17.255

Mayse, Henry. His boundry line. Also as wit. 26 Mar 1703. 17.9

Mayes, Henry. Will d 10 Feb 1708/9. Record of probate burned. To dau Mary Mayes plantation where Jno Wolfe lives. To dau Elizabeth. Refers to wife as possibly with child, her name not shown. Refers to his two daus Mary and Eliz and leaves "their Two Uncles Isaac Basie and Edmond Basie to be a Guide to them". Rerecorded 17 May 1711. Mr Edmond Basie and Mr Richd Nutt swearing this a true copy. 17.101

Mayes, Henry. Depo. 16 May 1717. Aged 26 yrs or th-abts. Says he was
    an evidence to the will of Jane Robinson. 17.237
  Henry Jr. Wit assignmt Mayes to Innis. 15 Apl 1702. Atty of Henry
    Mayes Sr and Litia his wife. 16 Apl 1702. 17.255
  Kesia, wife of Christopher Mayes. 16 May 1711. 18.29
  Mary, dau of Henry Mayes. Bequest from Isaac Weaver. 13th Jan
    1663/4. 15.116
  Tho. His land adj Leonard Howson. 19 July 1704. 17.255
  Tho. og G W par. P of A to his son Henry Mayes of same par to
    ack sale of 60 acres to Tho Berry. 18 Mar 1711/12.
    18.160
  Thos. of Wicco par. Sells Thos Berry of same par, for 5500 lb
    tobo, 60 acres in Wicco par, on S side G W river.
    This land sold by Jno Pinkard to Henry Mayes 26
    Oct 1680 who left it by will to Christopher Mayes
    who sold it to sd Thos Mayse by deed dated 19 Dec
    1710, who now sells it to Berry. 18 Mar 1711/12.
    18.158
  Tho. planter, sells Richd Lattimere 25 acres on N side Dennis
    Creek. 10 Dec 1712. 18.233
  Tho of G W par, sells Christopher Mayes for L 100, Sterl., 150
    acres. 19 Dec 1710. 18.24
Mayes, 'Mr Mayes path' adj land of Peter Knight. 28 Nov 1702. 17.175
Mayes plantation. Adj Jas Knight. 20 Nov 1705. 17.112
McCormac, Fra: Signs bond with Richd Hews who is admr of est of Robt.
    Barton. 17 May 1711. 18.48
McGregor. Patented land with Hugh Fough and sold it to Walter Moor on
    15 Oct 1656. 18.307
Meath, Jno. Gives bond for admr est of Danll Murphew decd. 19 Dec 1711.
    18.116
  Jno. Presented fro absence from Church in St S par. 15 May 1717.
    6.202
Medison, Jno. (Madison) Wit deed Embry to Tapscott. 19 Feb 1711/12.
    18.150
Meeks, Jno. Pat 1000 acres in what later became St S par. 6 May 1651.
    17.153 Another entry states that Jno Meeks in
    partnership with Wm Newman patented 1000 acres in
    St S par. 6 May 1651. 18.147
Meekes, Jno. His funeral last November. 21 July 1656. 14.86
Mehone, Thos. Regs mark for cattle. 21 Nov 1711. 18.113
  Tho. Owes Wm Pickerin 150 lb tobo for coffin plank. Ao 1712.
    18.222
Meloy, Charles. Regs mark for cattle. 31 Aug 1712. 18.227
Melton, Jno. Orphan son of Miles Melton aged 14, with his mother's
    consent, bound to Richard Hopwood to be taught
    the trade of hatter. 18 Sept 1717. 6.238
Melton, Michael decd. Will presented by Mary Melton extrx. 16 June 1714.
    6.41
Melton, Rd. Owes Wm Pickerin 20 lb tobo for an iron pot. Ao 1712.
    18.222

Merryday, John. Certificate of Marriage. 11 Sept 1656. Jno Merryday and Mrs Ann Nash als Mallett were married by Coll John Trussell, according to Act of Parliament 24th Aug 1653. Wit: Geo Colclough, Leonard Spencer and John Carter. Recorded 20 Sept 1656. 14.90

Meredy, Nathan. Wit deed Jno Crafford to Wm Davis. 20 Dec 1706. 17.94

Mereday, Nathan. Fined for absenting himself from Church. 21 Janry 1713/14. 6.16

Merrydith, John. "To all such whom it may concerne These are to certifie that John Meridith and Ann Nash being three times Published according to Law were married at Currotoman the 14th of this instant July 1657 per mee Samuell Cole minister ibidem 20th July 1657 this Certificate was Recorded". 14.111 See entry above John Merryday.

Meredith, John, shipwright of Christ Church par, Lancaster Co., and Dorothy his wife relict of Abram Byram. Cattle to remain on property for use of Byram's children, etc. 16 Oct 1668. 16.59

Meredith, Jno. Dorothy his widow. Gift to his child Joanna from Thos Hopkins who is now dec'd. 20 Nov 1669. 3.40

John who married Mary the relict of Wm Barry dec'd. Com of admr on Barry's est to him. 19 Apl 1693. 4.619

Merny, Tho. Servt to Mr Rhoden adj to be 14 yrs old. 6 Apl 1669. 3.60

Medcalf, Hen. (bro of Geo Medcalf) has bequest from Jno Tyngey. 1 Aug 1667. 16.30

Hen. Orphan of Wm Medcalfe. List of his cattle, 8 head, submitted by Wm Jolland. 22 August 1670. 16.144

Hen. Wit will of Saml Griffin 2 Feb 1702/3. Prov by oath 5th Sept 1703. 17.215

Henry (Henry Motcalf) married Phoebe Shippey, legatee of James Jones. 17 Feb 1714. 6.98

Jane. That Dennis the wife of Jno Clarke being now a servant to Danl Holland is unable to continue as guardian of Jane Medcalfe. Order that Wm Ruske who married a sister of Jane be appointed guardian. 22nd July 1661. 2.144

Medcalfe, Wm. Signs Oath to Commonwealth of England. 13 Apl 1652. 1.72

Wm. dec'd. Account of his estate. 18 Apl 1657. Personal property delivered some 2 yrs since to his children and heirs:
    To Wm Davis for Henry Medcalfe
    To Susan Davis a heifer loft her by the will
    To Eliz: Carpenter a cow left her by the will
    To Phill Carpenter for use of George Medcalfe
    To Richd Clare for use of Anne Medcalfe
    To Jno Kent for use of Kath: Medcalfe
    To Richd Clare and Anne Reynolds for use of Eliz Medcalfe.
    To Dennis the wife of Jno Clarke for the use of Jane Medcalfe with a cow allotted to Henry Medcalfe.
    To Charity Medcalfe. She of this date deceased. 14.105

Medcalfe, Wm. Wit will Saml Griffin. 2 Feb 1702/3. Proved it by oath 5 Sept 1703. 17,215
  Wm. To take inv of est of Peter Coutanceau at Cherry Point. 20 Apl 1709. 17. pp 216-221
Metcalfe, Wm. Signs bond of Jas Moulder to keep ordinary. 16 July 1712. 18,213
  Wm. Appraisor of est of Hugh Wallis. 12 March 1712/13.18,272
  Wm. Guardian of Ann Auveling. 16 June 1714. 6,38
  Wm. Chosen as her guardian by Priscilla Shippy. 21 July 1714. 6,56
  Wm. Security for Robt Vaulx. 21 Nov 1716. 6,185
  Wm. Exor of Parish Gardner. 18 March 1718/19. 6,308
Merriton, Matthew of London, Gent. Ref to as "my Cozen" and overseer of his est in England by Richd Wright. 16 Aug 1663. 15,114
Mew, Jno. Chain carrier on survey. 5 June 1710. 17,50
Michaell, Robt. Headright of Wm Sheares. 21 Aug 1678. 4,4
Middleton, Mary. See entry Adam Yarratt. 22 Oct 1667. 15,26
  Robt. Land now or lately belonging to him adj Jno Crump in Wicco par. 16 Sept 1707. 17,128
Miles, David. Residuary legatee of Simon Kirby who was his friend. 22 March 1666/7. 16,3
Mill Creek. Adj Tho Wms dwelling plantation. 2 Dec 1700. 17,70
  in Wicco par adj land of Leonard Howson. 19 July 1704 17,255
  Adj land of Tho Wms. 25 Nov 1706. 17,67
Mill Landing Point. in St S par. 15 May 1711. 18,84
Millerd, Mary. Admr bond on est of Tho Millerd decd. Signed by Mary x Millerd, William Price and Tho Millerd. 20 May 1713. 18,293
  Tho. Signs Richd Brown's bond as guardian of Edw Algood. 20th May 1713. 18,293
  Tho. decd. Appraisal of his est submitted by Mary Millerd his widow. 17 June 1713. 18,314
  Tho. Junr. of St S par, planter, buys 30 acres on branch of Mattapony River. 16 Aug 1712. 18,215
Miller, Christopher. Orphan son of Tho Miller decd, 13 yrs old last Nov, bound to Roger Wigginton till 21 to leard the trade of ship carpenter. 12 March 1713/14. 6,21
Miles (Michaell) Servt to Mr Jno Saffin. Fought with Thomas Barrett who was considered a bad character. Janry 1664. 16,10
  Michael "aged 22 years or thereabout" says Richd Rice taxing Jeremy Cannady servt to Mr Jno Saffin and Tho: Barrett for stealing pork which Constant Daniell had had in the woods. Cannady denied it saying he lay at Barretts being "twelfth day" 1664. That several times Cannady and Tho Young, another servt of Mr Saffin, had been absent from their business at Exeter Lodge, etc. No date but recorded January 1666/7. 16,10

Miller, Miles. aged 20 yrs. Headed thus and deposition signed Michaell
    Miller. Says abt 2 yrs ago he heard Jam Parker
    say - see under Parker's name just what he said.
    No date but recorded January 1666/7. 16.9

Miller, Randolph and Kath his wife ack sale of 250 acres to Edw Sanders.
    21 Dec 1698. 4.846

    Mr Randolph. 203 acres surveyed for him, part in Chicicocomoco
        par; Northumberland Co and part in Christ Church
        par, Lancaster Co. 2 June 1711. 18.166

    Mr Randolph. His line adj Edwd Sanders. 13 July 1711. 18.73

    Tho. Her dau Anne left to him till of age by Mrs Welthian
        Bonas. 20 Aug 1684. 4.236

    Tho. Wit deed Busslo to Straughan. 15 Sept 1703. 17.233

    Tho. Decd. His relict Winnefred Miller swears he left no will.
        Admr granted. 19 Aug 1719. 6.327

    Wm. Exor of Tho Percifull. 8 Sept 1714. 19.38

Milligan, Jamose. Headright of Mr Jno Harris. 15 July 1696. 4.733

Million, Eliz. Her servt boy Richd Kennedy 12 yrs old. 18 Dec 1717.
    6.251

    Eliz: Orphan dau of John Million decd makes choice of John
        Lancaster as guardian. 19 June 1717. 6.218

    Eliz: Orphan of John Million makes choice of John Ashburn as
        guardian. 21 Jan 1718/19. 6.297

    John. Petitions that the est of Benj Golson decd be appraised.
        19 Nov 1696. 4.748

    John. Nearest of kin to Richd Lankester dec'd. 18 Nov 1713.
        6.2

    John. Admr of est of Richd Lancaster decd. 18 Nov 1713. 18.346

    John. His mark for cattle recorded. 16 Mar 1714/15. 6.101

    Jno. decd. His relict Elizabeth Million swears he left no will.
        Admr granted. 19 June 1717. 6.218

    Mary. Indenture. 22 July 1668. Mary Million from par of Drury
        Lane in Co of Middlesex, spinster, being free,
        neither servant or apprentice, to go to Virginia
        on the a/c of Thomas Smith, marriner, in the good
        ship called the Salisbury, she to serve 4 years
        after arrival in Virginia to pay her passage, she
        to have double clothing, etc. 16.86

Minty, Edw. Formerly sold land in Westmorland Co to Geo Leasure. 17th
    Nov 1708. 17.59

Miryman, Francis. Wit agreement Kaye to Higginson. 31 Oct 1636. 14.66

Mitchell, Jas. Wit deed Hill to Chilton. 15 June 1709. 17.78

    Jas. Wit will Jos Rudnall. 9 July 1709. 17.58

    Matthew. Servt to Wm Nelms is judged to be 15 yrs old. 20th
        March 1716/17. 6.201

Mittchiles, Robt. His land adj Tho Rout and land sold by Jno Hill to
    Wm Dare this date. 20 Sept 1711. 18.152

Monning, Giles. Bequests to his now wife and his eldest son Francis.
    To Bro in Law Rd Feilding, also Bro in law Francis
    Monning and his now wife. 16 July 1666. 16.12

Monohory, Cornelius. Servt to Joice Holland judged to be 17 yrs of age. 17 Apl 1672. 3.144

Montgomerie, James. Wit deed Hudnall to Palmer. 5 June 1677. 17.28
    James. Wit deed Crawford to Legg. 15 June 1692. 17.212

Moon, Elenour. Widow of Tho Moon. Rerecords deed Dunaway to Moon. 16th Jan 1711/12. 17.150
    James. Married Sarah widow of Jno Mason prior to 19 July 1718. 6.371
    John. Fined for absenting himself from Church. 21 Jan 1713/14. 6.15
    Tho. Buys land from Dunaway at head of Great Wicco:. 11 March 1705/6. 17.150
    Tho. Will d 21 March 1711. p 16 Jan 1711/12. Wife Ellender. Son John (only child). 18.132

Moore, Hannah. Wife of Wm. 5 Sept 1707. 17 Sept 1707. 17.47
    James. See entry Loughly Conolin. Bought land from Anthony Lynton. 22 Dec 1673. 17.143
    James. Dec'd prior 21 July 1703. Bought 41 acres in Mattaponi Neck from Antho: Linton. 22 Dec 1673. 17.96
    James. To value buildings put on land to be ret'd by Geo Hutton to Antho Lynton. 16 Oct 1676. 4.7
    James. As wit proves will of Wm Hill. 20 May 1685. 4.269
    James. Late of this County dying intestate and no person near of kin, etc. 10 Oct 1692. 4.601
    James and Agnes. Wit deed Conolin to Hutson. 17 Apl 1700. 17.146
    James. Late of Northumberland Co now of Richmond Co, deed to Hutson. See entry Conolin. 21 May 1707. 17.148
    John. Wit deed Wm Smyth to Rd Lugg. 18 Nov 1677. 17.141
    John. His servt Richd Archer judged 14 yrs of age. 21 Dec 1698. 4.847
    John. Son of James Moore decd and his wife Sarah, now wife of Laughly Conolin. 21 July 1703. 5.256

Moor, Roger. Long entries. "a negro transported serv't (but no slave) to Richd Hudnall having been committed into the Sherriffs custody by precept from Mr John Ingram one of his Maj Justices" on complaint of Tho Eve that he had broken into his house, stolen goods, etc. 15 Aug 1716. 6.171

Moore, Sarah. Widow of James Moore. She had married Laughly Conolin prior to 21 July 1703. See Sarah Conolin. 17.96
    Mrs Sarah. Widow of James. She was married to Loughly Conolin at the date 17 May 1708. 17.143

Moor, Walter. Bought land from Jams McGregor and Hugh Fouch. 15th Oct 1656. 18.307

Moore, Walt. On Jury to div land Saffin and Hull. 29 Nov 1669. 16.63

Moore, Wm. Deed. 5 Sept 1707. of N Co., planter, to Timothy Canaday of Richmond Co., planter. 116 acres, part of a pat granted Jno Carpenter, Charles Carpenter and Wm West 24 Nov 1670, related in another deed betw John Hill of Rappa Co and Eliz his wife to James Gaynor of N Co dated 1691, etc. 17.47

Moorehead, Charles. His servt Andrew Farguson judged 11 yrs of age.
16 Nov 1698, 4,342
 Charles. Lives on land of Rd Nelmes. 13 Apl 1706. 17,98
 Charles. To teach Nicho Callan, now abt 12 yrs old, trade of cooper. 18 March 1713/14. 6,25
 Sarah. Her land adj Jno Crafford. 20 Dec 1706. 17,94
 Wm. Wit Smith to Nelmes. 16 Dec 1710
 Wm. Signs Jno Nelms bond to keep ordinary. 10 Sep 1711. 18,99
 Wm. "at present much weakened Lame and incapable of labour by means of some late sicknesse" excused from levy this year. 16 June 1714. 6,43
Morattico path. Adj land of Tho Towers. 8 Sept 1668. 16,38
 At head of G W River, adj land John Donaway. 11 July 1706. 17,99
Mordant, L'strange. See entry Wm Gradey. 17,152
Morgan, Mr Charles, dec'd. 4800 lb tobo to Mrs Jane Wildey for sundry expenses. See entry her name. 15 June 1681. 4,97
 Charles. Mrs Martha Jones obt judgt agt him 22 Nov 1677 for 16 bu salt. Mrs Eliz Morgan his admr not appearing, the order confirmed and Mrs Morgan ordered to pay. 20 Oct 1681. 4,107
 William. Wit will of Rd Feilding. 16 July 1666. 16,12
 Wm. Wit will of Rd Span. 16 Mar 1667/8. 16,64
 Wm. of Bristol sells Mary Mottley, widow, 100 acres that Henry Roach of Bristol, mariner, bought from Wm Betts. 24 Feb 1670/1. 16,158
 Wm. "an ancient impotent person" freed from levy. 19 Apl 1693. 4,619
Morphew, Patrick. (Patrick Murphy ?). Depo, age not shown. Says when servt to Mr Garlington abt 5 yrs since, etc. Date not shown but recorded in 1664. 15,136
Morrill, Tho. Witness. See entry Jno Ingram. 29 Apl 1670. 16,76
Morris, Antho: Age 24 yrs or th-abts. 5 Oct 1669. 16,94 Also 16,58A
 Antho: on Jury Saffin vs Thompson. 6 Apl 1669.
 Antho: P of A from Tho Lane. 23 Sept 1671. 16,214
 Eliz. Age 22 yrs or th-abts. 4 Aug 1665. 15,164
 Mrs Martha. Aged 46 yrs or th-abts. 4 Sept 1655. 14,62
Morrice, Mr Nicho: His land adj Peter Knight. 26 Nov 1651. 17,179
Morris, Nicholas. Signs oath to Commonwealth of England. 13 Apl 1652. 1, pp72-3
 Mr. Nicho. Justice. 20 July 1652. 1,76
 Nicho: Wit deed Saffell to Hudnall. 20 Nov 1655. 14,59
 Nicho. Alice Larritt makes sworn stmt before him. 19 Janry 1655/6. 14,67
 Nich: Will. d 21 Nov 1660, p 20 Jan 1664/5. To son Anthony Morris. To wife Martha, she extrx; To dau Jane Haney. Grandchildren Martha Haney, Elizabeth Haney and Richd Haney.
 Wit: Sam George. Jeffery George. 15,140

Morris, Mr Nicho: His land adj Jno Hudnall. 25 July 1665. 17.28
Morriss, Tho. Wit receipt Ingram to Harris. 29 Apl 1670. 16.128
    Tho. "was miserably drowned". His partner, Jno Turine, pd all debts, 21 Aug 1678. 4.1
    Tho. Owes Rd Hull 2900 lb tobo. 21 Aug 1678. 4.5
    Wm. Owes est of Tho Crowder 1000 lb tobo. 20 June 1711. 18.62
    Wm. Signs bond Eliz Tapico admr Wm Tapico. 17 June 1719. 19.61
Mortemore, Farragon. Aged 6 yrs the 24th of Oct next, one of the sons of James Mortemore dec'd. Bound by his mother Mrs. Margaret Mortemore to Tho Gill of St S par till 21. 15 July 1713. 18.326
    Jam: Servt to Mr Coutanceau (John) Sr judged 16 yrs of age. 18 March 1684/5. 4.256
Mortimore, Jas. Wit Price to Odohoty. See entry R Gibble. 8 Nov 1701. 17.156
Morton, Andr: Admr of est of Jno Bennett who on 1 Apl 1665 gave a bill for a heifer, etc. 11 Jan 1668/9. 3.50
    Andrew. His est owes Capt Jno Mottrom 366 lb tobo (prob levies and sheriff's fees) 21 Aug 1678. 4.4
Mosley, Hen: Signs oath to Commonwealth of England. 13 Apl 1652. 1.72
    Henry, dec'd. a/c of orphans' cattle submitted by John Tingey.
        son John   2 cows
        dau Anne   1 heifer
        son Wm   1 calfe   13 Apl 1657. 14.105
    Hen: Wit Jno Moseley's will. 18 May 1668. 16.74
    Hen: Sued by Geo Deacon for 323 lb tobo. 21 Jan 1668/9. 3.52
    Hen: See entry Wm Graddy. 17.152
Moseley, John. Will 18 May 1668. prob 19 Nov 1669. To bros Wm and Hen:. To "Cosen Tho Harden", to "cosen Anne Harden". To Robt Penell and his wife. Witt: Hen Moseley. Robt: Penell, Jane Penell. 16.126
    Wm. Chooses Tho Harding as his guardian. 6 Apl 1669. 3.61
    William, John and Henry. Bequests from Jno Tyngey. 1 Aug 1667. 16.30
Mottrom, Anne. married Richd Wright. His widow. 10 Dec 1663. 15.114
    John. Burgess. Nov 1645. Hening. Vol.1. page 299
    Mr John. Justice. 24 Aug 1650. 1.41
    John, Gent. To have admr of est of Mr Florentine Suningberke. 10 Jan. 1650/1. 1.46
    John. Store had been kept at his house by Tho Hawkins. 17 Jan 1651/2. 1.70
    John. Signs oath to Commonwealth of England. 13 Apl 1652. 1.72 (Note: 2 persons of this name signed this oath. It is also a fact that another person named John Mottrom, not Capt John Mottrom the son of Col Jno Mottrom, was in Northumberland Co after the death of old Col John Mottrom. See Va. Colonial Abstracts, Vol.2. I am uncertain as to the correct pronounciation of this name Mottrom. I came upon it at a later date appearing as 'Mottrom' and as 'Makum' in the same entry. B.F.

Mottrom, Jno. 200 lb tobo due him from Freeman Conaway. 13 Apl 1652. 1.75
    Col. Jno. Justice. 20 July 1652. 1.76
    Col. Jno. His widow Ursula, formerly relict of Richd Thompson, now wife of Geo Colclough. 3 Jan 1656/7. 14.123 and 14.124
    Col. Jno. dec'd. Capt Richd Wright admr. 21 July 1659. 15.27A
    Col. See depos of Wm and Eliz Grinsted and of Francis Clay Gent. 10 Oct 1660. 15.61
    John (Jr). Ref to as brother in will of Richd Wright. (that is his wife's brother). 16 Aug 1663. 15.114
    Col John. land adj Matthew Rodham. 17 Nov 1666. 16.22A
    Capt John. Justice. 21 Aug 1678. 4.1
    Mr John. Sworn Justice. 24 Aug 1669. 3.69
    Capt John. Est of Andrew Morton owes him 366 lb tobo. 21 Aug 1678. 4.4
    Capt Jno. Est of Mr Robt Jones owes him 4425 lb tobo levies and sheriff's fees. 21 Aug 1678. 4.3
    Capt Jno. Justice. 16 Oct 1678. 4.5
    Major John, dec'd. His orphan's estate managed by Hon Nicho: Spencer, who arranges that Danl Webb "a molatto" is set free. 5 Oct 1687. 4.405
    Major Jno. In his lifetime gave bill dated 29 Oct 1683 to Mr Geo Luke for 692 lb tobo. Judgt to Luke agt the est. 5 Oct 1687. 4.406
Mottrome, Capt Spencer. Justice. 21 Sept 1692. 4.599
                               Justice 15 July 1696. 4.731
                               Justice 16 July 1696. 4.734
Mottrom, Spencer. Orphan of Spencer Mottrom dec'd. Bond L 1000. Sterl. by Jos Ball his guardian. Bond also signed by Richard Ball and Geo Ball. 19 June 1712. 18.198
    Spencer. Orphan under 21. Jos Ball guardian. 12 March 1713/14. 6.22
Motly, Jno. Patent. 13 Jan 1661. 17.24
Motley, Jno. His land adj Capt Jno Whitty. 15 May 1661. 17 pp 224-229
    Mr Jno. Appoints Mr Jas Gaylord his atty. 11 Jan 1668/9. 3.50
    Jno. His servt Jno Farrar adj 13 yrs of age. 19 Jan 1675/6. 3.250
    Mr Jno of N. Co dec'd, land adj Jno Cockerill Sr. 30 Dec 1695. 17.135
    John, dec'd. Pat land 13 Jan 1661/2. Father of Mr Jno Mottley Junr and Grandfather of Mrs Eliz Wildey. 18 Dec 1706. 17.24
Mottley, Jno Jr. Dec'd. His will dated 8 Feb 1669/70. Son of John Sr and husband of Mary. Entry dated 18 Dec 1706. 17.24
    Mary. Widow and extrx of Jno Mottley of G W par, buys from Wm Morgan of the City of Bristol, mercht, 100 acres that Henry Roach of the City of Bristol, mariner, bought of Wm Betts. 24 Feb 1670/1. 16.158.

Mottley, Mary. Deed of Gift to her son Jne Mottley, land, etc. Wit: Jno Farnefold, Edw Cole. 23 Oct 1671. 16.198

Mary. Dec'd. Wife of John Mottley Jr. She was living 18 Decr 1671. This entry 18 Dec 1706. 17.24

Mottleys Neck. So commonly called. Patented 13 Jan 1661/2 by John Mottley decd. 13 Dec 1706. 17.24

Mould, Tho. P of A. 18 Feb 1669/70 to friend Dennis Eyes to cause Jam: Robinson to ack tfr of land from sd Mould and Tho Edwards. Wit Leo Howson, Jno Burkston. 16.170

Tho. Balance of est left him by Tho Edwards. 9 March 1669/70 16.71

Tho. Freed from future levies, being lame and incapable of maintaining his family by labor. 21 Aug. 1678. 4.3

Moulder, Jas. Lic to keep ordinary "att his mansion house". 16 May 1711. 18.44 . Also bond to keep ordinary at his mansion house. 16 July 1712. 18.213

Jas. Wit deed Nutt to Blackwell. 26 July 1712. 18. 224-5

Jas. Bond to keep ordinary. 16 Sept 1713. 18.340

Jane. Presented for charging excess prices for Rum, brandy, etc. 15 May 1717. 6.207

Moult, Joseph. Appointed Constable for Lower Fairfield. 18 May 1687. 4.394

Moulton, Wm. with Tho Grimstead next of kin to Jas Lookman decd. 18th June 1718. 6.269

Muckleslose, Turner. Servt to Peter Presly adj 13 yrs of age. 19 Janry 1675/6. 3.249

Mulberry Fields. See entry Capt Tho Brereton. 23 Mar 1698/99. 17.189

Mullis, Mr Jno. To assist settlemt Tho Brewer's est. 11 June 1697. 17.268

Mulloy, Charles. Servt to Mr Tho Gaskins adj 14 yrs of age. 16 Novr 1698. 4.842

Mulraine, Alex: Wit will Eliz Bledsoe. 13 Feb 1707/8. 17.55

Alex: Deposition. Age not shown. Swears that he wrote and wit will for Richd Nelmes Sr dated 13 Apl 1706. Deposition dated 16 May 1711. 17.98

Alex. Rerecords Inv of Est of Hugh Callan decd. 20 June 1711. 17.113

Alex: Appraisor of est of Jno Corbell decd. 18 July 1711. 18.72

Alex: Wit deed Cottrell to Prosly. 14 Jan 1711/12. 18.123

Alexr: Wit deed Murrow to Gator. 11 Mar 1711/12. 18.307

Alex: "a poor Ancient man" exempt from levy. 17 July 1717. 6.221

Munro, Alex. In county expense "for the ferry 3000 lb tobo". 2 Novr 1681. 4.681

Munroe, Andrew. Signs oath to Commonwealth of England. 13 Apl 1652. 1. 72-3

Munslow, Valentine. Bought land 6 Dec 1669. See entry Alex Cumins et als dated 7 Apl 1707. 17.116

Munslow, Valentine. Nuncupative Will. Sworn 18 June 1712 by Onesephorus Harvey and Jno Brown. Gives plantation etc to his Godson Vallentine Hester, he failing in heirs to Mary Hester, she failing in heirs to Jno Gouch. That Eliz Gaskins was an evidence. 18,185

Murdock, Geo. Deposition. 16 July 1712. Aged 36 or thereabouts. Says he was well acquainted with Robt Boyd, taylor. "and was at his wedding when he was Marryed to Ann Boyd now his relict and Admrx". Also well acquainted with John Boyd eldest son of Robt and Ann Boyd "and is now Very Nigh 9 years of age". 18,215

 Benj: Son of Geo and Mary. Grandson of Benj Browne. 16 Nov 1708. 17,158

 Geo. Wit deed Pope to Boyd. 1 Jan 1703/4. 17,194

 Geo: of Richmond Co. Wit deed Moore to Canaday. 5 Sept 1707. 17,47

 Geo. Ref to as "my Friend" in bequest from Robt Boyd. 10 Sept 1710 /18,42

 Geo. Husband of Mary who is dau of Benj Browne. 16 Nov 1708 Also rerecords deed Browne to Murdock. 19 March 1711/12. 17,158

 Geo: Court orders he lay out road thru land of Jno Thomas for Tho Laine. 18 June 1712. 18,210

 Geo: Deposition. 20 March 1716/17. Aged 40 yrs or th-abts. Re. Wm Howard's will. 17,236

 John. Servt to Geo Murdock judg'd to be 6 yrs old. 20 May 1719. 20 May 1719. 6,316

 Marg't. Wit will of Robt Boyd. Shown as Mary in proof of will. 10 Sept 1710. 18,42

Murphew, Daniel, decd. Inv of his est. Value 7140 lb tobo. Presented by John Moath and Mable his wife late relict and widow of Murphew. 16 Jan 1711/12. 18,144

 Maurice. A poor man exempted from levy. 15 June 1715. 6,112

Murray, Wm. His will presented by Abner Neal exor. 20 Jan 1719/20. 6,352

Murrow, Wm. Signs Jno Nelms' bond for ordinary. 10 Sept 1711. 18,99

 Wm and Anne his wife of St S par sell land to Matthew Gater. 11 March 1711/12. 18,307

Mutton, Eliz: Bequests from her father Jno Mutton Sr. 26 Sept 1675. 17,260

Mottoune, John. Court orders Certificate to be made to the Assembly "of his long aboad in this Colony his resolution to continue therein and his Civill Comportment towards his Majesty and his Majesties Leigh people that he may have his denizacon". 6th April 1669. 3,60

Mottoone, Jno. deceased. See entry Jno Lewis who married his daughter Frances. 24 Apl 1684. 4,93

Mutton, John. Living 9 Feb 1685/6. See entry Alex Cumins et als. 7th April 1707. 17,116

Mutton, John and Sarah his wife summoned as evidence in behalf of
    Peter Byram agt Jeffery Johnson. Failed to appear,
    are fined. 16 July 1685. 4.287
Mutton, Jno. dec'd. Alex: Cummings and Sarah his wife of Stafford Co.,
    sell Geo Dameron 100 acres she inherited from said
    Mutton. 4 Dec 1711. 18.117
    Jno. Jr. Only son of Jno. Sr, of tender age. Bro in Law John
        Lewis. 26 Sept 1678. 17.260
    Jno. Senr. Will of Jno Muttoone of G W par. dated 26 Sep 1678.
        prob. 2 Mar 1680/1. 17.260
    Sarah. Bequests from her father Jno.Sr. 26 Sept 1678. 17.260
Mutton Family detail: Jno Mutton was father of Jno Mutton who in turn
    was father of Sarah wife of Alex Cummings of
    Stafford Co, Mary wife of Henry Robinson. 4th Dec
    1711. 18.117
Myars, Jane. Says she brought up Christian Penny "a base born child
    from an Infant". Order that sd Penny serve her until
    she be 18 yrs of age. 20 Aug 1719. 6.334
Myars, Matthew of Whitechapple par, Lancaster Co., cordwaynar, buys
    100 acres in Mattapony Neck, Northumberland Co.,
    from Wm and Anne Lambert. 17 Dec 1707. 17. pp 130-5
    Matthew. Rerecords deed 17 Dec 1707 Lambert to Myars. 15 Aug
        1711. 17.pp 130-5
    Mathow, dec'd. Jane his relict swears he left no will. Admr of
        est to her. 21 Aug 1717. 6.235

Nash, Ann. Married to Jno Merrydith by Rev Saml Cole. 14 July 1657.
    (had already been married to him by Civil ceremony)
    14.111
Nash, Mrs Ann als Mallett wife of Jno Merryday. 11 Sept 1659. 14.90
    Robt. Wit will of Peter Knight. 28 Nov 1702. 17.175
    Robt. Atty for Mary wife of Jno Gooch. 7 Apl 1706. 17.195
    Robt. Wit deed Mayes to Mayes. 19 Dec 1710. 18.26
    Robt. of Wicco par. Fined for 2 mos absence from Church. Possibly
        a Quaker. 23 Sept 1715. 6.138
    Robt. Guardian of Farnifold Nutt. 18 Nov 1719. 6.346
    Tho. of Corotomen, Rappahannock Co., Virginia, boatwright, sells
        Mr Leonard Howson of G W par, 1/2 of 6000 acres
        granted Wm Vincent, sold by him to Jno Ingram, and
        by him to Nash. 17 Jan 1671/2. 16.219
    Wm. Wit bond Thos Hubbard of Christ Church par Lancaster Co to
        Jno Wright of same par. 9 March 1712/13. 18.287
Neale, Abner. Orphan son of Danl Neale late decd. Guardianship bond
    given by Tho Barnes. 20 Aug 1712. 18.219
    Abner. Presented to Grand Jury for absenting himself from Church.
        Dismissed, he being under age. 16 Aug 1716. 6.175
    Abner. Fined 50 lb tobo for absence from Church in St S par.
        16 May 1717. 6.213 (Note: The first entry omitted
        and the second subtracted from the third seems to
        equal 21)

Neal, Abner. with Robt Davis and Hugh Owen gives Guardianship Bond for
            Anne Lucas orphan of Tho Lucas decd. 18 Feb 1718.
            19.25
    Abner. Wit deed Jones to Lancaster. 10 Oct 1718. 19.8
    Abner. Chosen by Ann Lucas as guardian. 18 Feb 1718/19. 6.299
    Abner. Exor of Wm Murray. 20 Jan 1719/20. 6.352
Neale, Anne. Wife of Rodham Neale of St S par. P of A to David
            Straughan. 20 May 1713. 18.303
    Christo: His wife Hannah dau of Matthew Rodham. 17 Dec 1666.
            16.22
    Christo: Wit P of A Ellen Neale to Danl Neale. 21 Nov 1669.
            16.64
    Christo: Wit P of A LeBreton to Matthew. 3 Apl 1671. 16.192
    Mr Christo: Sec on bond of Mrs Mary Thomas admr Wm Thomas for
            70000 lb tobo. 16 Oct 1678. 4.6
    Mr Xpher. His hands (laborers) to be in charge of Victor Drew.
            17 Oct 1678. 4.10
    Mr Xpher. Justice. 18 Aug 1681. 4.101
            Justice. 18 Apl 1683. 4.176
            Justice. 18 May 1687. 4.493
            Justice. 20 July 1687. 4. 397
            Justice. 16 Nov 1687. 4.410
    Christo: Exor of Rev Jno Farnefeld. 3 July 1702. 17.234
    Christopher. Justice. 21 July 1703. 17.127
    Christo. Wit will Jno Bowers Sr. 29 Sept 1704. 17.167
    Christo. Justice. 13 Oct 1704. 17.165
    Christo. "Cozen" and exor of Rodham Kenner. 26 July 1706. 17.126
    Christo. Justice. 19 Dec 1706. 17.24
    Christo: Justice. 20 Apl 1709. 17. pp 216-221
    Capt Christo: Justice. 4 June 1709. 17.102
    Christo: Wit will Rebecca Price. 10 Dec 1709. 18.242
    Capt Christopher. Justice. 16 March 1712/13. 18.270
            Justice. 12 April 1711. 18.46
            Justice. 21 May 1713. 18.307
    Christo: Guardian of Richd Kenner. 15 June 1715. 6.116
    Christopher. The following items appear in the County charges
            against the levy 28 Nov 1715.   lb tobo
            To Capt Chr'phr Neale for Burg's charges   6610
            To Mr Richd Neale for ditto   6610
            To Collo Peter Presly for ditto last sessions 6820
            To Capt Chr'phr Neale for ditto   6220
                6.146
    Capt Christo: Justice. 18 April 1716. 6.153
    Christo: Exor of Rodham Kenner. See entry Richd Kenner. 16 Aug
            1716. 6.177
    Capt Christo. Justice. 15 May 1717. 6.206
Neale, Danl. Bought 250 Acres from Tho Garrard 1 Dec 1656. 17.91
    Danl and "my wife Hellen" assign rights to bill of sale to Jas.
            Robinson. 22 Sept 1668. 16.62

Neale, Danl. P of A. Ellen Neale to her husband Danl Neale of Fairfield par to ack sale of land to Rich Way.
Wit: Xpofhr Neale, Jno Upton. 21 9ber 1669. (Nov) 16.105

Dan: Wit agreemt Parker and Wood. 10 March 1669/70. 16.165

Dan. Wit will Hen: Lambert. 31 March 1670. 16.72

Daniel. His wife ref to as "Granny Neale" accused by Edward Coles of bewitching his wife. The depositions in this case are among the most absurd that appear in Virginia records. 20 May 1671. 16.181
See entry 'Witchcraft'

Danl. Wit deed Smith to Nipper. 14 Apl 1677

Mr Danl. Justice. 19 Apl 1693. 4.619

Danl. Judgt to him agt Edwd Feilding Exor of Mr Tho Jones decd. Jones in his life time being indebted to Mrs Patience Downing now wife of said Neale for 400. 21 May 1696. 4.726

Mr. Danl. His servt Matth: Simmons adj 11 yrs old. 21 Dec 1698. 4.847

Dan'l. Will. dated 4 Nov 1700. prob. 2 Feb 1700/1.
To younger bro Ebenezer Neale 500 acres on Hulls Creek, also land Bartholomew Shephard now lives on.
Sister Hannah Neale.
"my Mother in Law Mrs Patience —"
Brother in Law Jno Cockrill
to "my —" Elizabeth dau of sd Jno Cockrill silver spoons marked D.N.
to Andrew Cockrill 1000 lb tobo for looking after him in sickness.
Balance of est to be div equally betw his own natural brothers and sisters.
"My Cousin Mr Christopher Neale" sole exor.
Wit: Ann x White, Eliz x Amey and Jas Rogers.
The will recorded 16 Sept 1719 by Richd Lee.

Danl Senior. Disposed of a servt named Jno Wood to Sibbey Parker. 28 March 1671. 16.184

Ebenezer, deceased. Bond for admr his est given by Jno Cotrill and Jno Haynie Jr. Also signed by Rodham Neale and Joseph Humphris. 19 Dec 1711. 18.116

Ebenezer, deceased. Division of his estate betw Cotrel and Haynie. 14 Janry 1711/12. Vol.18. pages 133 plus. Indenture betw John Cotrell and Lucretia his wife one of the sisters and nearest of kin to Ebenezer Neale late deceased of St Stephens par of one part and John Haynie and Hanah his wife other sister and equal in blood with the said Lucretia to the said Ebenezer Neale, all of St S. par.

(continued next page)

Neale, Ebenezer, dec'd. Division of his estate (continued)

That whereas Daniel Holland late of Northumberland Co., deceased, died soized of various tracts of land in Northumberland Co., Va. and in Maryland, in fee, to wit:

379 acres in Newmans Neck, part of 814 acres granted Robt Newman 25 March 1651/2 and sold to sd Danl Holland by Newman and his wife by deed dated 6 Aug 1655.

And 2 other. One an assignment of the patent of 13 Apl 1659 and the other a deed dated 18 Feb 1658/9."both made over to the sd Holland by the sd Newmans successors by his will authorized thereunto"

The other tract in Newmans Neck, 550 acres granted by patent renewed by Holland the 7th Oct 1670, both tracts being in Newmans Neck.

And in Maryland the following. A great amount of detail concerning these properties. In outline:

"Commencement", patented 3 July 1667, and an addl 100 acres patented 17 July 1667 by Raymond Stapleford and sold in October 1671 to Danl Holland.

Also in Maryland 2 islands. 220 acres granted to Tho Taylor, known as Taylors Island. Also 80 acres known as St Johns Island which was granted Taylor 29 May 1668 and sold to Holland by 2 deeds dated 1 March 1669/70.

Also in Maryland 200 acres known as "Taylors Inheritance", sold by Taylor to Holland 28 Feb 1671/2.

All which Danl Holland owned at time of death, and by will dated 31 March 1672, proved in Northumberland 17 April 1672, gave all his lands to his wife Joyce Holland, excepting 20 acres to his daughter Elizabeth.

And the said Joyce Holland by Deed of Gift dated 12 June 1672, for natural affection she had for her daughter Elizabeth Neale, wife of Danl Neale, gave her all lands in Virginia at her death.

The sd Elizabeth dying and leaving 4 sons and 2 daus, towit: Daniel, William, Edward, Ebenezer, Lucretia Cotrell and Hannah Haynie. "the three eldest brothers abovesaid dying without issue" all the land descended to Ebenezer, who later died intestate. Therefore the lands descended to his sisters, Lucretia Cotrell and Hannah Haynie.

Entry dated 14 Jan 1711/12. Vol.18. pp 133 plus.

Neale, Edwd. Will. dated 4 Nov 1700. prob. 20 Feb 1700/1. Exor Danl
    Neale. Bro Ebenezer Neale. Sister Lucretia
    Cookrill. Bal of est to be div betw Daniel
    Neale, Wm Neale and sister Hannah Neale.
    Wit: John Cookarill, Wm Skinner and Jas Crosse.
    Re-rec 16 Sept 1719 by Rd. Lee. 17.251
 Mrs. Hannah. Wife of Christo: Neale. Dau of Matthew Rodham from
    whom Deed of Gift. 17 Nov 1666. 16.22A
 Mrs Hannah. Wit will Rodham Kennor. 26 July 1706. 17.126
 R. To view P Countanceau's inventory at Deeds Quarter. 20 Apl
    1709. 17. pp 216-221
 Richd. of G.W. par, gent. Buys 130 acres on S side G.W. River
    from John Gouch. 7 Apl 1706. Re-recs deed 20
    May 1713. 17.195
 Richd. Gent. App by Governor to be agent at Shapleigh Store
    House on Wicco River. Bondsmen Richd Lattemore
    and Tho Hobson. 17 Nov 1714. 6.88
 Mr. Richd. Justice. 21 Jan 1719/20. 6.353
 Rodham. Wit deed Arledge to Maley. 7 July 1703. 17.127
 Rodham. Wit delivery of land Gooch to Neale. 11 Oct 1706. 17.195
 Rodm. Signs appraisal of est of Vincent Garner. 16 May 1711.
    18.47
 Rodham. Appraisor of est of Robt Barton, decd. 20 June 1711.
    18.69
 Rod'm. Swears to inv of Jno Bowles Jr. 19 Jan 1713/14. 17.206
 Rodam of St S par, sells the Hon Robt Carter Esq of Lancaster
    Co, 300 acres in Wicco par, part of 700 acres
    granted James Pope the elder and by his son
    James Pope sold to Christopher Neale (father
    of sd Rodam Neale) on 13 Aug 1691. Christopher
    Neale left the land to his sons Rodam and John.
    John Neale is now dead and the land vested in
    Rodam the surviving brother. 9 Apl 1713. 18.297
Nelmes, Allice. Mother of Patience Nelmes who was an heiress of Partin
    Hudnall. 4 Dec 1698. 17.117
 Alice. An orphan, Henry Common age 12 yrs, bound to her.
    Ambrose Feilding sec. 15 May 1717. 6.209
 Charles. His servt Phill Clissen adj 15 yrs of age. 21 Decr
    1698. 4.848
 Charles. Wit Rev Jno Farnefold's will. Signs with a mark. 3rd
    July 1702. 17.234
 Charles. His land adj Jno Crafford 20 Dec 1706. 17.94
 Charles. Formerly sold servt woman to Wm Winder now decd. 20th
    June 1711. 18.67
 Charles and Wm. Both sign appraisal of est of Mary Walker decd.
    24 Nov 1711. 18.114
 Charles. deceased. Will presented by Alice Nelmes and Charles
    Nelmes exors. 12 March 1713/14. 6.18
 Charles. Conf Judgt to Mr Jos Tipton. 17 July 1717. 6.221
 Charles. Exor of Eliz Cookrill. 20 May 1719. 6.316

Nelmes, Elizabeth. Wife of Wm Nelmes, daughter of Mrs Elizabeth
    Bledsoe. 13 Feb 1707/8. 17.55
  Elizabeth. Wife of Charles Nelmes. Bequest from her mother,
    Mrs Elizabeth Cockerell. 25 Apl 1719. 19.42
  John. Freed from levies on account of lameness. 20 May 1685
    4.269
  Jno. Wit deed Saml Smith to Wm Nelmes of St S par. 19 Dec 1709.
    17. 53
  Jno. Bond to keep ordinary. 10 Sept 1711. 18.99
  Joshua. Makes choice of Isaac Edwards as guardian. 21 March
    1716/17. 6.201
  Rd. His servt Nath Gardoner to serve 6 yrs. His servt John
    Duckot to serve 4 yrs. 8 Oct 1662. 2.163
  Richd. Will. dated 13 Apl 1706, probate date not shown in
    record. Of St S par. To son Richd part of land
    that adjs Cowpen Swamp and also adj the path
    that was formerly called George Clarkes, that
    path to equally divide land betw son Richd and
    son Moses Nelmes. Daughter Lucrotia Nelmes, she
    under 18 and unmarried. To son John Nelmes land
    that Charles Morehead now lives on. Daughter
    Elizabeth Nelmes. Wife Sarah, she extrx. Bros
    Charles Nelmes and Wm Nelmes overseers of will.
    Signature not shown on record.
    Depo of Alexander Mulraine who swears he wrote
    Richd Nelmes will as above and that it was sign-
    ed in the presence of Dorothy Temple, Hannah
    Thropp and himself.
    Deposition of Alexander Rogers, about 18 yrs old,
    says with "asristance and command of his Father
    James Rogers this Deponent did Copy out a
    Written Will subscribed Rich'd Nelmes".
    Depo of Tho Strewton, age not shown. Swears that
    Richd Nelmes will was proved in Court by oaths
    of Alexander Mulraine, Dorothy Templar and
    Hannah Thropp. Sworn 16 May 1711.
    Copy of will rerecorded 16 May 1711 by Sarah
    Nelmes.   17. pp 98-99
  Richd. His land adj Jno Crawford. 15 July 1706. 17.229
  Nelmes als Maddox, Thomas decd. His admr Tho Trapo who married
    his mother. 20 Aug 1684. 4.235
  Wm. Wit Rev Jno Farnefold's will. 3 July 1702. 17.234
  Wm. Son in Law of Mrs Elizabeth Bledsoe and husband of Elizabeth
    Nelmes. 13 Feb 1707/8. Rerecords will of Eliz
    Bledsoe 22 March 1710/11. 17.55
  Wm. of St S par. Buys land from Saml Smith, Gent., 19 Dec 1709.
    Acquitted by Smith of all debt 16 Dec 1710.
    17.53
  Wm. Signs inv of est of Jno Wall decd. 20 June 1711. 18.67

Nelmes, Wm. Signs appraisal of est of Jas Rogers decd. 19 Sept 1711. 18.102
    Wm. of St S par. Overseer of will of his neighbor Wm Pickering 18.228
    Wm. Is pd 250 lb tobo for making a coffin for Mary Walker decd. 17 June 1713. 18.312
    Wm. Son of Charles Nelmes decd petitions to choose a guardian. He chooses Wm Nelmes his uncle. 17 Oct 1716. 6.183
    Wm. His servt Mathew Mitchell adj 15 yrs old. 20 Mar 1716/17. 6.201
    Wm. Will dated 28 Apl 1719. prob 19 Aug 1719. Sons Saml and Wm. Daughters Elizabeth, Winnsyfred, Angelica, Mary, Hannah and Sarah. Wife Elizabeth. Refers to his cousin Wm Nelmes son of his brother Jno Nelmes. 19.54 (Note: the 6 daus all under 21 and umm)
    Wm. Will presented by Elizabeth Nelmes his relict and Samuel Nelmes. 19 Aug 1719. 6.326
    Winifred. Grandaughter of Mrs Eliz Bledsoe. 13 Feb 1707/8. 17/55

Nepper see Nipper.

Netherton, Henry. Wit deed Cornhill to Cralle. 21 Dec 1711. 18.145

Newman, Mrs Eliz:. In dif with Capt Thos Burbage re cattle. 20th Nov. 1651. 1.68
    Mrs Elizabeth. Aged 80 or thereabouts. A midwife. 20 January 1655/6. 14.67 (Note: WHEW ! I'll bet this old lady could have told a tale or two that we would love to know. She saw 27 years of Queen Elizabeth's reign, for instance. B.F.)
    Elizabeth, widow. Gifts to Peter Presly Jr, Martha and Eliz: Haynie. 13 Apl 1659. 15.21A
    Hannah. Headright of Wm Presly. 21 Jan 1660/1. 2.136
    Robt. Sues Rice Maddox. 10 Jan 1650/1. 1.47
    Rob: Signs oath to Commonwealth of England. 13 Jan 1652. 1.72
    Robt and Eliz'a his wife sold 50 acres in Newmans Neck to Robt Smyth. 20 Dec 1652. 18.125
    Robt. Chirurgeon. 6 August 1655. 14.68
    Robt. deceased. Inv submitted by Wm Presly. 20 Sept 1659. 15.28
    Wm. Pat 1000 acres in what later became St S par. 6 May 1651. 17.153 Also another entry: Grant of 1000 acres in St S par in partnership with John Meeks. 6th May 1651. 18.147

Newmans Neck. Jos White lives there. 11 Nov 1698. 17.124

Newton, Christo: Wit will Tho Berry Sr 15 Apl 1700. Proved by his oath 17 July 1700. 17.106
    Christopher. Pays 435 lb tobo to orphans of John Games. (This may possibly be Gaines, but I don't think so. B.F.) 25 June 1710. 18.47
    Christopher. Appraises est of Jas Allen late decd at house of Ralph Beckly. 29 March 1711. 18.38
    Christopher. Wit deed Webb to Wright. 12 July 1712. 18.206

Newton, Christo: His land adj Geo Crosby in St S par. 18 Oct 1705. 17.192

    Christo: Rerecords deed Crosby to Purcell. 17 Dec 1712. 17.192

Nibbs, Danl. Headright of Mr Robt King. 10 March 1661/2. 2.154

Nickless - (Nichols) Land adj Gaskins in G W River. 16 Jan 1710/11 17.80

Nicklesse, Hancock. Wit will Jno Harris 23 Feb 1709/10. Proves it by oath 18 June 1713. 18.318

Nichollas, Elizabeth. Deed of Gift. 20 May 1670. Personal property.
    To son Thomas Baker
    To son Henry Heard (under age. 16.127)
    To son Theodore Baker
    To dau Eliz Nicholas, under 16.
    Wit: Randle Catherall, Pet: Tibbalds. 16.75

Nicholls, Geo. Land adj Geo Crosby in St S par. 18 Oct 1705. 17.192

    Hancock. Land "now in possession of Winters Orphans", adj Charles Ingram. 14 Oct 1707. 17.23

Nickless, Hancock. Wit deed Bledsoe to Ingram. 14 July 1708. 17.22

    Hancock. Wit will of Antho: Haynie 31 Jan 1709/10. Rerecords the will 20 June 1711. 17.107

Nichols, Jno. Appointed Constable for Deviding Creek. 22 June 1669. 3.64

Nickles, Jno. Heir of Theodor Baker decd. Deed Tho Brewer to said Nickles. 13 Dec 1671. 16.226

Nicholas, Jno. Wit deed Holland to Warner. 20 Feb 1671/2. 16.230

Nicholls, Jno. alias Corbell, father of Clem't Corbell, bought 50 acres in Newmans Neck. 28 June 1675. 18.125

Nickless, Jno. Wit deed Innis to Howson. 19 July 1704. 17.255

    Mr John. Was friend of Geo Bledsoe and wit his will. 23 Jan 1704/5. 17.16

Nickles, Jno. Wit deed Cockrill to Cockrill. 19 Nov 1706. 17.138

Nickhols, Jno. decd. Bond for admr his est given by Robert Gordon. Also signed by Tho Dameron, Hancock Nickhols and Christopher Dameron. 20 Feb 1711/12. 18.156

Nickless, Jno Senr. To assist settlemt of Tho Brewer's est. 11th June 1697. 17.268

Nicholls, Saml. Buys 300 acres with Clement Corbell. 11 Feb 1652/3. Having married the relict of Corbell he sells the land to Jno Haynie 20 May 1656. 14.80

    Saml. Age of 30 years. 20 Sept 1658. 15.10A Also 15.10

    Saml. Guardian for 12 yrs past of Prudence Pellam. 20 July 1663. 15.105

Nichols, Sam. Says he was given the name of "an outlandish man". He produces evidence to the contrary. He was from Gurnsey. See depositions of Jno Hull and Robert Island. 20 Dec 1667. 16.32

Nichols, Sam. Values est of Jno Hull decd. 11 Jan 1668/9. 3.51

Nicholls, Saml. Freed from Levy "being a Very Ancient man". 16 Oct 1676. 4.6 (Note: If this is the same Saml Nicholls who was 30 in 1658 he would now be 48 yrs old. The term "Very Ancient" suggests two generations here. B.F.)

Niggins, Richd. Six yrs old next Augt. Eliz Niggins of Lancaster Co.
		binds him apprentice to Henry and Ann Tapscott
		for 15 yrs 4 mos to be taught trade of Joyner and
		trade of Carpenter. 16 May 1711. 18,21
Nipper see Nepper.
Nipper, James. His dau Isabell given a heifer by Rd Span. 8 Sept 1668.
		16,55
Naper, Jas. His bill of sale agt Wm Alexander has priority over any
		other. 21 Jan 1668/9. 3,55
Nepper, Jas. Gives a heifer to his son James. 17 Apl 1672. 16,229
Naper, Jas. His servt Neale Dorhoty adj 15 yrs old. 19 Jan 1675/6.
		3,249
Nipper, Jas. of Fairfield par. Buys land from Rd Smith on Chicacoan
		River. 14 Apl 1677. 17,120
Nepper, Jas. Proves will of Hannah Bridgman by oath as wit. 21 Aug 1678.
		4,1
Nepper, James. Surveyor immediately prior to 15 Oct 1679. 4,47
Nipper, Jas. Wit deed Hobbs to Crawford. 6 Dec 1683. 17,212
	James. Will make his utmost endeavor to teach Wm Odohorty, age
		7, bound to him, to read and keep him at his books.
		20 July 1687. 4,398
	James. Assigns land in Fairfield par to Geo Dawkins. 19 Octr
		1700. 17,120
	Jane. Widow of James Nipper decd. Admr of est to her. 21 May
		1696. 4,725
	John. His land adj Saml Mchaines and Alex Love on the Mill
		Creek. 16 June 1711. 18,76
	Jno. P of A from Elilia Love wife of Alex Love to ack deed.
		17 July 1711. 18,81
	Jno. Presented "for drinking and singing on the Saboth day"
		21 Jan 1713/14. 6,17
	Jno. As exor presents inv of Charles Prichards est. 17th March
		1714/15 6,103
	Jno. deceased. By will designated Swanson Prichard, Charles
		Prichard and Mary Prichard, minors, his exors.
		Whereupon Richd Dennis and Jno Swanson, next of
		kin, came into Court and refused to take admr on
		the will during the minority of the children.
		Saml Heath the greatest creditor obt admr. 18th
		June 1718. 6,270
	Jno. Exor of Charles Prichard. See entry Rd Swanson. 21st Aug
		1718. 6,277
Neppers Plantation, now in possession of the Widow Gaskins. 9 June
		1711. 18,93
Norgate, Phill. His servt Jno Fagan adj 12 yrs of age. 28 Dec 1687.
		4,416
Norgatt, Phillip. deceased. His est appraised. 16 Apl 1711. 18,38
Norman, Jno. and Kath his wife one of the daus of Jno Boucher dec'd
		pet agt Kath Boucher admr of sd doc'd for a childs
		part of her father's est. 19 Oct 1715. 6,140

Norman, Mary. Deed of Gift. 27 Aug 1705. Cattle to 2 daus, Jane and
 Anne Norman. Wit: Tho Stretton, Clark Hobson.
 Rerecorded 20 July 1715 by Wm Popplewell. 17,223
 Mary. Deceased. Her will presented by Wm Popnwell her exor.
 Robert Jones and Cuthburd Bennett swear they wit
 the will. 21 Nov 1716. 6,184
Nornitt (?) Richd. Servt to Jos Hudnall adj 11 yrs of age. 21 Dec 1698.
 4,847
Norris, Wm. Wit deed Hill to Dare. 20 Sept 1711. 18,152
North, Matthew. Headright of - Bridges. 20 July 1652. 1,76 (see Va.
 Colonial Abstracts, Vol.2)
Northen, Soloman of Northumberland Co. "Being a poore Orphant of 16
 years of age and very small and weak of body at
 that age" bound to John Ingram. 17 Oct 1711.
 18,113
Northern Neck. Proprietors of: Margaret, Lady Culpeper, Thomas, Lord
 Fairfax, Katherine his wife and Alex: Culpeper,
 Esq. 10 Nov 1694. 17,142
Northumberland County. Precints.
 Mattapony
 Cherry Point
 Cone
 Newmans Neck
 Upper Fairfield
 Lower Fairfield.
 Upper Great Wiccomoco.
 18 May 1687. 4,394
Norwood, Edw. "a poor antient man", exempt from levy. 22 Nov 1716.
 6,185
Nott, Geo and John. Mrs Eliz Man their mother. See will of Saml Man
 dated 1 Jan 1664/5. 15,170 (see below)
Nowland, Cha: Servt to Robt Seoh adj 10 yrs of age. 20 May 1685. 4,268
Nott, Geo: Age 32 or th-abts. Deposition re Geo Thompson who says he
 is going out of this County. 20 Feb 1650/1. 1,58
 Geo: Wit Deed of Gift Lee to Rhoden. 8 Nov 1651.
Nott also as Knott.
Nutt, Mrs Anne. Wife of Richd Nutt who was son in law (I think this
 means step son in this case. B.F.) to Rev John
 Farnefold. 3 July 1702. 17,234
 Mrs Anne. Rerecords deed dated 19 Apl 1676 Knight to Farnefold.
 18 Apl 1716. 17,230
 Ann and Joseph Nutt, Exors of will of Rd Nutt, ack deed to Wm.
 Smith. 21 Nov 1716. 6,183
 Benj. Son of Richd. 16 July 1707. Rerecords Deed of Gift 21st
 Aug 1723. 17,269
 Mrs. Eliz: Com of admr of est of her late husband Capt Wm Nutt.
 20 Oct. 1668. 3,44
 Mrs Eliz: Her land adj Roger Walters. 29 Dec 1669. 16,69
 Farnefold. Son of Richd Nutt who was son in law (I think step
 son. B.F.) of Rev Jno Farnefold. 3 July 1702.
 17,234

Nutt, Farnefold. Son of Richd. 16 July 1707. 17.269
Farnifold. Orphan of Richd Nutt makes choice of Robt Nash as guardian. 18 Nov 1719. 6.346
Joseph. Complains that since the death of his father Richd Nutt the estate has been diminished by his mother, Ann Nutt, one of the exors, before her decease. Requests that appraisal be made. 19 Nov 1718. 6.297
Mary. Dau in Law to Capt Leonard Howson. Her Father and Mother both dec'd. 13 Dec 1704. 17.8
Mary. Account for her expenses in 1705 incl "To pd Mr Tho Gaskins for accomodating her six months in Mr Leonard Howsons lifetime 500 lb tobo". And "To pd Mr Robt Jones for her schooling in ditto 175 lb tob" a/c recorded 18 July 1711. 18.83
Mary, deceased. Her surviving exor Jno Tarpley, Gent. 18 June 1719. 6.325
Richd. His land adj Jno Farnefold. See entry Peter Knight. 19th April 1676. 17.230
Richd. Prob of will of Mr Richd Nutt deceased to him. 18th March 1684/5. 4.255
Richd. Son in Law to Rev Jno Farnefold who requests that he carry him to his grave. 3 July 1702. 17.234
Richd. His land adj Peter Knight. 28 Nov 1702. 17.175
R'd. Wit deed Crawford to James. 15 July 1706. 17.229
Richd. Deed of Gift. 16 July 1707. Gives his sons Benj: and Farnefold Nutt a negro slave each. Rerecorded by Benj Nutt 21 Aug 1723. 17.269
Richd. Wit will of Jos Hudnall. 9 July 1709. 17.58
Richd. Wit deed Blackwell to Hugh Lett. 20 March 1710/11. 18.13
Richd. Signs bond Hannah Smith admr Rd Smith decd. 22 Mar 1710/11 18.17
Mr Richd. Swears Hen: Mayes' will a true copy. 17 May 1711. 17.101
Richard. Family detail. Deed Nutt to Blackwell. 6 July 1712.
  Richd Nutt and Anne his wife, one of the daus and coheirs of Wm Downing Junr, dec'd.
  Wm Downing Jr decd, will dated 3 Sept 1682, devised to "Charles Downinge youngest sone of his the testators father Wm Downing and to Margery Downinge his the testators Daughter his Tract of land that he lived on", only an estate for life. Charles Downing, one of the legatees dying before partition, Margary became legally vested in the land for life, which after her death descends to nearest of kin.
  The testator at time of death left 3 daughters only: Anne (married Rd Nutt), Elizabeth and Margary, coheirs and equally related.
  Richd Nutt and Anne his wife now sell their int in the land (788 acres) to Saml Blackwell and Margery his wife, the said Margary the abovesaid

Nutt, Richard. Family detail (continued) daughter of Wm Downing Junr (and sister of Mrs Anne Nutt) and now living on the 788 acres in St Stephens parish. 18,222
    Richd. Rerecords patent dated 4 Feb 1662/3 to Wm Nutt. 20th Aug 1712. 17,177
Nutt, Richd (This name may be Hutt) Orphan of Richd Nutt decd chooses Jas Burberry as guardian. 18 Nov 1719. 6,345
    Richd, Jr. Son in Law to Rev Jno Farnefold. 20 Nov 1679. 17,230
    William. Wit deed Saffell to Hudnell. 20 Nov. 1655. 14,59
    Wm. His land adj Rich Gibble. 4 March 1657/8. 15,13
    Mr. Wm. Justice. 20 Sept 1658. 2,91
    Wm. Patent. 4 Feb 1662/3. 683 acres in Northumberland Co. on N side G W River, Lambdons Creek, Island Creek. Adj land of "Wm Tho", land of Tho Garratt, Hen Smyth, the land Richd Spann bought of Edward Coles. This land due by pat dated 4 June 1655, now renewed. Rerecorded 20 Aug 1712 by Richard Nutt. 17,177
    Capt William, deceased. His est to be appraised by Mr Edw Sanders. 20 Nov 1668. 3,48
    Capt. Wm, decd. Sym Dudson to pay arrears in levies from his est. 11 Jan 1668/9. 3,50
    Wm. His land adj Charles Betts. 10 Nov 1694. 17,142
    Wm. His land adj Geo Crosby in St S par. 18 Oct 1705. 17,192
    Wm. of St S par. Will. dated 12 Feb 1711/12. prob 18 Feb 1712/13. To dau Frances Nutt, under 18, and wife Hanah Nutt, all land. They failing in heirs to "my three Brothers Joseph Benjamin and John Nutt". 18,265
    Wm. decd. Appraisal of his est "brought to our veiw by Mrs Hannah Nutt". 17 June 1713. 18,313
    Wm. decd. Reference to land belonging to his orphan on Lambdons Creek. 19 June 1718. 6,272

Odie, Dennis. Hath begotten a servt of James Jones with child and fled out of the County, etc. 8 Oct 1662. 2,166
Odohorty, Wm. Age 7. See entry Jas Nipper. 20 July 1687. 4,398
Odohoty, Neal. His wife rerecords deed dated 1671/2 Gibble to Price. See entry Rd Gibble. 20 Feb 1711/12. 17,156
Odoughity, Sarah (also as Odohotys in entry) files mark for cattle. 19 Sept 1711. 18,100
Odyer, Gabriell. Certif for 100 acres for importing himself and his wife Mary. 20 Feb 1650/1. 1,49
Oldam, Jas. decd. Inv of his est presented by Ruth Oldam admr. 18 Feb 1712/13. 18,262
Oldham, James. Swears to inv of Jno Bowers Jr. 19 Jan 1713/14. 17,206
    James. dec'd. His orphans Geo, James and Abigall choose their uncle Richd Oldam as guardian. 19 Feb .717/18. 6,256

Oldham, Jno. His land adj Tho Towers on Morattico path. 8th Sept 1668. 16.38

Jno. To be pd 2000 lb tobo from County levy for the ferry. 5th Nov 1668. 3.47

Jno. Deeds of Gift from Abigall Oldham to Jno Oldham Jr and "For the girle" Abigall Oldham. No date for entry, but is recorded as of Jan 1668/9.16.71

Jno. His land in Bettys neck adj Edwd Barnes. 21 Oct 1702. 17.200

Jno. Senr. Deed of Gift. 15 Jan 1700/1. For Fatherly love and affection gives James Oldam "the said James being my son", 170 acres in St S par. Adjs Kings Creek, Tuckahoe Swamp. Wit Tho Hughlett, Teige Allen. Rerecorded 17 Sept 1712 by Ruth Oldham. 17.185

Ruth. Admr bond on est of James Oldham decd. Bond also signed by Wm Cornish and Geo Hill. 20 Aug 1712. 18.220

Mrs Ruth, deceased. Saml Smith and Jane his wife, she one of the daus of Ruth Oldam, swear she left no will. Admr granted. 21 Aug 1717. 6.236

Oldis, Tho. (prob of Elizabeth City Co). Phillip Mallory, clerk, his guardian. 17 March 1657. 15.4 (Note: Rev. Phillip Mallory was minister of Lynnhaven par Norfolk (later Princess Anne Co) Co in 1657. Chaplain of the General Assembly in 1658 and 1659, etc)

Oliver, Elinor. Will. dated 4 Sept 1719. prob 16 Sept 1719. Dau Eliz: Keen and son in law John Keen. Grandaus Eliz and Elinor Keen. Refs to "my white girl Mary Fletcher". Wit Jno Lewis. Matt Kenner. 19.56

Ignatius. Servant to Mr Tho Matthews adjudged 10 yrs of age. 17 March 1674/5. 3.224

Ignatius. To be pd 600 lb tobo from County levy for "the best peece of Cloth the Last Yeare". 19 Nov 1696. 4.748

Ignatious. deceased. Suit of his exors Elinor Oliver, Jno Keen and Eliz his wife agt Frat Kenner ref to next Court. 22 Nov 1716. 6.186

John. See entry Wm Gradey. 8 Oct 1705. 17.152

OLoth, Don'll. Servt to Phill Shaply adj 16 yrs old. 19 Jan 1675/6. 3.249

Omuddy, Danll. Servt to Pet: Presly adj 17 yrs old. 19 Jan 1675/6. 3.249

Omullion, Patrick. Servt to Mrs Jane Wildey adj 13 yrs of age. 28 Dec 1687. 4.416

Oneale, Arthur. Servt to Rich: Hull adj 15 yrs of age. 19 Jan 1675/6. 3.249

Roger. Free from levy. Lame and disabled. 21 Aug 1678. 4.1

Only. The word derived from 'one'. See entry Tho Ingram "his onely sonne". 16 Apl 1672. 16. 231

Opie, Jno., Gent., of St S par buys 124 acres in St S par from Phillip Rogers. 16 Feb 1711/12. 18.147
    Jno. Rerecords deed dated 1707 Jas Jones to Phillip Rogers. 20th Feb 1711/12. 17.153
    Jno. Appraises est of Tho Millerd decd. 17 June 1713. 18.314
    Mr Tho: Joane Willoughby widow assigns her int in thirds of land belonging to him formerly in poss of Mr David Lyndsay. 17 March 1674/5. 3.224
    Mr. Tho. His 3 servants accused by Mr Nicho Owen of hog stealing. 16 Oct 1676. 4.6
Orland, Richd and Margrett his wife. Her atty Jno Turberville to ack deed to Robt Davis. 16 Dec 1696. 4.752
Orley see Hawley.
Orley, Tho. His widow m Wm Jolland. 8 Oct 1662. 2.163
    Tho of London and Anne his wife. Their son Tho Orley of Cherry Point, Northumberland Co, now deceased. See entry George Hardinge. 22 Sept 1664. 15.144
Ortland, Sam. Servt to Mr Pot Knight adj 18 yrs old. 5 Nov 1668. 3.46
Otter, Rich. Headright of Mr Edw Sanders. 22 June 1669. 3.65
Outris, Mary. Headright of Capt Gylos Brent. 21 Jan 1651/2. 1.70
Oventon, Sarah. Servt to Christopher Garlington adj 13 yrs old. 20th May 1662. 2.157
Owen, Mrs Ann. Landlady to and bequest from Simon Kirby who leaves her "my silver tooth picker". Kirby also leaves Mr Nicho Owen his silver buttons. Nicho Owen wit the will. 22 Mar 1666/7. 16.13-
    Nicholas. Age 30 yrs or th-abts. 20 June 1663. 15.103
    Nicho: Age 32. 4 Aug 1665. 15.165
    Nich: Bequest from Jno Tyngey. 1 Aug 1667. 16.30
    Mr Nicho: To lay out land left by Henry Roach to Mrs Eliz Tyngey. 21 Jan 1668/9. 3.55
    Mr Nicho: Justice. 23 June 1669. 3.66
    Mr Nich: On vestry Chicacone par. 20 March 1671/2. 16.158
    Mr Nicho: Attachmt agt est of Wm Wood 1000 lb tobo. 16 Oct 1676. 4.7
    Mr Nicho. Accuses Mr Tho Opye's servants of hog stealing. 16th Oct 1676. 4.6
    Mr Nicho: Justice. 16 Oct 1678. 4.5
    Justice. 18 Aug 1681. 4.101
    Mr Nich: Prob of will of Mr Jno Julian to him. 18 Mar 1684/5 4.255
    Mr Nicho: Justice. 16 Sept 1685 4.291
    Justice. 18 May 1687 4.493
Owen, Rice. Wit tfr land Hutton to Groves. 22 Feb 1710/11. 18.2
Owens, Wm. Servt to James Magreger and Hugh Fouch adj 13 yrs old. 20th April 1660. 2.121

Paine, Edward. "an ancient poor man". To be free from levy. 19th Apl
    1693. 4.619
  Wm. His land adj Jno Bayles in Cupids Neck. 18 Jan 1705/6.
    17.180
  Wm and Susanna his wife. Give bond to admr est of John Husk decd.
    20 June 1711. 18.63
  Wm. Owes Wm Pickerin 100 lb tobo for coffin plank. Ac 1712.
    18.222
Payne, Wm. M'nalls est in his hands. 15 June 1715. 6.113
  Wm. married Susanna relict of Jno Feilding. See entry Owen
    Jones dated 19 Sept 1716. 6.182
Pallas, Mary. Age 19. 4 Aug 1665. 15.166
Palmer, Abraham of Charleton in New England app John Hillier of Appo-
    mattucke his atty to collect debts. 26th Febry
    1649/50. 1.69
Palmore, Alice. Wife of Joseph. 26 March 1703. 17.9
Palmer, Alice of Wicco par, widow. Buys 60 acres from Thos Downing.
    17 Nov 1708. 18.4
Palmer, Alice. Rerecords deed for land bought 5 June 1677 by Joseph
    Palmer from Jno and Alice Hudnall. 15 Mar 1710/11
    17.28
Palmore, Benj: Son of Joseph. 26 March 1703. 17.9
  Isaac. Son of Joseph. To be cared for by brothers. 26th Mar
    1703. 17.9
Palmer, Jno. Age 32. 4 Aug 1665. 15.166
  Jno. Bought land from Partin Hudnall prior to 5 June 1677.
    17.28
  Jno. Owes Jno Harris 1200 lb tobo. Jno Hudnall his atty. Also
    owes Jno Cooke of Bristol mercht 511 lb tobo.
    21 Aug 1678. 4.2
  Jno. His atty Jno Hudnall confesses judgmt to Mr Edw Feilding
    for 6000 lb tobo. 17 Oct 1678. 4.8
Palmore, Jno. Son of Joseph. 26 Mar 1703. 17.9
Palmer, Jno. Sold 100 acres in G W River in Feilding Neck to David
    Jennings 14 March 1667/8. This land by various
    transfers is now sold to Hon Robt Carter of
    Lancaster Co. 11 Oct 1712. 18.246
Palmor, Joseph. cooper. Buys land from Jno Hudnall and Alice his wife.
    5 June 1677. 17.28
  Joseph. Wit will of Hen Mayos. 12 Apl 1702. 17.205
Palmore, Joseph of Wiccomico par, Gentleman, cooper. Will dated 26 Mar
    1703. prob 21 June 1704. Refs to Henry Mayse's
    line. Sons John, Joseph, Thomas, Benjamin, Isaac.
    Refs to Thos Downing's line and Geo Downing's line.
    Wife Alice Palmore. Exors: Friend Richd Wright,
    Bro: Robt Palmore and Mr Tho Downing. Wit Henry
    Mayse, Tho Downing, Dennis Coudre. 17.9
Palmer, Joseph. Wit deed Downing to Alice Palmer. 16 Jan 1710/11.18.6
Palmer, Jos. decd. 398 acres of his land surveyed by order of his
    relict and extrx Allice Palmer. 2 Apl 1711.18.165

Palmer, Mrs Kath: Rerecords Peter Coutanceau's will. 22 Feb 1710/11. 17.21

    Kath: Guardian and nearest friend of Peter and Ann Coutanceau. 17 Feb 1714/15. 6.96

    Sarah. Wit Price to Odohoty. See entry R Gibble. 8 Nov 1701. 17.156

    Tho: See entry Adam Yarratt. 21 Oct 1667. 16.25

    Tho. Will dated 28 March 1709, prob 15 June 1709. "In the name of God Amen I Thomas Palmer of St Maries County in the Province of Maryland doe make this my last Will and Testamt in manner and forme following (Vizt) Imp'rs I doe give to Thomas Waughop my Bridle and saddle I give to Anne Waughop my two Wearing R- - give to Katherine Cannadies Daughter Katherine Twenty shillings I appoint my Loveing Wife my Exec'rx as Witness my hand this 28th - March 1709

    Test M Mason   Tho Palmer
        Tho Manning
        Geo Guyther

Die Junii 15 1709 This will was proved in Northumberland County Court to be the - Will and Testament of Thomas Palmer by Matthew Mason one of the witnesses thereto and is admitted to Record   Test Tho: Hobson Cl Cur

Vera Copa Test Tho: Stretton Dep Cl Cur

Die Aust 15 1711. The within attested Copy was presented to the Court by Mr Thomas Waughop (and by the Court Admitted the Originall being burnt) and upon his mo'con the said Copy is admitted to Record   Test Tho: Hobson Cl Cur 17. 127

Palmer's land. Adjoins Peter Knight. 26 Nov 1651. 17.179

Pargater, Mary. Servt to Robt Lord. Bequest from him. His will dated 1 Dec 166-, prob 10 March 1661/2. 15.71

Parker, Azricum. Wit deed Brewer to Bleeker. 15 Apl 1672. 16.229

Parker, James. In deposition of Miles Miller, aged 20, he says abt 2 yrs ago next May he heard Jam: Parker say that "he must give the Widdow Hickman a spell of work for 3 small pigs about 2 dayes old which were brought up by and fed with a spoon". No date but recorded Jan 1666/7. 16.9

    James. Wit deed Edwards to Edwards. 19 Sept 1711. 18.107

    James. Deceased. Inv of his est submitted by Peter Hack Admr. 18 June 1713. 18.317

    Jonathan. His servt Jno Holland age 13. 6 June 1661. 2.142

    Jonathan. His burial at Exeter Lodge abt middle of Jan 1664/5. 16.10

    John. planter. Overseer of Jno Wobber's will. 12 Feb 1670/1. 16.166

Parker, Sibbey. Agreemt that Jno Wood serve her. Wit Florence Driscoll,
    Dan: Neale. 10 March 1669/70. 16.165
    Sibbey, Age 30 or th-abts. Exchanged a servant named Jno Wood
        with Danl Neale senr. 28 Mar 1671/2. 16.184
    Thomasine. Dau of Tho Ingram. Sister of Jno, Charles and Abra:
        Ingram. 12 Oct 1700. 17.21
    Wm. Wit will of Peter Hammond. 18 Jan 1711/12. 18.151
    Wm. deceased. Jane Parker his relict swears he left no will.
        19 Feb 1717/18. 6.255
Parkes, Tho. Servt to Mr Tho Phillpot to serve 8 yrs. (13 yrs old ?)
    8 Sept 1662. 2.161
Paris, Nich: Proves, as witness, will of Henry Wicker decd. 22 June
    1669. 3.65
Parris, Nicho: of St S par. Bought land near the church from Tho Berry
    Senior betw 1682/3 and 1700. See entry Thos
    Berry. 17.183
Parry, Hen: Wit will Mrs Jane Wildey. 11 Apl 1701. 17. pp 224-229
Tarre, Tho: See entry Jno Reed. 21 Mar 1716/17. 6.201
Parry, Jno. of St S par. Presented for absence from Church. 15 May
    1717. 6.202
Parse, Jno. Will. no date. Recorded 20 May 1667. To dau Eliza: Parse,
    among other things 2 pewter dishes "one large
    and the other the likely dish". To 2 sons 500
    acres of land, to son in law John Grimsted the
    part called hog towne and to son in law Wm
    Grimsted the part called long neck. He refers
    to them affectionately as sons and as sons in
    law, my children, etc. All 3 under age. Hugh
    Statham to raise and educate them. 16.16
Parvin, Jno. Owed 400 lb tobo by Francis Posey. 20 Nov 1651. 1.67
Pascall, Jno., of G W, pewterer. Power of Atty to his wife Hanah. 14th
    Feb 1671/2. 16.225
Pasquee, Walter. Wit deed Jno to Charles Ingram. 14 Oct 1707. 17.23
Pasquett, Walter. Wit deed Hill to Chilton. 15 June 1709. 17.78
Pate, Thoroughgood. As wit proves will of Robt Pritt. 18 Mar 1684/5.
    4.255
Peacox, Rd. Headright of - Bridges. 20 July 1652. 1.76
Peake, Tho: Appraises est of Jno Hampton decd. 7 Mar 1649/50. 1.49
Pease, Jno. See entry Jno Saffin. 21 Aug 1669. 16.62
Peirce, Richd. Carpenter. Scrvt to Col Rd Lee. Rev David Lindsey fined
    for marrying him to a servt of Tho Brewer.
    20 Jan 1661/2. 2.150
Perce, Richd (also as Peirce) of Northumberland Co, carpenter, sells
    a mare to Dominick Theriatt now running on his
    plantation at Curratomen in Lancaster Co.
    16 Jan 1663/4. 16.6
Pearse, Richd. Wit P of A Madring to Flowers. 1 Dec 1666. 16.24
Pearse, John. Owed 200 lb tobo by bill by Rd Eaton. 17 Feb 1667. 16.37

Pearcie, Richd. Depo, age not shown, re P of A Madrin to Flowers. No date but entered 22 Oct 1667. 16.26

Peirce, Tho. Wit deed Ironmonger to Griffin. 20 Dec 1667. 16.32

Pearce, Henry. Servt to Edwd Sanders adj 15 yrs old. 20 July 1687. 4.397

Pellam, Prudence. Orphan. Account of her cattle submitted by Samuel Nicholls her guardian "Twelve years since I received one cow" etc. 20 July 1663. 15.105

Pemberton, Anne. Daughter and sole heir of Dr Richard Pemberton. She married Jno Claughton prior to 18 Jan 1707/8. 17.89

    Eliz: Appears as a witness 4 Apl 1703. 17.12

    Rich. Wit P of A LeBreton to Matthew. 3 Apl 1671. 16.192

    Richd. of Matapony, Chirurgeon. Deed 345 acres from James Claughton. 17 Feb 1679/80. 17.87

    Doctor. Ordered to pay Jno Scripture "his kersey suite shooes stockins and shirt", also 200 lb tobo. 2 March 1680/1. 4.84

    Dr Richd. Arrests Ralph Spilman for 650 lb tobo. 21 April 1681. 4.93

    Rd. As witness proves will of Wm Hill. 20 May 1685. 4.269

    Richd. Wit deed Smith to Sims. 11 Sept 1703. 17.104

    Richd, deceased, chirurgeon. His dwelling plantation adj Wm Lambert, Back Creek in Mattapony Neck. 16th Dec 1707. 17. pp 130-5

    Dr. deceased. His land adjoined Josiah Dameron. 17 March 1712/13. 6. pp 78-81

Penell, Robt and Jane. Wit will of Jno Mosely. 18 May 1668. 16.126

    Robt and his wife. Bequest from Jno Mosely. 18 May 1668. 16.126

Pengelty, Margritt. Bequest from her brother Jno Harris of St S par. 20 Sept 1718. 19.44

Penny, Christian. Bound to Jane Myars who brought her up from infancy. 20 Aug 1719. 6.334

Persyfull, Elizabeth. Shows that her son, Wm Persyfull of this Co decd, by his will left her competent maintenance. Tho Everitt and Charles Craven, exors, ordered to pay. 18 June 1718. 6.269

Percifull, Jno. decd. Mary his relict swears he left no will. Admr to her. 15 May 1717. 6.209

Percifull, Mary. Admr of Tho Percifull decd. 18 Feb 1718/19. 19.32

Percifull, Tho. Will. dated 8 Sept 1714. prob 18 Mar 1718/19. Wife Mary. "All my children" not named. Exors Bro. Wm Percifull, Wm Miller. 19.38

Percivall, Tho. decd. Mary Percivall his relict swears he left no will. Admr granted. 18 Feb 1718/19. 6.299

Percivall, Tho. decd. Admr to his relict Mary Percivall. The will presented by Jno Webb one of the witnesses, the exor being dead. 18 March 1718/19. 6.309

Peircivale, Tho. Orphan of Tho Peircivale, age 12 yrs last December, bound to Jno Webb to be taught trade of shoe maker. 20 Jan 1719/20. 6.351

Perseyfull, Wm. 481 acres surveyed for him in G W par. 5 Feb 1710/11. 18.165

Wm. Will presented by Tho Everitt and Charles Craven exors. 19 March 1717/18. 6.262

Peircifull, Wm Jr. Brother of Jno Webb. 5 Oct 1700. 17.265

Peircifull, Wm Sr. Ref to as "my father" by John Webb. 5 Oct 1700. 17.265

Perriman, Wm. decd. Admr of his est to Jno Atkins. 16 Oct 1676. 4.6

Perry, Eliz: An orphan, now under Guardianship of Mr James Hauley, at his request put in care of Abraham Joyce who married the orphan's sister. She, Eliz, to be at her own disposal after 3 yrs. 20 Sept 1658. 2.94

Perry, Sam. Age 60 years or th-abt. Says "about five yeares agoe Thomas Barret now resident in Northumberland in Virginia having inticed one Dinah the daughter of one Natha Hickman, and as this depon't is Informed the wife of one Wm Lyndsay, whom he alsoe brought into the County of Rappahannock and unlawfully kept hir Company and after as this Depon't is informed, went down into Virginia and marryed her".
No date. Recorded Jan 1666/7. 16.10
(Please note that Samuel Perry was born the year before Jamestown was settled. B.F.)

Perry, Wm. Wit Deed of Gift, Mrs Ursula Thompson in Eliz City Co. 25th March 1649/50. 15.61

Perryn, Thomas. Aged 44 or th-abts. Says the latter end of Jan 1664 (1664/5) Tho Barratt came to borrow a canoe to go aboard Mr Haskins ship. That he going aboard took Barratt, who stopped at Richd Rice's plantation to assist James Cannady Mr Saffins servt to runaway to Maryland, which he did.
No date but recorded Jan 1666/7. 16. pp 10-11

Peryn, Tho. His wife Sarah Pereene. 21 Sept 1668. 16.54

Perryne, Tho. Sued by Steph Wells. 20 Apl 1681. 4.90

Peters Valley. Land left Richd Robinson at head of. 13 Jan 1700/1. 17.108

Peterkin, Grace. Her Godmother, Mrs Span, gives her "a browne pyde calfe". 15 Sept 1670. 16.140

Peterkin, Jam: On Jury Presly vs Matthew. 21 Jan 1668/9. 3.53

James. Gives a heifer to "my Eldest Daughter Elizabeth", 15 Sept 1670. 16.149

Peterson, Jane. Headright of Capt Jno Haynie. 15 July 1696. 4.733

Pettigrew, Andrew. Who married the widow of Gervase Dodson. 8 Octr 1662. 2.163

Andrew "and Isabella my wife" of G W Par, sell 750 acres in G W par to Thomas Salisbury. This land originally granted Mr Gervise Dodson decd 27 Apl 1658 and devolved to Isabel the widow and heir of Dodson "and now wife to me the sd Andrew Pettigrew". 17 May 1671. 16.223

Pettigrew, Isabell. Mother and guardian of Thos Salsbury. 16 Dec 1662. 15.96

Petigrew, Isabel. Deposition. Age 37 or th-abts. Date not shown. Recorded latter part of 1664. 15.135

Pettigrew, Isabell. Age 40, 4 Aug 1665. 15.163

Pettus, Wm. Servt to Col Richd Lee adj 12 yrs old. 21 Jan 1660/1. 2.136

Peyton, Valentine. Wit P of A Henry Corbin to Capt Peter Aston. 29th Aug 1663. 17. pp 224-9

Phillips, David. Certif for 100 acres for importing himself and Anne his wife. 10 Jan 1650/1. 1.47

 Edw. Buys land from Jno Lee, tailor, and Sarah his wife. 19 Feb 1671/2. 16.218

 James. His servt, Wm Dowlane age 19, urged by Tho Barratt to steal clothes from him and runaway to "Deloway". No date. Recorded Jan 1666/7. 16.9

 Joseph and Mary his wife. Fined for absenting themselves from Church. 21 Jan 1713/14. 6.15

 Joseph, of St S par. Presented for absence from Church. 15th May 1717. 6.202

 Margaret, wife of Tho Phillips, tailor, lately deceased, gives 2 heifers to her young dau Margaret Phillips. 10 Aug 1066. 16.2

 Mathew. Servt to Col Rd Lee adj 12 yrs old. 21 Jan 1660/1. 2.136

 Robt. Statement re James Jones' will which was burned. 17th Feb 1714. 6.98

 William, deceased. Father of Mrs Sarah Wildy. Grandfather of Michael Wildy. 9 July 1729. Lancaster County Records. No.8. p 114.

Phillpott, Joan, widow. Prenuptial agreemt with Jno Howell, planter, of Northumberland Co. 30 Dec 1649. 1.40

Philpott, Jno. Servt to Mr Peter Presly punished for running away. 17 Apl 1672. 3.144

Phillpott, Tho. His wife Racher not guilty of the murder of her late servant Hannah Dyer. 14 Nov. 1660. 2.134

Phillpot, Tho. His servt Tho Parkes 13 yrs old. His servt Ed Jennings 16 yrs old. 8 Sept 1662. 2.161

 Tho. Refers to events "about 21 or 22 years since" concerning Capt Rogers building a church. 22 June 1669. 16.152

Phispound, Peter. Appraises est of Jno Hampton decd. 7 March 1649/50. 1.49

Pickerill, Hen: To serve Nicho: Jurnew 9 yrs (therefore prob 12 yrs old). 8 Oct 1662. 2.163

 Sarah. Dau of Jno Pickerill. Bequest from Moore Price. 23 March 1662/3. 15.99

Pickering, Edw. Registers his mark for cattle. Also Geo: Pickering registers his mark. 17 Apl 1672. 16.230

Pickerine, Wm of St S par. Will. dated 18 June 1712. prob 20 Aug 1712. Sons: Wm, Geo and Isaac. Daus Elizabeth, Katherine and Susannah. Overseers, neighbors William Nelmes and Simon Bowley. 18,221.

Pickering, Wm. By his Atty, Geo Eskridge, produced an order of Court dated 19 March 1706/7, which his father, William Pickering late of this Co dec'd, obtained concerning a bridge, etc. 17 May 1716. 6,163

Pickering, Wm. Richd Lancaster, orphan of Rd Lancaster, age 14 bound to him to be taught shoemaking. 16 Sept 1719. 6,336

Pinchard, Marg't. Wife of Tho: Pinchard. 23 Dec 1701. 17,245

Tho. Bequest from Jno Eustace. 23 Dec 1701. 17,245

Jno. Bought 1000 acres on N side of a branch of Dennis Creek from David Whitford. 3 July 1677. 18,27

Jno. See entry Edw Potoes. 1677. 18,158

Mr Jno. He and Capt Leonard Howson ordered to div est of Christo: Garlington betw widow and the children. 21 Aug 1678. 4,2

Mr. Jno. To be pd 200 lb tobo for a gun that was pressed. Also for 2 bu corn. 21 Aug 1678. 4,1

Jno. See entry Thos Mayes. 26 Oct 1680. 18,158

Jno. Bought 500 acres in Wicco par 3 July 1677 from David Whitford and sold it to Henry Mayes 26 Oct 1680. 26 Oct 1680. 17,255

John. of Lancaster Co., Will. dated 20 March 1689/90. prob 10 Dec 1690. Sons John, Thos, James. Wife and daughters mentioned but not named. Wit: William Jones, Tho Gillet, Jas Shelton. Lancaster County Records. No.35. p.7

Tho: Chosen by Eliz: Brereton as her Guardian. 18 Nov 1714. 6,90

Pine, Margaret. To serve her master, Mr Saml Heath, 3 mos and 3 weeks for his charge of 250 lb tobo pd Dr Thornton "Occasioned by the said servants laying Violent hands on herself". 20 Aug 1719. 6,334

Place, Jno. "The Body of the said Place is to be under the tuition of Henry Hurst of Wiccomoco till hee bee of age to make choice of his Guardian". 22 May 1656. 14,83

Platt, Peter. Wit Jno Bearemore's will. 20 Jan 1676/7. 17,109

Peter. Wit Col Tho Brereton's will 11 Oct 1675. Retd to England prior to 1683. 6. pp 83-6

Mr Peter. Who wit Col Tho Brereton's will is now dead. 4 June 1684. 4,231

Plum Tree Swamp. at Fleet's Bay, Northumberland Co. 14 Jan 1675/6. 17,244

Podle, Corbell. Appears as Corboll Pidwell, etc. Left papers with Wm Wildey in 1659. 15,14

Pollin also appears as Pullen. circa 1650. See next page.

Pollen, Roger. Signs oath to Commonwealth of England. 13 Apl 1652. 1.72
Pollick, Patrick. Will 4 Dec 1702. Prob date missing. Exors Wife Jane and her son John who is now under 18. All est to wife. Wit: John Harris, Antho Haynie and Onecepherus Harvey. Rerecorded 16 Jan 1716/17 by Abra: Ingram, Jno Ingram and Onecephorus Harvey. 17. 235 (Quakers)
Pollusk, Patrick. (Pollick). Wit will Jno Muttoone. 26 Sept 1678. 17.260
Poole, Henery. Wit Deed of Gift Mrs Ursula Thompson in Eliz City Co. 25 March 1649/50. 15.61
Poole, Henery. Deposition. That Mrs Ursula Thompson gave her son Richd stock, her dau Sarah stock and her dau Elizabeth stock. That Mr Jno Mottrom was present and the gifts were in Elizabeth City Co. Depo dated 27 Sept 1658. 15.61
Poole, Sam. Wit relinq of title by Rd Coke. 16 Sept 1671. 16.200
    Saml. App Constable of Cone. 18 May 1687. 4.394
    Saml and his wife. An orphan, Mary Baker age 11 bound to them till 17 "to be taught to read the bible perfectly". 5 Oct 1687. 4.402
Poor, Jno. Exor of Patrick Keeve. 18 June 1718. 6.266
Pope, Jas. Pat land on S side Wicco: River. 16 Apl 1668. 17.194
    Jas. Pat land now in G W par prior to 1670. Sold it to Jno Bound 6 Jan 166--. 17.76-8
    James. His widow now married to John Higginson who has much impaired the est of the children, etc. 19 Febry 1678/9. 4.21
    James. His plantation adjs "the Run or Stream of the main branch that falleth down from between the plantation of James Hill and said James Popes plantation into the Maine Swamp that falls into Great Wicocomoco River", near Feildings Bridge, etc. 9 April 1713. 18.297
    James, Jr and Sr. See entry Rodham Neale. 9 Apl 1713. 18.297
    John. Deed. 1 Jan 1703/4. Sells Robt Boyd of N Co 150 acres on S side main branch of Wicco River. Granted to James Pope father of the sd Jno 16 Apl 1668. 17.194
    John. Ref to as "my Brother in Law" in will of Robt Boyd. 10th Sept 1710. 18.42
    Jno. Upon Court order lays out road through land of Jno Thomas. 18 June 1712. 18.210
    John of N Co. Deposition. Aged 36 or th-abts. says "your depon't was very well acquainted with Robt Boyd Taylor of the County aforesaid dec'd and alsoe with Jno Boyd Eldest son of the aforesaid Robt Boyd and Anne Boyd formerly Wife of the aforesaid Robt and that the aforesaid Jno Boyd was borne since the intermarriage between the said Robt and Anne his
(continued next page)

Pope, Jno. Deposition. (continued) Wife the Naturall mother of the aforesaid Jno and is now 9: years of age or theirabouts and further your depon't saith not etc " John Pope
Dio July 16th 1712
    Jur Cur North'd and rec'd
    per Tho Hobson Cl Cur for North'd"
18.214

Pope, Jno. Owes 600 lb tobo to Mrs Esther Webb. - Nov 1712. 18.242
 Jno. Admr of Simon Thompson. 16 June 1714. 17.221
 Mr Nathaniel. Justice. 10 Jan 1650/1. 1.46
 Mr Nathl. Justice. 20 July 1652. 1.76
Peplar Neck. Adj land of Richd Rice Sr. 19 Dec 1681. 17.212
  400 acres belonging to Mrs Jane Wildey there. 11 Apl 1701. 17. pp 224-9
Popplewell, Wm. Rerecords deed of gift dated 1705 Norman to Norman. 20 July 1715. 17.223
Popnwell, Wm. Exor of Mary Norman decd. 21 Nov 1716. 6.184
Porter, Anne. dau of Elinor, wife of Tho Dorrell. 13 Aug 1663. 15.167
 Wm. Signs inventory Tho Shapleigh decd. 29 Sept 1703. 17.11
Portees, Edw. Bought 1000 acres from David Whitford 16 Mar 1674/5 and sold it on 5 Aug 1675 to Saml Mahan who sold it back to him 30 Nov 1675. Then Portees sold it back to David Whitford 20 Apl 1677. 18.27 This land then sold by Whitford to Jno Pinkard 3 July 1677 and by him to Henry Mayes 20 Octr 1680. 18.158
Porteus, Edw. Bought 500 acres from Da Whitford 16 March 1674/5 and sold it back to Whitford 20 Apl 1677. 17.255
 John. Atty of Da: Whitford. 3 July 1677. 17.255
Posey, Francis. Owes John Parvin 400 lb tobo. 20 Nov 1651. 1.67
Potter, Lt Col Cuthbert. Judgt to be confessed to him for 2359 lb tobo by Antho Morris atty of Tho Lane. 23 Sept 1671. 16.214
Potts, Wm. Headright of Mr Edw Sanders. 22 June 1669. 3.65
Poultry, Andrew. His dau Hannah Poultry is given a calf by Jno Waddy. 20 May 1658. 14.143
Powell, Joane. Deposition. Aged 40 and upwards. 10 Jan 1650/1. 1.47
 Jo. Signs oath to Commonwealth of England. 13 Apl 1652. 1.72-3
 Jno. Swears Wm Thomas owes Saml Bonham rent. 14 Nov 1660. 2.133
 William, son of Edm'd Powell, being 4 yrs old the 11th day of March next, bound, with his father's consent, to Jno Houghton and Dorothy his wife till 21. Jno Downing Security. 5 Oct 1687. 4.404
Power Danl. Wit deed Williams to Champion. 2 Dec 1700. 17.70
Power, Danl. Wit deed And: Salsbury to Wm Barrett. 3 July 1701. 17.95
Powlter, Hannah. Dau of Andrew Powlter dec'd chooses Robt Crowder her guardian. 21 Jan 1660/1. 2.137

Powlter see Poultry.

Preist, Tho. A servt boy belonging to David Straughan agrees to serve 2 extra yrs in return for being taught "to Write and Cypher to the Rule of three". 19th Feb 1717/18. 6.255

Presly. A heifer is given by Tho Kedby to Peter Presley Junior now the eldest son of Wm Presly. Ack in Court by Peter Presly Senior. 15 May 1658. 14.143

Peter. Signs oath to Commonwealth of England. 13 April 1652. 1. 72-3

Peter. Married Eliz Thompson. See entry Richd Thompson. Confirms sale 48 acres in N. Co from Eliz Thompson, Tho and Sarah Willoughby. 20 June 1664. 15.124 (therefore we would judge married betw 20 Feb 1663/4 and 20 June 1664)

Mr Pet: pd 400 lb tobo from Co levy "for a wolf in a trap". 5 Nov 1668. 3.47

Peter. On Jury to div land Saffin and Hull. 29 Nov 1669. 16.63

Mr Peter. His servt Jno Philpott punished for running away. 17 Apl 1672. 3.144

Peter. His servts: Turner Muckleslose adj 13, Carmock Castide adj 13, Danl Omuddy adj 17. 19 Jan 1675/6. 3.249

Mr Peter. Justice. 16 Oct 1678. 4.5
Mr Pet: Justice. 20 Nov 1678. 4.12
Mr Peter. Justice. 18 Apl 1683. 4.176
Mr Peter. Justice. 19 Apl 1693. 4.619
Mr Peter. Justice. 16 July 1696. 4.734
Peter. Land adj Peter Knight. 28 Nov 1702. 17.175
Peter. Signs Inv of Peter Coutanceau. 20 Apl 1709. 17.216-221
Col. Peter. His line adj Wm Short late decd and Mr Richd Nutt. 20 June 1711. 18.62
Mr. Peter. Justice. 18 July 1711. 18.71
Peter of St S par buys 75 acres on Newmans Neck from John Cottrell. 14 Jan 1711/12. 18.121
Peter. Bond as sheriff of Northumberland Co. Signed by Peter Presly, Phillip Shapleigh and Peter Presly Jr. 18 June 1712. 18.197
Peter. Rerecords inv of Nichs Edwards. 18 June 1712. 17.169-171
Peter. Bond as Sheriff L 1000. Sterl. 19 June 1713. 18.319
Col Peter. Pd 6220 lb tobo from Co levy for Burgess' charges the last sessions. 28 Nov 1715. 6.146
Col Peter. Justice. 15 May 1717. 6.206
Peter. Churchwarden St S Par sues Geo and Patience Curtis. 16 May 1717. 6.215
Coll Peter. Justice. 18 Feb 1718/19. 6.297
Capt Peter. On motion of Danl McCarty Esq in behalf of Mr Wharton Ransdale and Charnock Cox, Col Peter Presley came into Court and made oath that he wrote Capt Peter Presley's will and that the dec'd intended to give his negroes not bequeathed to his two sisters Ursula Ransdale and Mary Cox. 21 Jan 1719/20. 6.353

Presley, Col Peter. Justice. 21 Jan 1719/20. 6,353
    Peter Jr. Gift from Eliz Nowman. 13 Apl 1659. 15,21A
    Mr. Pet Jr. Justice. 16 Sept 1685. 4,291
    Mr Peter Junr. Justice. 18 May 1687. 4,493
    Peter Junr. Justice. 20 July 1687. 4,397
    Mr Peter Jr, Justice. 16 Nov 1687. 4,410
Presly, Peter Junr. Deceased. Will presented by Ursula Ransdell and
        Mary Cochs his exors and proved by oaths of wit: Rd
        Haynie Jr, Jno Bridgman and Jas Magoon. 19 Nov 1718.
        6,296
    Peter Senr. Justice. 16 Nov 1687. 4,410
    Wm. Burgess. Nov 1647. Hening Vol.1. page 340
    Wm. Very brief abstract of will. Dated 15 Aug 1650. Prob 20th
        Jan 1656/7. To be bur beside deceased wife. Son Wm
        to be guardian of Peter. Son Peter exor, he under 21.
        To grandchild Wm Presly. 14,95
    Mr Wm. Justice. 24 Aug 1650. 1,41
    Wm. His will drawn by Tho Wilsford. 15 Aug 1650. 14,96
    Willm. Signs oath to Commonwealth of England. 13 Apl 1652.
        1, 72-3
    Mr Wm. Justice. 20 July 1652. 1,76
    Wm. Whereas it was the desire of Elizabeth Newman widow of this
        Co that Peter Presly Jr and Martha and Eliz Haynie
        should have some part of her estate, this deed to
        them. Signed Wm Presly, Jno Haynie. 13 Apl 1659.
        15,21A
    Wm. His a/c of estate of Mr Robt Newman dec'd. Includes items
        "my Aunt sold". 20 Sept 1659. 15,28
    Wm. Certificate for 450 acres for importing:
        Himselfe and Jane his wife   Thomas Underhill
        Joseph Beavan   Wm Bancroft
        John Lane   Wm Boles
        Roger Lane   Hannah Newman
    Wm. Pd 1000 lb tobo from Co levy for 5 wolves. 5 Nov 1668.
        3,47
    Wm. Says 4 or 5 years since he carried a "Denizacon" to James-
        town issued by King James to Jacob Coutincoau father
        of Jno Coutancoau, etc. 5 Oct 1669. 16,96
    Mr Wm. His servt Jas Russell adj 15 yrs of age. 17 Apl 1672.
        3,144
    Mr Wm. Justice. 17 March 1674/5. 3,224
    Mr. As Justice dissents from Court order. 16 Oct 1676. 4,6
    Mr Wm. Justice. 21 Aug 1678. 4,1
    Mr Wm. Justice. 16 Oct 1678. 4,5
    Mr Wm. Justice. 20 Nov 1678. 4,12
    Mr Wm. Justice. 18 Aug 1681. 4,101
    Winnifred. See entry Saml Griffin. 2 Feb 1702/3. 17,213
Price, Flora. See entry Rd Gibble. 8 Nov 1701. 17,156
    Jno. Buys 50 acres from Richd Gibble. 16 Jan 1671/2. 17,156

Price, Jno. Gives a heifer to dau Anne Price. If she die before age
 to his son Jno Price. Wit: Wm Flowers, Hugh
 Baker. 17 Janry 1671/2. 16.215
 Mary. Swears to Tho Hobson's statement. 20 Apl 1709. 17.21
 Moore. Will dated 23 March 1662/3. prob 20 Apl 1663. To William
 Raven son of Jno Raven practically whole est.
 To Sarah Pickerill dau of Jno Pickerill. No
 other heirs. 15.99
 Rebecca. Will dated 10 Dec 1709. prob 17 Dec 1712. To Ann
 Shirley (under 16) dau of John and Jane
 Shirley, clothing, etc. Relationship if any
 not shown. To friend Jacob Bayly residue of
 estate, he exor. Wit: Christopher Neale and
 Jeremiah Greenham. 18.242
 Rebecca, Dec'd. Inv of her est presented by Jacob Bayly admr.
 21 May 1713. 18.307
 Richd. Wit deed Wright to Crump. 16 Sept 1707. 17.128
 Tho: Wit P of A Edmunds to Sech. 17 Feb 1664/5. 16.13
 Waltor. Arrested at suit of Edw Williams and no cause appearing,
 non suit granted. 20 Nov 1868. 3.49
 Walter. Entertained Mr Nich Hale's runaway servt. Hale wants
 satisfaction. 11 Jan 1668/9. 3.50
 William. Signs admr bond of Mary Millerd on est of Tho Millerd.
 20 May 1713. 18.293
Prichard, Charles. Wit Robinson to Embry. 28 July 1704. 17.153
 Charles of Wicco par gives his son Charles Prichard a cow.
 6 June 1713. 18.316
 Charles. Presented "for drinking and singing on the Saboth
 day". 21 Jan 1713/14. 6.17
 Charles. Fined for not going to Church. 21 Jan 1713/14. 6.15
 Charles. Presented for not going to Church in Wicco parish.
 19 May 1714. 6.35
 Charles, deceased. Jno Nipper exor presents inv. 17th March
 1714/15. 6.103
 Charles and Mary. See entry Rd Swanson their guardian. 21st
 August 1718. 6.277
Prickett, Ellenor. Orphan of Thos Prickett. 16 July 1663. 15.105
 John. Son of Tho Prickett. Jno Bennett gives him a calf. 18
 Jan 1664/5. 15.144
Prichat, John. Servt to Jno Muttoone. 26 Sept 1678. 17.260
 Rich'd. "   "   "   "   "   "
Prichard, Swanson, Charles and Mary. All minors, exors of John Nipper.
 18 June 1718. 6.270
Prickett, Tho. Signs oath to Commonwealth of England. 13 Apl 1652. 1.72
Pride, Benj. Attachmt for 595 lb tobo agst his est to Tho Holbrooke.
 20 Nov 1668. 3.49
Prim, Jno. Wit deed Williams to Gascoyne. 27 Mar 1703. 17.45
 Jno. Wit deed Williams to Lattimore. 15 May 1705. 17. 252-4
 Jno. Wit will Tho Williams 11 March 1706/7. Proved it 23rd May
 1707. 17.72

Prior, Walt: Owes Jno Evans 372 lb tobo. 21 Jan 1668/9. 3.55
Pritt, Robt dec'd. Prob of his will to Rich Rice. 18 Mar 1684/5. 4.255
Proverb, Richd. Wit P of A Gradey to Vanlandingham. 8 Oct 1705. 17.152
Pullen also appears as Pollin. Circa 1650.
Pumfrett, Richd. Reported for strikeing fish contrary to law. 22 June 1669. 3.65
Purcell, Tobias of Lancaster Co., planter, buys 316 1/2 acres in St S par Northumberland Co from Geo Crosby. 18 Oct 1705. 17.192
Pursly, Tobias. Wit deed Wildey to Chichester. 19 Nov 1706. 17.224-9

Quakers. Gervase Dodson, David Cussin, Robert Lambdon, John Smith and Thomas Shields met at the house of David Cussin contrary to Law. To receive 20 stripes apiece on their bare backs. Cussin fined L 100. Sterl. 26 June 1660. 2.126.
Cussin's estate seized by the sheriff 29 June 1660. Includes a Bible and "Perkins his works" 2.126
Quakers Persecuted. See entry Onecephorus Harvey. 18 Nov 1713. 6.5
Quick, Tht "a poor man was in the parish levy", "lately fell sick and dyed". Wm Dawson to be pd for careing for him. 13 March 1684/5. 4.257
Quife, Patrick. Wit deed Boyles to Gill. 18 Jan 1705/6. 17.180
Quiffe, Patrick. 50 acres on Little Wicco to be made over to him by Jno. Webb. 4 June 1709. 17.102
Patrick. License to keep an ordinary "att his Mansion house" 16 May 1711. 18.44
Patrick. Signature on bond appears as "Patrick Keeve". 16 May 1711. 18.44
Patrick. Signs bond of Jno Meath for admr of est of Danll Murphew decd. 19 Dec 1711. 18.116
Quintennecke in Richmond Co. See entry Saml Griffin. 2 Feb 1702/3 17.213
Quintoncake. Adj land of Jno Adams. 13 Feb 1701/2. 17.151

Radford, Mr. deceased. Land formerly his adj Capt Jno Whitty. 15 May 1661. 17. pp 224-229
Jno. dec'd. a/s of cattle belonging to his orphans (their names do not appear) signed Walter Weekes. 20th July 1663. 15.104
Tho: Conf judgt for present paymt 165 lb tobo to Tho Barratt. 20 Nov 16--. 3.49
Ram, Ebenezer. Servt to Mr Jno Hanye adj 11 yrs old. 16 Nov 1698. 4.842
Rankin, Jno. Age 38 yrs or th-abts. 2 Nov 1704. Richmond Co. Misc. Records page 28-A.
Jno. Wit will Jno Thomas. 15 Aug 1710. 18.266
Ransdell, Ursula. Sister and exor of Peter Prosly Jr. 19 Nov 1718. 6.296

Raven, Jno. A lame impotent person freed from levies. 20 May 1659. 2.106

    Jno. His estate attached for 2020 lb tobo by Jas Hoback. 6 Apl 1669. 3.62

    William son of Jno Raven inherits practically all est of Moore Price. 23 March 1662/3. 15.99

    William. Son of Jno Raven. 2 Jan 1655. 14.63

    Wm. Bought 50 acres in Newmans Neck from Wm Cornish 1st March 1658/9 but resigned it to Cornish 20th Febry 1659/60. 18.125

Raymonds Creek. In St S par adj land of Saml Smith. 19 Dec 1709. 17.53

Rayner, Mary. See entry Tho Cane. 3 June 1658. 15.2

Reason, Geo. Wit will Rev David Lyndsey. 2 Apl 1667. 16.12

    Jno. Appointed Constable in Jno Bennett's place. 4 Apl 1672. 3.144

    Jno. Land adj Jno Cockorill Sr. 30 Dec 1695. 17.135

    Jno. Aged abt 40 yrs. See his interesting deposition in appendix under Bashford. 26 July 1712. 18.254

    Jno. Fined for absenting himself from Church. 18 Nov 1713. 6.5

    Jno Sr. His land adj Wm Tignor. 28 Nov 1698. 17.160

Reed, Andrew. Owes Wm Pickerin 1000 lb tobo as per a/c Jno Wilkins. An'o 1712. 18.222

Read, Edward son of Jno Read. Gift of cattle from Mrs Graciana Span. 15 Nov 1671. 16.210

Read, Jno and Anne his wife of Little Wickocomicoe and par of Fairfield sell Mrs Graciana Span 200 acres, part of 600 acres sold by Jas Magregor to Mr Richd Span decd, which 200 acres was by will of Mr Richd Span decd bequeathed to his dau Anne wife of the said Jno Read. 30 Jan 1670/1. 16.159

Reede, Jno. Registers mark for cattle. 8 June 1672. 16.235

Reed, Jno. A Court Order, on the petition of Garvis Elistone, that Tho: Parre bring "Jno Reed a poor orphan child in his possession" to next Court. 21 March 1716/17 6.201

Reade, Tho. Bill from Capt Henry Fleet for 2000 lb tobo. 20 Mar 1654/5. 4.127

Reade, Wm. Land formerly sold to him adj Jno Wright in Wicco par. 16th Sept 1707. 17.128

Reed, Wm. His relict Anne swears he died without will. Admr granted. 20 March 1716/17. 6.199

Reeves, Robt. Servt to Peter Presly Jr adj 9 yrs of age. 17 Mar 1674/5 3.224

    Robt. His land adj Vincent Garner. 18 June 1706. 17.202

    Robt. Signs appraisal of est of Vincent Garner. 16 May 1711. 18.47

    Robt. Buys 50 acres in Bettys Neck from Edwd Barnes 21 Octr 1702. Rerecords the deed 15 July 1713. 17.200

    Robt. Signs appraisal of Bowers est. 17 Dec 1705. 17.167

    Robt. Deed from Vincent Garner 18 June 1706. Rerecords it 15 July 1713. 17.201

Reeves, Robt. Swears to inv of Jno Bowes Jr. 19 Jan 1713/14. 17.206
Reily, Jno. As wit proves will of Patrick Keeve. 18 June 1718. 6.268
Revoire, Peter and Ann his wife ack deed to Wm Buck. 24 July 1714.
  6.74
Reynolds, Anne. With Rd Clare in chg of Eliz orphan of Wm Metcalfe. Was
  pd 2 yrs since. 18 Apl 1657. 14.105
  Mrs Ann. Bequest from Simon Kirby "my ring and Davids re-
   pentance". Kirby also leaves Wm Reynolds "my
   practice of piety". 22 March 1666/7. 16.13
Reynalds, Jno. Headright of Mr Edw Sanders. 22 June 1669. 3.65
Renolds, Peter. "a poor lame decrepid man" exempted from levy. 20 June
  1716. 6.170
Reynolds, Wm. Signs oath to Commonwealth of England. 13 Apl 1652. 1.72
  Wm. deceased. Richd Clare his exor sets over 92 acres granted
   Wm Reynolds 13 Oct 1653 to Anne Reynolds one of
   his daughters. 24 Sept 1656. 14.100
  Wm. His land adj Nicho: Jernew. 20 Jan 1656/7. 14.98
Rhodon prob same as Rodham.
Rhodon, Mathew. A cow is given by Mrs Hanah Lee to Mathew Rhoden for
  use of his dau Hannah Rhoden. To be delivered to
  her when she is 16. If she die to descend to the
  next child of Matthew Rhodon and Elizabeth his
  wife. Wit: Geo Nott, Wm Walker. 8 Nov 1651. 1.69
Rhoden, Matthew. Signs oath to Commonwealth of England. 13 April 1652.
  1. 72-3
  Matthew. Aged 33 yrs or th-abts. 20 Sept 1653. 14.34
Rhedon, Mr Matth: Justice. 26 May 1656, 14.84
Rhodon, Matthew. His wife Elizabeth. 9 Sept 1668. 16.53
Rhoden, Mr Math: His servt Tho Marny adj 14 yrs old. Also his servt
  Jno Whitney adj 17. 6 Apl 1669. 3.60
Rhoden, Mr Mathew. His servt "Guillian an Irish wench" adj 14 yrs of
  age. 22 June 1669. 3.65
Rhoden, Mr Math: On Vestry Chisacone parish. 20 March 1671/2. 16.158
Rhodes, Augustine, deceased. Rachel wife of Adam Yarratt his extrx.
  21 Aug 1678. 4.5
Rhodes, Augustine, deceased. Nuncupative will produced by Edw Barnes
  17 Apl 1678. Declared void in favor of his sister
  Mrs Rachell Yarratt. 17 Oct 1678. 4.8
  Nicho. "a poor child being three yeares of age in October next"
  given by his mother to John Freeman to serve him
  till 21. 15 July 1685. 4.274
Rhotheram, Jno. Sues Jas Claughton but fails to appear. Nonsuit to
  Claughton. 20 Nov 1668. 3.49
Ribton, Jno. of Whitehaven in County of Cumberland, merchant. P of A
  to Isaac Langlon of Whitehaven to settle a/cs in
  Virginia and Maryland. 10 Jan 1710/11. 18.64
Rice's Bridge. The main road to adj Vincent Garner's land. 18th June
  1706. 17.201
Rice, Hannah. Relict of Richd Rice says he made no will. 24 July 1714.
  6.67

Rice, Richd. Aged 32 yrs or th-abts. Says Henry Toppin said if Tho:
          Adams would live with him and remain a bachelor
          he would leave him his whole estate. 21 July
          1660. 2.127
     Richd. Reference to his plantation. Jan 1664. 16.10
     Richd and Anne his wife sell 100 acres to Jno Saffin of Boston
          in New England. Dated 16 Apl 166-. Recorded 20
          Janry 1666/7. 16.7
     Richd. Survey of 188 acres entered for him at Jamestown by Richd
          Thompson. 7 March 1665/6. 16.94
     Richd. Aged 37 yrs or th-abts. Entry not dated but recorded in
          January 1666/7. 16.11
     Richd. His land adj Tho Towers on Morattico path. 8 Sept 1668.
          16.38
     Richard. In regard to building houses. See entry Adam Yarratt.
          22 Oct 1667. 16.25
     Richd. Age 38 yrs or th-abts. Statement regarding Glebe land.
          22 June 1669. 16.152
     Richd. See entry Jno Saffin. 21 Aug 1669. 16.62
     Richd. 188 acres entered for him 7 Mar 1665/6 by Richd Thompson.
          Richd Coke relinq all right and title. 16 Sept
          1671. 16.200
     Richard, Senior. Deed. 19 Dec 1681. of N Co, planter. 100 acres
          on Chickacone, adj Poplar Neck. Signed Richd x
          Rice. Elizabeth x Rice wife. Wit Jno Hughlett,
          Peter Flynt. The deed to Robert Hobbs of N. Co.
          Robt Hobbs and Anne his wife assign the land to
          John Crawford on 6th Dec 1683. Wit by David
          Lindsey and Jas. Nipper. Jno Crawford assigns the
          land to Jno Legg on 15 June 1692. Signed Jno x
          Crawford, Elizabeth x Crawford. Witnessed James
          Montgomerie, Josias Long. Rerecorded 15th Sept
          1714. 17.212
     Rich: Probate of will of Robt Pritt dec'd to him. Proved by oaths
          of wit: Thoroughgood Pate and Jer Thornton. 18th
          March 1684/5. 4.255
     Richd. Atty of Edw Williams who was heir to Temperence Bradshaw.
          15 July 1685. 4.274
     Richd. His land adj Jno Adams. 2 Jan 1702/3. 17.161
     Richd. His land adj Geo Dawking. 16 Dec 1707. 17.114
     Richd. Signs inv of est of Jno Wall dec'd. 20 June 1711. 18.67

Rice, Tho. In legal dif with Jno Essex. 20 Feb 1651/2. 1.50
Richards, Jno. Suspected, with Jno Jones, of murder. To touch corpse
          of Tho Rolph and that of Tho Bayles before a Jury.
          20 Nov 1669. 3.41
     Jno. His suit agt Mr Phillip Shapleigh to next Court. 16 Oct
          1676. 4.6
     Peter. Headright of Wm Sheares. 21 Augt 1678. 4.4
Richardson, Ja: Wit deed Jones to Claughton. 16 Nov 1699. 17.88

Richardson, James. Wit tfr Scott to Rose. 7 Sept 1702. 17.202
    Jas. Wit deed Conolin to Alverson. 21 July 1703. 17.96
    Jas. A friend of Geo Bledsoe. Wit will. 23 Jan 1704/5. 17.16
    Jas. Wit P of A Dameron to Waddy. 20 Feb 1705/6. 17.55
    Jas. Wit deed Cockrill to Cockrill. 19 Nov 1706. 17.138
    Jas. Wit agreemt Bickley and Ingram. 2 July 1707. 17.24
    Jas. "On the petition of John Brewer the aforesaid James Richardson was admitted Guardian to him". Bond 20000 lb tobo also signed by Richard x Ruth. 18th Feb 1712/13. 18.261
    Jas. and Eliz: his wife, produce will of Wm Sheirs. 17th July 1717. 6.219
    Simon. Deceased. 11 Sept 1702. 17.4
    Symon. His servt Geo Harris age 17. 24 Aug 1669. 3.35
    Also the same entry 24 Aug 1669. 3.69
    Simon. Signs oath to Commonwealth of England. 13 Apl 1652. 1. 72-3
    Simon. His will proved by oath of one wit., Tho Sudler. The others going out of the country. 17 March 1674/5. 3.114

Ricketts, Benj: Headright of Mrs Jane Wildey. 19 Oct 1681. 4.105

Riddan, Thaddeus of Lynn in Newengland. P of A to Tho Hobson to transact all business in Virginia. Wit Christopher Moss. Sam Anderson. 5 Apl 1667. 16.21

Ridge Path. in Fairfield par. Adj land Danl Chandler. 22 Jan 1673/4. 17.120

Ring, Ellenor. See entry Capt Giles Russell. 18 Nov 1719. 6.346

Roberts, Danl. "About the age of 26 Yeares". That in 1649 William Lewis of Virginia being in England, brought a bill of Exch from Virginia of Everard Roberts for L 25. Sterling to the father of the said Everard. And that Lewis said at that time to Mr John Roberts, the father of the sd Everard, that that was all that he (Everard) owed him (Lewis). That he was paid and satisfied. 20 Sept 1656. 14.89

Roberts, Edw. His children, Francis and Edward Jr receive gift from Richd. Holden. 21 Sept 1658. 15.11
    Eliz: "an orphant left when very young to the tutele and oversight of the said Mr Wm Wathen". Bound to him for 7 yrs, "not to worke in the ground". 9 Dec 1669. 16.141
    Francis. Headright of Wm Betts. 20 Feb 1651/2. 1.50
    Francis. Wit will of Richd Span. 16 Mar 1667/8. 16.64
    Francis. Entered as "Fran Robts". To be pd 100 lb tobo from county levy "for a wolf shott". 5 Nov 1668. 3.47
    Francis. His wife Rosamond Roberts. 3 July 1668. 16.52
    Fran: As wit proves will of Mr Rd Span. 11 Jan 1668/9. 3.51
    Francis. Sells land to Ralph Waddington. 10 Oct 1671. 16.200

Roberts, Fran: Wit deed Salsbury to Barrett. 3 July 1701. 17.95
    Richd. Age 21. 4 Aug 1665. 15.166

Roobert, Wm. Servt to Francis Clay to serve 7 yrs. 8 Sept 1662. 2.161
Robinson, Cornelius. Signs Oath to Commonwealth of England. 13 Apl 1652 1. -72-73
Robinson, Mrs. Eliz:. Extrx and heiress of "Loveing friend" Col. Geo: Cooper. 18 Nov 1708. 17.123

    Henry. Assignment. 28 July 1704. Title of land to Jno Embry. Wit by Tho Williams, Chas Prichard and Robt Robuck. Note in margin says this land was sold by Thomas Williams to Stephen Robinson 3rd May 1690. 17.153

    Henry. of Wicco par. See entry Alex Cumins at als. 7th Apl 1707. 17.116

    Hen: Wit deed Mayes to Dameron. 15 May 1711. 18.41

    Henry. Wit deed Alex Cummings (who m his wife's sister) to Dameron. 4. Dec 1711. 18.117

    James. Assigned rights to bill of sale by Danl Neale and Hellen his wife. 22 Sept. 1668. 16.62

    James. Gives his dau Frances Robinson a heifer. Wit by Tho. Hobson and Sar: Hobson. 20 July 1668. 16.36

    Jas. His servt Jos Atkins adj 15 yrs of age. 20 Nov 1668. 3.48

    James. Owes Jno Garner 982 lb tobo. 20 Nov 1668. 3.48

    Jam: a/c agt him 1450 lb tobo exhib by Jas Claughton admr of Edw Salmon. 20 Oct 1668. 3.45

    James. Regarding tfr land from Tho Mould to Tho Edwards. 18 Feb 1669/70. 16.70

    James. Sold land to Tho Edwards prior to 9 March 1669/70. 16.71

    John. Wit P of A Salisbury to Salisbury. 21 Jan 1670/1. 16.147

    John. To appraise est of Jno Lee dec'd. 16 Oct 1676. 4.6

    John. Evidently of Fairfeild par. Will dated 13 Jan 1700/1. Probated 19 Feb 1700/1. Sick and weak. To eldest son, Rich'd Robinson, land where he now lives, adj Jno Wornom, the head of Peters Valley, land of Wm. Blundle. To sons Antho: and Tho Robinson land adj Mr Downing, Mr Wildie's land, land bought of Peter Taylor. To 2 youngest sons Joseph and Benj: Robinson. Exor son Thos. Signed Jno x Robinson. Wit: Jno Blundle, Edw x Atkins and Tho. Hobson. Proved by Hobson and Blundle. Re-recorded 20 June 1711 by Thos Robinson. A division of the land 12 Aug 1703 betw Antho and Tho Robinson, wit by Tho Hobson, Nicholas Hack and Clark Hobson. 17. 108

Robinson, Jno. Security on Mrs Sarah Lee's bond 30000 lb tobo. 16 Oct. 1676. 4.7

    Jno. To appraise estate of Wm Perriman, decd. 16 Oct 1676. 4.7

Robinson, Joseph and Frances his wife, late Frances Waddington, relict of Jno Waddington, decd. 18 Mar 1713/14. 6.24

Robinson, Mary. Wife of Henry. See entry Alex Cumins et als. 7th Apl.
1707. 17.116
    Richd. Bequest from Jno Webb. Wit his will. 5 Oct 1700.
17.265
    Richd. Deed of Gift to his brother Saml Robinson. 50 acres
in St Stephens par. 14 July 1702. 17.105
    Richd. Wit tfr Scott to Rose. 16 Jan 1702/3. 17.202
    Richd. Wit will Tho Barnes. 5 May 1712. 18.265
    Richd. dec'd. Will produced by Francis Robinson, Exeuyx.
18 Jan 1716/17. 6.188
    Robt. Son of Cornelius Robinson, decd. Given a cow by Doctor
Saunder (Edward Sanders). 20 June 1664. 15.125
Robinson, decd. Saml Robinson swears he left no will. Admr
granted. 20 Jan 1719/20. 6.353
    Stephen. Bought land from Tho Williams. 3 May 1690. 17.153
    Saml. Deed of Gift from his brother Richd. Robinson, 50 acres
in St S. par. 14 July 1702. 17.105
    Saml. Signs bond with Ralph Bickley admr Jas Allen. 20 Mar
1710/11. 18.16
    Saml. Re-records will of Col Geo Cooper. 18 July 1711. 17.123
Also records oath of Jno Copedge regarding will of
Geo Cooper. 19 Dec 1711. 17.143
    Saml and Eliz'a his wife, exors of will of Geo Cooper decd.
18 March 1713/14. 6.27
    Stephen. Bought 50 acres on S side Wicco River 3 May 1690
from Tho Williams and sold it to Jno Embry 26th
July 1704. 18.149
    Susanna. Dau of Tho Gill Sr. 10 Feb 1707/8. 17.97
    Tho: Deposition. Age not shown. Says Jane Robinson by her
will gave land to Martha Robinson and land to Wm
Robinson. That he was an exor and that Henry Mayes
was an evidence. 16 May 1717. 17.237
    William, deceased. Will presented by Joseph Robinson his exor.
18 Jan 1716/17. 6.188
Robuck, Robt. Wit Robinson to Embry. 28 July 1704. 17.153
    Robert. Owes est of Tho Crowder 515 lb tobo. 20 June 1711.
18.62
Roche, Henry. Age 55 or th-abts. 4 Aug 1665. 15.164
Roach, Henry of City of Bristol, marriner. Mary Mottley widow, of G W.
parish, buys from Wm Morgan of Bristol, 100 acres
the said Roach bought of Wm Betts. 24 Feb 1670/1.
16.158
    Capt Henry. Has bill dated 11 Apl 1678 signed by Mr Wm Thomas
decd for 607 lb tobo. 21 Aug 1678. 4.2
    Henry, deceased. Father of Jno Roach. Left land to Mrs Eliz:
Tyngey until his son comes to age. 21 Jan 1668/9
3.55
    John. Bequest to Wm Short. 10 Dec 1688. 17.13
    Laurence. Servt to Mrs Kath: Coutanceau adj 11 yrs of age.
4.412

Roberts, Mary. Deed. 16 Dec 1707. Mary Roberts, widow, of Westmorland Co. and Thomas Timmonds of the Middle parish in Stafford Co son and heir apparent of Tho Timmonds late deceased, sell Geo Dawking of St S par, N Co, for 6000 lb tobo, land near Bebe's Neck. Adjs land of Rd Rice and Tho Addams, Chicacone branch, part of a tract of land which Wm Garner bought of said Richd Rice and by him sold to Thos Timonds, father of Tho Timonds party of these presents by deed dated 9 Oct 1674 and ack 18 Nov 1674. The land adjoins Wm Addams, Bates Branch, Tho Adams and Rd Rice. Does not show relationship of Mary Roberts. Signed by Mary x Roberts and Thomas Timmons. Wit by Wm x Warwickm Wm Warwick Junr and Wm Dawkins. Rerecorded 20 June 1711 by Geo Dawkins. 17,114

Robins, Jeremiah. As witness swears to will of Dan Holland dec'd. 17th April 1672. 3,145

Rock, Jno. Wit P of A LeBreton to Matthew. 3 Apl 1671. 16,192

Rodham prob same as Rhoden.

Rodham, Matthew. Deed of Gift. 17 Nov 1666. To daughter Hannah Neale wife to Christopher Neale, plantation formerly Mr Hugh Lee's in N. Co. 393 acres. Adj land of Hugh Lee, James Claughton, Kings Creek, Col Jno Mottrom, Capt Jno Rogers and Jno Trussell. Refers to his wife Elizabeth. Signed Matthew Rodham, Eliz x Rodham. Wit: Rich Kenner, Wm Thurnbury. 16,22-A

Roe, Thos. Bought 50 acres in Newmans Neck from Wm Cornish 20 Febry 1659/60 and assigned it to Tho Sadler and Joseph Dowling 8 Jan 1668/9. 18,125

Rogers, Alex: deceased. His widow Eliz now married to Timothy Selcheverill. 16 May 1717. 6,212

    Alex. Deposition. About 18 yrs old, says "with assistance and command of his Father James Rogers this Deponent did Copy out a Written Will Subscribed Richd Nelmes". 16 May 1711. 17,99

    Alexander. Wit deed White to Davis. 16 July 1711. 18,88

    Isabella. Bequest from Danl Suilevant. 29 Aug 1704. 17,261

    James. Wit Danl Neale's will. 4 Nov 1700. 17,249

    James. Bequest from Danl Suilevant. 29 Aug 1704. 17,261

    James of St S par. Will dated 3 March 1707/8. prob 17 Sept 1712. Land to wife Susanna Rogers (she exor) till son Alexander Rogers be of age, he failing in heirs to "my Brother Richard Rogers". To son Jno Rogers and dau Judith Rogers. Trustees Capt Geo Eldridge, Capt Tho Hobson and Tho Stretton. Wit: Tho Lucas, Thos Stretton. 18,230

Rogers, Doctor James. Deceased. Inventory presented by Robt Davis and Susanna his wife, late Susanna Rogers, relict and admr. 19 Sept 1711. 18,102

Rogers, Capt. Jno. Justice. 26 May 1656. 14.84
John. Age 45. Then Churchwarden. 4 Aug 1665. 15.163
Capt. Jno. His land adj Matthew Rodham. 17 Nov 1666. 16.22-A
Capt Jno. Justice. 20 Oct 1668. 3.44
Capt Jno. Took up land and built a church "about 21 or 22 yeares since". 22 June 1669. 16.152-3
Capt Jno. Holds land at head of Yeacomico river in right of his wife Anne, relict of Mr Francis Clay and relict of Mr Jno Temple. No date but recorded 22 Aug 1670. 16.143
Capt Jno. Vestryman Chicacone parish. 20 March 1671/2. 16.158
Capt Jno. Was landlord to Tho Swan deceased. Swan left him his chest and all therein. 11 Jan 1668/9. 3.51
Capt Jno. Miles Gorham petitions for his child who he says was bound to Rogers in his absence. 21 Aug 1678. 4.3
Capt Jno. Ordered to deliver Miles Goreham's son to him. 17th Oct 1678. 4.8
John Junior. Arrested at suit of Wm Crab. No cause, nonsuit. 21 Nov 1678. 4.15
John Junior. By a bill dated last of April 1679, at the time of his decease he owed Edw Elliott 1302 lb tobo, of which 704 lb is pd. Judgt agt Joane the admr of Jno Rogers for the bal. 20 Apl 1681. 4.92
Philip. An heir of Danl Suilevant. 29 Aug 1704. 17.261
Phillip. Buys 124 acres in St S par from Jas Jones. 19 August 1707. 17.153
Phillip. Wit will of Tho Hall Sr. 10 Feb 1708/9. 17.163
Phill of St S par, mariner, sells Jno Opie of same par, Gent, 124 acres in St S par, part of 1000 acres granted Wm Newman and John Meeks on 6 May 1651. 16 Feb 1711/12. 18.147
Mr. Richd. Justice. 16 Sept 1685. 4.291
Mr. Richd. Justice. 18 May 1687. 4.493
Richd. Sued for 550 lb tobo by Geo Groves who married the admr of Jas Seabury. 20 Nov 1696. 4.751
Roles, Matthew. Servt of Richd Cox of Chicacone parish, to be whipt for having a bastard child by her master. Col St Ledger Codd paying her fine she is acquitted. 16 Oct 1678. 4.5
Rolfe, Tho deceased. Inv of his est. No date but is entered as though of Jan 1668/9. 16.84
Tho. Appears to have been murdered. Jno Jones and Jno Richards to touch his corpse before a jury. 20 Nov 1669. 3.41
Rookes, Mr Geo. Merchant in London. Father of Mary wife of Rev John Farnefold. 3 July 1702. 17.234
Rookwood, John. Headright of Capt Gyles Brent. 21 Jan 1651/2. 1.70
Ropier, Sarah. Married Tho Colles. See entry Nicho Britton. 20th Jan 1664/5. 15.149
Rose, Jno. Wit will Mrs Jane Wildey. He prob married Mary Blackerby. 11 Apl 1701. 17. pp 224-9

Rose, Jno. With Mary his wife, late Mary Blackerby, proves by oath
                will of James Wildey they being wit:. 19th Nov
                1701. 5.180
        Jno. Buys 50 acres from Jno Scott. 16 Jan 1702/3. Re-recorded
                by Rose 16 Sept 1713. 17.202
        Jno of Wicco par. Buys 50 acres from Hugh Campball. 6 Sept 1713.
                18.343
Rosier, Jno. Signs oath to Commonwealth of England. 13 Apl 1652. 1.72
Rodham, Matthew. Gives to "my Daughter Hannah Neale wife to Christopher
                Neale" the plantation that was formerly Hugh Lee's.
                393 acres, etc. Wit: Rich Kenner, Wm Thornbury.
                17 Dec 1666. 16.22
Rotheram, Jno. P of A from Michael Huggall. 25 Oct 1668. 16.55
        Jno. Having misbehaved in Court ordered to sit in the stocks.
                21 Jan 1668/9. 3.53
        Jno. Wit sale 2 servts Courtnell to Howson. 27 Jan 1668/9.
                16.69
Rout, Mr. His land adj Wm Moore. 5 Sept 1707. 17.47
        Frances. Exhibits inv of est of her dec'd husband Richd Rout.
                12 March 1713/14. 6.20
        Frances, deceased. Will produced by Geo Rout her exor. 20 June
                1716. 6.170
        Richd. of Fairfield par. His land adj Rd Smith and Jas Nipper.
                14 Apl 1677. 17.120
        Richd. As marrying Frances Adams is sued for 680 lb tobo by Jno
                Downing atty of Sam Tipton. 6 Oct 1687. 4.407
Routt, Richd. Senior of St S par. Will. dated 26 Feb 1710/11. probated
                17 June 1713. To sons Tho Routt and Richd Reutt
                300 acres each. Refs to son Wm Routt now deceased.
                To grand-daus Elizabeth Routt and Anne Routt the
                daus of dec'd son Wm Routt. To wife Fran: Routt
                and the 4 children had by her, viz: Geo Rout, dau
                Ann Conway, dau Mary Crosby and dau Fran Rout.
                18.316
Rout, Richd. deceased. Inv submitted. 12 March 1713/14. 6.20
        Tho. Wit deed Adams to Shirley. 13 Feb 1701/2. 17.151
        Tho. Wit deed Adams to Harrison. 2 Jan 1702/3. 17.161
        Tho. Wit deed Crosby to Purcell. 18 Oct 1705. 17.192
        Tho. The land he now lives on adj Robt Mittchiles land and the
                land sold by Jno Hill to Wm Dare this date. 20th
                Sept 1711. 18.151
        Tho of St S par. Buys from Jno Hill and Ann his wife of Farnham
                parish, 23 acres on N side G W river, etc. 19th
                March 1711/12. 18.161
        Tho. deceased. Will presented by Eliz Rout, extrx. 18 May 1715.
                6.108
        Wm. Wit will of Rd Routt senr. 26 Feb 1710/11. 18.316
Rowe, Tho. On jury to div land Saffin and Hull. 29 Nov 1669. 16.63
Rowland, Luke who married Anne, admr of Tho Harding. 22 May 1696.
                4.728

Rowland, Robt. Presents nuncupitive will of Jno Thomas. Admr granted. 19 June 1718. 6.272

Rowley, Joane. Age 20 yrs or th-abts. 19 July 1670. 16.132

Rowling Road. Adj land Dunaway at head of Great Wicco. 11 March 1705/6 17.150

Royston, Betts. Under 17. Son of Charles. 1 Oct 1709. 17.100
    Jonath: On jury to div land Saffin and Hull. 29th Nov 1669. 16.63

Ruberd, Wm. Age 24 or th-abts. 22 June 1671. 16.186

Rule, Wm. Headright of Lau Dameron. 21 Feb 1658/9. 2.102

Rumley, Jno. Servt to Tho Matthew adj to be 16 yrs of age. 22nd June 1669. 3.64

Rumney, Abra. Deposition, age not shown. Long entry regarding papers stolen by a runaway servant. No date but as of 22 Oct 1667. 16.28

Runkin, Geo. Headright of Mr Jno Harris. 15 July 1696. 4.733

Ruske, Wm. Appointed guardian of Jane Metcalfe (in place of Mrs Dennis Clarke) he having married her sister. 22 July 1661 2.144

Russell, Capt Giles. Commander of the ship Brimpton swears that the Indentures of Jno Gray, Edwd Welch, Mary Maheon and Elliner Ring for 7 years were real Indentures. He produces papers wherein several persons are ordered for transportation according to act of Parliament, etc. 18 Nov 1719. 6.346
    James. Servt to Mr Wm Presley adj 15 yrs of age. 17 Apl 1672. 3.144
    Jno. Wit deed of gift Burrell to Burrell. 19 May 1670. 16.75
    Peter. Lives on land of Jno Bowers Senior. 29 Sept 1704. 17.167
    Peter. Sold Jno Webb land in St S par prior to 4 June 1709. 17.102
    Richd. His land adj Dunaway at head of G W. 11 Mar 1705/6. 17.150
    Richard, deceased. Inv of his est taken by Court Order dated 16 Feb 1709/10. Presented by Hannah Russell his relict 16 May 1711. 18.35

Rust, Wm. Present paymt of 960 lb tobo conf to by Miles Gorham. 20th Nov. 1668. 3.49

Ruth, Mary. Dau of Rd Ruth deceased chooses Mr Jno Copedge as her guardian. (He admr of her father's estate) 18th March 1718/19. 6.308
    Richd. Wit P of A Champion to Lattimore. 15 Feb 1709/10. 17.186
    Richd. Signs bond Jas Richardson as Guardian of John Brewer. 18 Feb 1712/13. 18.261
    Richd. His wife the mother of Edward Bowen. 19 Oct 1715. 6.141
    Ruth. Will. dated 26 Jan 1718/19. prob 18 March 1718/19. To daus Mary, Eliz and Alice, To John Bowen. Exor Richard Hackney. Wit Tho Cunningham, Loughly x Welsh. 19.31

Ryan, Edw: Servant to Tho Gill adj to be 8 yrs old. 18 Nov 1713. 6.3
    Laughlin. Servant to Edw Sanders adj 18 yrs old. 21 Dec 1698.
        4.848
Ryder, Josian. Wit deed Murrow to Gater. 11 Mar 1711/12. 18.307

St Marys White Chappell. This entry concerns the bapt of Mary Orley
        in London on 25th April 1622. See Geo Hardinge
        of London. 29 Sept 1664. 15.145
St Stephens Creek. On N side G W River adj Tho Saffell. 20 Nov 1655.
    14.59
St Stephens Parish. Presented for not going to Church:
        Jam Fulks
        Edwd Cockrill
        Jno Parry
        Sylvester Welsh
        Jes Phillips
        Laurence Fletcher
        Wm Williams and Jno Williams
        Jno Meath
        Jno Taylor, smith
        15 May 1717. 6.202
St Thomas Creek. On N side G W River, adj Tho Saffell. 20 Nov 1655.
    14.59
Sacheverill, Timothy. Nearest relative of Jos Long deceased. Swears
        he left no will. Admr to him. 18 Nov 1719. 6.345
Sadler, Tho. On jury to div land Saffin and Hull. 29 Nov 1669. 16.63
    Tho. His servt Mommey Macklaugn adj 13 yrs old. 19 Jan 1675/6.
        3.249
    Tho. Pd 200 lb tobo from County levy "for a Gunn Lost". 21st
        Nov 1678. 4.17
Saffell, Tho. Grant from Ri Hennett, 850 acres adj S on G W river, W
        upon St Johns Creek, NW and N on the main woods,
        E and NE on Saffells Creek and St Stephens Creek.
        This land formerly granted Saffell 3 Sept 1651.
        Now dated 1 June 1654. 14.58
    Tho. of Northumberland Co. Sells Jno Hudnall of Ile of Wight
        Co 500 acres on N side G W river beginning at St
        Thomas Creek and ext to St Stephens Creek.
        Wit: Jne Fausitt, Will Nutt, Nicho Morris.
        20 Nov 1655. 14.59
Saffin, Jno of Boston. Buys 100 acres from Rd Rice and Anne his wife.
        16 Apl 166-. Recorded 20 Jan 1666/7. 16.7
Saffin, Jno. Accused of exporting English goods out of this Country
        contrary to Law. Tried before jury. Verdict not
        shown. 21 Jan 1668/9. 3.53
Saffin, Jno. Owed a balance of 917 lb tobo by Jno Evan. 21 Jan 1668/9.
    3.52

Saffin, Jno. of Boston in the Massachusetts Colony of New England, merchant, and Martha his wife, sell for L 100. to Jno Hull of Boston, merchant, 1/2 of 400 acres in Northumberland Co, on W side of Mattaponi river, known as Exeter Lodge. 200 acres pur by sd Saffin from Richd Rice and another 100 pur of Robt Hickman. Wit: Jno Pease, Geo Ellistone. 21 Aug 1669. Robt Howard Notary Public, Mass. 16.62

Power of Atty. 30 Sept 1669. Martha Saffin wife of Jno Saffin of Boston to Mr Tho Smith to ack above in the Court of Northumberland Co. 16.63

By order of Court there is a div of property belonging to Jno Hull deceased into 3 parts, btw Richd Smith who married the relict of Jno Hull decd and Richd Hull. Refers to land of Tho Kitchin, to an agreemt for building a house, etc. 29 Nov 1669. 16.62

Salmon, Edw. His admr, Jas Claughton, exhibits a/c agt Jam: Robinson for 1450 lb tobo. To be used for Salmon's children. 20 Oct 1668. 3.45

Hugh. deceased. Richd Booth next of kin to his orphans. 17th June 1714. 6.44

Middleton. deceased. His daughter Sarah, wife of Tho Thomas, swears he died without a will. 16 Nov 1715. 6.142

William. Orphan of Edw Salmon. List of his cattle, 10 head, submitted by Adam Yarret. 22 Aug 1670. 16.144

Salsbury, Andrew of G W par, carpenter, sells Wm Barrett 150 acres. 3rd July 1701. 17.95

Salisbury, Barbara. Appointed to admr est of Jno Jones deceased. Tho Hobson security. 19 Jan 1675/6. 3.250

John. Owes Mr Jno Hainie 1002 lb tobo. 20 Nov 1668. 3.48

Tho. Signs oath to Commonwealth of England. 13 Apl 1652. 1. 72-3

Tho. Land on S side G W River adj Martin Cole. 1 July 1654. 14.92

Tho. Will. dated 3 March 1656/7. prob 20 July 1657. Eldest son Thomas, youngest son John, both under 21. To wife Isabell. If need be David Cussin and John Bardon to have charge of sons. To Eliz dau of Jno Hulett a sow. Wit: Jno Haynie, Jno Bennett. 14.112

Thomas. His mother and guardian Mrs Isabella Pettigrew. 16 Dec 1662. 15.96

Thomas. P of A to "my loving Bro: Jno Salisbury" to appear in Court for him. Wit. Jno Robinson. Alexr Fleming. 21 Jan 1670/1. 16.147

Tho. Buys 750 acres in G W par from Andrew Pettigrew and Isabella his wife. 17 May 1671. 16.223

Salisbury Park, Northumberland Co. P of A from there dated 28 Sept 1654. Westmorland Co records, 1653-9. p 28

Salisbury Park, Northumberland Co. Owned by Richd Cole. 30 Aug 1658. 15.11

Salter, Jno. Wit will Rd Foilding. 16 July 1666. 16.12
Sanders, Capt. His land adj Saml Downing. 9 June 1711. 18.93
    Ebenezer. Son of Mr Edwd Sanders decd, petitions for land and
        cattle left him by his father. Delivery ordered.
        21 August 1678. 4.2
    Ebenezer and Edward. Admrs of Mrs Mary Thomas. See entry Wm
        Thomas. 17 Sept 1684. 4.244
    Ebenezer. Justice. 21 Sept 1692. 4.599
    Ebenezer. Deceased. His widow Mrs Eliz Sanders ordered to
        produce inventory of his estate. 19 Apl 1693. 4.619
    Ebenezer. "Saml Downing and Elizabeth his wife Daughter of
        Mr Ebenezer Sanders dec'od" regarding the div of
        her father's land amongst the heirs. 2 April 1711.
        18.55
        In the division of the land there is reference his
        daughter Elizabeth Sanders, his son Edwd Sanders and
        his brother Edward Sanders. Refers to the land hav-
        ing been patented 5 March 1662/3 by his father Mr
        Edward Sanders chirurgeon. 5 Apl 1711. 18.55
    Edward. Who married the widow and admrx of John Hudnall decd.
        18 Sept 1660. 2.132
    Edward and Mary his wife. Deed 8 Dec 1662. 16.70
    Dr. Edward. Gives a cow to Robt son of Cornelius Robinson.
        20 June 1664. 15.125
    Mr Edw of Wicocconico, chirurgeon. P of A from Geo Tuchingham
        of Bristol, mercht. 18 June 1667. 16.23
    Edw. Wit will of Richd Span. 16 March 1667/8. 16.64
Saunders, Dr. Pd 2000 lb tobo from County levy "For the Ferry". 5 Nov.
    1668. 3.47
Sanders, Mr Edw. To appraise est of Capt Wm Nutt dec'd. 20 Nov 1668.
    3.48
Saunder, Edw. As wit proves will of Richd Span. 11 Jan 1668/9. 3.51
Sanders, Edw. To appraise est of Tho Rolph decd. 10 Mar 1668/9. 3.58
    Mr. Edw. Certificate for 600 acres for importing 12 persons.
        22 June 1669. 3.65
    Mr Edw. This day sworn Justice. 22 June 1669. 3.64
    Edw. Wit will Roger Walters. 29 Dec 1669. 16.69
    Edw. Wit will . ger Walters. 29 Dec 1669. 16.115
    Doctor Edw. Al. g with others suspected Granny Neal of bewitch-
        ing rs Coles. 11 Apl 1671. 16.187
    Edw. Aged 50 yrs or th-abts. Deposition regarding the Coles -
        Neale witchcraft case. 20 May 1671. 16.81
    Edw. Chirurgeon. Will dated 4 Oct 1669. Prob 19 June 1672.
        Leaves land to one of his sons, Edward Sanders.
        18.75
    Edward. Makes choice of his mother, Mrs Mary Thomas, to be his
        guardian. 21 Aug 1678. 4.2
    Dr. Edw. deceased. Wm Flower trustee for his children demands
        cattle from estate of Wm Thomas deceased. 17 Oct
        1678. 4.10

Sanders, Edw: His servt Henry Pearce adj 15 yrs old. 20 July 1687. 4.397
 Edw: His servt Laughlin Ryan adj 18 yrs of age. 21 Dec 1698. 4.848
 Edw: Buys 250 acres from Randolph Miller and Kath: is wife. 21 Dec 1698. 4.846
 Capt Edw: Land lately possed by him adj Jas Loughman. 7 Sept 1702. 17.202
 Edw: His land adj Geo Crosby in St S par. 18 Oct 1705. 17.192
 Capt Edw: 1200 acres, part in Wicco par Northumberland Co and part in Christ Church par Lancaster Co, surveyed by Court Order dated 16 Aug 1710. 18.165
 Edw: Wit assignmt Burbury to Cepedge. 21 Mar 1710/11. 17.50
 Edward of St S parish. Sells Alex Love 100 acres, part of 365 acres bequeathed to him by will dated 28th Feb 1692/3 of his brother Ebenezer Sanders dec'd. The 365 acres being part of 2000 acres bequeathed to sd Ebenezer by will dated 4 Oct 1669 of his father Edward Sanders. The 2000 acres being part of 2900 acres granted on 5 March 1662/3 to the said Edward Sanders. 16 April 1711. 18.50
 Capt Edw: Referred to in John Webb's will as "my Cozen Edward Sanders". 4 June 1709. He rerecords the will 17 May 1711. 17.102
 Edw: Signs bond of Tho Hobson as admr of Wm Winder. 17 May 1711. 18.46
 Capt Edw: Rerecords deed Saml Smith to Tho Sims for Ann Sims. 18 May 1711. 17.104
 Capt Edw: He and Capt Francis Kenner, Churchwardens of St Stephens parish, order survey of 467 acres in Cherry Point Neck for a Glebe. 19 May 1711. 18.166
 Edw of St S parish sells Edwin Conway of Christ Church parish Lancaster Co, 200 acres, part in N Co and part in Lanc Co. 13 July 1711. 18.73
 Edwd: Son and heir of Ebenezer Sanders. 1 Apl 1712. 18.188
 Capt Edw: Presented for not keeping Cone Mill dam in repair. Dismissed. 21 Jan 1713/14. 6.16
 Edw: Exor of Jno Webb deceased. 17 Feb 1714/5. 6.99
 Edw: Bequest from his mother Mrs Eliz Cockerell. 25 Apl 1719. 19.42
 Edward Jr of Wicco par sells Jno Ingram, for L 45., 100 acres. This land known as Sanders Quarter, was granted 15 March 1662 to Mr Edward Sanders chirurgeon deceased, who left it by will dated 4 Oct 1669 to his youngest son Edw Sanders uncle to said Edw Sanders Jr. Bal of land given to Ebenezer Sanders who by will dated 28 Feb 1692/3 devised it to his son . . . . (Note: The balance of my note on this entry has become misplaced. I shall have to offer it thus, without date, volume or page reference. B.F.)

Sanders, Elizabeth. Wife of Edwd S, relinq dower rights in land sold Alex Love. 17. May 1711. 18.54
    Elizabeth. Daughter of Ebenezer Sanders and gr-dau of Edward Sanders, now wife of Saml Downing. 9 June 1711. 18.93
    Mrs. Mary. Deposition. "Mary the wife of Capt Edward Sanders maketh oath that the Munday after twelfth day Mr Edward Coles came to the house of the said Sanders this Depont asked the said Coles how his wife did and he replyed that shee was dead, And your Deponent said, she was sorry for that, and the said Coles replyed againe that shee was not dead but bewitched, and that Mrs Neale was the woman hee did suspect, and further sayth not Jurat' Curia 19 July 1671". 16.179
    William, deceased. Inventory of est taken 13 Oct 1704 by order of Court dated 21 Sept 1704. Sworn before Captain Christopher Neale. Totals 11679 lb tobo. Signed by Wm Warrick, Jno Webb, Vincent Garner and John Bowes.
    A further inventory, not valued, submitted 18 Jan 1704/5. Includes a sword "given by word of mouth by my deceased Husband to his Godson, two bibles also given to his Son in Law". Signed Thomas Harrison, Mary x Harrison. Submitted by "Tho Harrison and Mary his wife late Mary Sanders Executrix of the said Wm Sanders dec'd". Rerecorded by Mary Harrison relict of Wm Sanders decd. 17.165

Sanders family detail in deed Downing to Schriever. 9 June 1711. 18.93
Sander's line. In G W parish adj Geo Chilton and Saml Mahane Jr. 16 July 1705. 17.122
Sandy Valley. Adj Jno Webb. 5 Oct 1700. 17.265
Samford, Saml and Isabell wit will of Mrs Dorothy Spann. 11 Feb 1711/12 18.157
Sanford, Saml who married Eliz Keen the extrx of Edw Elliott. 16 Sept 1685. 4.291
Sanson, Jno. Wit P of A DeConti to Gaylard. 20 July 1671. 16.194
Scaffold Point. Adj land of Tho Wms. 15 Mar 1704/5. 17.67
School. See entry Rev Jno Farnefold. 3 July 1702. 17.234
Schrever (Schreever) Barth and Mary his wife exors of Capt Wm Lee decd. 18 Nov 1698. 4.845
    Barth: Wit deed Wms to Mahan. 15 Mar 1704/5. 17.67
    Barth: Buys 199 acres from Tho Crowder on W side Corotomen River. 18 Sept 1705. Re-recorded 20th Feb 1711/12. 17.155
    Barth: Wit deed Williams to Maurice Jones. 22 Feb 1705/6. 17.164
    Mr Barth: L 3. from a "Gentlewoman in Maryland" mentioned in Hancock Lee's will. 20 May 1709. 17.29

Schrever, Barth: Overseer of will of Isaac Gaskins 22 Oct 1709.
        Rerecords the will 18 June 1712. 17,167
    Bartholomew. Appears in entry as Scriever and as Schreever.
        Buys 365 acres in Wicco parish from Saml Downing and Eliz his wife, 9 June 1711. 18,92
    Barth: Admr of Mr Tho Urquhart late decd presents inv of his
        est. 19 March 1711/12. 18,168
    Barth: Appears as Schriever. Guardian of Jno Brewer orphan
        of Tho Brewer decd petitions the Court in favor
        of his pupil agt Jno Burne and Eliz his wife.
        They ordered to appear. 18 Mar 1713/14. 6,28
    Barth: Guardian of Jno Brewer orphan son of Tho Brewer decd
        agt Jno Burn continued. 22 July 1714. 6,60
    Barth: Admr Tho Urquhart decd. 17 Feb 1714/15. 6,99
    Barth: Junr. Wit will of Mrs Sarah Jones. 26 Jan 1719/20.
        19,98
    Dennis, deceased. Appears as Schriver. His will presented
        by Tho Waddy exor. 15 May 1717. 6,208
Scoggin, Tho. His land adj Peter Knight. 26 Nov 1651. 17,179
Scoggins Creek. Adj land of Peter Knight as above.
Scotland Mill Creek. Adj land of Tho Williams. 27 Mar 1703. 17,45
Scotland Mill Swamp. In Gr Wic Par. 5 June 1710. 17,50
Scott, Mr Jno. His servt Zachariah Coynia adj 14 yrs old. 16 Nov 1687.
        4,410
    John of Wicco parish. Cooper. Buys 50 acres from Jas Loughman
        7 Sept 1702. The land sold by Jno Scott and
        Anne his wife to Jno Rose 17 Feb 1702/3. 17,202
    Samman. Wit deed Fleet to Baker. 15 Nov 1655. 14,58
    William. Servt to Col Rd Lee adj 13 yrs old. 21 Jan 1660/1.
        2,136
Scotts branch. Adj land of Tho Crowder on W side Corotomen River. 18th
        Sept 1705. 17,155
Scripture, John. Order that Dr Pemberton pay him "his Kersey suite,
        shooes, stockins and shirt", also 200 lb tobo.
        2 March 1680/1. 4,84
Seaburn, Mr Nicho: See deposition of Mrs Hannah Smith. 17 Aug 1713.
        18,335
Seabury, James. Geo Groves as marrying his admr sues Rd Rogers for
        550 lb tobo. 20 Nov 1696. 4,751
Seagrave, Robert, deceased. His inventory appraised by Jno Spiller,
        Francis Gray, John Delahay and Robert Cole.
        20 March 1649/50. 1,48
Seaham, Jno. Servt to Mr Peter Coutanceau adj 15 yrs of age. 21 Dec
        1698. 8,847
Searle, Tho. A poor impotent person freed from levy. 18 March 1684/5.
        4,256
Sech, Rob: P of A from Jos Edmonds. 17 Feb 1664/5. 16,13
    Robert. Age 34 or th-abts. 4 Aug 1665. 15,161
    Robt. Gives a cow to Mary Hitchcock dau of Robt Hitchcock. 7th
        March 1667/8. 16,42

Sech, Robt. "Aged 37 yeares or therabouts". 11 Jan 1668/9. 3.51
    Robt. As witness proves will of Tho Swan. 11 January 1668/9.3.51
    Robt. His servt Cha Nowland (who later ran away) adjudged 10
        yrs of age. 20 May 1685. 4.268
    Robt. To "Assort" dower for Mrs Eliz Evans, widow. 6 Oct 1687
        4.407
    Robt. His land adj Patrick Maley on main swamp of Mattaponi.
        7 July 1703. 17.127
Seddon, Tho. of St S par sells to Wm Tyney of Cople par, Westmorland
    Co., 110 acres in St S par which he purchased on 12th
    Feb 1696/7 from Edw and Jno Lewis. 18th March 1711/12
    18.166
Selcheverill, Setchiverill, Selchiverile, etc, etc,
    Timothy and Elizabeth his wife. Give bond as admrs of
    estate of John Dawson deceased. Bond also signed by
    Theoffilus Setchiverele and Wm Betts. 15 Aug 1711. 18.98
Selcheverill, Timothy and Elizabeth his wife present inv of est of Jno
    Dawson decd. 14 Sept 1711. 18.105
    Timothy and Eliz his wife. She late Eliz Rogers relict
    of Alex Rogers decd, state Rogers died without a will.
    Admr granted. 16 May 1717. 6.212
Serves, Jno. Servant to Geo English adjudged 13 yrs old. 21 Jan 1660/1.
    2.136
Sewards, William. An indenture is presented by Tho Hobson with said
    William, that his children, John and Mary Seward, serve
    the said Hobson, etc. 22 July 1714. 6.60
    It is difficult to estimate this kind of entry. Did he
    sell his children ? - no I don't think so. It is as
    though he had placed them with the most responsible
    man in the community for safe keeping.   B.F.
Shapleigh, Shapley, Shippy. This last the pronunciation. The name often
    appearing thus.
    Elizabeth. Daughter of Tho Shapleigh deceased. She makes
        choice of her uncle, Mr Jno Shapleigh, as guardian. 12
        March 1713/14. 6.18
    Hannah. Signs inv of est of Mr Tho Shapleigh 29 Sept 1703.
        17.11
    Jno. Appears as guardian of Eliz dau of Tho Shapleigh decd.
        19 May 1714. 6.36
    Jno. Suit, as guardian of Eliz Shapleigh, sole dau of Tho
        Shapleigh dec'd, against Jno Hattsie and Hanah his wife,
        she relict and admr of sd dec'd. Referred to next
        Court. 19 Oct 1715. 6.141
    Phill (Shaply) His servants' ages adj as: Lawrence Keire
        13, Don'll OLoth 16 and Humphrey Eale 13. 19th Janry
        1675/6. 3.249
    Mr Phillip. Suit agt him by Jno Richards to next Court. 16
        Oct 1676. 4.6

Shapleigh, Mr (doubtless Philip Shapleigh) Sued by Jno Kyrke. Ref to
    next Court "the said Mr Shapley being taken sicke
    and gone from this Court". 21 Aug 1678. 4.4
    Phillip. Judgt agt Jno Laurence 1452 lb tobo. 17 Oct 1678.
    4.9
    Mr Phillip. Justice. 20 Nov 1678. 4.12
    Mr Phillip and Mr John Haynie. They to have liberty to set
    up and keep an Ordinary near the new Courthouse.
    15 June 1681. 4.97
    Mr Phillip. Justice. 20 July 1687. 4.397
    Mr Phill. Justice. 16 Nov 1687. 4.410
    Capt Phillip. His land adj Saml Smith, Great Pond, Flyntts
    Pond. 11 Sept 1703. 17.104
    Capt Phillip. Rerecords inventory taken 29 Sept 1703 of est
    of Mr Tho Shapleigh. 22 Feb 1710/11. 17.12
    Phillip. Gives a heifer to Elizabeth dau of Tho Hobson who
    is his wife's God-dau. 18 July 1711. 18.82
    Phillip. Signs bond L 1000. Sterl of Peter Presly as Sheriff
    of Northumberland Co. 18 June 1712. 18.197
    Phillip. Signs bond of Hon Robt Carter as guardian of John
    Bashford. 17 June 1713. 18.309
    Phillip. Deceased. Will presented by Hannah and John
    Shapleigh his exors. Proved by oaths of wit
    Tho Hobson and Rainsford Smyth. 15 May 1717.
    6.203
    Phoebe. (the name appears as Phoebe Shippey in the entry.)
    As legatee of James Jones. She married Henry
    Metcalfe. 17 Feb 1714/15. 6.98
    Priscilla. (Appears as Priscilla Shippey in entry) as
    legatee of James Jones. She married Jno Turner.
    17 Feb 1714/15. 6.98
    Priscilla (as above) Chooses Wm Metcalf to be her guardian.
    21 July 1714. 6.58
    Mr Tho. Deceased. Inv of est. Signed by Hannah Shapleigh as
    admr. Also signed by Thos Gill, Wm Porter, John
    Graham, Geo Crosby. Sworn before Peter Hack.
    29 Sept 1703. 17.11
    Tho. Deceased. 12 March 1713/14. 6.18
Shapleighs Quarter. In St S par. Road from adjs Saml Smith's land.
    19 Dec 1709. 17.53
Shapleigh Storehouse. On Wicco River. Rd Neale appointed agent there.
    17 Nov 1714. 6.88
Sharecropper. "an Jobe lease fellow not suffered to be admitted in any
    Civill Company". Certificate from the Court that
    Dennis Carter is no such person. 17 Oct 1678.
    4.8
Sharpe, Mr Jno. Appointed Sub-sheriff by the Governor. (Mr Wm Lee sher.)
    26 Apl 1687. 4.394
Sharp, Jno. Who had wit will of Jno Cookerill Sr on 30 Dec 1695 had
    died prior to 18 Nov 1704. 17.135
    Jno. Wit Tho Brewer's will. 11 June 1697. 17.268

Sharp, Jno. Atty of Mrs Alice Williams. 19 Jan 1700/1. 17.70
    Jno. Son of Mrs Mary Knight. 1 Oct 1706. 17.43
    Linsfield. Son of Mrs Mary Knight. 1 Oct 1706. 17.43
Sharpe, Mary. Widow of Robt Sharp decd. 20th -- 1655. 14.84
    Mary. Dau of Mrs Mary Knight. 1 Oct 1706. 17.43
    Mary. Daughter of Eliz the wife of Jno Jemmison bound to Robt
        Davis and Susanna his wife till 18. 16 June 1714.
        6.42
Shaw, Jno. Buys 300 acres on S side G W River from Tho Hipkins. 20th
        May 1657. 14.92
    Jno. Deposition. Age 40 yrs or th-abts. Exact date not shown but
        recorded the latter part of 1664. 15.135
    Jno. Age 42 or th-abts. 4 Aug 1665. 15.162
    Jno. Registers mark of cattle. - (May ?) 1667. 16.14
    Jno. Deceased. Jno Hainie admr. Wm Flowers owes the estate 846
        lb tobo. 11 Jan 1668/9. 3.50
    Jno. Bequest from Jno Lewis. 4 July 1702. 17.223
    Jno. Patents land formerly sold to Wm Thomas now dec'd. 20 Sept
        1709. 17.177
Shawe, Kath: Headright of Lau: Dameron. 21 Feb 1658/9. 2.102
Shaw, Tho. He accused, last March, Antho: Lenton in "scandellous and
        opprobieus terms" of being a Runaway from York.
        20 May 1656. 14.77
    Tho. Freed from levies "by reason of his age and disability".
        24 Aug 1669. 3.69
    Tho. late of Chicacone parish. Inventory of est. 24 Mar 1671/2.
        16.163
Sheapard, Shepherd, etc.
    John, Headright of - Bridges. 20 July 1652. 1.76
    Lewis. Owes Jos Jepsen 650 lb tobo. 21 Jan 1668/9. 3.54
    Lewis. Formerly owned land sold by Tho Brewer Sr to Richd
        Linsfield on S side Div Creek. 21 Oct 1681. 17.204
    Thos. Age 30 yrs or th-abts. 17 Jan 1651/2. 1.70
    Tho: Signs oath to Commonwealth of England. 13 Apl 1652.
        1. 72-3
Sheares, Sheers, Shirs, Shear, etc. In certain instances this name
        appears exactly as though it were Shores. So much
        so that some of my notes were taken as Shores. B.F.
Sheares, Abra: As wit swears to will of Tho Williamson Jr dec'd. 18th
        April 1683. 4.176
    Elizabeth. Aged 56 yrs or th-abts. She and her husband, Geo:
        Knott being forced off the Isle of Kent and forced
        to fly for succour into these parts happened to
        pitch upon that land now called the Glebe land and
        remained there for a time, and would have taken it
        up but it would not be suffered. Your deponent's
        husband requested Mr Cook the surveyor to survey it,
        but he declined "for he said he would not Answer to
        the Governor and Council for it was Glebe land"
        22 June 1669. 16.153

Sheares, Elizabeth (here as Sheeres) widow. Her servant Terrence
        Bourne adj 18 yrs of age. 16 Nov 1698. 4.841
    Sarah. (here as Shiers) relict of William applies for admr
        but refuses to take oath. She thinks James Rich-
        ardson and Eliz his wife have a copy of the will.
        They ordered to produce it. (p.220 the will pro-
        duced). 17 July 1717. 6.219
    Thos. (here as Sheers) Reference to his house. 18 June 1706.
        17.1
    Tho. Wit deed Gaskins to Gaskins. Signed with mark. 16th Jan
        1710/11. 17.80
    Tho. Sells Wm Garlington 7 acres. Sarah Shears wife of Tho.
        relinq her dower rights. 20 June 1711. 18.59
    William. Pre nuptial agreement. Wm Shearer of Cherry Point,
        planter, and Elizabeth Tingey, widow, of Cherry
        Point. "whereas there is a marriage intended" 26
        Jan 1668/9. 16.67
    Wm. (here as Shear) His servant Wm Jetts adj 13 yrs of age.
        10 March 1668/9. 3.58
    Wm. Appointed Constable for Matopony. 22 June 1669. 3.64
    Wm and Eliz his wife disclaim all interest in land at head of
        Yeacomico river (Wiccomicoo River) now in tenure
        of Capt Jno Rogers, which he holds in right of his
        wife Mrs Anne Rogers relict and admr of Mr Francis
        Clay and also relict of Mr Jno Temple. No date
        but recorded 22 Aug 1670. 16.143
    Wm and Eliz his wife sell Tho Matthew 67 acres given by John
        Tingey in his will proved 21 Oct 1661 to abovesd
        Elizabeth then his relict, now the wife of Wm
        Sheares. 22 Feb 1670/1. 16.164
    William. On vestry Chicacone parish. 20 Mar 1671/2. 16.158
    Wm. His servt Edw Smyth came without indentures. To serve 9
        years. 21 Aug 1678. 4.1
    Wm. Atty of Geo Carter. 21 Aug 1678. 4.4
    Wm. Certificate for 600 acres for importing 12 persons. 21st
        Aug. 1678. 4.4
    Wm. His plantation adj Saml Downing. 9 June 1711. 18.93
    Wm. Wit deed Sanders to Ingram. 1 Apl 1712. 18.191
Shelton, Robt (prob a Quaker) Wit will of Tho Steed. 2 Apl 1670.
        16.149
Shelton, Steph: Senr (prob Chilton) To assist settlement of Thomas
        Brewer's estate. 11 June 1697. 17.268
    Tho. Deputy Clerk N. Co. 15 June 1709. 17.19
    Wm. Wit Tho Brewer's will. 11 June 1697. 17.268
Shenton, Jno. Servant to Abra Joyce adj 15 yrs old. 21 Apl 1662. 2.156
Sherwood, Alexr. See entry Adam Yarratt. 22 Oct 1667. 16.25
Sheilds, Tho. Persecuted. See Quakers. 26 June 1660. 2.126
Shirley, Anne. Under 16. Dau of John and Jane Shirley. Bequest of
        clothing from Rebecca Price. 10 Dec 1709.
        18.242

Shirley, Jno. Deed. 60 acres from Jno Adams. 13 Feb 1701/2. Rerecorded 20 Feb 1711/12. 17.151
    Richd. His land adj Jno Shirley. 13 Feb 1701/2. 17.151
    Tho. Deceased. Prob of his will to Richd Shirley. 15 July 1696 4.731
Short, Judith. Orphan of Wm Short decd. Aged 7 the 7th of April last. Bound to Mary Hornsby till 18. Jos Knight Sec. 21 July 1714. 6.56
    Wm. Land sold prior to 4 Apl 1703. 17.12
    Wm. His land adj Jas Knight. 20 Nov 1705. 17.112
    Wm. Formerly sold land to Geo Leasure. 17 Nov 1708. 17.59
    Wm. of St Stephens parish, carpenter. Deed. 1 Oct 1702. Short sells to Charles Dormott of same parish, planter, land, acerage not shown, devised to him by will of John Roach dated 10 Dec 1688. Adj land of Mr Tho Flynt deceased and land of Hugh Stathams. Wit: David Straughm, Samuel Godwyn. Deed rerecorded by Robt Bradley 22 Feb 1710/11. 17.13
    William. Late deceased. His property adj Mr Richd Nutt. 20 June 1711. 18.62
Shorter, William. Aged 30 yrs or th-abts. Says in 1664 "being at Exeter Lodge at Mr Gaskins plantation on that day Jonathan Parker was buried I saw Thomas Barrett with his fist strike Miles Miller, servant to Mr Saffin at least three times in the house". Exact date not shown. Recorded in January 1666/7. 16.10
    Wm. Will proved by oaths of witnesses James Johnson and Hugh Harris. 21 Aug 1678. 4.1
Shortes, Wm. Formerly bought land from Jas Claughton. 17 Feb 1679/80. 17.87
Silvester, Phill: His land surveyed. 20 Jan 1656/7. 14.98
Simmons, Simons, Simonds, Symmons, etc.
    Elizabeth. Deed of Gift to her 3 children John, Elizabeth and Frances Simmons. 15 Aug 1663. 15.112
    Eliz: Will. Entry mutilated. Dated 20 Jan 1663/4. Prob 8th March 1663/4. Various bequests. Refers to her deceased husband Francis Simmons. 15.121
Simons, Edw of Stepney in Co of Middlesex. P of A to his son George of same place to transact business in Virginia. 30 March 1659. 15.20
Simmons, Francis. Bequest to his god-son Tho son of Tho Keene. 16 Apl 1661. 15.93
Symmons, James. His servt Rd Casly adj 15 yrs old. 16 Nov 1698. 4.842
Simmons, Matthew. Servt to Mr Danl Neale adj 11 yrs of age. 21st Dec 1698. 4.847
Simonds, Matthew. Servant to Capt Jno Graham prior to 17 Dec 1712. 17.193

Symmons, Jno. Order that Mr Ambrose Fielding atty for Mr Edw Fielding pay him a feather bed and other goods that "the said Mr Edw Fielding did not send in". 6 April 1669. 3.62

Symons, Jno. Security for Edyth Way admr of her husbands estate asks release from bond. 20 Apl 1681. 4.92

Simpson, Jno. Headright of Wm Wildey. 8 Sept 1662. 2.161

    Percifull. Bought land from Christo: Bayles 10 Dec 1688 and sold it to - - 10 March 1689/90. 19.3

Sims, Ann. Rerecords deed Saml Smith to Tho Sims dated 11 Sept 1703. Capt Edw Sanders her atty. 17.104

    Joane. Age 22 or th-abts. 4 Aug 1665. 15.161

    Sam: Age 31 or th-abts. 4 Aug 1665. 15.161 Also 15.163

    Tho. of St S par, cooper. Pays Saml Smith 5000 lb tobo and one gray horse for 50 acres on Potomac River. 11th Sept 1703. 17.104

Singer, Edwd. of St S par. Will. Dated 6 Jan 1711/12. Probated 18th Feb 1712/13. Very sick and weak. Estate to be div betw wife Jane Singer and Children (not named individually). 18.261

    Edwd. Deceased. Admr bond given by Thos Earth and Jane Earth his wife. Also signed by John Chilton. 18 Feb 1712/13. 18.262

Site, George Jr. Wit Nathl Wildy's will probated 10 June 1730. Lancaster Co records. No 8. p 173

Skinner, Wm. Wit Edw Neale's will. 4 Nov 1700. 17.251

Skipworth, Saml. Went to York well clothed and with a castor hat while he lived with Adam Yarratt. See entry his name. 22 Oct 1667. 16.25 (Note: is a beaver hat. B.F.)

Smith, Smyth, etc.

    Alice. Wife of Saml. 11 Sept 1703. 17.104

    Anne. Wife of Richd. 20 Mar 1677/8. 17.120

    Bryant. Wit will Jno Thomas. 15 Aug 1710. 18.266

    Edw. Headright of Wm Sheares. 21 Aug 1678. 4.4

    Edw: Servant to Wm Sheares. Came without indentures with Capt Tho Smyth. To serve 9 yrs with consent of both parties. 21 Aug 1678. 4.1

    Hen. His land adj Wm Nutt. 4 Feb 1662/3. 17.177

    Hannah. Bond for admr est of Richd Smith deceased. 22 March 1710/11. 18.17

    Hannah. "The deposition of Hannah Smith aged Sixty years or therabouts being sworn saith.
That Nathaniel Bradford of Accomack County came to Henry Franklings house this Deponents former husband and the (said) Bradford had with the said Frankling some Communication whether he would not goe Over with him and see his Sister Joan Bradford and accordingly the said Frankling together with this Deponent his then wife went and Landed at Charles Scareborrows and then went

Deposition of Mrs Hannah Smith (continued)
to one of the said Bradfords plantations and Taried till the said Bradford sent horses for us and wee tooke horse and came to Bradfords house within night and the said Bradfords wife came out and asked If her Brother was come and the said Henry Frankling hearing her voice said that shee (to witt Bradfords wife was his sister saying I know her by her voice and the said Henry with this Deponent his then wife Tarried at the said Bradfords almost Eight weeks during which time they acknowledged each other as Brother and Sister and during the said Franklings life he acknowledged the said Joan Bradford for his Sister and sometime before the said Franklings Death the said Frankling desired Mr Nicho Seaburn to write for him to his Sister Joan Bradford to send her son John Bradford to him and he would Leave him all his Estate when he died but had noe Return and therfor the said Frankling said he thought they slighted his kindness and therefore he would devise his Estate otherwise and further this Deponent saith not

Hannah x Smith "
Sworn before Richd Spann and Richd Hull 17 Aug 1713 Presented in Court by Tho Smith.

Ibid. Deposition of James White, aged 53 yrs or thabts Deposition about as that of Mrs Hannah Smith. Indicates that Henry Franklin and his sister Joan were not born in this country. A quaint entry. Says Henry Frankling was "distasted" with his nephew's behavior. Sworn 16 Sept 1713.   18.335

Smith, John. Persecuted. See Quakers. 26 June 1660. 2.126
    John. To serve Edw Humpston 6 yrs. 10 Feb 1662/3. 2.168
    John of Purton in Gloucester Co. In agreement with Wm Tapptice King of the Wicccomoco Indians in the year 1695/6. 19.95
    John. Wit deed Knight to Knight. 19 June 1710. 17.198
    Joseph. Order that he be pd L 6. Sterling due from est of Tho Urquhart decd. 17 Feb 1714/15. 6.99
    Rainsford. (this name appears as Smith and Smyth) Was left land in St S parish by his grandfather James Austen in his will dated 7 March 1696. 18.84
    Ransford. Wit deed Saml Smith to Wm Nelmes of St S par. 19 Dec 1709. 17.53
    Rainsford of St S par. Sells Tho Gill 50 acres in St S parish. 15 May 1711. 18.83
    Rainsford of St S par. Sells Tho Gill 100 acres in St S par, adj land of sd Smith and Gill. Part of land left him by his grandfather Jas Austen. 15 July 1712. 18.210

Smith, Rainsford. of St S par. Sells Wm Berry 100 acres in St S parish. 17 Nov 1712. 18.255
    Rainsford. Sued by Tho Hobson admr of Wm Winder dec'd. 17 March 1714/15. 6.107
    Rainsford. Eldest son of Saml Smith late of St S par deceased. 18 Jan 1716/17. 6.188
    Rainsford. Swears he wit Phillip Shapleigh's will. 15 May 1717. 6.208

Smith, Richard. Buys 30 acres from Richd Gibble. 4 Mar 1657/8. 15.13
    Rd. Married widow of Jno Hull. See entry Jno Saffin. 29 Novr 1669. 16.62
    Richd. Aged 44 yrs or th-abts. A neighbor of Edw Coles. Depo re witchcraft. 20 May 1671. 16.180
    Richd. of Fairfield Par. Sells Jas Nipper land adj Chicacoan River. 14 Apl 1677. 17.120
    Richd. Deed. 20 March 1677/8. Sells James White one of the orphans of Rd White late of this Co, 200 acres being 1/2 of 400 acres the sd Smith bought from Daniel Chandler 22 Jan 1673/4, the other half being sold to James Nipper of N Co. Anne wife of Richd Smith relinq her dower rights. Wit: Tho Ashley, Tho Webb. Ack 15 May 1678.
    James White assigns above to Geo Dawkins. 4 Sept 1680. Wit: Will Downing, Margtt' x Downing. Recognit 2 March 1681/2.
    Re-recorded 18 July 1711 by Geo Dawkins. 17.120
    Richard. Security for Tho Barnes when Wm orphan of Edw Algood is bound to him. 5 Oct 1687. 4.403
    Richd. Chosen by his brother-in-law John, son of Richd Way, as guardian. 16 Nov 1687. 4.410
    Mr Richard. Attachment agt goods of Steph Gibbons for 5 pair of shoes due by bill dated 4 Jan 1695/6. 15 July 1696. 4.732
    Richd. Wit will of Partin Hudnall. 4 Dec 1698. 17.117
    Richd. Wit deed Salsbury to Barrett. 3 July 1701. 17.95
    Richd. Wit will of Henry Mayes. 12 Apl 1702. 17.205
    Richd. Wit will of Wm Tignor 28 Nov 1698. Proved it by oath 15 April 1702. 17.160
    Richd. Wit deed Williams to Mahan. 15 March 1704/5. 17.67
    Richd. Power of Atty from Dorothy Mahane 16 July 1705. 17.122
    Richd. Wit will of Eliz Bledsoe. 13 Feb 1707/8. 17.55
    Richd. Gift to his wife's children. She formerly Mary Betts. 18 March 1713/14. 6.25
    Richd. Guardian of Jno Davis an orphan. 16 June 1714. 6.40
    Richd. Security, with Sarah relict of Jno Mason decd, for admr of estate. The said Sarah since married Jas. Moon. Smith desires payment of part of the estate to protect the orphans. 19 June 1718. 6.271

Smith, Richd. of G W par buys 50 acres from Josias White of North
                Carolina. 17 Dec 1718. 19.3
    Richd. Signs bond of Elizabeth Taptico admr of Wm Taptico. (Wm
                Taptico was King of the Wiccomicoe or Wiccocom-
                icoe Indians). 17 June 1719. 19.61
    Robert, Signs oath to Commonwealth of England. 13 Apl 1652.
                1.72-3
    Robt. Bought 50 acres in Newmans Neak from Robt Newman and Eliz
                his wife 20 Dec 1652 and assigned it to William
                Cornish 20 Jan 1658/9. 18.125
    Robt. His widow now married to Jno Aires. 6 June 1661. 2.141
    Robt. His widow Anne now widow of Jno Aires. His orphans Robt,
                Nicho:, Eliz: and Jane Smith. Recorded 16 June
                1663. 15.100
    Samuell. Signs oath to Commonwealth of England. 13 Apl 1652.
                1. 72-3
    Mr. Saml. Justice. 20 July 1652. 1.76
    Lt Coll Samuell. Elected Sheriff of N Co at James Citty.
                Test Tho Brereton. 14.78
    Lt Coll Saml. Justice. 20 Nov 1668. 3.48
    Col Saml. Justice. 17 March 1674/5. 3.224
    Lt Col Samll. Justice. 21 Aug 1678. 4.1
    Lt Coll. Abused and his collar bone broken by Xpfer Garlington
                who is heavily fined for it. 2 March 1680/1.
                4.85
    Lt Col Sam. Justice. 18 Apl 1683. 4.176
    Saml. of St S par. Sells Tho Sims 50 acres in St S parish on
                Potomac River. 11 Sept 1703. 17.104
    Saml Sr, Gent, deceased. Late father of Saml Smith Gent of St S
                parish. 19 Dec 1709. 17.53
    Saml, Gent, of St S par. Deed to Wm Nelmes 19 Dec 1709. Acquits
                Nelmes of all debt 16 Dec 1710. 17.53
    Saml. Wit deed Webb to Wright. 12 July 1712. 18.206
    Saml. Guardian of Mary Garratt an orphan. Wm Wildey Sec. 17th
                June 1714. 6.46
    Saml and Jane his wife. She one of the daughters of Ruth Oldam
                deceased. 21 Aug 1717. 6.236
    Sarah. Daughter of Lt Col Saml Smyth receives gift of a cow
                from Richd Iland. 21 July 1656. 14.85
    Tho. Wit deed Wildey to Hobson. 8 Nov 1664. 16.125
    Tho. Wit deed Rice to Saffin. 16 Apl 166-. Recorded 20th Jan
                1666/7. 16.7
    Thos. Marriner. Commander of the 'Salisbury'. 22 July 1668.
                16.86
    Mr. Tho. See entry Jno Saffin. 30 Sept 1669. 16.63
    Capt Tho. Marriner or merchant. See entry Jno Webber. 12 Febry
                1670/1. 16.166
    Capt Thos. Ship Captain. Reference to his last arrival. 21 Aug
                1678. 4.1
    Tho. Wit deed of gift Waddington to Waddington. 20 Oct 1678.
                17.118

Smith, Tho. one of the orphans of Richd Smyth makes choice of his brother Wm Smyth as guardian during his minority. 19 Feb 1678/9. 4.26

Capt Tho. Sued by Rd Thompson for 600 lb tobo for keeping John Stone 'chirurgions Mate' of his ship for 6 weeks while sick. 21 Apl 1681. 4.93

Tho. of St S par. Deed for 100 acres from Tho Leechman. 8 Febry 1708/9. Rerecords it 16 May 1711. 17.91

Thos. Wit deed Geo Hutton to Geo Groves. 8 Jan 1710/11. 18.2

Tho. Rerecords will Hen Franklin. 19 July 1711. 17.124

Tho. Signs appraisal of est of Arther Bridgeman decd. 29 Aug 1711. 18.101

Tho. Signs bond of Jno Meath for admr est of Danl Murphew decd. 19 Dec 1711. 18.116

Thos. Part of entry torn away. Appears that Smith buys from Jno Bradford of Somerset Co Maryland, planter, for 7000 lb tobo, 400 acres in St S parish, formerly in possession of Henry Franklin. Appears to have been inherited by Bradford through a sister of Franklin. The doubt in this entry may be cleared by reference to the deposition of Mrs Hannah Smith. 16 July 1713. 18.327

Tho. His servt Tho Gardner age 11. 20 Feb 1717/18. 6.258

William. Headright of Wm Wildey. 8 Sept 1662. 2.161

Wm. His wife Frances daughter of Roger Walters. 29 Dec 1669. 16.115

Wm. of G W parish. Deed. 18 Nov 1677. Sells Richd Lugg 1/2 of his land. Wit John Moore, Thos -. Acknowledged 17 Apl 1678 by John Smyth attorney of Wm Smyth. Rerecorded 15 Aug 1711 by Rd Cockrell. 17.141

William. His wife Frances dau of Roger Walters. See entry Tho Berry. Sold him land. 14 Feb 1682/3. 17.183

Wm. His land adj Charles Betts. 10 Nov 1694. 17.142

William and Elizabeth his wife. She one of the daughters and coheirs of William Downing Jr deceased. They sell to Saml Blackwell of St S parish, 788 acres in St S par. That Wm Downing Jr by will dated 3rd Sept 1682 left his father's youngest son Charles Downing and his own youngest daughter Margery Downing this land. Charles Downing having died the land reverts to Anne, Elizabeth and Margary. Elizabeth now the wife of Wm Smith and Margary wife of Saml Blackwell, etc. 20 Oct 1712. 18.304

Wm. Ann and Jos Nutt exors of Rd Nutt ack deed to him. 21 Nov 1716. 6.183

Wm. Will presented by Alice Smith his exor. 18 June 1718. 6.267

Soape, Benj. Servt to Wm Jones adj 17 yrs of age. 16 Sept 1696. 4.740

Southerland, Jno. Constable in G W parish. 20 Apl 1681. 4.92

Southern, James. Wit deed Lambert to Myars. 16 Dec 1707. 17.130-5
Sowell, Jno. Deed for 100 acres from Hugh Harris. 20 Apl 1681. 17.251
Span and Spann. Of this family·Rev John Span (Spann) Son of Cuthbert
      of Virginia. Queen's College, Oxford. Matriculated 20 March 1704/5, age 18. King's Bounty, Virginia, 25 Oct 1710. Minister St Stephens parish, Northumberland Co., 1712-22. This from the Colonial Church in Virginia, p. 308. This gentleman must have been much beloved for his name has come down the generations in a number of families. B.F.
Span, Mrs. Godmother of Grace Peterkin. Gives her a calf. 15 Sept 1670. 16.140
Spann, Mrs. Her land adj Jno Bayles in Cupids Neck. 18 Jan 1705/6. 17.180
  Cuthbert. Prays that the estate left by his mother to his brother Richard and to him be divided, his bro Richd being dead. The Court orders him to live on the Plantation "have his subsistance out of the profitts" and not to dispose of it till he be 21. 2 March 1680/1. 4.84
  Cuthbert. Petitions that a division of the estate be made betw him and his brother John. 18 Mar 1684/5. 4.259
  Mr Cuthbert. Exor of Capt Tho Brereton. 23 March 1698/9. 17.189
  Cuthberd. Died betw 16 Aug 1699 and 2 July 1703. 17. 238-243
  Mr. Cuthbert. See entry Capt Tho Brereton. 17. 238-243
  Mrs Dorothy. Will of Dorothy x Spann. Dated 11 Feb 1711/12. Probated 19 March 1711/12. Sick and weak. All bequests are of personal property.
  To grandson Jno Webb son of Giles Webb. To other grandchildren Isaac Webb and Elizabeth Webb children of Giles Webb. To dau Elizabeth Webb and to "my son" Saml Span. To son Richd Span and to his child Francina Span. Exors sons John Span and Saml Span. Wit: Isabell x Samford, Edwd Jones, Samll Samford, 18.157
  Graciana. Gives land to "my eldest son Richard Span" 14 Novr 1671. 16.207
  Graciana. Late wife to Richard Span of Fairfield parish, N Co. Gives to "my two dear sons" Samuel and John Span, servants, silver and other property. Both of her sons under 16. 14 Nov 1671.16.208 She also gives 2 heifers to each of the boys on 15 Nov 1671. 16.209
  Graciana. Gives a mare to her son Cuthbert Span. Also gives cattle for "love and affection" to Edward Read son of John Read. 15 Nov 1671. 16.210
  Richard. Certificate for 100 acres for importing himself and George Aldridge. 20 Feb 1650/1. 1.49

Spann, Richd. His land adj Wm Nutt. 4 Feb 1662/3. 17.177
    Richd of Fairfield parish. Will. Dated 16 Mar 1667/8. Probated 11 Jan 1668/9. To daughter Anne. To sons Cuthbert, Saml, Henry (he under age) and Richard. Wife Grace. Witnesses: Jas Austen, Francis Roberts, Edw Sanders, Wm Morgan. 16.64
    Richd. Father of Cuthbert and Grandfather of Richd Spann and John Spann. Bought 100 acres in little Wicco river from Andrew Bowyer. 10 May 1667. 18.174
    Richd. Deed of Gift. A cow to Ann dau of Rd Gibble. 20 May 1667. 16.17
    Richd. Gives a heifer to Isabell Nipper dau of James Nipper. 8 Sept 1668. 16.55
    Mr Richd. Will proved by oaths of witnesses Edwd Saunder (sic), Fran Roberts and Jas Austen. 11 Jan 1668/9. 3.51
    Richard, deceased. See entry Jno Read and Anne his wife dau of said Richd. 30 Jan 1670/1. 16.159
    Rich: Appraises est of Wm Harcum decd. 17 Dec 1711. 18.171
    Richd of St S parish, Gent. Deed. 19 May 1712. Richd Span sells to Jno Span Gent, 350 acres where he now lives, late the plantation of Cuthbert Span, Gent., the father of the said Richd and John Span. The same land where Richard Span father of Cuthbert Span and grandfather of Richard and John Span lived at time of his death. Is in the Little Wicco River, St S par., etc. Signed Richard Spann. Wit: Giles Webb, Tho Hobson, Saml Spann. 18.174
    Richard. Deed of Gift to his brother Saml Spann. 600 acres in Cupids Neck in St S par. 19 May 1712. 18.181
    Richd. Justice. 17 Aug. 1713. 18.335
    Capt Richd. This day sworn Justice. 17 Feb 1714. 6.94
    Richd. Churchwarden in St S par. 16 Mar 1714/15. 6.102
    Capt Richd. Justice of N Co. 18 Apl 1716. 6.153
    Capt Richd. Justice. 15 May 1717. 6.207
    Capt Richd. Justice. 21 Jan 1719/20. 6.353
    Mr Samll. Chosed by Jno Graham as guardian. 21 Mar 1716/17 6.202
    Mr Sam: His land adj Owen Jones. Wit deed Jones to Lancaster. 10 Oct 1718. 19.8
Sparkes, Wm. Deposition, age not shown. Date also not shown but recorded latter part of 1664. 15.135
Sparks, Wm. Servant to Tho Hobson to serve extra time for running away. 10 Mar 1668/9. 3.58
Spe, George. Wit Deed of Gift Goohe to Johnson. 4 Dec 1663. 16.2
Speke, Ann. Wife of Tho Speke. Age 42 yrs or th-abts. 4 Nov 1653. 14.36
    Mrs Anne. Wife of Thos Speke. At the house of Col Mottrom when Jno Kaye was there prior to 20 Jan 1655. 14.67

Speks, Mr Thomas, Justice. 24 Aug 1650. 1.41
    Tho: Signs oath to Commonwealth of England. 13 Apl 1652. 1.72
    Mr. Tho. Justice. 20 July 1652. 1.76
    Tho. Gent. Aged 30 yrs or th-abts. 4 Nov 1653. 14.36
    Tho. Gives a heifer to John Langford. 25 Sept 1654. Westmorland Co Records. 1653-9. p.28
Spellman, Clement and Ralph of Westmorland Co. See entry Jas Jones, prior to 19 Aug 1707. 17.153
    Mrs Hannah. Presentment for absenting herself from Church dismissed. 18 Nov 1713. 6.5
Spence, David. Signs appraisal of est of Jas Rogers decd. 19 Sept 1711. 18.102
    David. Signs inv of Danl Murphew decd as appraisor. 16th Jan 1711/12. 18.144
    David and Ann his wife. Their suit as admrs of Nicho: Edwards deed agt Frances Clifford to next Court. 17 June 1714. 6.47
    David and Ann. Ordered to answer petition of Charles Edwards son of Nicho: Edwards. 16 Sept 1719. 6.337
    Patrick. Wit deed Cornhill to Cralle. 21 Dec 1711. 18.145
    Patrick. Robert Carter of Lancaster Co Esqr sends Greeting. Whereas suits are likely to be raised betw Capt Geo Eskridge of Westmorland Co, one of the exors of Patrick Spence dec'd and guardian to Mary Spence sister of the said Patrick and only surviving daughter of Alexander Spence of said Co deceased, and Mr Richd Neale of Northumberland Co and Mr Mathew Mason of the Province of Maryland the husbands of the two other daughters of the said Alexander Spence, both deceased, in Right of their children by the said daughters. That Robert Carter settle properties involved in the estate.
    The "said Patrick Dyed - illegible - he being but of the age of 19 years", his land should by Common Law descend to his 3 sisters or their heirs. Dated 27 May 1712. 18.320
    Patrick Spence lately departed this life age 19. 15 July 1713. 18.322
Spencer, Leonard. Wit marriage of Jno Merryday to Ann Nash on 11 Sept 1656. 14.90
    Nicho: Referred to as brother in will of Richd Wright. 16 Aug 1663. 15.114
    Hon. Nicholas. Manages est for orphans of Major Jno Mottrom. 5 Oct 1687. 4.405
    Robert. Wit Hancock Lee's codicil 18 May 1709. Proves it by oath 20 July 1709. 17.29
Spicer, Wm. He and Tho Coggin called to testify in cause betw Tho Rice and Jno Essex. Each pd 50 lb tobo. 20 Feb 1651/2. 1.50

Spicer, Wm. Signs oath to Commonwealth of England. 13 Apl 1652. 1.72
    Wm. Aged 38 yrs or th-abts. - Sept 1652. 14.11
Spiller, David. Signs oath to Commonwealth of England. 13 Apl 1652. 1.72
    David. Guardian of orphans of Jno Dennis. 13 Apl 1657. 14.105
    David. Will. Date missing but recorded 21 Oct 1658. Entry badly damaged but this perfectly clear "I give my whole estate to be equally devided betweene my sonnes Jno Swanson Richard Dennis Pasco Dennis Jno Dennis Excepting one Cowe called Florence which I alsoe give - my youngest sonne Jno Dennis". "I give unto Susanna Holling my Brothers Childe" a cow. Tobacco to James Magregory. Witnesses Tho Gaskins, Jno Tayler.
    Appraisal of estate follows. This headed "by Nathaniell Holling". Dated 21 8br 1658. (Oct). 15.11
Spiller, Jno. Appraisor of est of Robt Seagrave decd. 20 Mar 1649/50. 1.48
Spilman, Ralph. Arrested at suit of Dr Rd Pemberton for 650 lb tobo. 21 Apl. 1681. 4.93
    Tho: Pd 400 lb tobo from County levy (under Fairfield parish) "To the French Dr for looking after Tho Spilman". This entry does not seem clear. Actually the French doctor was pd for looking after Spilman. 5 Nov 1668. 3.47
    Tho. "being a very poore and impotent man" to be pd 600 lb tobo for maintenance. 20 Nov 1668. 3.49
    Tho. also Mary Spilman. Headrights of Mrs Jane Wildey. 19th Oct 1681. 4.105
Sprigg, Kath: deceased. See entry Saml Griffin. 2 Feb 1702/3. 17.213
Spring Cove. Wicco par. Adj land of Tho Williams. 15 May 1705. 17.252
Spry, Jno. Wit will of Tho Webb 11 Sept 1702. 17.5
    Jno. Wit deed Smyth to Gill. 15 July 1712. 18.212
    Jno. Granted permission to build a water mill on Lambdons Creek. 17 Feb 1714/5. 6.99
Squire, Jno. Has served his full term to estate of Col Rd Lee and myselfe. Signed Francis Lee. 5 Jan 1670/1. 16.149
Staney, Tho. Age 30 or thereabouts. 2 Mar 1680/1. 4.85
Stanford, Edw: Headright of Law Dameron. 21 Feb 1658/9. 2.102
Stanley, Francis. Makes oath regarding Mrs Mary Barnes' child held by Richd Cox. 19 Oct 1681. 4.106
Standley, Jno. Age 35 or th-abts. 20 March 1655/6. 14.73
Stanley, John. Signs bond Honor Dermott admr of Hugh Dermott. 17 Dec. 1712. 18.241
Stanly, Jno and Eliz his wife, sister of Jno Wall late of this County dec'd. Their suit agt Dan'l Dunaway and Jane his wife late widow of the sd Jno Wall dec'd to the next Court. 18 Mar 1713/4. 6.29

Statham, Hugh. To raise and educate children and step children of Jno Parse. No date but will recorded 20 May 1667. 16.16

Hugh. Went with Mrs Hanah Abram to the Indian Cabbin to obtain a servant. See entry Adam Yarratt. 22 Oct 1667. 16.26

Hugh. His land ref to. 1 Oct 1702. 17.13

Staynies Neck. Adj land of Wm Harcum. Prior to 15 Mar 1709/10. 17.111

Steed, Tho. (prob a Quaker). Will dated 2 Apl 1670. Prob 20th Dec 1670. To wife Sarah all estate except a colt to Jno Yealke. To friend Jno Cussins 50 shillings for a ring. To friend Thomas Delahay 10 shillings. Wiwe extrx. Cussins overseer. Wit Robt Shelton, Eliz Carter. 16. 149

Steevens, Stevens, Stephens, etc.

Steevens, Arthur. Agreement 3 Nov 1666 with Bennett Madring. 1 Dec 1666. 16.24

Arth: Servant to Bennett Madrim. 22 Oct 1667. 16.27

Stevens, Jne. P of A from Lt Col Henry Fleet. 12 Sept 1657. 15.10

Stephens, Mary. Headright of Rd Haynie. 15 July 1696. 4.733

Stevens, Ralph. Assigns land to Jno Garner. 1 Apl 1667. 16.15

Stephens, Ralph. Appointed Constable Cherry Point. 18 May 1687. 4.394

Steppman, Jonoth: Also appears as Stepping in same entry. "Jonathan Stepping dec'd lately come forth of England in Capt Samll Tilghman March 30th 1657". Inventory shows exactly clothing and equipment brought by a colonist at this date. 14.104

Steptoe, Jne. Exor of Jno Eustace. Bequest from him. 23 Dec 1701. 17.245

Jno. Wit will of Jno Lewis. 4 July 1702. 17.223

Jno. Signs inv of Hancock Lee. No date but rerecorded 21st March 1710/11. 17.38

Mr. Jno. Justice. 17 Feb 1713/14. 6.17

John and Eliz his wife, late Eliz Eustace widow of Jno Eustace of N Co. 16 Nov 1719. 19.73

Sterling, Walter. Servt to Tho Ashburne adj 13 yrs old. 23 July 1714. 6.65

Stick Branch. Adj land of Jne Bayles in Cupids Neck. 18 Jan 1705/6. 18.180

Stiles, Robt. Servant to Geo English adj betw 16 and 17 yrs of age. 14 Nov 1660. 2.134

Stone, Dr John. Rd Thompson petitions Judgt agt Capt Tho Smith for 600 lb tobo "for entertaining John Stone Chirurgions Mate, of the said Capt Smith his ship six weekes sick at his house" 21 Apl 1681. 4.93

Stowe, Tho. Headright of Mr Robt King. 10 March 1661/2. 2.154

Stowell, Jno. Wit P of A Madring to Flowers. 1 Dec 1666. 16.24

Straughan, David. Wit deed Barnes to Reeves. 21 Oct 1702. 17.200
David. Wit deed Dermott to Gill. 20 Mar 1702/3. 17.119
David. Buys 75 acres in Mattaponi from Phillip Bussle and Jane his wife. 15 Sept 1703. 17.233
David. Gent. Buys 100 acres in Mattaponi Neck from Richd Booth. 15 Sept 1703. 17.232
David. Wit deed Bayles to Gill. 18 Jan 1705/6. 17.180
David. Wit deed Gooch to Neale. 7 Apl 1706. 17.195
David. Wit deed Jones to Rogers. 19 Aug 1707. 17.153
David. Wit deed Lambert to Myars. 16 Dec 1707. 17.130-5
David. Wit deed Claughton to Claughton. 18 Jan 1707/8. 17.89
David. Wit deed Wiggins to Tulles. 8 July 1708. 17.204
David. Wit will of Tho Hall Sr. 10 Feb 1708/9. 17.163
David. Swears to Tho Hobson's statement. 20 Apl 1709. 17.21
David. Wit will Vincent Garner. 30 Sept 1710. 18.12
David. Wit deed Rogers to Opie. 16 Feb 1711/12.
David. Swears he wit will of Edwd Woolridge decd. 16 March 1714/15. 6.100
David. Rerecords deed Booth to Straughn. 17 Mar 1716. 17.232
David. Tho Preist his servant. 19 Feb 1717/18. 6.255

Streator, Streeter, etc.
Streator, Capt Tho. Married the relict of Col Tho Burbage prior to 17 March 1657. 15.4
Streeter, Barth: As witness. 18 June 1706. 17.3
Barth: Wit will Barth: Dameron. 8 Aug 1708. 17.57
Tho: Wit Deed of Gift Norman to Norman. 27 Aug 1705. 17.223

Stretton, Tho. Wit delivery Gooch to Neale. 11 Oct 1706. 17.195
Tho. Wit deed Wildey to Chichester. 19 Nov 1706. 17.224
Tho. Wit deed Wildey to Ingram. 13 Dec 1706. 17.24
Tho. Eit deed of gift Webb to Wornum. 16 May 1707. 17.209
Tho. Deputy Clerk. 15 June 1709. 17.127
Tho. Wit deed Saml Smith to Wm Nelmes of St S par. 19 Dec 1709. 17.53
Tho. Deposition. Age not shown. Swears Richd Nelmes' will was proved in Court. Sworn 16 May 1711. 17.99
Tho. Rerecords deed Lee to Lee. 16 May 1711. 17.60
Tho. Deposition. "Aged thirty yeares or thereabouts". That at a Court for N Co 15 Mar 1709/10, this deponent then Deputy Clerk, the will of Mr Wm Harcum was proved by oaths of Tho Gill, Jno Way and Wm Godwyn. Agrees with Tho Gill in detail of will. 20 June 1711. 17.111
Tho. Wit deed White to Davis. 16 July 1711. 18.88
Tho. Deposition. "aged thirty yeares or thereabouts". (15 Aug Regards Downing properties. 17.125   (1711
Tho. Wit deed Jonathan to Isaac Edwards. (This is an important item to anyone interested) 20 Sept 1711. 18.107

Stretton, Tho. Deceased. Bond for admr of his est signed by Robt x Davis. 19 Dec 1711. 18.115

Sudden, Tho. (Sutton ?) His land adj Dennis Cornhill in St S par. 21st Dec 1711. 18.144

Sudler, Tho. Wit will Simon Richardson. 17 March 1674/5. 3.114

Sullivan in various spellings.

Swillivant, Danl. Sued by Mr Richd Kenner for wages due his son Rhodon Kenner. 18 Nov 1687. 4.414

Suilevant, Danl. of St S par. Will. Dated 29 Aug 1704. Prob 22 Febry 1704/5. To my Cousin George Hutton (under 21) the plantation at Rappahannock except 100 acres to Cousin Rebecca Hutton. To Philip Rogers and Vincent Cox land bought of Tho Freshwater, 4031 acres, except 200 acres to James Thomas near where he now lives. They exors. Gives to Vincent Cox his servant boy Richd Baker. To Isabella Rogers. To Ann Cox. His Cousin Margaret to inherit lands if George and Rebecca Hutton fail in heirs and if she fail in heirs the lands to James Rogers and Winnefred Cox. Wit: Jno Kean, James Thomas, Joseph Willgrass. Rerecorded 21 March 1721/22 by Danl McCarty. 17.261. (All actual relationships shown in original entry are shown in this abstract)

Swillevend, Timothy. Wit will Jno Bisick. 25 March 1706. 17.173

Summars, Henry. Proves, as witness, will of Henry Wicker dec'd. 22nd June 1669. 3.65

Suningberke, Mr Florentine. Admr of his estate to Jno Mottrom, Gent. 10 Jan 1650/1. 1.46

Sutton see Sudden.

Sutton, Richd. Judgt agt him to Mr Richd Ward for 400 lb tobo. 24 Aug 1669. 3.69

    Richd. Wit deed Williams to Lattimore. 26 Sept 1702. 17.252-4

    Richd of Wicco par. Will. Dated 1 Feb 1702/3. Probated 17 Mar 1702/3. Eldest son Wm Sutton, Sons Jno and Wm. Dau Mary. Whole estate to Anne Sutton. The will does not state that she is his wife or the mother of his children. We would presume that she was. Wit: Tho English, Dennis Conway, Rerecorded 16 July 1712 by Jno Taylor. 17.172

    Richd. Wit deed Mayes to Dameron. 15 May 1711. 18.41

    Richd. Wit P of A Alex Cummins of Stafford Co to Tho Berry to ack sale of land in N Co. 3 Dec 1711. 18.120

    Wm. Wit deed Champion to Curtis. 3 Dec 1709. 17.186

    Wm. (here as Suttum) Wit deed Cummings to Dameron. 4 Dec 1711 18.117

Surveys. List of surveys made in Northumberland County from June 1710 to June 1711. 18.165. List from June 1711 to June 1712. 18.225

Swaine, Tho. Age 22 yrs or th-abts. 23 Oct 1658. 15.14
    Tho. Age 21 or th--abts. 23 Nov 1658. 15.14
    Thos of Northumberland Co. "being a poor man and near related to the said John Ingram and being destitute of meanes whereby to subsist and having noe place of Residence", Ingram pays 1000 lb tobo and Swaine becomes his servant for 7 yrs, etc. 28 Dec 1712. 18.258

Swainie, Isaac. "an Orphant child" of Charles Swainie dec'd, abt 3 yrs old, is bound to Mary Davis till 21. 12 March 1713/14. 6.18

Swan, Tho. His nuncupative will probated by oaths of witnesses Robert Sech and Jno Coutanceau. 11 Jan 1668/9. 3.51
    (He left his chest and all therein to his landlord Capt Jno Rogers)

Swanson, Jno. Ref to as "my sonne" in David Spiller's will. Was prob his stepson raised by him. The will probated 21 Oct 1658. 15.11
    Jno. His servt Jno Travers adj 10 yrs of age. 21 Aug 1678. 4.1
    Jno, deceased. Prob of his will to his widow Mary Swanson. 17 Sept 1684. 4.239
    Jno. deceased. Referred to as having sold land to Wm Coppage Sr. 4 June 1698. 17.15
    Jno. Wit deed Champion to Curtis. 3 Dec 1709. 17.186
    Jno. Next of kin to Jno Nipper deceased. 18 June 1718. 6.270
    Richd. Declines to act as exor of Mary Bryan. Jno Swanson and Dennis Swanson appointed. 17 June 1714. 6.45
    Richard. Guardian and nearest friend to Charles and Mary Prichard. Saml Heath ordered to appear and answer his petition. 20 Aug 1718. 6.275
    Richd. Guardian of Charles and Mary Prichard. That Mary Bryant left certain property to them which was committed to John and Dennis Swanson who delivered it to Charles Prichard father of Charles and Mary. The property then came to John Nipper exor of Charles and since the death of Nipper came to Saml Heath. Swanson desires the property delivered to his wards. 21 Aug 1718. 6.277

Swanson's land. Near the Church in Wicco parish. Adj land of Thomas Bonum. 20 Sept 1709. 17.177

Sweethall. Adj Mulberry Point and Fleet's Point. 23 March 1698/99. 17.189

Sweetland, Ric: Wit will of Andrew Delabriere. 24 June 1670. 16.137

Tabb, Humfry. Admr of the est of Simon Domebielle ordered to pay him a debt of 450 lb tobo. 10 Jan 1650/1. 1.46
Tanner, Tho. Judgt agt him 2474 lb tobo to Geo Carter. 21 Aug 1678. 4.4
Tapscott, Henry and Ann his wife. Richd Niggins bound apprentice to them. 16 May 1711. 18.21
Tapscot, Henry. Wit will of Peter Hammond. 18 Jan 1711/12. 18/151.
Tapscott, Henry of G W par. Buys from Jno Embry and Sarah his wife, 50 acres, part of 1000 acres formerly in poss. of Tho Williams dec'd as by patent dated 11 Feb 1663/4. On S side Wicco River. 19 Feb 1711/12. 18.149
    Henry. Complaint that he has failed to teach Jno Maddison the trades of "Cooper, Carpenter and Joyner" 18 May 1715. 6.109
Taptico, Elizabeth. Bond L 200. Sterling as admr of Wm Taptico dec'd. Signed also by Richd Smith and Wm Morris. 17 June 1719. 19.61
Tapptico, William. "King of the Wiccocomoco Indians". This entry in regard to a land agreement with John Smith of Purton in Gloucester County in the year 1695/6. "Wm Tapptico Elinder his wife and Wm Taptico Junr". Witnesses: Maurice Jones, Bridgett Ward. 31 Dec 1718. 19.95
Taptico, Wm. Admr of est to Eliz Taptice. 17 June 1719. 6.321
Tarpley, Mr. See entry Rev Jno Farnefold. 3 July 1702. 17.234
    Elizabeth. Dau in law to Rev Jno Farnefold. 3 July 1702. 17.234
    John the younger, grandson of Jno Tarpley Senior. 19 Febry 1718/19. Lancaster Co records. No. 12, Deeds etc 1726-1736. p 60.
    John, Gent. Surviving exor of Mary Nutt. 18 June 1719. 6.325
Taylor. This name appears throughout the records either as Taylor or as Tayloe. Tayloe being the old manner of spelling the name. All quibbling on this subject may be settled by one word - NONSENSE.
Taylor, Elizabeth. Deposition. Age not shown. She is referred to on p 26 as "goody Taylor". The deposition is in regard to Arth Steevens servant of Bennett Madrim. No date but is of 22 Oct 1667. 16.27
Taylor, John. Wit David Spiller's will. The will probated 21 Oct 1658. 15.11
    Jno and Anne. See entry Jno Bradley. 21 Oct 1658. 2.94
    John. Deposition. Age not shown. Says when he was servant to Mr Garlington, about 5 yrs since, etc. - 1664. 15.136
    John. Assigned interest by Jas Hill in certain land. 10 Augt 1667. 16.70
    John. Trustee of will of Andrew Delabriere. Also wit the will. 24 June 1670. 16.137

Taylor, Mr Jno Jr. Exhibited 56 yds "of Linnen Cloth about three quarters wide" and took oath it was his own growth and manufacture. 16 Mar 1683/4. 4.226

Jno. Wit assignment Champion to Mahane. 5 Feb 1704/5. 17.71

Jno. Divides land betw Capt Jno Howson and the orphan of Capt Wm Howson. 15 Apl 1706. 17.42

Jno. Wit deed Williams to Mahane. 25 Nov 1706. 17.67

Jno. Wit deed Jno Crafford to Wm Davis. 20 Dec 1706. 17.94

Jno. Wit will Tho Williams. 11 Mar 1706/7. 17.72

Jno. Wit bond Tho Byram. 19 May 1708. 17.72

Jno. See entry Wm Howard. Late 1709 or early 1710. 17.236

Mr John. Justice of Northumberland Co. 18 July 1711. 18.70

Jno. Justice. 19 Sept 1711. 18.101

Jno. Divides land betw Tho Eves and Graves Eves, sons of Wm Eves dec'd as by his will proved 20 June 1688. To son Thos Eves 80 acres, etc. 21st Jan 1711/12. 18.215

Jno. Rerecords will dated 1702/3 of Rd Sutton. 16 July 1712. 17.172

Jno. Deputy Clerk of Northumberland Co. 18 Oct 1712. 18.250

Jno. Blacksmith. Fined for absenting himself from Church. 21st Jan 1713/14. 6.15

Jno. Runaway servant to Jno Copedge ret'd by Wm Barnes. 22nd Sept 1715. 6.135

Jno. Blacksmith. of St S par. Fined for 2 mos ab from Church. Wm Mason enters himself as security. 23 Sept 1715. 6.138. He is again presented for absence from Church 15 May 1717. 6.202

Tayloe, Joseph. Wit deed Mahane to Chilton. 16 July 1705. 17.122

Jos. Wit deed Dunaway to Chilton. 3 Sept 1708. 76.78

Jos. Wit deed Hill to Chilton. 15 June 1709. 17.78

Mr Jos. His line adj Edwd Sanders. 13 July 1711. 18.73

Taylor, Joseph. Appears in bond concerning property taken by him from "John Right" (Wright). 9 Mar 1712/13.18.287

Lazarus. Wit deed Mahane to Love. 21 Feb 1704/5. 17.51

Lazarus, Jr. Wit agreemt Bickley and Ingram. 2 July 1707. 17.24

Lazarus. Deposition. Age 44 yrs or th-abts. Says in 1703 he appraised the estate of Wm Fletcher late of this County deceased, etc. 18 July 1711.18.91

Peter. Sold land to Jno Robinson prior to 13 Jan 100/1. 17.108

Tho. Age 21 or th-abts. 22 June 1671. 16.185

Tho. Divides land betw Capt Jno Howson and the orphan of Capt Wm Howson. 15.Apl 1706. 17.42

Tho. als Wm Harmwood. Runaway servant to Mark Harden ret'd by Wm Barnes of Maryland. 22 Sept 1715. 6.135

William. Gives his son William Taylor a calf. 26 Oct 1665. 15.167

Taylor, William with consent of his wife Anne sells Wm Addams 240 acres 16 Jan 1670/1. 16.151

Wm. Tho Grinstead age 7 and Jno Grinstead age 4 bound to him till 21 with consent of their father. Also as Grimstead. 18 March 1684/5. 4.256

Tayloe, Col Wm. See entry Saml Griffin. 2 Feb 1702/3. 17.213

Taylor's land. Adj Rd Gibble. 16 Jan 1671/2. 17.156

Teague, Mr Jno. Master of the ship Phenix of Bristol. 14 Feb 1669. 4.26

Temple, Mrs Anne. Now married to Francis Clay. There is 500 lb tobo due her from the estate of Jno Washington dec'd. 5 Sept 1660. 2.130

Dorothy. This name also appears as Templer in the entry. Wit the will of Rd Nelmes Sr. 13 Apl. 1706. 17.98

Tempest, Edw. Arrested Wm Bedlam (who did not appear) for debt. 20 Feb 1651/2. 1.50

Temple, Jno. His widow married Francis Clay. 8 Oct 1662. 2.164

Mr Jno. His relict Anne, also relict of Mr Francis Clay, now wife of Capt Jno Rogers. No date but recorded 22 Aug 1670. 16.143

Templar, William. Ordered to clear the many trees he has fallen across the highway. 18 Mar 1684/5. 4.258

Terrell see Turrill.

Terrell, Arthur. Certificate for 200 acres for importing: Himselfe, Eliza: his wife, Arthur Terrell and Eliza Terrell. 20 Feb 1651/2. 1.50

Tew, Eliz. Buys a heifer from Tho Brereton. 23 Jan 1671/2. 16.216

Jno. Files mark for cattle. 18 Dec 1651. 1.70

John. Signs oath to Commonwealth of England. 13 Apl 1652. 1.72-3

Jno and his wife Grace Baldridge als Tew and widow of Major Thos Baldridge of Westmorland Co, obtain letters of admr for Tho Baldridge's est. Witnesses Walter Brodhurst, Tho Wilsford. 21 Aug 1654. Westmorland Co records. 1653-9. p 28

Thacker, C. C. Signs patent for Tho Gascoine. 15 Sept 1649. 17.80

Thackrell, Thos. Wit Dennis Conaway's will. 15 June 1709. 17.19

Thatcher, Wm. with Andrew Bouer buys land from Tho Brewer and sells it to Jno Essex prior to 16 March 1674/5. 18.39

Theriatt, Dominick of Curratomen, Lancaster Co. Buys a mare from Richd Perce (also as Peirce). 16 Jan 1663/4.16.6

Dominick. P of A to Tho Maddison to represent him at N Court in suit agt Richd Pearce. 9 May 1665. 16.19

Thomas, Danll. Servt to Mr Tho Matthews adj 9 yrs of age. 17 March 1674/5. 3.224

Eliz: Headright of Wm Sheares. 21 Aug 1678. 4.4

Henry. Age 20 yrs. 6 March 1668/9. 16.84

Hump: Wit will Steph Wells 31 Oct 1712. Proved by his oath 21 Jan 1718/9. 19.12

Thomas, James. Wit will of Danl Suilevant who leaves him 200 acres. 29 Aug 1704. 17.261

Jeremiah. Servant to Walter Dinnie adj 17 yrs old. 19th Jan 1675/6. 3.249

Jno. Servant to James Dasheild coming without indentures adj to be 13 yrs old. 20 Apl 1660. 2.112

Jno. Age 17 or th-abt. 4 Aug 1665. 15.163

Jno. Wit deed Moore to Canaday. 5 Sept 1707. 17.47

Jno. Will. Dated 15 Aug 1710. Prob 18 Feb 1712/13. Sick and weak. Sons Richd, Wm, Peter, John, all to have land. Wife Eliz'a. 2 daus Eliz and Jane, under age. Gives to dau Elizabeth "my Orphant Girle Anne Fitzgerreld". 18.266

Jno. Court order that road be laid out through his land for Tho Laine. 18 June 1712. 18.210

Jno. Complains of Rebecca Fulk, an orphan bound to him, who continually runs away. 16 March 1714/15. 6.100

Jno. of Wicco par. Fined for 2 mos ab from Church. Prob a Quaker. 23 Sept 1715. 6.138

Jno. Nuncupative will presented by Robt Rowland and proved by oaths of James Magoone and Mary his wife. Admr granted. 19 June 1718. 6.272

Jno. His relict, Tamor Thomas, swears he left no will. Admr granted. 19 Aug 1719. 6.327

Mrs Mary. "Upon the petition of Mrs Mary Thomas Widdow of Mr William Thomas It is ordered that a feather bed, Bolster pillowes, one blanchett one Ham'ock one Rugg, a Suite of Curtains and Gallens, two paire of sheets, one pillow beare and one Warmeing pann, be allowed to her for her Paraphanalia. 16 Oct 1676. 4.3

Mrs Mary. Chosen by her son Edward Sanders as his guardian. 21 Aug 1678. 4.2

Mrs Mary. Com of admr of est of her dec'd husband Mr Wm Thomas. 21 Aug 1678. 4.2

Mrs. Mary. Gives bond 70000 lb tobo as admr of est of her dec'd husband Wm Thomas. Mr Wm Downing and Mr Christ: Neale go security. 16 Oct 1678. 4.6

Richd. Wit deed Moore to Canaday. 5 Sept 1707. 17.47

Rog: Headright of Tho Lane. 23 June 1669. 3.66

Roger. Wm Flowers ordered to deliver him a maid servant. 21st Nov 1677. 4.2

Tho of St S par sells Jno Hadock 100 acres in branches of Cupids Creek. 18 Oct 1712. 18.249

Tho and Sarah his wife. She dau and sole heir of Middleton Salmon dec'd swear he left no will. They obtain admr. 16 Nov 1715. 6.142

William. There appear to have been two persons of this name at the same period in Northumberland Co. William Thomas who was a Justice and William Thomas referred to in the records as the "Fiddler".

Thomas, William. Headright of Jno Vaughan. 20 Nov 1651. 1.67
    Will: Signs oath to Commonwealth of England. 13 Apl 1652. 1.72
    Wm. Age 25 yrs or th-abt. Says he pd Mr Hallowes 1800 lb tobo
        the last year and took a bill from him
        which he passed to Wm Freake. 21 Oct 1654.
        Westmorland Co records. 1653-9. p 28
    Wm. Paid from Co levy "For his Burgess charges". 1 Nov 1656.
        14.94
    Wm. Wit deed Gibble to Smyth. 4 March 1657/8. 15.13
    Wm. Wit Mich: Brooke's statemt re Wm Wildey. 28 Mar 1658.
        15.14
    Wm "Fidler". Dif betw "Wm Thomas, Fidler" and Francis Clay
        admr of Wm Bacon gent dec'd, regarding
        land decided by Jury in favor of Clay.
        21 July 1660. 2.128
    mr Wm. Justice of Northumberland Co. 18 Sept 1660. 2.132
    Wm. Justice. 14 Nov 1660. 2.133
    William. "by the oathes of mr Wm Thomas and mr John Powell that
        William Thomas of Yeocomoco fidler" stands
        indebted to Saml Bonham for rent of land,
        etc. 14 Nov 1660. 2.133
    Wm. His land adj Wm Nutt. 4 Feb 1662/3. 17.177
    Wm. Buys 50 acres from Jno Johnson in April 1660. Also sells
        279 acres to Rd Way 12 March 1663/4. 17.91
    Wm. His land adj Jno Hudnall. 25 July 1665. 17.28
    Wm. P of A to "my Loving wife Rebeccah Thomas". 5 Apl 1667.
        16.21
    Wm. To value buildings on land to be retd by Geo Hutton to
        Antho: Lynton. 16 Oct 1676. 4.7
    Mr Wm. deceased. Signed bill on 11 Apl 1678 for 607 lb tobo
        to Capt Henry Roach. 21 Aug 1678. 4.2
    Wm. deceased. Wm Flower trustee for children of Dr Edw Sanders
        demands cattle from his estate. 17 Oct 1678.
        4.10
    Wm. Ebenezer and Edw Sanders admrs of Mrs Mary Thomas who was
        admr of Mr Wm Thomas, arrested at suit of
        Edwd White and Benj Cotman husbands of Mary
        and Elizabeth daughters of Mrs Mary Thomas
        for their share of the estate, etc. 17th
        Sept 1684. 4.244
    Wm. deceased. His dau Rebecca wife of Tho Bonum. 20 Sept 1709.
        17.177
    Wm. Land in Wicco par on S side G W river descended from him
        to Rebecca Bonum his dau and sole heir.
        This appears as a former tfr of the land
        in a deed Hudnall to Lunsford dated 16th
        Sept 1712. 18.227
Thompson, Elizabeth. Married Peter Presly betw 20 Feb 1663/4 and 20th
        June 1664. 15.124
    George. To take inv of est of his friend Edw Walker. 2 Dec
        1650. 14.92

Thompson, George. His wife was told by James Claughton of his unfaithfulness to her, etc. Henry Haler also made a deposition in the case as did George Nott. 20 Feb 1650/1. 1.58

Mary, Boquest from Saml Griffin. 2 Feb 1702/3. 17.213

Phillip. orphan of Simon Thompson, he being 11 yrs old last June 11th, bound to Ann Heath. He to learn trade of shoemaker. 18 Nov 1719. 6.345

Richd and Sarah. Their guardians are Geo Cololough and Ursula his wife. (Mrs Ursula Cololough being their mother). 29 Sept 1657. 15.8

Richd. His widow, Ursula, married next Col Jno Mottrom and next Geo Cololough. 20 Nov 1658. 2.95

Richd. See depositions of William and Eliz Grinsted and of Francis Clay Gent. 10 Oct 1660. 15.61

Richd. Orphan. Having arrived at legal years to choose a guardian selects Mr Tho Willoughby. 8 Sept 1662. 2.161

Richd. Patented 48 acres in Northumberland Co 15 Dec 1651. This sold by Tho Willoby and Sarah his wife and Elizabeth Thompson to Wm Thomas. 20 Feb 1663/4. 15.124
See entry Peter Presly who married Elizabeth Thompson on the same page.

Richd. Age 33 yrs or th-abts. 4 Aug 1665. 15.161

Rd. Wit deed Rice to Saffin. 16 Apl 166-. Recorded 20 Janry 1666/7. 16.7

Richd. Abused by Jno Walters who ack his scandlemongering in Court. 22 Oct 1667. 16.31

Richd. Says he entered a survey of 188 acres at Jamestown for Rich Rice 7 March 1665. Sworn 25th Aug 1669. 16.94
Rd Coke relinquishes all right to the 188 acres. 16 Sept 1671. 16.200

Richd. Petitions judgt agt Capt Tho Smith for 600 lb tobo for care of Jno Stone when sick. 21 Apl 1681. 4.93

Sim. Wit deed Hill to Taylor. 10 Aug 1667. 16.70

Simon. Wit Rev Jno Farnefold's will. 3 July 1702. 17.234

Simon. Inventory of estate. Dated 16 June 1714. Signed by Dennis Conway, Tho Hughlett and Jno Conway. Presented by Mr Jno Pope admr of Simon Thompson deceased, the original being burned, etc. 17.221

Mrs Ursula (who married 2nd Col Jno Mottrom and 3rd Major Geo Cololough. B.F.) of Kiquohton widdo of Richd Thompson gent, gives cattle to her children. To son Richd (under 21). To daus Sarah and Elizabeth Thompson. Wit Henery Poole and Wm Perry. 25 March 1649. 15.61

Thompson, Wm. Will. Dated 13 Dec 166-. Prob. 20 Jan 1665/6. To daus
                Mary and Elizabeth. 15.175
Thornton, Dr. Margaret Pine his patient. 20 Aug 1719. 6.334
        Jer: As witness proves will of Robt Pritt. 18 March 1684/5.
                4.255
Thornbury, Wm. Wit deed of gift Rodham to Neale. 17 Nov 1666. 16.22
           Wm. Wit deed of gift Rodham to Neale. 17 Dec 1666. 16.22
Threlkeld, Christopher. Will. Dated 10 Feb 1707/8. Prob 16 Jan 1711/12.
                Wife Mary. Sons Wm, Christopher, Henry, James.
                Dau Elizabeth. All children under age. 18.131
Thropp, Hannah. Wit will of Rd Nelmes Sr. 13 Apl 1706. 17.98
        Robt. Fined for not going to Church. St S par. 21 Aug 1718.
                6.280
Tibbalds, Peter. Wit deed of gift Mrs Eliz Nichollas to her children.
                20 May 1670. 16.75
Tignall, Wm. His wife Kath: 24 Oct 1668. 16.58
         Wm. His servt Chas Harry adj 12 yrs of age. 6 Apl 1669. 3.60
         Wm. Churchwarden of Fairfield par. 4 June 1684. 4.233
Tignall. Is it not possible that this name may be a form of Tignor ?
Tignor, Dennis. Orphan of Phillip. To be brought to Court by George
                Dameron. 19 Sept 1716. 6.182
        Denis. Orphan son of Phillip Tignor, with his mother's consent,
                bound to George Dameron till 21. Mr Robert
                Jones security. 16 Jan 1716/17. 6.187
        Elizabeth. Orphan of Phillip Tignor, about 9 yrs old, bound to
                Mr Tho Hughlett and Mary his wife till 18.
                21 Nov 1716. 6.184
        Mary. Relict of Phillip Tignor deceased, swears he died with-
                out will. Admr granted. 18 Apl 1716. 6.154
        Phillip, son of Phillip Tignor makes choice of Dennis Fallin
                as guardian. 20 Jan 1719/20. 6.352
        Sarah. Age 35 or th-abts. See deposition under Reason. 29 July
                1712. 18.255
        William. Will. Dated 28 Nov 1698. Prob 15 Apl 1702. To eldest
                dau Mary Hughlett wife of Tho Hughlett. To
                dau Mabel Hill. To eldest son Phillip Tignor
                land called Hollise oldfield adj land of Jno
                Reason Sr. Wife Anne Tignor she sole extrx.
                To son James. To daus Eliz Tignor and Anne
                Tignor, both under 20 yrs. Wit Richd Wright,
                Richd Smith. Proved by both wit. Rerecorded
                19 March 1711/12 by Dennis Fallin. 17.160
        William. Late owned land adj Tho Loechman. 8 Feb 1708/9. 17.91
Tilghman, Capt Saml. Lately came forth of England. 20 March 1657.
                14.104
Tillitt, Tho. Headright of Rice Maddox. 10 Jan 1650/1. 1.47
Timmons, Tho. Late deceased. Father of Tho Timmons of Middle parish in
                Stafford Co. 16 Dec 1707. See entry Mary
                Roberts. 17.114
Tindall, Mary. Dau of Jne Besick. Disinherited. 25 Mar 1706. 17.173

Tingey see Tyngey.
Tipton, Joseph. See entry Capt Tho Brereton. 17.238-243
Typton, Mr Joseph. Admr of his est to Eliz Typton the widow. 19 Feby 1678/9. 4.22
Tipton, Jos. Wit will Jno Bisick. 25 Mar 1706. 17.173
 Jos. Wit deed Rainsford Smyth to Tho Gill. 15 May 1711. 18.86
 Jos. Proves by oath, as witness, will of Saml Downing dec'd. 19 Oct 1715. 6.141
 Mr Jos. Mr Charles Nelms and Mrs Eliz Downing confess judgt to Mr Jos: Tipton fer a feather bed, 8 ewes and 4 cows which were conveyed to sd Tipton by deed of gift by his deceased mother Mrs Eliz Tipton dated 21 Sept 1683. This entry dated 17 July 1717. 6.221 Perhaps the explanation of this entry is that he gave or sold the property to Nelms and Mrs Downing and that this entry is to pay him.
 Richard. Wit deed Gibson to Downham (sic) and Gilbert. 3 Dec 1666. 16.3
 Samuel. 840 lb tobo owed to him by Jacob Cotanceau. 21 Augt 1678. 4.1
 Sam: Sues Rd Rout who married Frances Adams for 680 lb tobbo. 6 Oct 1687. 4.407
Todwell, Richd. Receives pmt for crop from Dr Edmd Helder for Samuel Leverton. 25 Oct 1671. 16.201
Tope, Thomas. This name also appears as Tap and Tapp. He was overseer for Tho Hobson and in difference with him. Hobson is ordered to pay according to agreemt. 24 Aug 1678. 4.5
Tapp, Tho. deceased. Probate of will granted Jno Lewis. 18 May 1687. 4.394
Toppin, Henry. Signs oath to Commonwealth of England. 13 Apl 1652.1.72
 Henry of Cherry Point. Registers mark for cattle. 13 Apl 1652. 1.75
 Henry. deceased. Tho Adams his heir. 21 July 1660. 2.127 See entry Rd Rice.
Topping, Jno. Sworn under-sheriff. 18 Apl 1683. 4.176
Totaskey Ferry. Main road to adj Saml Churchill's land. 19 Dec 1705. 17.161
Toulson, Tho. An orphan, Edw Bennitt age 15, bound to him to be taught shoemaking. 22 Aug 1718. 6.290
Tower, Tho. Deposition. Age not shown. Says 3 yrs since packing tobo at Adam Yarratt's etc. 22 Oct 1667. 16.25
 Tho. Carpenter and freeholder ef N Co, sells Tho Colton planter, 125 acres on Morattico Path, adj Jno Oldham, Tho Adams and Rd Rice. Wit: Wm Barton, Adams Yarrets marke. 8 Sept 1668. 16.38
 Tho. Sells land to Tho Dyer. 18 Oct 1670. 16.201
 Tho. deceased. Prob of his will to Dorothy the widow and extrx. 15 July 1685. 4.275

Tower, Tho. Land lately his in Betty's Neck adj Edwd Barnes. 21 Octr 1702. 17.200

Tho. His land adj Jno Adams. 2 Jan 1702/3. 17.161

Trape, Tho. On his petition com of admr to him of est of Tho Nelmes als Maddox decd. 20 Aug 1684. 4.235

Trapnell, Phillip. Wit deed Rogers to Opie. 16 Feb 1711/12. 18.148

Travers, Jno. Servant to Jno Swanson adj 10 yrs old. 21 Aug 1678. 4.1

Mr Raw: Justice. 18 Dec 1696. 4.755

Rawleigh. In the will of Rev Jno Farnefold he refers to "my cozen Rawleigh Travers wife" and leaves to Rebecca Travers "my wifes picture". 3 July 1702. 17.234

Trip, Tho. (also as Treip). Says Ezekial Genesis left several things to The Nelms als Mattocks, but the greater part of his estate to sd Trip and to his wife who was mother of said Tho deceased. He prays judgt agt Alice Hudnall for Tho Nelms part of the estate. 19 Sept 1684. 4.242

Troth, Matthew. "a poore Impotent Distempered person" freed from levy. 21 May 1696. 4.726

Trussell, Jne. Commander of Northumberland Co. 31 Jan 1644/5. (This is the earliest known record of Northumberland Co as such) 4 Archives of Maryland. Provincial Court. 301

Jno. Burgess. October 1649. 1 Hening 359.

Mr John. Justice. 24 Aug 1650. 1.41

Jno. Signs oath to Commonwealth of England. 13 Apl 1652. 1. 72-3

Mr Jno. Justice. 28 May 1652

Collo Jno. Justice. 26 May 1656. 14.84

Coll Jno. As justice marries Jno Merraday and Ann Nash in civil ceremony. The first, in fact the only instance of this I've come upon in these records. B.F. 11 Sept 1656. 14.90

Col Jno. deceased. Admr to Mary Trussell the relict. 20 Feb 1659/60. 2.119

Jno. His land adj Matthew Rodham. 17 Nov 1666. 16.22

Col Jno. See entry Wm Gradey. Prior to Mar 1705/6. 17.152

Mary. Wit deed Conolin to Hutson. 17 May 1708. 17.143

Robert. Son of Col Jno Trussell. Received land by deed of gift dated 20 June 1683. He dying without issue the land reverted to his father and on his death it descended to Jno Trussell son of Jno and brother of Robt, who sold it 20 Dec 1711. 18.142

Jno of St S par. Buys 100 acres from Tho Barecroft in St S par. On the same date Trussell sells Barecroft 50 acres on Kings Creek, part of land formerly granted Col Jno Trussell. 20 Dec 1711. 18.140

Trussell, Jno of St S par sells Tho Millard Junior of same place, 30 acres on a branch of Mattapony river, etc. Acknowledged by Jno Trussell and Jane his wife. 16 Aug 1712. 18.215

    Wm. Admr of Henry Hutson. 16 Jan 1716/17. 6.188

    Jno. deceased. His relict Jane married Jno Harding. 18 Sept 1717. 6.241

Tuckahoe Swamp. in St S par. Adj land of Jno Oldam Sr. 15 Jan 1700/1. 17.185

Tucker, John and Rose his wife. P of A to Jas Claughton. 7 Aug 1667. 16.31

Tuckingham, George of Bristol, marcht. P of A to Edw Sanders. 18 June 1667. 16.23

Tullos in various spellings. The first name 'Cloud' may be taken as Claudius or Claude. B.F.

Tulley, Cloud. Age 24. 4 Aug 1665. 15.165

Tullos, Cloud. His suit agt Jno Lawrence to next Court. 17 Oct 1678. 4.9

Tullus, Cloud. Son of Cloud Tullos "being both deaf and dumb" cleared from the levy. 18 July 1683. 4.188

Tulles, Claudius. Owned land with Jno Donaldson 25 July 1680 and on 20 July 1687. 17.127

Tullos, Cloud. With other inhabitants to clear the road called the Ridge Path on Cherry Point. 20 Nov 1696. 4.750

Tulles, Jno. Appraises est of Phillip Norgatt dec'd. 16 Apl 1711. 18.38

    Jno. Appraises est of Robt Barton dec'd. 20 June 1711. 18.69

    Richd. Wit Gradey to Shirley. 12 Mar 1705/6. 17.152

    Richd of St S par. Jno Wiggins age 3 bound to him to be taught trade of cooper. 6 July 1708. 17.204

Tullos, Richd. His land adj 60 acres in St S par sold by Robt Banks and Eliz his wife to Allen Hunter. 19th May 1713. 18.295

    Richd. Refuses admr of est of Mrs Sarah Tullos. 12 Mar 1713/14 6.19

    Mrs Sarah. Late deceased. Her dau Sarah wife of James Fulks. 12 March 1713/14. 6.19 They appointed admrs of her estate. 17 Mar 1714/5. 6.104

Tully, Wm. Servant to Jos Humphrey adj 11 yrs old. 20 May 1719. 6.316

Turberville and as Turbervile.

Turbervile, Mr Jno. Justice. 21 Sept 1692. 4.599

    Mr Jno. Justice. 19 Apl 1693. 4.619

Turberville, Jno. Atty of Margarett wife of Rd Orland. 16 Dec 1696. 4.752

    Jno. Sheriff. To collect 53870 lb tobo from 1016 tythables in the County at 53 1/2 lb per poll. 19 Nov. 1696. 4.748

    Jno. Acts for Mrs Eliz Lee, widow of Charles Lee Sr, in having will probated. 17 Dec 1701. 17.248

Turbervile, Jno Gent of Lancaster Co sells Robert Carter Esqr of Lancaster Co Gent, plantation that Wm Lester Gent of Northumberland Co died possessed of, which was bequeathed to him by his mother Dorothy Jackson. 600 acres. Escheated for want of heirs and granted Turbervile. 21 June 1713. 18.337

Turine, Jno. Was partner of Tho Morris who "was miserably drowned" has paid all bills, etc. 21 Aug 1678. 4.1

Turner, Jno. Married Priscilla Shippey legatee of Jas Jones. 17th Feb 1714/15. 6.98

Turrill, Jno. Headright of Rd Haynie. 15 July 1696. 4.733

Tyeer, Richd. "a poor man" exempt from levy. 15 May 1717. 6.211

Tynan, Wm. To teach shoemaking to Wm and Jas Grace orphan sons of Jno Grace who are bound to him. 20 May 1719.6.316

Tyney, Wm of Cople par Westmorland Co buys 110 acres in St S par from Tho Seddon. 18 March 1711/12. 18.166

Tyngey also as Tingey.

Tyngey, Mrs Eliz: Awarded judgt 20 Dec 1667 for 1480 lb tobo agt est of Mr Jno Fountayne. Now retd executed on 335 lb in hands of Wm Fisher and 440 lb in hands of Tho Hickman, etc. 21 Jan 1668/9. 3.54

    Mrs Eliz: formerly Eliz Man widow. 21 Jan 1668/9. 3.55

    Mrs Eliz: Says Henry Roach in his will bequeathed her sufficient ground for 4 servants to plant until Jno Roach son of said Henry Roach comes to age. Mr Nicho Owen and Jas Johnson ordered to lay out the land. 21 Jan 1668/9. 3.55

    Elizabeth, widow. Prenuptial agreemt with Wm Sheares. 26 Jan 1668/9. 16.67

    John. Guardian of orphans of Henry Moseley. 13 Apl 1657.14.105

    John. Age 55 yrs or th-abts. 20 June 1663. 15.103

    Jno. Wit will of Simon Kirby. 22 Mar 1666/7. 16.3

    Jno. Will. Dated 1 Aug 1667. Prob 21 Oct 1667. To son in law Wm Moseley. To John Moseley. To Hen Moseley. To Tho Hardings eldest boy. To Henry Medcalf land bought of his brother Geo Medcalfe when he is 21. To God dau Mary Henly. To God son Jno Bayley. To Jno Landman. To Friend Nich Owen. Balance of estate to wife Eliz. 16.30

    Jno. deceased. His will proved 21 Oct 1667. His widow Eliz now wife of Wm Sheares. 22 Feb 1670/1. 16.164

Underhill, Tho. Headright of Wm Presley. 21 Jan 1660/1. 2.136

Upton, Jno. Wit P of A Neale to Neale (of Fairfield par) 21 Nov 1669. 16.105 also 16.64

Urquhart, Mr Thos late deceased. Inv of his est presented by Barth Schrever admr. 19 Mar 1711/12. 18.168

    Tho. dec'd. Owed Jos Smith by Bills of Exch drawn on David Arbuthnot mercht in Weymouth dated 4 June 1710 L 6. Sterl. 17 Feb 1714/15. 6.99

Valey, Cornelius. Servt to Wm Downing adj 15 yrs of age. 17 Apl 1672 3.144

Valleys Three. in Fairfield par. Adj land of Danl Chandler. 22nd Jan 1673/4. 17.120

Valon, Charles. Wit will Tho Edwards. 9 Mar 1669/70. 16.71

Vanlandingham, Francis. Petitions that his sister's son Phillip Clowes left very young fatherless and motherless and distempered and no estate friend or relation that offered to take care of him either for his maintenance or cure but himself. That he spent 1300 lb tobo for the cure of his "scald head", and had him 8 or 9 yrs. That he is now 17 yrs old. Jno Walters was chosen his guardian, etc.
The Court orders the orphan to remain with Vanlandingham one year for restitution of the tobacco expended. 17 Nov 1696. 4.844

  Fra: Acks deed Gradey to Shirley. 20 Mar 1705/6. 17.152

  Francis. Signs appraisal of est of Vincent Garner. 16th May 1711. 18.47

Van Landigam (Michael). An alien. Hath long lived in this country and behaved himself "made a free Denizen of this Country of Virginia". 20 Sept 1664. 16.37

  Michael. Naturalization Certificate. 20 Sept 1664. 16.51

Vanlandegham, Mich: Pd 400 lb tobo from County levy "for a wolf in a pitt". 5 Nov 1668. 3.47

Vanlandeyham, Richd and Francis. Give bond as admrs of est of Phillip Norgate. 22 May 1711. 18.18

Vanlandingham, Richd. Winneyfred Britt age 11 bound to him. 16 Sept 1719. 6.336

Varley children. All servants of Mr Tho Winter. Their ages adj by the Court to be:

  Christopher Varley 8 years
  John Varley 10 "
  James Varley 6 "
  Jennett Varley 14 "
  Elizabeth Varley 12 "

21 August 1678. 4.3
(It would be most interesting to know what became of these children. Prob they were French. The item to follow is all that I see concerning them. B.F.)

Varley, Jno. "a poor Decreped man" exempt from levy. 19 Sept 1716. 6.181

Vaughan, Christopher. Headright of Wm Wildey. 8 Sept 1662. 2.161

  John. Certificate for 150 acres for importing 3 persons. 20th Nov 165½. 1.67 (1651)

  William. Servant to Mr Tho Brereton adj 13 yrs old. 26th Feb 1660/1. 2.137

Vaulx, Robt. Appointed guardian of Rd Kenner by the Gen'l Court. Tho Gill and Wm Metcalf securities. 21 Nov 1716. 6.185

Vawter, Jno. Servant to Mr Tho Opie. To be punished for killing a hog belonging to Mr Nicho Owen. 16 Oct 1676. 4.6

Vestry for Chicacone parish. Names listed. 20 Mar 1671/2. 16.158

Vincent, Wm. Signs oath to Commonwealth of England. 13 Apl 1652. 1.72

    Wm. Granted 6000 acres. Sold it to Jno Ingram who sold it to Tho Nash. Of this 3000 acres is now sold to Mr Leond Howson. 17 Jan 1671/2. 16.219

Voss, Richd. Indenture with Jno Cary of Bristol to serve 4 years in Virginia. 5 Feb 20th yr Charles II. 16.87

Vulcans Creek. Adj land of Jno Gooch. 7 Apl 1706. 17.195 Also ref to as being in Wicco par. 19 Nov 1707. 17.38

Waddington, George. Son of Ralph Sr and bro of Ralph Jr. 20 Oct 1678. 17.118

    Geo. Appointed Constable this day. 21 Mar 1716/17. 6.202

    Geo. Son and heir of Geo Waddington dec'd, late of this County. 19 June 1717. 6.218

    Frances. Daughter of Tho Gill Sr. 10 Feb 1707/8. 17.97

    John. deceased. His widow Frances now married to Jos Robinson. 18 March 1713/14. 6.24

    Ralph. Buys land from Francis Roberts. 10 Oct 1671. 16.200

    Ralph of Fairfield parish. Deed of Gift. 20 Oct 1678. To son Ralph Waddington land bought of James Allen. Refers to his son Geo bro of Ralph Jr. Wit: Thos Smith, Alexander Brodie. Ack 8th Oct 1680. Rerecorded 18 July 1711 by John Lancaster. 17.118

Waddy, Eliz. Wit deed Dameron to Dameron. 19 Feb 1705/6. 17.55

    Mr James. His servants Jno Birk adj 13 yrs of age and Symon Holland adj 14 yrs of age. 16 Nov 1698. 4.841

Waddey, Jas. Wit deed Williams to Gaskins. 18 Dec 1699. 17.44

Waddy, Mr Jas. A friend of Geo Bledsoe. 23 Jan 1704/5. 17.16

Waddey, Jas. Wit deed Dameron to Dameron. 19 Feb 1705/6. 17.55

    Jas. Wit deed Williams to Mahane. 25 Nov 1706. 17.67 To ack this sale 11 Mar 1706/7. 17.72 He does ack it 21 May 1707. 17.67

    Mr James. His land adj Charles Ingram. 14 Oct 1707. 17.23

    Mr Jas. His land adj that of Ebenezer Sanders dec'd. 2nd Apl 1711. 18.57

    James. His plantation adj Saml Downing. 9 June 1711. 18.93

    Jas. Owes est of Tho Crowder 555 lb tobo. 20 June 1711. 18.62

Waddy, Jno. Signs oath to Commonwealth of England. 13 Apl 1652. 1.72

    Jno. Age 40 yrs or th-abts. 20 May 1656. 14.76

    Jno. Gives Hannah dau of Andrew Poultry a calf. 20 May 1658. 14.143

    Jno. Guardian of Martha Graham. Claims land for her. 22 July 1711. 2.145

    Jno. His son Thos Waddy given a mare by Tho Hobson. 20 May 1670. 16.74 Also 16.126

Waddy, Mr Jno. His land referred to. 11 June 1680. 17.14
Waddey, The. Wit deed Brewer to Linsfield. 21 Oct 1681. 17.204
Waddie, Mr Tho. His plantation referred to. 14 July 1708. 17.22
Waddey, Tho. Appraises est of Tho Urquhart late dec'd. 19 Mar 1711/12
                18.169
Waddy, Tho. Exor of Dennis Schriver dec'd. 15 May 1717. 6.208
Wake, Matthew, dec'd. Admr of his est to Mr Charles Ashton. 5 Nov 1668.
                3.46
Wale, Geo. Married Mary daughter of Robt Jones dec'd. Petitions for
                division of estate in right of his wife. 21st
                August 1678. 4.2
   Geo. John Pinckard's will (Lancaster Co) refers to plantation
                Geo Wale formerly lived on. 20 Mar 1689/90.
                Lancaster Co records. No.35 p. 7
   Geo. Bequest from Jno Eustace. Wit his will. 23 Dec 1701. 17.245
Walker, Edw. Will. Dated 2 Dec 1650. Prob 20 Sept 1656. All estate
                to son John Walker. Inv to be taken by friends
                Henry Hayler and George Thompson. Wit: Anne
                Compton, Grace x Holden, Geo Thompson. Proved
                by oaths of Anne Compton and Henry Hayler.
                14.92
   Elizabeth. Age 48 or th-abts. 20 March 1655/6. 14.71
   Emanuell, Reference to his house. 2 July 1707. 17.24
   Frances. Wit deed Nutt to Blackwell. In the entry the name
                appears "Frances x Walker his marke".
                26 July 1712. 18.224
   James. Pd a bonus from the County levy of 400 lb tobo "For a
                peece of Linning Clothmakeing". 19 Novr 1696.
                4.748
   Mary "the late wife of Robert Sharpe dec'd, aged 25 years or
                thereabouts". 28 Jan 1655. 14.64
   Mary. deceased. Inventory of her estate incl an item "about
                3 1/2 bushell Meale Eaten by the children after
                their (mother) Dyed". Inv submitted by Saml
                Blackwell admr. 24 Nov 1711. 18.114 Also an
                inv of her est submitted by Blackwell 17 June
                1713. 18.312
   Nath'l. Rerecords will dated 1706 of Jno Bisick. 16 July 1712.
                17.173
   Richd. Signs oath to Commonwealth of England. 13 Apl 1652. 1.72
   Richd. Assigns 200 acres of land, pat 6 May 1651, to Phill
                Carpenter and Edw Henley. 10 June 1652. 1.76
   Saml and Jane his wife. She relict of Jacob Bayly decd, say
                he died without a will, etc. 24 July 1714.
                6.68   They present an inventory 17 Feb 1714/5.
                6.99
   Symon. Headright of Wm Sheares. 21 Aug 1678. 4.4
   Wm. Wit Deed of Gift Lee to Rhodon. 8 Nov 1651. 1.69
   Wm. Age 33 yrs or th-abts. 20 March 1655/6. 14.71

Walker, Wm. His wife insulted her brother Wm Jeffers at a funeral last November. See entry ; Mary Laud, 21 July 1656. 14.86

    William. Will. Dated 10 March 1656/7. Prob 20 May 1657. Eldest son John. Under 18.
        Middle son Wm. " (sic)
        Youngest son Wm. " (sic)
    Wife Mary.
    (Note: There is either an error in the original or the two youngest boys had the same name. B.F.) 14.108

    Wm. His widow married Steph: Bailey. See entry Wm Jeffers. 21 July 1660. 14.86

    Wm. Cleared of accidentally having killed Danl Crosby. "homicide by misadventure". 16 Oct 1676. 4.7

Wall, Jno. dec'd. Bond for admr of his est given by Jno Dunaway and Jane his wife. 17 May 1711. 18.47

    Jno. dec'd. Inv of his estate. 20 June 1711. 18.66

    Jno. dec'd. His widow Jane married Danl Dunaway. His sister Eliz married Jno Stanly. 18 Mar 1713/14. 6.29

Waller, Anne. Headright of Geo Colclough. 21 Jan 1651/2. 1.71

Wallis, Hugh. Will. Dated 11 Feb 1712/13. Prob - Feb 1712/13. All est to Henry Boggess of N Co. he exor. 18.260

Walter, Dorcas, Katherine and Elizabeth. All 3 referred to as "my cousins" in will of Jno Coutanceau. 17 Dec 1718. 19.10

Walters, Ester. As wit proves will of Rd Jones. 15 July 1685. 4.275

    John. Asks he has scandalously abused Richd Thompson in saying he had stolen Jas Claughton's chest. 22nd Oct 1667. 16.31

    John. Found guilty of hog stealing. 6 Apl 1669. 3.62

    John. Certificate for 350 acres for importing: John Walters, Hester Walters, Phoebe Walters, Diana Walters, Mary Walters, Easter Walters, John Walters. 19 July 1682. 4.138

    Jno. Exor of Richd Jones dec'd. To have prob of will which is proved by oaths of wit: Jeffery Addamson and Ester Walters. 15 July 1685. 4.275

    Jno. Chosen guardian for Phillip Clowes age 17. 17 Nov 1696. 4.844

    Jno. of St S parish. Fined for absenting himself from Church. 18 Nov 1713. 6.4

    Jno Jr. For some time past an inhabitant of this County. Certificate for leaving the Colony. 22 Apl 1714. 6.358

Walter, Roger. Had pat land sold to Richd Aylett. 22 Apl 1659. 17.192

Walters, Roger. Will. Dated 29 Dec 1669. Prob 20 Jan 1669/70. To Jno Jones son of Hugh Jones, taylor, land where sd Hugh now lives. To dau Sarah land betw John Jones and Jno Wood adj land Mrs Eliz Nutt. To son Roger Walters. To dau Frances wife of Wm Smyth. To Dorothy wife of Jno Alloway. Ellinor wife of Jno Yeates. Wife Ellinor extrx. Wit Jno Allen, Edw Sanders. 16.69. Also 16.115

Walters, Roger. Patented 1000 acres. See entry Tho Berry. His will dated 29 Dec 1669. 17.183

Roger. In will dated 29 Dec 1669 left land to be div betw his son Roger Walters and Frances the wife of Wm Smith. Roger the son dying without issue, Wm and Frances Smith sold the land 14 Jan 1682/3 to Tho Berry, who by will dated 15 Apl 1700 gave it to his 2 sons Tho and Wm Berry, etc. 18.243

Roger. Grandfather of Jno Jones formerly left him 100 acres in St S parish. 10 Feb 1707/8. 17.97

Walton, Jno. Signs oath to Commonwealth of England. 13 Apl 1652. 1.72

Jno. He leaving Westmorland Co with unsettled a/cs, there is "A Huy and Cry after" him. 21 Oct 1654. Westmorland Co records, 1653-9. p.28

Walton, Robt, Gent. Lengthy will. 3 1/2 pages. Dated 14 Jan 1669/70. Probated 19 July 1671. Refers to his overseer Ralph Clifford, at plantation at head of Potomac Creek. "my most dear Relations in England". "my dear spouse Mrs Elizabeth Walton". "my two dear children Charles and Elizabeth Walton". Charles under 21. "my sister Elizab: Walton". "to my sister Frisis Matthew" (sic). "Well beloved Brother Thomas Matthew of Northumberland Co in Virginia", he sole exor. Wit: Christopher Hargill, Jane Head, Thomas Hobson, Thomas Brereton. 16.188

Ward, Bridgett. Wit entry re Wm Tapptico, King of Wicocomoco Indians. 31 Dec 1718. 19.95

James. Headright of Mr Jno Harris. 15 July 1696. 4.733

Jno. His land adj Vincent Garner. 18 June 1706. 17.201

Mr Richd. Obtains judgt agt Richd Sutton 400 lb tobo. 24 Aug 1669. 3.69

Warder, Wm. Signs oath to Commonwealth of England. 13 Apl 1652. 1.72

Wm. Age 47 yrs or th-abts. 20 March 1655/6. 14.73

Wm. His widow married Richd Browne. 9 Sept 1661. 2.147

Warner, Jno and Prue his wife buy 100 acres from Danl Holland formerly belonging to Rd Gibble. 20 Feb 1671/2.16.230

Jno. Judgt to Phillip Shapleigh agt him for 3660 lb tobo. 17th Oct 1678. 4.9

Warnem, Jno. His land adj Rd and Saml Robinson in St S par. 14 July 1702. 17.105

Warr, Susanna. Dau in law to Jno Haynie. Gift from him. 20 May 1659. 15.22

Warrick, Mrs Anne. Extrx of her husband applied for admr but has since died. Admr of est to Wm Warrick and Geo Dawkins Junr. 21 Mar 1716/17. 6.202

George. Orphan son of Wm Warrick dec'd, aged 14 in July next, bound to Wm Lewis till 21 to be taught the trade of brick layer. Jno Lewis and William Grimstead securities. 21 Mar 1716/17. 6.204

Warwick, Tho. Adjudged 10 yrs old. 9 May 1660. 2.122
Warwick, Wm. Signs Inv Wm Sanders est. 13 Oct 1704. 17.165
Warwick, Wm. His will presented by Anne Warwick his exor. 15 Aug 1716. 6.172
Warwick, William and William Jr. Wit deed Roberts and Timmons to Dawking. 16 Dec 1707. 17.114
Warrington, Eliz: "aged 38 yeares or thereabouts sayth that Sam: Nichols is a Gurnsey man and that she did know his Friends there and that she lived there seaven yeares close by his Friends in the Towne of Gornsey
       the mark of Eliz: Warrington"
No date but evidently sworn 20 Dec 1667 from like depositions. 16.32
Washington, Jne. Dec'd. Owed Mrs Anne Temple 500 lb tobo. Attachment agt his est to Francis Clay who married Mrs Temple. 5 Sept 1660. 2.130
 Jno. 1200 lb tobo and cask of his est attached. This in the hands of Isaac Foxcroft mercht at suit of Mrs Anne Brodhurst admrx of her husband Walter Brodhurst, gent., dec'd., in part satisfaction for a mare, etc. 20 July 1660. 2.127
Waterland, Mich: Servant to Mrs Joyce Holland, has runaway, etc. 17th Apl 1672. 3.145
Waterman, Tho. Headright of Mr Edw Sanders. 22 June 1669. 3.65
Waters, Roger. His land adj Capt Jno Whitty. 15 May 1661. 17.224-9
 John Junr. Appraises est of Phillip Norgatt, dec'd. 18.38
 Dorothy. Claims for 10 days attendance as witness in suit Owen Dermott vs David Gill. She to have 60 lb tobo per day. 16 May 1717. 6.215
Wathen, Wm. Wit P of A Lyndsey to Bridges. 6 Apl 1667. 16.13
 Wm. Exor of Mr David Lyndsey pets for 1178 lb tobo due from Chas Ashton. 21 Jan 1668/9. 3.55
 Wm. Sued by Jno Evans. 23 June 1669. 3.68
 Wm. An orphan, Eliz Roberts, left to him when very young. Now bound for 7 yrs. "not to worke in the ground" 9 Dec 1669. 16.141.
Watkins, Edw. Security in bond of Wm Paine and Susanna his wife to admr est of John Husk. 20 June 1711. 18.63
Watson, Nathl. Sold a servant named Jno Marson, age 11, to Mr Edward Coles. 21 March 1716/17. 6.204
 Tho. Assigns 200 acres to Jno Garner. 14 Feb 1667/8. 16.42
Watts, Henry. Appointed guardian of Thos, John and Francis Webb, sons of Tho Webb dec'd, he having married their mother. 20 May 1659. 2.106
 Hen: Is building a mill at head of Chicacone. 20 Oct 1668. 3.45
 Henry. Deed of Gift. A mill house and 25 acres, "little Wiccomico mill house" to "my Grandson in Law Thomas Hobson son of Thomas Hobson" 9 Jan 1668/9. 16.47 also 16.72

Watts, Hen: Admr of Wm Anderson dec'd. 6 Apl 1669. 3.61
  Henry. Will. Dated 9 June 1670. Prob 20 July 1670. To wife
      Eliz Watts. To 3 sons in law Thos, Jno and
      Francis Webb. etc. 16.79
  Henry. Late of this Co dec'd. Was granted 650 acres 16 Janry
      1661/3. He devised 200 of it in his will d.
      9 June 1670 to his son in law Fra: Webb who
      left it to Jno Webb for life. It then descend-
      ed to Tho Webb (who sold 58 acres to Richard
      Wright 12 July 1712) the eldest son and heir
      of Tho Webb dec'd who was the eldest brother
      of Francis Webb legatee of Watts. 12 July 1712.
      18.206
  Richd. Wit deed Mayes to Mayes. 19 Dec 1710. 18.26
  Richd. Wit will of Edw Singer of St S par. 6 Jan 1711/12.
      18.261
  Robt. Runaway servt to Jno Copedge retd by Wm Barnes of Md.
      22 Sept 1715. 6.135
  Tho. deceased. Late of Nansemond Co. Sold 300 acres in
      Northumberland Co to Tho Garrett. Tho Alderson
      admr confirms sale, his atty being Wm Wildey.
      11 Dec 1654. 14.79
Waughop, Anne. Bequest from Tho Palmer of Md. 28 March 1709. 17.127
  Tho. Wit bond of Jas Moulder. 16 May 1711. 18.44
  Tho. Bequest from Tho Palmer of Md. 28 March 1709. Rerecords
      Palmer's will 15 Aug 1711. 17.127
  Tho. Rerecords inv of Peter Coutanceau. 17 Feb 1714/5. 17.216
  Tho. Died without will. Admr to Rd Wright the greatest
      creditor. 15 May 1717. 6.210
Way, Edyth. Admr of her husband's est. 20 Apl 1681. 4.92
  Elizabeth. Wife of Jno Way relinq dower rights in land. 12 Decr
      1719. 19.108
  Jno. Son of Richd Way, late of this Co dec'd, this day made
      choice of his bro in law Richd Smyth to be
      his guardian. 16 Nov 1687. 4.410
  Jno. His land adj Tho Leechman. 8 Feb 1708/9. 17.91
  Jno. Wit will of Wm Harcum. Proved it by oath 15 Mar 1709/10
      17.111
  Jno. Fined for absenting himself from Church. 18 Nov 1713. 6.5
  Jno. Judgt for 320 lb tobo agt him by admrs of Henry Dawson.
      17 March 1714/15. 6.104
  Richd. Bought 229 acres from Wm Thomas 12 March 1663. Also 50
      acres from Danl Neale in Oct 1669. Sold 100
      acres to Richd Gralesse on a date not shown.
      17.91
  Richd. Bought land from Danl and Ellen Neale in Fairfield parish.
      21 Nov 1669. 16.105 also 16.64
  Wm. "a poor Ancient man and almost blind" excused from paying levy.
      19 May 1714. 6.34
Wayland, Wm. Servant to Tho Gill adj 10 yrs old. 18 Nov 1713. 6.3

Weatherstone, Maurice, deceased. Jno Kean, his nearest of kin, appointed admr, 17 Mar 1714/15. 6,106

Weaver, Isaac. Signs oath to Commonwealth of England. 13 Apl 1652. 1,72

    Isaac. Will. Dated 13 Jan 1663/4. Prob 20 Jan 1663/4. (Not much time lost here). All estate to Godson Tho Gaskins Jr, excepting a cow to goddaughter Mary Mayes. 15,116

    Jno. Age abt 30 yrs. 1 Feb 1667/8. 16,43

    Richd. Pd 186 lb tobo from est of Tho Crowder. 20 June 1711. 18,62

Weaver's line. Ref to. 18 June 1706. 17,1

Webb. The complications here are so involved that I've always looked upon the preposition as 'the tangled web'. A good deal was done by the late Lyon Gardiner Tyler in his "The Webb and Allied Families", which most unfortunately was misprinted, further adding to the general confusion. There are some rather horrid details concerning persons in no way related to the family (or if so in a left handed manner) which I have, in the main, omitted, although this is ordinarily against my rule. One instance is included here. I can only offer in this volume a part of what I found. B.F.

Webb, Anne. Widow of Thomas. Swears to inv of his est. 14 Dec 1702. 17,8

    Mrs. Anne. To keep Hannah dau of Capt Leonard Howson. 13 Dec 1704. 17,8

    Ann. Will. Dated 21 Sept 1710. Prob 16 Mar 1719/20. All estate to Ann Howson. Capt Jno Howson and Richard Wright executors. 19,89

    Mrs Ann. Presented for not going to church in Wicco par. 19th May 1714. 6,35

    Danl. "a molatto son of an Engl woman serv't to the orph'ts of Maj Jno Mottrom dec'd", being 21 asks for his freedom. This granted. Hon Nicholas Spencer who manages the estate of the orphans agrees that Danl be immediately free. Richd Haynie acts as attorney for Danl Webb. 5 Oct 1687. 4,405

    Elizabeth. Deed of Gift. 16 May 1707. Widow. Late relict and admr of Jno Wornum dec'd of this Co, gives to her son Jno Wornum personal property. Wit names worn away. P of A Eliz Webb to Tho Hobson 16 May 1707 wit by Clark Hobson and Tho Stretton. All rerecorded 19 May 1714 by Jno Wornum. 17,209

    Elizabeth, Giles, Isaac and John. See will of Mrs Dorothy Spann. 11 Feb 1711/12. 18,157

    Eliz: Deed to her son Jno Wornom. 19 May 1714. 6,33

Webb, Mrs Esther. Nuncupative Will. Sworn 17 Dec 1712. Deposition of Thos Webb aged abt 28 yrs. Says in month of Novr 1712, some short time before his mother died, she desired to make her will in the presence of John Burgin and himself. To 2 sons Thos and Saml Webb. To son John Webb 600 lb tobo due from Jno Pope. To son William 500 lb tobo due from Christopher Conway. To son James Webb 500 lb tobo. Jno Burgin age 40 or th-abts swears as above. 18.242

Webb, Francis. Orphan son of Jno Webb dec'd chooses Wm Hughlett his guardian. Sarah Webb orphan daughter of Jno Webb dec'd chooses Tho Ashburn her guardian. 17 Janry 1716/17. 6.191.

Francis. Makes choice of Yarratt Hughlett as guardian. 19 June 1717. 6.219

Giles. Wit deed Spann to Spann. 19 May 1712. 18.174

John. Pd from County levy "To John Webb for making a Bridge at Cone 800 lb tobo". 2 Nov 1681. 4.681

John. Will. Dated 5 Oct 1700. Prob 16 Oct 1700. To son John plantation betw mine and Saml Mahaines. To son Richd neck of land adj Wm Coppedge. To youngest son Peircifull a neck of land running from Sandy Valley to Wheeler's line. Daus Eliz: and Ann. To William Peircifull "my best hatt". To Jno Wo- a Coat that I bought of Widow Page and a pair of breeches. To Richd Robinson saddle and bridle bought at Colonel Cooper's. "unto my brother Wm Peircifull" full keeping of wearing clothes for use of my 2 eldest sons. He desires his father Wm Peircifull and his father's son William Peircifull, his (John Webb's) brother to care for the children and be exors. Wife Eliz:. Wit: Roger x Jones, Jno Blundle, Richd x Robinson. Rerecorded 20 Apl 1726 by Jno Webb. 17.265

Webb, John. Atty for Alice wife of Saml Smith. 11 Sept 1703. 17.104

Jno. Signs inventory Wm Sanders estate. 13 Oct 1704. 17.165

Jno. Signed appraisal Bowers est. 17 Dec 1705. 17.165

John of St S parish. Will. Dated 4 June 1709. Prob 20 July 1709. To son Francis, water grist mill at head of Coan River purchased from Jno Boaze, also land 'I now live on' purchased from Peter Russell. He under 18. To dau Sarah Webb 150 acres bought of Jno Boaze on which Thos Harrison now lives. To son John Webb land on Little Wiccocomoco except 50 acres to be made over to Patrick Quiffe. Sister Sarah Dickinson. Exors "my Cozen Edward Sanders, my Nephew Thomas Webb and my Loveing sister Sarah Dickinson". Wife not mentioned. Wit: Richd Wright, Jno Allen, Jno Harvie, James Badger.
Rerecorded 17 May 1711 by Capt Edward Sanders.
Inv of est 17 Aug 1709. Appraisors names do not appear. Were sworn before Capt Christo Neale. 17.102

Webb, John. Deceased. Suit by his exors, Edw Sanders, Tho Webb and Sarah Dickinson agt Enoch Hill and Jno Dunaway dismissed. 17 Feb 1714/15. 6.99

John. As witness presents will of Tho Percivall. 18 Mar 1718/19 6.309

John. Ordered to bring an orphan boy, Tho Peircival son of Tho Peircival dec'd, to be disposed of according to Law. 19 Nov 1719. 6.348

Jno. Tho Percivale age 12 bound to him. 20 Jan 1719/20. 6.351

Richd. His land adj Wm and Charles Copedge. 5 June 1710. 17.50

Robt. Wit will of Jno Hull of Fairfield par. 4 May 1667. 16.97

Saml. Adj 13 yrs old. 9 May 1660. 2.122

Saml. Headright of Wm Wildey. 8 Sept 1662. 2.161.

Saml. His spring branch adj land of Charles Fallon. 17 Dec 1700. 17.159

Samuel and Eliz: his wife, she relict of Stephen Chackalate, swear he left no will. Admr granted. 21 August 1718. 6.278

Sarah. Orphan of Jno Webb dec'd. 15 June 1715. 6.114

Thos. Is owed 600 lb tobo and 3 bbl corn by Jeremy Cooper. 21 Jan 1651/2. 1.70

Tho. His widow married Henry Watts who is appointed guardian of his children Tho, Jno and Francis Webb. 20 May 1659. 2.106

Tho. His servant Hen Howard to be free having served 4 yrs since his arrival in this country, according to indenture. Webb protests but is overruled. 16 Octr 1676. 4.6

Tho. Wit deed Rd Smith to Jas White. 20 Mar 1677/8. 17.120

Thomas. Will. Dated 11 Sept 1702. Prob 16 Sept 1702. Children: Thos, Jno, Elizabeth, all under 18. Mentions land formerly belonging to Simon Richardson dec'd. Refers to son Thomas' grandfather Mr James Austen. John Bowler's land in Maryland. Bro John Webb. Bro Francis Webb deceased. Wife Anne. Overseers friend Richd Wright and nephew Tho Hobson. Son Tho. exor. Wit John Spry, Tho Hobson, Issabella Fletcher.
In this will he leaves to his eldest son Thomas "my Water Grist Mill with what land belongs to me adjacent thereto scituate in the Ile of Weight County on the South side of James River". 17.3

Thomas. Inventory of his est. Lengthy. A good deal of silver, etc. 13 Nov 1702. 17.5

Tho. His land adj Jno Bayles in Cupids Neck. 18 Jan 1705/6. 17.180

Tho. His land adj Wm Wildey. 18 Dec 1706. 17.24

Thos. Appraises est of Jas Allen late dec'd at house of Ralph Bickly. 29 March 1711. 18.38

Webb, Tho. Appraises est of Wm Dow dec'd. 18 July 1711. 18.71
  Tho. Appraises est of Wm Harcum dec'd. 17 Dec 1711. 18.171
  Tho. Signs bond of Anne Hoult admr of Joseph Hoult dec'd. 18th
    June 1712. 18.194
  Tho of St S par. Sells Rd Wright of same par, 58 acres in St S
    par. See entry Henry Watts. Dower rights relinq
    by Charity Webb wife of Thos. 12 July 1712. 18.206
Webb's Branch. Adj land of Wm and Chas Copedge. 5 June 1710. 17.50
Webb's land. Adj land of Tho Crowder on W side Corotomen River. 18th
    Sept 1705. 17.155
Webb's land. Adj land of Ralph Bickley. 2 July 1707. 17.24
Webb family detail. See entry Henry Watts. 12 July 1712. 18.206
Webber, John. Will. Dated 12 Feb 1670/1. Prob 28 Mar 1671. Overseers
    Edw Franklin and Jno Parker of N Co planters. To
    son Peter Webber.
    Tobacco "to be shipt home in my Cosen Georg Baker,
    if he came not in to be shipt home to England by
    Capt Tho Smyth to my Bro Samuell Webber". Wit:
    Robt Brierley, Fra Brierley, Jno Keene. 16.166
Weekes, Susanna. Dau of Walter Weekes. 14 Mar 1664/5. 15.151
  Walter. Signs oath to Commonwealth of England. 13 Apl 1652.
    1.72-3
  Walter. Age 43 yrs or th-abts. 22 May 1658. 15.19
  Walter. Guardian of orphans (not individually named) of John
    Rodford. (this name may mean either Radford or
    Rutherford) 20 July 1663. 15.104
Wells, Richd. Sued by Saml Mahon. 17 Oct 1678. 4.8
  Steph: Sues Tho Perryne. 30 Apl 1681. 4.90
  Stephen. Wit deed Trussell to Millard. 16 Aug 1712. 18.217
  Stephen. of St S par. Will. Dated 31 Oct 1712. Prob 21 Janry
    1718/19. To children of my dau Mary Faver dec'd.
    To son Stephen Wells. To grandson Stephen Wells
    he under 21. Wit Tho Williams, Humph: Thomas, Tho
    Dickinson. Proved by oaths of Williams and Thomas.
    19.12   This will presented by Steph: Wells Junr
    the exer. 21 Jan 1718/19. 6.296
Welch, Edw. See entry Capt Giles Russell. 18 Nov 1719. 6.346
Welsh, Jas. Servt to Mr Henry Brereton adj 13 yrs of age. 21 Dec 1698.
    4.847
  Loughly. Mentioned. 26 Jan 1718/19. 19.31
  Matthew. Servt to Mr Wm Harcum adj 15 yrs old. 21 Dec 1698.
    4.847
  Sylvester. Appointed Constable for Newman's Neck. 17 June 1714.
    6.55   He was presented for absence from Church
    15 May 1717. 6.202
  Tho. Servt to Christo: Garlington adj 15 yrs old. 20 Mar 1716/17.
    6.201
West, Wm. Pat land later belonging to Wm Moore. 24 Nov 1670. 17.47
  Majr. Jno. Judgt to him agt the Sheriff who arrested Wm Eves,
    who owed 2115 lb tobo and failed to appear. 17th
    Oct 1678. 4.9

West, Jno. Deceased. At request of Susan West his widow the estate to be appraised. 20 May 1696. 4.723

Wm. Wit deed Crafford to Davis. 20 Dec 1706. 17.94

Weston, Edwd. Wit will of Jno Lewis. 4 July 1702. 17.223

Wetherstone, Alex and Jane his wife. Rebecca Maudley age 2 bound to them with consent of her father. Richd Haynie goes security. 6 Oct 1687. 4.407

Whay, Eliz: Claims for attendance of 5 days as witness in suit of Kean agt Dameron. She to have 30 lb tobc per day. 16 May 1717. 6.215 See deposition under Reason.

Wheeler, Jno. Wit Tho Brewer's will. 11 June 1697. 17.268

Wheelor's line. Adj Jno Webb. 5 Oct 1700. 17.265

Wherrett, Sus: Headright of Mr Edw Sanders. 22 June 1669. 3.65

White, Ann. Headright of Capt Gyles Brent. 21 Jan 1651/2. 1.70

Ann. Wit Danl Neale's will. 4 Nov 1700. 17.249

Edw: of Gloucester Co. See entry Nisho Britton. 20 Jan 1664/5 15.149

Edw. Married Mary dau of Mrs Mary Thomas. See entry Wm Thomas. 17 Sept 1684. 4.244

James. Orphan of Richd White. List of his cattle (19 head) submitted by Hugh Fouch. List of 15 head sub: by Jno Bearmore. 22 Aug 1670. 16.144

James. Orphan of Richd. Buys 200 acres from Rd Smith 20 March 1677/8. Sells 200 acres to Geo Dawkins 4 Sept 1680. 17.120

James of St S par. Sells Robt Davis tailor, 100 acres. 16 July 1711. 18.86

James. Age 53 yrs or th-abts. See entry Mrs Hannah Smith. 16th Sept 1713. 18.335

Jame. Swears he wit will of Elis Downing dec'd. 19 Oct 1715. 6.140

Joseph. of Newmans Neck. Father of Richd and Henry White who were heirs of Henry Franklin. 11 Nov 1698. 17.124

Josias. Of parish of "Cerryluck" in No Carolina sells Richard Smith of G W par, 50 acres, being part of land sold by Capt Leonard Howson dec'd on 19 Febry 1665/6 to Tho Bayles and by Bayles will dated 4 Janry 1684/5 to be div betw his 3 sons, John, Christopher and Je- Bayles. Whereas Christo: Bayles the 2nd son, by deed dated 10 Dec 1688, sold to Percifull Simpson of this County Dec'd, and the said Simpson by deed dated 10 March 1689 delivered the land to the abovesaid Richd Smith, etc. The land joins that of Wm Fletcher dec'd, the line of Robt Davis, line of Isaac Foster and the land of Thos James. Wit: Pitts Curtis, Thos Blanch, Tho Eves. 17 Dec 1718. 19.3. (I think this entry is in error. The land prob sold to White or some member of his family by Simpson)

White, Richd. Aged 80 yrs or th-abts. 2 March 1658/9. 15.19 (If this
    entry is correct, and there seems no good reason
    why it should not be, his birth would be circa
    1579.)
  Richd. Headright of Wm Wildey. 8 Sept 1662. 2.161
  Richd. Deceased. Father of James White. 20 Mar 1677/8. 17.120
  Simon. He, Thos Cole and Edmond Cole were sons of Mrs Margritt
    Davis, dec'd. 19 Feb 1717/18. 6.254
  Tho. On jury Saffin vs Thompson. 6 Apl 1669. 3.63
  Tho. Sold 50 acres to Saml Mahane prior to 21 Feb 1704/5. 17.51
  Tho. Bought land from Tho Bayles and left it to his son Thomas
    White who sold it to Saml Mehaines all prior to
    21 Feb 1704/5. 18.76
Whitford, David. Merchant of Edinburgh in Scotland. Buys 1/2 int in
    water mill from Tho Lane, tailor. 18 Jan 1669/70.
    16.154
  David. Bought 500 acres on 1 Nov 1671 from Tho Lane. Sold it
    to Edwd Porteus on 16 March 1674/5. 17.255
  David. Sold 1000 acres to Edw Portees on N side of a branch
    of Dennis Creek. 16 March 1674/5. 18.27
  David. See entry Edw Potees. 16 Mar 1674/5. 18.158
  Da--. Sold 500 acres in Wicco par to Jno Pinkard. 3 July 1677.
    17.255
  David. His admr Jno Harris sues Jno Gouch son and heir of
    Saml Gouch. 21 May 1696. 4.724
Whitthall, Erasmus. Age 16 yrs. 19 July 1670. 16.78
Whitehall, Rasmus. Wit deed Smith to Nipper. 14 Apl 1677. 17.120
Whitehead, Tho. of Wicco par. Buys 50 acres from Tho Downing. 20 Feb
    1710/11. 18.7
Whitney, Jno. Servt to Mr (or Math) Rhodon. Adj 17 yrs old. 6 Apl 1669.
    3.60
Whittington, Capt Wm. Age 37 or th-abts. Being at Midleburgh in
    Zealand was there requested by Mr Richd Wright to
    go with him to Flushing regarding Mrs Hugh Lee,
    etc. 14 May 1653. 14.145
Whitty, Capt Jno. Patented 1400 acres. See entry Wm Wildey. 5 May 1661.
    17.224-9   Also pat 1450 acres on N side G W river.
    15 May 1661. 17.224-9 Also sold 1450 acres to Wm
    Wildey prior to 8 Nov 1664. 16.74
Wiccomico Church. Road to passes Tho Williams' house, Spring Cove, etc.
    15 May 1705. 17.252-4
Wicoocomoco Indians. All persons in this County having any guns belong-
    ing to the Indians of Wicoocomoco Indian Towne to
    deliver them "to Robert the Greate man of the said
    Towne". 19 Feb 1678/9. 4.23 Also: Wm Tapptico,
    King, in the year 1695/6. 19.95
Wiccomico (Little) Mill House. See entry Henry Watts. 9 Jan 1668/9.
    16.47
Wiccocimocoe Parish. Ref to 24 Feb 1670/1. 16.162

Wiccomocce parish. The Vestry complains that Wm Hartland agreed 3 July 1678 to finish the church. He has done nothing about it. The Court orders him to finish it by Christmas. 16 July 1685. 4.289

Wiccocomoco parish. The following fined for absence from church for 2 months. Wm Arledge, Robt Nash, Meredith Mahens, Tho Laurence, Lawrence Gaskins, Wm Cox, Richd Crawford, Jno Thomas. 23 Sept 1715. 6.138. (Prob Quakers)

Wicker, Henry. Aged 45 or th-abts. 20 May 1656. 14.77

Henry. Deceased. Prob of will to Jno Hainie and Sam Goohe overseers and proved by oaths of wit: Nich: Paris and Henry Summars. 22 June 1669. 3.65

Wiggins, Anne. of St S par. Deed. 6 July 1708. To Richd Tulles of St S par, for 800 lb tobo paid to James Magow of St S par for 14 months accomodation of Jno Wiggin, son of said Anne. The said Anne Wiggins binds her son John, aged 3 yrs the 5th Feb last, as servant to Tulles until he be 22 yrs of age. Tulles to teach him to read, write and cypher and the trade he now follows, ie cooper. Wit David Straughan, Robt Maukin. 17.204

Wigginton, Roger. To teach Christo Miller, age 13, trade of ship carpenter. 12 March 1713/14. 6.21

Wildey. There are so many of these notes and they are so involved that to include them it will be necessary to change the arrangement of this volume.

Wildey, Mr. Pd 400 lb tobo from County levy for "clearing the Court house. 5 Nov 1668. 3.47. Also pd 100 lb tobo from County levy "for a paire of Pistolls spoyled". 21 Nov 1678. 4.17 Also as "Mr Wildie" his land adj Antho and Tho Robinson. 13 Jan 1700/1. 17.108

Wildey, Mrs Eliz:. Wife of Wm Wildey and dau of Jno Mottley decd. 19th Dec 1706. 17.24-8

Wildey, James. His will prob by Henry Fleet exor. 19 Nov 1701. 5.180

Wildey, Mrs Jane. Extrx of Wm Wildey deceased. To have 4800 lb tobo from the estate of Mr Charles Morgan "for her Charge and Trouble in Tending Mr Charles Morgan in the tyme of his Sickness and Funerall Expenses after his decease, and six hundred pounds of Tobacco and Caske for so much paid to Mr Farnefold for a Funerall Sermon, And two hundred pounds of Tobacco to Mr Edward Husbands for medicines Administered to the said Mr Morgan in the time of his Sicknes". 15 June 1681. 4.97 (Note: There is some Wildey-Morgan family connection not made clear by any records I have seen. B.F.)

Wildey, Mrs Jane. Certificate for 250 acres for transportation of Tho: Spilman, Mary Spilman, Benj Ricketts, Jno Cunny, Owen Macgaaine. 19 Oct 1681. 4.105

Wildey, Mrs Jane. Arrested at suit of Jno Harris. He not appearing non suit to Mrs Wildey. 16 Aug 1682. 4.141

Wildey, Mrs Jane. "Whereas Mrs Jane Wildey and Mrs Eliz: Fleet were both sumoned to this Court to give in their Evidence in difference depending between Xphr Kirk and Eliz Williams, and not appearing, It is ordered that they be fined according to Act" 18 July 1683. 4.190

Wildey, Mrs Jane. Attachmt to her agt est of Saml Jones 800 lb tobo. 18 Nov 1685. 4.308

Wildey, Mrs Jane. Her servt Patrick Omullion age 13 yrs. 28 Dec 1687. 4.416

Wildey, Mrs Jane. Judgt to her agt Joseph Humphreys 850 lb tobo as by his bill dated 6 July 1691. 15 June 1692. 4.594

Wildey, Mrs Jane. Judgt to her agt the sheriff who arrested James Blackberby at her suit for 1522 lb tobo and he (Blackberby) not appearing. 15 June 1692. 4.594

Wildy, Michael. Son of Nathl and Sarah (Phillips) Wildy. Grandson of Wm Phillips. 9 July 1729. Lancaster Co Records No. 8. p 114

Wildy, Nath'l. of Lancaster Co. Deposition. Aged 62 yrs or th-abts. Says Micheal Wildy, now in full life, is his son by Sarah his late wife, the only daughter of Wm Phillips. That he often heard his wife Sarah say there was 150 acres in Elizabeth City Co near Hampton, now or lately in possession of one Curle of that place, which legally descended to her, and that the said Michael is the only surviving heir. 9 July 1729. Lancaster Co Records. No 8. p 114

Wildy, Nathl. Will. No date shown. Probated 10 June 1730. Son Hopkins exor. Son Wm not of age. Sons Mail and Job. Daus Sarah, Cath:, Darkis. Wit Geo Site Jr, Jno Pines. This Nath'l was a boat builder and cooper (carpenter) and was of St Mary's White Chapel parish. Lancaster Co Records. No 8. p 173.

Wildey, Wm. Aged 38 yrs or th-abts. "Jurat in Cur 25 Novem: 1652".14.11

Wildey, Wm. Pof A. 11 Dec 1654. Whereas Tho Watts late of Nansemond Co dec'd sold Tho Garrett a tract of 300 acres in Wicco. Thos Adderson, admr of Watts, appoints "my friend" Wm Wildey to secure the land for Garrett. 14.79 Wildey, in behalf of Tho Adderson, assigns the land to Tho Garratt. 20 May 1656. 14.79

Wildey, Wm. Michael Brooke testifies he drew a release "some nine years since" for a parcel of bills and writings left by Corbell Pidwell in the hands of Wm Wildey. 26 Mar 1658. 15.14

Wildey, Wm. Records his mark for cattle. 29 Oct 1659. 15.30

Wildey, Wm. His servt Richd Jackson age 14. 21 Jan 1660/1. 2.136

Wildey, Wm. Certificate for 650 acres for importing: Christopher Vaughan, Tho Mash, Henery Clark, - Williams, Rich White, Samll Webb, Richd Jackson, Wm Smyth, Wm Boharry, Jane Fuller, John Simpson, Joseph Harrington and "one mayde serv't not named" 8 Sept 1662. 2.161

Willdy, Wm. of Great Wickecomicoe, N Co., planter. Sells Mr Tho Hobson, for 2000 lb tobo, 135 acres on N side Little Wicco. Adj house of Hugh Fouch and is part of 1450 acres sold by Captain John Whitty to sd Willdy. Jane, wife of Wm Willdy consents. Wit Jas Gaylord, Tho Smith. 8 Nov 1664. 16.125

Wildey, Wm. P of A to Jas Gaylord. 21 Dec 1666. 16.5
Wildye, Wm. On Jury Presly vs Matthew. 21 Jan 1668/9. 3.53
Wildey, Wm. Wit P of A Michaell DeConti to Jas Gaylord. 20 July 1671. 16.194
Wildey, Mr Wm. His will proved by oath of Owen Bradley one of the wit:, The other wit Mr Jas Gaylord being dead. 15 June 1681. 4.96

Wildey, William. of St S par. Deed. 19 Nov 1706. Wildey sells Richd Chichester of Lancaster Co, for L 150. already pd, 385 acres in St S par. Adj land of Tho Hobson, the head of a branch falling into the Easterly main branch (or Apes hole branch ?) of Hulls Creek, land of Joseph Hoult, land of The Barnes near Barnes Bridge, other land of Wildey. This land being part of a patent of 1400 acres granted Capt John Whitty 5 May 1661, and by Peter Aston Gent atty of Henry Corbin Esq who was atty of said Capt Whitty, sold to Wm Wildey late of this Co dec'd, who by will dated 1 Dec 1680 devised all his land to his wife Jane Wildey, all which by the said deed from Ashton atty dated 21 Jan 1664 and the said will proved in Northumberland Court 16 June 1681. Mrs Jane Wildey dieing and not disposing of the land it descended to Wm Wildey party to these parts. The deed refers to "the said William with Eliz: Wildey his now wife". Wit: Geo Cooper, Tobias x Pursly, Tho Hobson, Tho Stretton. Deed ack by Wm Wildey unto Mr Danl McCarty atty of Richard Chichester 20 Nov 1706. Rerecorded by Mr Jno Chichester, the original record being burnt, 15 Feb 1715/6.   17.224-9
On page 226. P of A. 20 Nov 1706. Richd Chichester to "my trusty friends" Geo Eskridge or Daniel McCarty or Wm Dare, Gent, to accept the deed.
P of A. Eliz Wildey to Eskridge and McCarty. 19 Nov 1706.

Wildey, Wills of William and Jane Wildey.
page 227. "In the name of God amen I William Wildey of Fairefields in Northumberland County in Virginia being sicke and weak in body but of perfect mind and memory (praised be God for the same) doe make this my last will and Testament in manner and forme following (Vizt) I committ my Soul to God that gave it me my body to the Earth from whence it came in an assured hope and confidence that the body and Soule through the merits of Jesus Christ my blessed Saviour and Redeemer shall have a Joyfull Resurrection at the last day I give my Deare and Loveing wife Jane Wildey all my Temporall Estate both reall and personall as Lands Tenements Goods and Chattles of what nature or kind soever the same shall be To have and to Hold to her and to her heirs Executors Administrators and Assignes for Ever desireing my said wife to Gratifie my children as shee shall find them deserveing and doe appoint my said wife to be the Executrix of this my last will and Testament Witness my hand and Seale this first day of December 1680.   (signature not shown on record)
Sealed in the presence of James Gaylord, Owen Bradley his marke.
June the 16 1681. This was proved to be the last will and

Wildey. Wills of William and Jane Wildey (continued) Testament of Wm Wildey by the oath of Owen Bradley and is Recorded Vera Cop'a Test The Hobson Cl Cur Northumberland"
Rerecorded 15 Feb 1715/16 by Mr Jno Chichester on behalf of his father Richard Chichester Esq.

p 228. "In the name of God Amen I Jane Wildey widdow of Northumberland County in Virginia being ancient and feeble and very sick and weake in body but of sound and perfect memory praise be God for it doe make and ordaine this my last will and Testament in manner and form following Imprs I comitt my soul into the hands of Almighty God - - (etc) - - and as Touching my Temporal Estate I dispose thereof as followeth Item I give and bequeath unto my daughter Elizabeth Fleet all my personall Estate of what quality or condition so ever to her and her heirs for Ever Item it is my will and desire that in case my son William Wildey assigne Transferr and make over the land and plantation whereon he now lives unto my said daughter Elizabeth Fleet and her heirs for Ever the Land aforesaid containing by Estimation Four hundred acres commonly called Poplers neck Then it is my will and desire that my sone William have an Equall proportion of my Estate with my said Daughter Elizabeth Excepting what is hereafter nominated the negro woman all my pewter and my made up Linnen and the rest of my goods and chattles to be Equally divided betweene my sone William and my daughter Eliz: in case my said sone shall make over the land called poplars neck as aforesaid to my said daughter Elizabeth and in case he refuses soe to doe to have noe part or portion out of any of my Estate Item: I give and bequeath unto my daughter Elizabeth all my wearing apparell. Lastly I doe constitute and ordaine and appoint my sone Henry Fleet and my said daughter Elizabeth Executors of this my last will and Testament In Testimony therto I have hereunto set my hand and seale this 11th day of Aprill 1701
Signed sealed   sign Jane Wildey (the seale)
declared and published
in the presence of us
John Rose,   sign Mary Blackeby
Henry Parry   "
Proved 19 Nov 1701 by oaths of Jno Rose and Mary his wife and Henry Parry.
Rerecorded 15 Feb 1715/6 by Mr Jno Chichester for his father Richd Chichester, Esq.

Wildey, William. His land at Fairfield. p.228. Patent. 15 May 1661.
Sir Wm Berkeley to Capt John Whitty. 1450 acres in Northumberland Co., on N side of Great Wiccocomoco River, "bounding Southward on the land of Mr John Berdon Mr Radford dec'd and Mr Downing (bought of Martin Cole John Edwards and others) and Easterly upon the lands of John Motley and Roger Waters Westerly and Northerly upon the maine Woods being a Quadrangular figure and Extending Northerly upon the first mentioned bounds", this land formerly granted Jane the daughter of Col William Clayburne by pat 10 Feb 1657 and now assigned over to

Wildey, Wm. His land at Fairfield (continued) said Jno Whitty by the said Collo Wm Clayborne, Capt Wm Clayborne and "Thomas Brereton who marryed the said Jane".
Assignment of above 21 Jan 1664/5, Peter Aston Gent atty of Henry Corbin Esq atty of Capt Jno Whitty to Wm Wildey. Signed Peter Aston. Wit: Sam: Smith, John Rogers.
p 229. P of A. 29 Aug 1663. Henry Corbin of Rappa River, mercht and atty of Capt Jno Whitty to Capt Peter Aston to sell "a Seate of Land called Fairefields". Signed Henry Corbin. Wit: Richard Lee, Val Peyton.

Wildey, William of St S par and Elizabeth his wife. Deed. 13 Dec 1706. They sell to Mr Jno Ingram of Wicco par, 200 acres of land on "Wiccocomoco River otherwise called Wiccocomoco Creek". Adjs line of Tho Webb, land of Ralph Bickley. Is part of land "commonly called Mottleys neck formerly granted by Pattent dated the 13 of January 1661 to John Mottley dec'ed" for 600 acres. "William Wildey in Right of his said Wife Elizabeth and by Vertue of his the said Wildeys Intermarrying the said Elizabeth the Daughter and sole heire of John Mottley dec'd the son of the aforesaid John Mottley and Donee of Mary Mottley his mother the Relict Legatee and sole Exer'trix of his said Father (as by the Will of the said first menconed John dated the 8th of February 1669/70 and by Deed from the said Mary to her said sone dated the 13th of October 1671 may more Largely appeare) obteyned a Grant from the Right Honourable the Proprietors of the Northern Neck of Virginia x x dated the third day of August 1704". Signed William Wildey, Elizabeth x Wildey. Wit: Tho Hobson, Tho Stretten, John x Hadwell. Various entries, bond, etc follow. 17. p 24-8 ('Donee' he to whom lands were given. This in old English law.)

Willdy, Wm. Appraises est of Wm Winder decd. 20 June 1711. 18.67
Wildy, Wm. Appraises est of Wm Dow decd. 18 July 1711. 18.71
Wildy, Wm. Appraises est of Mary Walker decd. 24 Nov 1711. 18.114
Wildey, Wm. Owes Wm Pickerin 70 lb tobo. Ao 1712. 18.222
Wildey, Wm. Security for Saml Smith. 17 June 1714. 6.46
Wildey, Wm. Arrested at suit of Tho Hobson for 440 lb tobo. 18 May 1716. 6.169
Wildeys land. In St S par, near the Church. See entry Tho Berry. 17th Feb 1708/9. 17.183

Wilkins, Jno. dec'd. His admr now Jane the wife of Tho Barnes. 20 Nov 1696. 4.751
Wilkins, Peter. Wit will of Tho Barns. 5 May 1712. 18.265
Wilkins, Tho. Wit deed Saml Smith to Wm Nelmes of St S par. 19 Decr 1709. 17.53
Wilks, Mr Tho. His suit agt Capt Peter Knight to next Court. 16 Oct 1676. 4.7
Willgrass, Jos. Wit will Dan'l Suilevant. 29 Aug 1704. 17.261

Williams. These notes will have to be somewhat crowded in order to
include them in this volume.
Williams, Mrs Alice. Wife of Tho. Deed to Jno Champion. 2 Dec 1700
17.70 Also as wife of Tho 18 Dec 1699;17.44 and as wife of
Tho 27 March 1703. 17.45 Also as wife of Tho acks deed to
Mahan 18 July 1705. 17.67
Williams, David. Son of Rog: Williams, abt 12 yrs old, bound, with his
father's consent, to Jno Wornam till 21. 17 May 1682. 4.128
Williams, David. Overseer to Capt Leonard Howson. Wit his will. 13 Dec
1704. 17.8
Williams, Edw. Arrests Walter Price and no cause appearing is nonsuit-
ed. 20 Nov 1668. 3.49
Williams, Edw. Bought 345 acres from Robt Bradshaw. Sold it to James
Claughton prior to 17 Feb 1679/80. 17.87
Williams, Edwd. Judgt to Richd Rice atty of said Williams who is heir
to Temperance Bradshaw deceased, and who brought action agt
Robt Bradley who married Anne dau and heir of Robt Bradshaw
deceased, for 345 acres, producing an obligation of Robert
Bradshaw dated 22 Oct 1654 to deliver the land to Temperance
Bradshaw. 15 July 1685. 4.274
Williams, Eliz: In legal dif with Xphr Kirk. 18 May 1683. 4.190
Williams, Jno. Headright of Capt Gyles Brent. 21 Jan 1651/2. 1.70
Williams, Jno. His servt Geo Edmonds age 13. 21 Jan 1660/1. 2.136
Williams, Jno. Servt to Mr Jones adj age 9 yrs. 19 Jan 1675/6. 3.249
Williams, Jno. Servt to John Hughlett adj 9 yrs of age. 15 Jan 1678/9.
4.18
Williams, Roger. Since 28 Nov 1667 has owed Jno Evans 450 lb tobo.
11 Jan 1668/9. 3.50 Also Roger Williams Jr who was son of
Roger Williams Sr. 20 Jan 1676/7. 17.109
Williams, Tho. His serv't Wm Hartington age 16 yrs. 21 Jan 1660/1.
2.136 Also his servt Owen Fell age 9. 10 Mar 1661/2. 2.153
Williams, Tho. He married the widow of Capt Richd Budd. 8 Oct 1662.
2.163
Williams, Tho. Sues Wm Brudenall. 21 Jan 1668/9. 3.52
Williams, Tho. His servt Alice Dryer ran away for 10 weeks and 3 days.
She ordered to serve extra time. 6 Apl 1669. 3.62
Williams, Tho. Wit deed Ingram to Winter. 16 Apl 1672. 16.231
Williams, Mr Tho. Court order that he inquire regarding Jno Mottoone's
estate. 21 Apl 1681. 4.93
Williams, Tho. Sold 50 acres on S side Wicco River to Steph: Robinson.
3 May 1690. 18.149 Also sold land to Steph: Robinson 3 May
1690. 17.153
Williams, Tho. of Wicco par. Deed. 18 Dec 1699. Son and heir to Thos
Williams deceased, sells to Tho Gaskins of same par, 100
acres on Dennis Creek. Signed Tho Williams, Alice Williams.
Wit: Jas Waddy, Richd Lattimore. P of A, Alice wife of Thos
Williams to Tho Hobson. Deed rerecorded by Mr Tho Gaskins 21
March 1710/11. 17.44
Williams, Tho. Sells dwelling plantation on Mill Creek to Jno Champion.
2 Dec 1700. 17.70
Williams, Tho. Wit Robinson to Embry. 28 July 1704. 17.153
Williams, Tho. Deed to Saml Mahan. 15 Mar 1704/5. 17.67

Williams, Thomas. Deed. 27 March 1703. Tho Wms and Alice his wife of Great Wicco: par., planter, sell Thos Gascoyne, planter, of same par., for 500 lb tobo., 50 acres on Scotland Mill Creek, on S side Great Wicco: River, part of a greater tract granted Mr Tho Williams deceased, father of sd Tho Williams on 30 Jan 1650/1, and by last will of Thos the Elder, devised to Thos the Younger. Adjoins land sold by Tho Jr to sd Thomas Gascoyne, the land of Jane Coppage widow, land of Tho Byram. Signed Thomas Williams, Alice x Williams. Wit: John x Lock, John Prim, Sarry x Lock. Rerecorded 21 March 1710/11 by Mr Tho Gaskins. 17.45

Williams, Tho. of Wicco par, planter and Alice his wife. Deed. 15 May 1705. Sell Rd Lattimore 20 acres adj the road to Wiccocomoco Church from sd Wms' house. Also adj Spring Cove. Part of 500 acres where Tho Wms now liveth, formerly patented by Thomas Wms deceased, father to Tho Wms party to these parts. Wit Jno Prim, Jeremiah Bell. Rerecorded 18 Feb 1719/20 by Rd Lee in behalf of Rd Lattimore. 17.252

Williams, Tho of G W par and Alice his wife. Deed. 26 Sept 1702. Sell Rd Lattimore 50 acres on Dennis Creek in G W par, etc. 17.254

Williams, Tho. of N Co., labourer. Deed. 22 Feb 1705/6. Sells Maurice Jones, Gent., for 7000 lb tobo, 100 acres where he (Wms) now lives, being bequeathed to him by will of Tho Banks of N Co deceased in words "I give and bequeath unto Tho Williams my Son in Law". Wit Bartho Schrever, Richd Hull. Ack by Eliz: Williams wife of Tho. Rerecorded 21 Mar 1711/12 by Maurice Jones Gent. 17.164

Williams, Thomas. Will. Dated 11 March 1706/7. Prob 23 May 1707. Mr Tho Hobson and Mr Jas Waddy to ack sale of 100 acres to Mr Saml Mahane. To eldest son Tho Wms. To youngest son Jno Wms, he under 21. Dau Eliz Wms cut off with a shilling. Movable est to be div betw wife Alice Wms (she extrx) and 4 children: Thos, Mary, Anne and Jno Williams. Wit John Prim, Ro Gordon, Jne Taylor. Proved by 3 wit. Rerecorded 16 May 1711 by Mr Saml Mahane. 17.72

Williams, Tho. Wit P of A Champion to Lattimore. 15 Feb 1709/10.17.186

Williams, Tho. Wit will Steph Wells 31 Oct 1712. Proved it by his oath 21 Jan 1718/19. 19.12

Williams, Tho Sr. Deceased. Father of Tho Jr. 18 Dec 1699. 17.44

Williams, Tho Sr. Deceased. Entry dated 27 Mar 1703 states that he patented land 30 Jan 1650/1. 17.45

Williams, Wm and Jno. of St S par. Presented for ab from Church. 15th May 1717. 6.202

Williams, Wm. Sued by Robt and Eliz Jones for 7200 lb tobo. 20 Febry 1718/19. 6.306

Williamson, Thos Jr. Probate of will of Tho Williamson dec'd to him. Proved by oaths of wit: Capt Tho Jones and Abra Sheares. 18 Apl 1683. 4.176

Willis, James. Gives Mary Earle the younger a heifer. 22 Jan 1651/2. 1.71

Willis, James. Signs oath to Commonwealth of England. 13 Apl 1652.1.72

Willoughby, Joane. The relict of Henry Willoughby, the relict of Robt Hitchock, the relict of Edw: Henly, assigns her interest of thirds of land belonging to Mr Tho Opie, formerly in posses: of Mr David Lyndsay. 17 March 1674/5. 3.224

Willowbye, Kath: Headright of Richd Hawkins. 20 Feb 1651/2. 1.50

Willoughby, Tho. Selected by Rd Thompson as guardian. 8 Sept 1662. 2.161

Willoby, Tho and Sarah. P of A to "oue Loveinge Brother Mr Isaac Allerton" to ack sale of 48 acres in N Co to Wm Thomas. See entry Rd. Thompson. 20 Feb 1663/4. 15.124

Wills, Saml. Headright of Wm Sheares. 21 Aug 1678. 4.4

Wilsford, Tho. Appointment from Sir Wm Berkeley, Governor, etc, etc, as Clerk of the Court of Northumberland Co. 22 Oct 1650. 1.48

Wilsford, Th: Signs oath to Commonwealth of England. 13 Apl 1652. 1.72

Wilsford, Tho. Wit entry re Jno Tew. 21 Aug 1654. Westmorland Co records. 1653-9. p 28

Wilsford, Tho. Aged 39 years or th-abts. Swears he drew will dated 15 Aug 1650 for Wm Presly Sr. 20 Jan 1656/7. 14.96

Wiltsheire, Wm. Signs bond Honor Dermott admr of Hugh Dermott. 17 Dec 1712. 18.241

Willshire, Wm. "a poor ancient feeble person" exempt from any levy. 19 May 1714. 6.36

Wiltshire, Wm and Kath his wife, Henry Dawson and John Conway, admrs of Henry Dawson dec'd. obt judgt agt Jno Way for 320 lb tobo. 17 March 1714/15. 6.104

Wiltshire, Wm. ref to "Catherine the late widdow of Hen Dawson dec'd since the wife of the said Wiltshire". 16 Nov 1715. 6.144

Wilson, Robt. Married widow of Jno Oliver. See entry Wm Gradey. 17.152

Wilson, Tho. Marriner. His land adj Col Rd Lee on Div. Creek. 21 May 1651. 17.65

Wilson, Tho. Wit P of A Essex to Bayly. 9 Feb 1671/2. 16.226

Willson, Tho. Marriner. See Rd Lee. 15 Feb 1707/8. 17.60

Winborough, Paul. As wit proves will of Dan Holland decd. 17 Apl 1672. 3.145

Winchester School. See entry Rev Jno Farnefold. 3 July 1702. 17.234

Winder, Capt. See entry Capt Tho Brereton. 17.238-43

Winder, Eliz. See entry Capt Tho Brereton. 23 Mar 1698/9. 17.189

Winder, Wm. Nuncupative Will. Dated 1 Oct 1701. "a short time before he dyed". Prob 5 Oct 1710. To brother Mr Jno Winder in Somersett Co in Md, all property there. Property in Va to Jno Hobson son of Tho Hobson except 2 silver spoons to Judith daughter of said Tho Hobson. To Tho Stretton his coat. J18.49 Also: Admr of his est to Tho Hobson during minority of John Hobson son of sd Jno. 17 May 1711. 18.45. Also inv of his est. 20 June 1711. 18.67

Window, Jno. Wit deed Bradford to Smith. 16 July 1713. 18.328

Winder, Mrs Eliz: widow. See entry Col Tho Brereton. 17 Sept 1714. 6.83

Winder, Wm, decd. His admr Tho Hobson agt Rainsford Smith to next Court. 17 Mar 1714/5. 6.107

Winlow, Mrs John. Overconscientious. See entry Adam Yarratt. 22 Octr 1667. 16.25

Winn, Tho. His mistress Mrs Eleanor - - accused of murdering him. His body dug up and she is vindicated. 1 Jan 1655/6. 14.67

Winter, Eliza. A mulatto woman sold by Leond Howson to Jno Bisick prior to 25 Mar 1706. Set free 19 Mar 1706/7. 17.173

Winter, Thos. Mercht. Appointed trustee for Kath: Ingram by Jno Ingram. 29 Dec 1671. 16.216

Winter, Tho. of Rappa. Buys 600 acres from Tho Ingram and Kath: his wife. 16 Apl 1672. 16.231

Winter, Tho. Ordered, with Erasmus Withers and Barth Dameron, to div est of Robt Jones decd betw the heirs. 21 Aug 1678. 4.2

Winter, Mr Tho. Ages of his 5 servants, all children, adj by the Court. 21 Aug 1678. 4.3 See entry Varley

Winter, Thos. of Dividing Creek. Deed of Gift to Tho youngest son of Charles Ingram, 200 acres. 11 June 1680. 17.14

Winter, Mr Tho. Agreemt re boundry line. 14 Oct 1707. 17.23

Witchcraft. Coles - Neale case. An absurd item. Depositions of Thomas Bandmill, Wm Barry, Wm Hartland, Fran: Hawkins, Tho Hobson, Edw: LeBreton, Clement Lempriere, Dr Edw Sanders, Mrs Mary Sanders and Richd Smyth. 20 May 1671. 16.179-181 and 16.187

Witham, Cuthbert. Wit deed of gift Lenton to Lenton. 26 Jan 1668/9. 16.67

Withers, Erasmus. To div est of Ro Jones betw heirs. 21 Aug 1678. 4.2

Withers, Erasmus. Nuncupative will. Sworn 15 June 1681 by Gervase Hatfield and Wm Jones. Wm Chapman also heard the will which was of 1 Nov 1680. To wife Francis and his 5 children all est except a black mare to Erasmus Allen. To son Erasmus Withers "his Gould Seale ring". 4.94

Withers, Mr Erasmus, late dec'd. His admr now married to Mr Jno Curtis. Her bondsmen Wm Jones and Jno Eustace request release. 20 July 1687. 4.460

Wittcliffe, David. Registers mark for cattle. 20 Nov 1651. 1.66

Woldridge, Edw. Servt to Jas Claughton adj 15 yrs old. 19 July 1671. 3.124

Wooldridge, Edw. His land adj Jno Claughton in Mattaponi Neck in St S par. 18 Jan 1707/8. 17.89

Wooldridge, Edw decd. His will presented by Ruth Wooldridge his extrx. Proved by oaths of wit: David Straughn, Ann Auveling, John Kemmys. 16 March 1714/15. 6.100

Wooldridge, Eliz: Wit will of Saml Churchill. 4 June 1702. 17.229 Also she appears as a witness 4 Apl 1703. 17.12

Wooldridge, Eliz. She and Jam Johnson complained against for trespass by Josiah Dameron. 17 Mar 1712/13. 6. pp 78 to 81.

Wooldridge, John. Son of Edw Wooldridge decd makes choice of Mr Matthew Kenner as guardian. 20 Jan 1719/20. 6.351

Wooldridge, Ruth. Div of land betw her and Henry Auvelin. 15 June 1715. 6.110

Wolfe, Jno. Lives on plantation owned by Henry Mayes. 10 Feb 1708/9. 17.101 He files mark for cattle 15 Aug 1711. 18.96

Wolf Pitt Neck. Adj land of Wm and Chas Copedge. 5 June 1710. 17.50

Wood, Jane. Wit will of Ro Boyd. 10 Sept 1710. 18.42

Wood, Jno. His land adj Roger Walters. 29 Dec 1669. 16.69

Wood, Jno. Sibbey Parker binds herself to serve him. 10 Mar 1669/70 16.165

Wood, Jno. A servt exchanged by Danl Neale Sr to Sibbey Parker. 28 Mar 1671. 16.184

Wood, Jno. Judgt agt him to Hen Burdett 710 lb tobo. 21 Aug 1678. 4.3
Wood, Jno. Agrees to serve Tho Gill one year. 15 July 1713. 18.327
Wood, Moses. Ref to as Godson in will of Ro Boyd. 10 Sep 1710. 18.42
Wood, Peter. Wit deliv of land to Purcell by Crosby. 18 Oct 1705. 17.192
Wood, Wm. His est attached by Mr Nicho Owen for 1000 lb tobo 16 Oct 1676. 4.7
Woodman, Jos. Servt to Hen Corbin adj 14 yrs old. 26 Feb 1660/1. 2.137
Wooll, Wm. Servt to Mr Jno Cralle. Agrees to serve 8 yrs rather than the 5 of his indentures in order to remain with Cralle if sold to him. 21 Dec 1698. 4.848
Wornam, Jno. David Williams abt 12 yrs old, bound to him till 21. 17th May 1682. 4.128
Wornom, Jno. His land adj that left to Rd Robinson. 13 Jan 1700/1. 17.106
Wornum, Jno. Was father of Jno Wornum who is now living and former husband of Mrs Eliz Webb widow. 16 May 1707. 17.209
Wornom, Ann. To be pd 30 lb tobo "for knitting a pair of Coton Gloves for Mary Walker in her lifetime". 17 June 1713. 18.312
Wornom, Jno. Deed from his mother Mrs Eliz Webb. 19 May 1714. 6.33
Wornom, Jno. Sworn Deputy Clerk of Northumberland Co. 19 Dec 1716. 6.187
Wren, Wm. Owes est of Tho Crowder 545 lb tobo. 20 June 1711. 18.62
Wright, Richd. At Midleburgh in Zealand. Went to Flushing with Capt Wm Whittington, etc. 14 May 1653. 14.145
Wright, Richd. Aged 22 or th-abts 20 Aug 1655. 14.52 He died betw 16 Aug and 10th Decr 1663. 15.114 Therefore aged abt 30.
Wright, Richd. Admr of Col Jno Mottrom. Objects to Geo Colclough, who married Ursula, widow of Col Jno Mottrom, and formerly widow of Richd Thompson, becoming admr of Thompson's estate. 20 Nov 1658. 2.96
Wright, Capt Richd. Admr of est of Col Jno Mottrom decd, assigns to Wm Grenstead a maid servant formerly belonging to Mottrom's est called Elizabeth Key, now wife to sd Grensted. 21 July 1659. 15.27
Wright, Richd. Will. Entry mutilated. Dated 16 Aug 1663. Prob 10 Decr 1663. Wife Anne. Son Francis, the only name of child appearing, but refers to 'my children'. Est div in 3 parts so evidently another child. Overseers in Va brothers Nicholas Spencer and Jno Mottrom. Overseer in England "my Cozen Matthew Merriton of London merchant". Wit Jno Fountaine, Edmund Helder. 15.114
Wright, Jno. of Cople parish, Westmorland Co, blacksmith. Patents 250 acres, thought to be in Westmorland Co but now found to be in Wicocomoco parish, Northumberland Co. 7 Sep 1691. 17.128
Wright, Richd. Wit will Wm Tignor 28 Nov 1698. Proved it by oath 15th Apl 1702. 17.160
Wright, Richd. Friend to and overseer of will of Tho Webb. 11 Sep 1702 17.5 Also friend and exor of Jos Palmore 26 Mar 1703. 17.9 Exor of Capt Leonard Howson 13 Dec 1704. 17.8 Wit will of Jno Webb 4 June 1709. 17.102 Exor of Ann Webb who leaves whole est to Ann Howson 21 Sept 1710. 19.89 Wit will of Charles Betts Sr dated 1 Oct 1709. Swears he wrote it for him when rerecorded 16 May 1711. 17.100

Wright, Richd. Exor of Leond Howson. 18 July 1711. 6.325. Swears he wrote will dated 18 Nov 1708 for Col Gee Cooper. 18 July 1711 17.123 Appraises est of Wm Dow decd 18 July 1711. 18.71

Wright, Richd. of St S par buys 58 acres in St S par from Thos Webb 12 July 1712. 18.206 Exor of Eliz Howson decd.16 Mar 1714/15. 6.101. Exor of Capt Jno Howson decd 17 Aug 1715.6.128 Exor as greatest creditor of Tho Waughop 15 May 1717.6.210 He re-records assignment Innis to Leon'd Howson 18 May 1720. 17.255

Yarratt, Adam. Various depositions and entries.
Thomas Gilbert. Deposition. Age not shown. Says "being once in Compa with Dennis Ize, when he was rooming of Hannah Abraham: and the old woman understanding the said Ize was like to have her daughter she said that if her daughter did goe along with Dennis Ize, she would not leave her house, and would tarry in it and furnish it, for she built it and paid for it, soe Yarrett understanding it, said she should not be there for he would fire the house". 22 Oct 1667. 16.25

Alexander Sherwood. Deposition. Age not shown. Says "Living at the house of Dennis Ize, his mother in law being at the house of James Johnson, he desired your deponent to fetch her down and she being ancient and not able to travel wee lay at Adam Yarratts and said Yarratt was gone to said Izes at that time, and next day being Sunday and not going to said Izes wee met Adam Yarrett coming home soe they gave each other the time of the day, and Izes mother in law desired (if he had bin at home) to have had the key of her Room doore, and Yarrett answered she was nere like to come there noe more upon which she tooke a small violl out of her pockett and drunke a dram to him soe they dranke to each other and parted" No date, but other depositions in this group are of 22 Octr 1667. 16.25

Rice, Richard. deposition. Age not shown. Says working at Adam Yarratt's he built 3 houses. That he was pd in part by Adam Yarratt and part by Hannah. That Hannah was at great pains in the affairs of the house. Took care of Adam when sick, etc. That while sick Adam Yarratt made his will "and gave Joan Winlow and Hanah Abram house and ground for their lifetime and Joan Winlow was something troubled at that she should take that for gift, which they had bin at soe much Cost and charge. And the said Hanah replyed Mother the man hath done that he promised us". The deponent has done other work for them, etc. 22 Oct 1667. 16.25

Palmer, Tho. Deposition. Age not shown. Says several times Adam Yarrett told him Hannah Abram and her mother were to have the land for their lives. 21 Oct 1667. 16.25

Tower, Tho. Deposition. Age not shown. Says that 3 yrs since, packing a hhd of tobo at Adam Yarratt's, etc. 22 Oct 1667. 16.25

Eaton, Richd. Deposition. Age not shown. Says that he and Adam Yarratt "joined mates" and bought land of Mr Francis Clay "and my motherlaw Joan Winlow living at the plantation called the

Yarratt, Adam. Various depositions and entries (continued) Glebe my wife said unto your Deponent - (Richard) - is convenient that if my mother will goe to the head of the river and live she would live more convenient for - and pay no rent. Your depon't answered I cannot doe it of my selfe, by reason the land is betwixt us both but if Adam will give consent, your deponent was very willing. Soe Adam Yarratt gave consent for her and her daughters coming upon condition (to the best of my rememberance) that they should have house and land for their lives. See when my mother removed your deponent helpt her to the head of the river with six head of cattle and in two Caneoes your deponent did helpe her up likewise". Etc, etc. He also gave "a Caster hatt with a green oyle case and old hattcase to my Bro-in law Wm Abrams, who after some time I asked why he did not weare his hatt and he said he had sold it to Adam Yarratt: and further saith that Sam'l Skipworth that lived with Adam Yarratt, when the said Yarratt sent him downe to Yorke I heard Yarratt say he had sent him down well clothed, and with a good hatt, and further sayth that when they came up to the head of the river, that that Hanah Abram did werke in the ground as well as in the house and there was crops went in her name and further saith not". 22 Octr 1667. 16.25

Statham, Hugh. Deposition. Age not shown. Says he went with Hanah Abram to the Indian Cabbin and "she did tell the Indian that she would give him a new hatt and a new pare of frenoh falls and a suit of clothes if he would come and live with them againe". So he came, etc. 22 Oct 1667. 16.26

Yarret, Adam. Submits a/c of cattle of Wm Salmon orphan of Edw Salmon. 22 Aug 1670. 16.144

Yarratt, Adam and Rachell his wife. She admrx of Augustine Rhodes decd bring suit agt Edw Barnes. 21 Aug 1678. 4.5

Yarratt, Adam. In behalf of Rachell his wife, sister of Augustine Rhodes decd. Admr of est granted 20 March last. Nuncupative will preduced 17th Apl by Edw Barnes declared void and he ordered to produce what est he had in his hands. 17 Oct 1678. 4.8

Yarrat, Adam. "did at the tyme when our men were up in Armes to suppress the Rebells, a considerable tyme entertine a considerable number of our men" to be pd 1000 lb tobo from next levy. 15 Jan 1678/9. 4.20

Yarratt, Adam. Surveyor up to 15 Oct 1679. 4.47

Yarratt, Alice. This name appears to be Larrett. It may be Yarratt. Age 38 or th-abts. 19 Jan 1655. 14.67

Yarratt, Wm and Jane his wife. Jno Greenstone, 9 yrs old, bound to them till 17 with consent of his father. 18 Mar 1684/5.4.256

Yarratt, Wm. Appointed Constable upper Fairfield. 18 May 1687. 4.394

Yealke, Jno. Has bequest of a colt from Tho Steed. 2 Apl 1670. 16.149

Yeates, Jno. His wife Ellinor has bequest from Roger Walters. 29 Dec 1669. 16.69 Also 16.115

Yeats, Wm. Wit deed Rainsferd Smith to Wm Berry. 17 Nov 1712. 18.257

Yewets, Adams. Wit deed Towers to Colton. 8 Sept 1668. 16.38
Youlle, Thos. To take charge of cattle belonging to the children of
    Thomas Allen. 10 Jan 1650/1. 1.46
Young, Wm. Referred to as uncle in will of Jno Coutanceau, who also
    leaves bequest to "my cousin Jno Young". 17 Dec 1718. 19.10
Yowell, Capt. See entry Capt Pet. Knight. 21 Aug 1678. 4.4

Appendix.

The items to follow properly belong in Virginia Colonial Abstracts, No. 19. However they were not available when that volume was released. They contain so much genealogical data that it seemed best to include them even if out of place.   B.F.

Abbott, Anne. Given a heifer "for my good will and affection by Henry Hurst. 24 May 1650. 1.40

Adams, Kath: Married Rd Rout who is sued by Tho Tipton for 680 lb tobo. 6 Oct 1687. 4.407

Adams, Summar. In dif with Wm Flowers. Settled by Jury. 21 Jan 1668/9. 3.55

Adams, Tho. On vestry Chicacone par. 20 Mar 1671/2. 16.158 Also to settle est of Tho Bennett lately decd at his house. 18 March 1684/5. 4.257   Also To 'Assort' dower for Mrs Eliz Evans widow. 6 Oct 1687. 4.407

Addamson, Jeffery. As wit proves will of Rd Jones. 15 July 1685. 4.275

Adington, Benj. Servt to Mr Tho Opie to be whipt for killing a hog belonging to Mr Nicho Owen. Ran away. 16 Oct 1676. 4.6

Adlam, Jos. Aged abt 20 yrs. 1 Feb 1667/8. 16.43

Aldridge, Clemt. Joiner. Garaves Garrett son of Tho.G. decd asks indentures to serve him and learn the trade. 21 Aug 1678. 4.1

Aldridge, Geo. Headright of Rd Span. 20 Feb 1650/1. 1.49

Aldwell, Tho. Wit deed Eyes to Fallon and Atkins. 26 Oct 1671. 16.201

Algood, Edw. dec'd. His orphans Jno and Richd bound to Peter Flynt. 5 Oct 1687. 4.403.   Also his orphan Wm bound to Tho Barnes. 5 Oct 1687. 4.403

Allen, Erasmus. Has bequest of a mare from Erasmus Withers. 1 Nov 1680. 4.94

Allen, James. Headright of Mr Edw Sanders. 22 June 1669. 3.65

Allen, Jno. Wit will Roger Walters. 29 Dec 1669. 16.115

Allen, Ralph. Servt to Theo Baker adj 14 yrs old. 21 Dec 1698. 4.847

Allen, Tho. Tho Youlle to take charge of cattle belonging to his children. 10 Jan 1650/1. 1.46

Allenson, Wm. Signs oath to Commonwealth of England. 13 Apl 1652. 1.72

Algrove, John. 5 yrs old the 26th of next May. Son of Nicholas Algrove, with consent of his mother Eliz Algrove, bound to Tho Hughlett and Mary his wife till 21. 19 Nov 1696. 4.748. (this name may be Argrove therefore possibly Hargrove)

Allgrove, Nicholas. A servt sold by Geo Courtnall to Leond Howson. 27 Jan 1668/9. 16.69

Algrove, Tho. Son of Nich: Algrove. 8 yrs old 8 May next. Bound with consent of his mother, Mrs Eliz Algrove, to Tho Gill till 21. 19 Nov 1696. 4.749

Alloway, Jno. His wife Dorothy left a calf by Roger Walters. 29 Dec 1669. 16.115

Anderson, Wm. Admr of his will to Henry Watts. 6 Apl 1669. 3.61

Anketell, Francis. Headright of Capt Gyles Brent. 21 Jan 1651/2. 1.70

Archer, Richd. Servt to Jno Moore adj 14 yrs old. 21 Dec 1698. 4.847

Armstrong, Henry. Headright of Mr Jno Harris. 15 July 1696. 4.733

Ashton, Charles. Signs oath to Commonwealth. 13 Apl 1652. 1.72

Ashton, Col. Pet: Justice. 5 Nov 1668. 3.46

Ashton, Mr Charles. Dec'd. Mrs Isabella Ashton his relict. 4 Apl 1672. 3.144

Appendix.

Atkins, Jno. To admr est of Wm Perriman. 16 Oct 1676. 4.6
Atkins, Joseph. Servt to Jas Robinson adj 15 yrs old. 20 Nov 1668. 3.48
Atkins, Joshua. He and Charles Fallon buy 370 acres from Dennis Eyes. 26 Oct 1671. 16.201
Austen, Jas. Wit will of Rd Span. 16 Mar 1667/8. 16.64
Auckland, Sam. Age 19 or th-abt. 19 July 1670. 16.132
Ayres, Jno. Admr of Simon Domibielle. Ord to pay debts. 10 Jan 1650/1. 1.46
Aires, Jno. (sic) Signs oath to Commonwealth. 13 Apl 1652. 1.72-3
Bady, Jane. Headright of Hugh Fouch. 22 June 1669. 3.65
Baineham, Alex: Certif for 150 acres for importing "Himselfe, Anne his wife, Alexand'r Baineham". 20 Feb 1650/1. 1.49
Baker, Geo. Marriner or merchant. Cousin of Jno Webber of N Co. 12 Feb 1670/1. 16.166
Baker, Hugh. Wit deed Nash to Howson. 17 Jan 1671/2. 16.219
Baker, Mary. An orphan child abt 11 yrs old bound to Sam'll Poole and his wife till 17. "to be taught to read the bible perfectly". 5 Oct 1687. 4.402
Baker, Tho and Theodore. Deed of Gift from their mother Mrs Eliz Niccolas. 20 May 1670. 16.127 Also Tho Baker's servant David Cavanah adj 14 yrs old. 16 Nov 1698. 4.842 and Theodore Baker's servt Ralph Allen adj 14 yrs of age. 21 Dec 1698. 4.847
Baldridge, Jas Jr. Given a calf by Jno Hallowes. 21 Jan 1650/1. 1.48
Baldridge, Mr Thomas. Justice. 24 Aug 1650. 1.41 Also as Major Tho Baldridge. Justice. 20 July 1652. 1.76
Ball, Sarah. Wife of Richd Ball. Ref to as "my aunt" in will of John Coutanceau. He also leaves a diamond ring to "my cousin Sarah Ball" the dau of Richd Ball and a bequest to Mr David Ball. Jos Ball Jr executor. 17 Dec 1718. 19.10
Bandmill, Tho. Depo re witchcraft. He evidently came in ship from Barbadoes with LeBreton. 11 Apl 1671. 16.186 /4.731
Bankes, Thos. Justice 21 Sept 1692. 4.599. Also Justice 15 July 1696.
Barnes, Edw. Sued by Rachel wife of Adam Yarrett and extrx of Augustine Rhodes. 21 Aug 1678. 4.5 Also: He produces nuncupative will of Augustine Rhodes brother of Mrs Rachel Yarrett on 17 Apl 1678. The will declared void in favor of Mrs Yarrett. 17 Oct 1678. 4.8
Barnes, Edw and Mary his wife complain that Richd Cox detained from them a child of the sd Mary. Phil Drake and Francis Stanley swear that Mary demanded the child within 2 mos after it's father's death but was refused. Cox is ordered to deliver the child to it's mother and Barnes ordered to pay him 300 lb tobo for keeping it. 19 Oct 1681. 4.106
Barnes, Hen: signs oath to Commonwealth. 13 Apl 1652. 1.72-3
Barnes, Tho. Wm Algood orphan son of Edw Algood bound to him. Richd Smyth security. 5 Oct 1687. 4.403 Also Tho Barnes and Jane his wife admr of Jno Wilkins decd. 20 Nov 1696. 4.751
Barratt, Tho. Ref to his character. Distressing but highly entertaining. 24 July 1665. 16.8
Barry, Wm. Age 25 (?) yrs or th-abts. Entry almost faded out. Depo re witchcraft. 20 May 1671. 16.181 Also Wm Barry wit deed Ingram to Winter. 16 Apl 1672. 16.231

Appendix.

Barry, Wm. Admr of his est to Jno Merrydith who married Mary his widow. 19 Apl 1693. 4.619

Bashaw, Wm. Age 27 or th-abts. 17 Feb 1667/8. 16.38

Bashford entries. Vol.18 page 251 plus.
Deed. 3 Nov 1697. Simon Bashford of Westwick in the County of Kent Linemaker only son and heir of Jno Bashford of Woolwich, Rope maker deed sells Mary Bashford of Woolwich widdow, for L 40. "Good and lawfull money of England" a tenement or messauge "known by the name and sign of the three Doves" late in occupation of Ambrose Capell. Refers to "in the now dwelling house of her the said Mary Bashford scituate in Woolwich" etc. Signed "The mark of Mary Bashford". Wit: Amy Hooper, John Hooper. This deed proved in Northumberland Co Court in Virginia by Christopher Dameron 18 Dec 1712.

p.254. Northumberland County in the Colony of Virginia July the 26th 1712. Mr Jno Cockrill aged forty three years or thereabouts saith upon his Oath that about therty years agoe he went with his father and mother to the Wedding feast of Simon Bashford and Grace his wife further this Deponent remembers that the Genterey at the Weding made a Gathering to sett up the young marryed Cople and they ever went for man and wife and that the said Simon Bashford some time after his marriage went whome to England and returned back with severall goods for his wife and children this I remember and further saith not
Jno Cockrill

July 26th Anno 1712 Then mr John Cockrill made Oath to the above before me   Peter Hack.

p 254. Northumberland County in the Colony of Virginia July the 26th 1712. Jno Reason aged about Forty years or therabouts sayth upon his Oath that about therty years agoe Simon Bashford came to his the said Reasons father and asked liberty for this Deponent to come and turn the spitt att the said Bashfords Wedding which this Deponent did further he remembers the people Wished Simon Bashford and his wife Grace Joye and that hee see the said Bashford waight on the table as bridgrom and that the Gentery made a Gethering to sett up the young married Cople and they ever went for man and wife and the said Bashford some time after his marriage went whome to England and att his Returne brought with him severall Goods for his wife and children this I remember and further sayeth nott
July the 26th Anno 1712.   Jno Reason R his mark
x x Dio December 18th 1712. Then Christopher Dameron came into Northumberland County Court and presented the within Copies to the said Court which are approved, etc.

p 255. Northumberland County Sct   The Deposition of Elizabeth Whay aged therty seven years or therabouts being Examined sworn sayth that she was at the labour of Grace Bashford the wife of Simon Bashford when she was delivered of (a) Son which this Deponent was afterwards Surety for when he was baptised and that he was called Jno and further saith that Christopher Dameron is now Guardian and tuto to the Afore-

Appendix.

Bashford entries (continued) said Jno Bashford and further sayth not. Eliza E Whay her mark
The above Deposition was made Oath to by Eliza Whay the 29th of July 1712 before mee Jno Howson

p.255. Northumberland County Sc. The deposition of Sarah Tignor aged therty five or thereabouts being Examined sworn sayth That she was at the labour of Grace Bashford wife to Simon Bashford when she was delivered of a son which was called Jno and further saith that Christopher Dameron is Guardian and Tutor to the aforesaid Jne Bashford and further saith not   Sarah x Tignor her mark
The above Deposition was made oath to by Sarah Tignor this 29th of July Anno 1712 before mee Jno Howson.

Northumberland in the Colony of Virginia July 16th 1712. Elenor Shaw aged sixty five years or thereabouts saith upon her Oath that about therty years agoe shee being at the Wedding feast of Symon Bashford and Grace his wife did here them declare that they were lawfully Marryed and did see them bed together And further sayth that Jno Bashford to whome Christopher Dameron is admitted Guardian is true and lawfull son of the said Simon Bashford and that she knew him the said Jno Bashford from his infancy and further this deponent saith not
The mark of Eleanor x Shaw
Die July 16th 1712 Jur in Cur Nor Test Tho Hobson Cl Cur Nor'ld

Northumberland Co., Va. Vol.18. p 309. Bond. 17 June 1713. L 600. Sterling. Hon Robt Carter Esqr, upon petition of John Bashford orphan son of Simon Bashford decd, is appointed his guardian.

Basouth, Wm. als Woodamore. Servt to Pet. Knight. 16 July 1685. 4.287
Bayles, Eliz. Orphan of Jno Bayles. List of her cattle, 21 head, submitted by Jos Feilding. 22 Aug 1670. 16.144
Bailes, Jno. (sic) Signs oath to Commonwealth. 13 Apl 1652. 1.72-3
Bailes, Tho.   "   "   "   "   "
Bayles, Tho. By his will dated 4 Jan 1684/5 div land betw his 3 sons, John, Christopher and Je- Bayles. That Christo: the 2nd son sold his share to Persifull Simpson 10 Dec 1688. 19.3
Bayly, Saml. P of A from Jno Essex. 9 Feb 1671/2. 16.226
Beane, Wm. Exor of Mrs Welthian Bonas. Her son Robt to him till 21. 20 Aug 1684. 4.236
Beane, Wm. Bonus for linen. Gets the booby prize. Actually the 2nd prize. In County expenses the record reads "the worst peece Last yeare" 400 lb tobc. 19 Nov 1696. 4.748
Beard, Jno. Headright of Capt Jno Haynie. 15 July 1696. 4.733
Bearmore, Jno. Submits a/c of cattle of James White orphan of Richd White. 22 Aug 1670. 16.144
Bedlam, Wm. Arrested by Edw Tempest for debt but did not appear. 20th Feb 1651/2. 1.50
Bennett, Jno. Signs oath to Commonwealth. 13 Apl 1652. 1.72-3
Bennett, Jno. deceased. On 1 Apl 1665 gave a bill for a heifer. Andr Morton his admr. 11 Jan 1668/9. 3.50

Appendix

Bennett, Jno. Jno Reason appointed Constable in his place. 4 Apl 1672. 3.144

Bennett, Tho. Lately dec'd at house of Tho Adams "and left noe knowne relations behind him, in this Country". Adams to settle estate. 18 March 1684/5. 4.257

Beorane, James. Servt to Tho Berry adj 15 yrs old. 21 Dec 1698. 4.847

Betts, Wm. Certif for 150 acres for importing: Himselfe, Robt Casleton and Francis Roberts. 20 Feb 1651/2. 1.50

Betts, Wm. His father by will left an estate to him and his bro Charles Betts, etc. 15 July 1685. 4.279

Bird, Christian. To be pd as evidence in suit Steph: Wells vs Thomas Perryne. 20 Apl 1681. 4.90

Bird, Timothy. Servt to Mr Jno Curtis adj 15 yrs old. 16 Nov 1698. 4.482

Birk see Burke.

Bishop, Sebene. (Cyprian Bishop) Signs oath to Commonwealth. 13 April 1652. 1.72-3

Blackerby, Jas. Sued by Mrs Jane Wildey for 1522 lb tobo. 15 June 1692. 4.594

Blackwell, Charles. Servt to - Downing adj 11 yrs old. 19 Jan 1675/6. 3.249

Blackwell, Saml and Margary his wife. See entries under Nutt.

Blanch, Tho. Wit deed White to Smith. 17 Dec 1718. 19.3

Bland, Joseph. Headright of Capt Jno Haynie. 15 July 1696. 4.733

Blecker, Geo. Buys land from Brewer. 15 Apl 1672. 16.229

Boggus, Hen and Kath his wife. Sell 100 acres given him by Gervase Dodson, gent, decd, to Eliz Hughlett. 24 Feb 1670/1. 16.162

Bonas, Welthian. Probate of her will to Wm Beane. She disposes of her 3 children as follows: Her son Robt Bonas to Wm Beane till 21, her dau Elizabeth Bonas to Mrs Rebecca Mathew and her dau Anne Bonas to Tho Miller. 20 Aug 1684. 4.236

Bourne, James. Servt to Jos Humphreys adj 14 yrs old. 16 Nov 1698. 4.842

Bourne, Terrence. Servt to Eliz Sheeres widow, adj 18 yrs of age. 16th Nov. 1698. 4.841

Bowen, Jno. To appraise est of Tho Rolph decd. 10 Mar 1668/9. 3.58

Bowen, Jno. His servt Jam: Cox adj 10 yrs old. 21 Jan 1684/5. 4.252

Bowen, Jno. Bequest from Rd Ruth. 26 Jan 1718/9. 19.31

Boy, Jno. Servant to Henry Lambert. His exor and main heir. 31 March 1670. 16.119 Also signs inv of Lambert's est. 26 Apl 1670. 16.124 Also: John Boy "of Chepnam in the County of Wilts Admr of the estate of Hen Lambert dece'd". P of A to Capt Tho Brereton to collect a/cs in Va and Md. 26 Apl 1670. 16.142

Boy, Tho. Left a gun by Mr Tho Matthew "a sick man in the service agt the Susquehannoughs". 21 Aug 1678. 4.4

Boyd family detail. See entries Pope and Murdock. 16 July 1712. 18.214.

Bradford, John, his wife Joan, his son John. See entry Mrs Hannah Smith 17 Aug 1713. 18.335

Bradley, Owen. As wit proves will of Wm Wildey. 15 June 1681. 4.96

Bradley, Robt. His wife Anne dau of Robt Bradshaw decd, See entry Edw Williams. 15 July 1685. 4.274

Bradley, Saml. Sues Fran Fisher but fails to appear. 20 Nov 1668. 3.48

Appendix.

Bradshaw, Jno. Signs oath to Commonwealth. 13 Apl 1652. 1.72-3
Bradshaw, Robt. " " "
Bradshaw, Temperence, dec'd. Her heir Edw Williams. See entry his name
    re Anne dau of Ro Bradshaw who m Ro Bradley.15 July 1685. 4.274
Brassill, Morris. Headright of Rd Haynie. 15 July 1696. 4.733
Brent, Capt Gyles. Certificate for 900 acres for importing 18 persons.
    The headrights include: Capt Gyles Brent, Mrs Margaret Brent, Mrs
    Mary Brent, Mrs Mary Brent wife to Capt Brent, Margaret Kendall.
    21 Jan 1651/2. 1.70

Brereton. Here are more of these notations which will have to be crowded in. Tho. Brereton, wit will Ro Walton Gent, 14 Jan 1669/70. 16.188. Tho Brereton gives personal property to son Thos (under 18) and dau Eliz: Wit Tho Hobson and Wm Brereton. 15 Nov 1671. 16.206. Major Tho Brereton includes in a gift to his dau Eliz, 4 silver spoones marked P.A. 1 Coker nut cupp with silver marked I.C., other gold and silver items. No date but recorded in Jan 1671/2. 16.224. Maj Tho Brereton as Justice dissents from Court order. 16 Oct 1676.4.6 Major Tho Brereton appears as Justice 21 Aug 1678.4.1 also as Justice 20 Nov 1678.4.12 Col Tho. appears as Justice 18 Apl 1683.4.176. Col Tho Brereton sworn high sheriff with Jno Topping as undersheriff 18 Apl 1683. 4.176
Mr Tho Brereton as Justice 16 Sept 1685. 4.291. Capt Tho Brereton as Justice 16 July 1696.4734. Capt Tho Brereton as Justice 16 Nov 1698. 4.841. Wm and Jane Brereton wit deeds 20 Jan 1668/9. 16.68

Brewer, Tho. Signs oath to Commonwealth. 13 Apl 1652. 1.72-3
Brewer, Tho. Deed to Jno Nickles heir of Theo Baker decd. 13 Dec 1671.
    16.226. Also Tho Brewer and Sarah his wife dell Geo Blecker land.
    15 Apl 1672. 16.229
Bridges, Francis. Headright of - Bridges (prob Hercules Bridges) 20
    July 1652. 1.76
Bridges, Hercules. Headright of - Bridges (prob himself) 20 July 1652.
    1.76
Bridgeman, Hannah. deceased. Eliz wife of Geo Hamilton her heiress. 21
    Aug 1678. 4.1
Brierley, Robt and Fra. Both wit Jno Webber's will. 12 Feb 1670/1.
    16.166 Also Robt Brierly's servant Benj Browne adj 16 yrs old.
    17 March 1674/5. 3.224
Brodhurst, Walter. Certificate for 200 acres for importing Himselfe,
    Anne his wife, Eliza Brodhurst, Susan Brodhurst. 10 Jan 1650/1.
    1.47 Also Walter Brodhurst signs oath to Commonwealth 13 Apl
    1652. 1.72
Brooks, Jno. Headright of Mr Edw Sanders. 22 June 1669. 3.65
Brooks, Jno. Servt to Jno Corbell adj 18 yrs old. 19 Jan 1675/6. 3.249
Broughton, Tho. Signs oath to Commonwealth. 13 Apl 1652. 1.72-3
Browne, Benj. Servt to Ro Brierly adj 16 yrs old. 17 Mar 1674/5.3.224
Browne, Geo. Servt to Mr Presly adj 12 yrs old. 19 Jan 1675/6. 3.249
Brudenall, Wm. Sued by Tho Williams and also by Mr Ro Jones. 21 Jan
    1668/9. 3.52
Bryan, Jno. Servt to Pet: Coutanceau adj 12 yrs old. 21 Dec 1698.
    8.847
Bryant, Jno. His wife Anne abused with vile language by Ann Cammell
    who is ordered to beg her forgiveness in Court. 22 Dec 1681.
    4.117

Budd, Rich: Signs oath to Commonwealth. 13 Apl 1652. 1.72

Burbage, Capt Tho. In dif with Mrs Eliz Newman re cattle. 20 Nov 1651. 1.68

Burgesse, Richd. Headright of Capt Jno Haynie. 15 July 1696. 4.733

Burgin, Jno. Age 40 yrs or th-abts. 17 Dec 1712. 18.242

Burke, Eliz: Servt to Jas Hill adj 14 yrs old. 16 Nov 1698. 4.842

Birk, Jno (sic) Servt to Jas Waddy adj 13 yrs old. 16 Nov 1698. 4.841

Burke, Wm. Servt to Jno Curtis adj 14 yrs old. 16 Nov 1698. 4.842

Burwell, Robt. Chirurgeon. Deed of Gift to "my welbeloved and only son John Burwell". 19 May 1670. 16.128

Bushrod, Jno. Appeals a decree agt him of 19 Sep 1711 in favor of Geo Eskridge, Guardian of Richd Bushrod, an infant son of Richd Bushrod decd who was son of Tho Bushrod decd. etc. Has to do with a div of slaves betw Eskridge as guardian and Griffin Fauntleroy who married Anne dau of sd Tho Bushrod. 10 Jun 1712. 18.196

Butler, Wm. a/c of his cattle submitted by Francis Gray. Westmorland Co records. 1653-9. p.28

Byram, Abra. Signs oath to Commonwealth. 13 Apl 1652. 1.72-3
Also Dorothy his relict now married to Jno Meredith of Lancaster Co. 16 Oct 1668. 16.59

Byram, Peter: His wife Ann was, on 10 Nov 1683, Mrs Ann Goche widow. 17 Sept 1684. 4.240

Byram, Peter. Complains that Jeffery Johnson, being brother of his wife was requested to stay at his home with his wife and children. That he misbehaved himself and abused them to their great sorrow, etc. 16 July 1685. 4.287 Also his wife extrx and widow of Saml Gouch and mother of Jno Gouch. 21 May 1696. 4.724

Cadany, Kath: Headright of Wm Sheares. 21 Aug 1678. 4.4

Cale, Susan. Headright of Rice Maddox. 10 Jan 1650/1. 1.47

Callan, Hugh of St S par. Late deceased. 16 July 1711. 18.86

Cammell, Alex. Servt to Tho Hobson adj 16 yrs old. 19 Jan 1675/6. 3.250

Cammell, Ann wife of Wm. Sued for slander. 22 Dec 1681. 4.117

Cammell, Samll. Servt to Dennis Eyse adj 12 yrs old. 19 Jan 1675/6. 3.249

Carpenter, Phillip. Signs oath to Commonwealth. 13 Apl 1652. 1.72-3

Carpenter, Phill. With Edw Henley buys 200 acres from Rd Walker. 10 June 1652. 1.76

Carter, Dennis. Whereas Dennis Carter Complained to this Court that he was by some person in the County, where he lived aspersed to have been generally looked upon here, as a vagabond, and an Jobe lease fellow not suffered to be admitted in any Civill Company, and prayed this Court to give Certificate what his behavior and Carriage was, whilst he lived here. The Court doth declare that during the many yeares of his abode in this County he had the repute of a Civill Just person, of a modest and good behavior. Neither did any of this Court, at any time here, or know of any Evill Carriage, or any misdemeanor of the said Carter. 17 Oct. 1678. 4.8

Carter, Eliz: Wit will of Tho Steed. 2 Apl 1670. 16.149

Cartwright, hinery. Signs oath to Commonwealth. 13 Apl 1652. 1.72-3

Casleton, Robt. Headright of Wm Betts. 20 Feb 1651/2. 1.50

Casly, Richd (or Casey) Servt to Jas Symmons adj 15 yrs of age. 16th Nov 1698. 4.842

Appendix.

Castide, Cormock. Servt to Mr Pet: Presly adj 13 yrs old. 19 Jan 1675/6 3.249

Cavanah, David. Servt of Mr Tho Gaskins ajd 14 yrs old. 16 Nov 1698. 4.842

Challenge, Saml. Headright of Rd Hawkins. 20 Feb 1651/2. 1.50

Chapman, Will. Aged 40 yrs. 15 June 1681. 4.94

Charmell, Sam: Age 25 yrs or th-abts. No date but recorded Jan 1666/7. 16.9

Chicacone parish. Vestry meeting to settle boundries of Glebe. 20 Mar 1671/2. 16.158

Church. Depositions re early Church. 22 June 1669. (1649) 16.152

Claiborne, Wm. "Whereas Mr James Gaylord hath informed the Court that the Honourable the Secretary is dead". 16 Oct 1676. 4.6 (Alas, this was the end of one of our great Virginians of the early period, the Hon. William Claiborne. B.F.)

Clare, Rich: Signs oath to the Commonwealth. 13 Apl 1652. 1.72-3

Clark, Geo. Appointed Constable for N side G W. 22 June 1669. 3.64

Claughton, Jas. Mischief maker. He told Mrs Geo Thompson of her husband's unfaithfullness. 20 Feb 1650/1. 1.58   Also he signs oath to Commonwealth. 13 Apl 1652. 1.72   Also admr of est of Edw Salmon. 20 Oct 1668. 3.45 Also mentioned 19 July 1671. 3.124

Clay, Tho. Age 69 or th-abts. 3 Oct 1712. 18.269

Clerke, Wm. Headright of Capt Gyles Brent. 21 Jan 1651/2. 1.70

Clissen, Phillip. Servt to Charles Nelmes adj 15 yrs of age. 21 Dec 1698. 4.848

Clowes, Phillip. Age 17. Nephew of Fran: Vanlanglingham. See entry his name. 17 Nov 1696. 4.844

Cocke, Wm. Wit deed of gift Hurst to Abbott. 24 May 1650. 1.40   Also signs oath to Commonwealth. 13 Apl 1652. 1.72-3

Cook, Mr. Surveyor circa 1650. See entry Mrs Eliz Sheares. 16.153

Cockerill, Andr. Values est of Jno Hull decd. 11 Jan 1668/9. 3.51

Cockerell, Elizabeth. of St S par. Will 25 Apl 1719. Prob 20 May 1719. To son Presly Cockerell. To dau Hannah Cockerell "plates that was my sister Hannah Cockerells". To dau Eliz Nelmes. To son Edward Saunders. To 3 sons John, Willoughby and Presly Cockerell. Youngest son and dau to live with son in law Cha Nelms, he exor. 19.42

Cockerel, John. His wife Hannah. 20 Nov 1668. 16.60

Cockrell, Jne. "Cosen" of Edw Coles' wife (nephew) had slight dif with Granny Neale wife of Mr Danl Neale. Started the absurd witchcraft case. 20 May 1671. 16.181

Cockerell, Jno. Son of Adr Cockerell decd. Chooses Jno Downing as guardian. 19 Oct 1681. 4.105

Cockerell, Jno. His servt Jno Hayes adj 14 yrs of age. 21 Dec 1698. 4.847

Cockrill, Tho. Headright of Rice Maddox. 10 Jan 1650/1. 1.47

Codd, Col St Ledger. His forgiveness asked in Court by Corderoy Ironmonger for spreading scandle regarding his treatment of servants. 17 Apl 1672. 3.146   Also appears as Justice 17 Mar 1674/5. 3.224   also as Justice. Dessents from Court order 16th Oct 1676. 4.6   Also appears as Justice 16 Oct 1678. 4.5 Also pays fine for a maid servant sentenced to be whipt. She then acquitted. 16 Oct 1678. 4.5

Appendix.

Coggin, Tho. Signs oath to Commonwealth. 13 Apl 1652. 1.72-3

Coke, Richd. of N Co. "doe let fall" right and title to 188 acres entered by Rd Thompson for Rd Rice 7 Mar 1665/6. Wit Tho Colton, Sam: Poole. 16 Sept 1671. 16.200

Colclough, Geo. Signs oath to Commonwealth. 13 Apl 1652. 1.72-3

Coles, Edw. Accuses Granny Neale the wife of Mr Danl Neale of bewitching his wife. 29 May 1671. 16.179-181. Further: he said his wife "was under an ill tongue" and "she lay speechless and further said that he did verily believe she was bewitched". Mrs Coles, as the center of attraction, kept up this fraud for some time. Then Edwd Coles says he is sorry he called Mrs Neal a witch and a whore, that the words "were passionately spoken and not malitiously". Pays all Court charges, etc. The whole affair is exceedingly comical. 5 Aug 1671. 16.187

Coles, Elinor wife of Edw Coles was widow of Tho Darrell. 15 Jan 1678/9. 4.18

Cole, Robt. Appraises est of Ro Seagrave decd. 20 Mar 1649/50. 1.48

Collins, Wm. "an impotent aged person" freed from levy. 19 Apl 1693. 4.619

Compton, Anne. Aged 27 or th-abts. Depo re Geo Thompson. 20 Feb 1650/1. 1.56

Conaway, Dennis Jr. "prest to Carry Letters to Coll Wormelyes" 19 Nov 1696. 4.748

Canaway, Freeman. Ack judgt to Jno Mottrom 200 lb tobo. 13 Apl 1652. 1.75

Conepesacke, Thomas. Headright of Capt Gyles Brent. 21 Jan 1651/2. 1.70

Cooper, Capt Geo. Justice 19 Apl 1693. 4.619 also as Justice 16 July 1696. 4.734 and as Justice 18 Dec 1696. 4.755

Cooper, Jeremy. Owes Tho Webb 600 lb tobo etc. 21 Jan 1651/2. 1.70

Cornish, Wm. Age 26 yrs or th-abts. 20 Nov 1651. 1.68 Also signs oath to Commonwealth 13 Apl 1652. 1.72-3. Also Walter Dunne gives his dau Mary Cornish a heifer 20 Dec 1671. 16.214. Also as deceased, his extrx married Tho Ham't. 5 Oct 1687. 4.402

Cotesford, Picard. Headright of Capt Gyles Brent. 21 Jan 1651/2. 1.70

Cotman, Benj. married Eliz: dau of Mrs Mary Thomas. 17 Sept 1684. 4.244

Cotoon, Anth: Servt to Clem: Latemore adj 17 yrs old. 21 Jan 1684/5. 4.252

Cottrill, Jno. Signs appraisal of est of Jas Rogers decd. 19 Sep 1711 18.103 Also gives bond for admr est of Ebenezer Neale dec'd. The bond signed by Jno x Cotrill, Jno Haynie Jr, Rodham Neale, Jos x Humphries. 19 Dec 1711. 18.116

Cottrell, John of Newmans Neck, St S par. Deed. 14 Jan 1711/12. Sells Peter Presly 75 acres. This land was sold by Rd Island on 21 July 1656 to Andrew Cotrell the father of the sd Jno Cotrell. Lucretia wife of Jno Cottrell reling dower rights. 18.121

Court House. Specifications in detail for new Court House. Incl "to be be seiled with boards (and arched as Fairefeilds Church is)" etc. 11 March 1680/1. 4.89

Courtnall, Geo. Atty of his father Geo Courtnall. 20 Nov 1668. 3.48 Also on Vestry Chicacone par. 20 Mar 1671/2. 16.158

Coutanceau, Jacob. Signs oath to Commonwealth. 13 Apl .652. 1.72-3 Also appointed Constable Newmans Neck. 18 May 1687. 4.394

Appendix.

Coutansheau, Jno. "aged 34 yeares". 11 Jan 1668/9. 3.51

Coutanceau, John. He requested Wm Presly, 4 or 5 years since, to carry a parchment and have the Assembly confirm it. That it was a "Denizacon" granted his father Jacob Coutanceau by King James and had a great seal affixed. The Assembly said it was better than any they could issue. It was left with Mr Francis Kirkman to be recorded, etc. 5 Oct 1669. 16.96

Coutanceau, Jno. Will. Dated 17 Dec 1718. Prob 21 Jan 1718/9. To uncle Wm Young. To aunt Sarah Ball wife of Richd Ball. Refs to each of the following 6 persons as "my cousin". Dorcas Walter, Jno Young, Jos Ball Jr, he exor, Kath Walters, Eliz Walter, Eliz Hack. Bequest to Mr David Ball. A diamond ring to his cousin Sarah Ball dau of Richd Ball. 19.10

Coutanceau, Mrs Kath: Her servt Laurence Roach adj 11 yrs old. 17 Nov 1687. 4.412

Coutansheaw, Oliver. Headright of Mr Edw Sanders. 22 June 1669. 3.65

Cotanco, Oliver. To give evidence for Saml Mahon at next Court. 17th Oct 1678. 4.8

Coutanceau, Mr Peter. Reference to his servants. 21 Dec 1698. 8.847

Coutanceau, Wm. His servt Wm Macktire adj 14 yrs old. 19 Jan 1675/6. 3.249

Cox, Jam: Servt to Jno Bowen adj 10 yrs old. 21 Jan 1684/5. 4.252

Cox, Richd. of Chicacone par. Fined for having a bastard child by his maid servant. 16 Oct 1678. 4.5

Cox, Richd. To be pd 300 lb tobo for keeping child of Mary wife of Edw Barnes. 19 Oct 1681. 4.106

Cox, Richd. Dec'd. Lucy Furnett his admr. 20 July 1687. 4.397

Coynia, Zachariah. Servt to Mr Jno Scott adj 14 yrs old. 16 Nov 1687. 4.410

Crab, Wm. Arrests Jno Rogers Jr. No cause. Nonsuit. 21 Nov 1678. 4.15

Cralle, Mrs Hannah. Formerly Hannah Hull. 18 May 1720. 19.105

Craze, Jno. Servt to Edw Coles adj 15 yrs old. 19 Jan 1675/6. 3.249

Cromwell, Gershom. Signs oath to Commonwealth. 13 Apl 1652. 1.72-3

Crosby, Danl. Accidentally killed by Wm Walker. 16 Oct 1678. 4.8

Cunliffe, Rd. Acks deed of gift to his son Richd Cunliffe. 18 Nov 1698. 4.841

Cunny, Jno. Headright of Mrs Jane Wildey. 19 Oct 1681. 4.105

Curtis, Mr Jno. married admr of Mr Erasmus Withers. 20 July 1687. 4.400

Curtis, Jno. Foreman of Jury. 18 Nov 1687. 4.414

Curtis, Mr Jno. Reference to his servants. 16 Nov 1698. 4.842

Downing family detail. See entry Rd Nutt. 6 July 1712. 18.222

Dyer. See Odyer. Gabriell and Mary his wife. 20 Feb 1659/1. 1.149

Farnefold. Arms. Sa. a chev. engr. betw 3 buck's heads erased ar. attired or. Burke's Encyclopedia of Heraldry or General Armory.

Feilding, Edw. Dec'd. Will presented by Mrs Winifred Feilding Extrx. 16 June 1714. 6.41

Fluker, David, deceased. Entry re dif betw Pitts Curtis who married the relict and admrx of David Fluker decd and Jno Champion Guardian to David Fluker son of sd Fluker decd. A settlement of the estate reached. 22 Oct 1712. 18.259

Appendix.

Franklin, Henry. Deceased. Ref to his wife Hannah and his sister Mrs Joan Bradford. See entry Mrs Hannah Smith. 17 Aug 1713. 18.335

Gaskins, Tho. Deed of Gift. A slave to his grand-dau Sarah Hull dau of Richd Hull. 14 March 1711/12. 18.315

Harris, John. Will. Dated 23 Feb 1709/10. Prob 18 June 1713. "Having through gods Mercy lived to a Great age". To daughter Sarah Haynie any slave she may choose. Refers to her husband Anthony Haynie and their daughter Grace Ball "my grandaughter". Exors daughter Sarah Haynie and grandson Geo Ball. 18.318

Helder alias Spicer. See Genealogia Bedfordiensis, 1538 - 1700 by Frederick Augustus Blaydes. Refer to index page 479. Many entries. There were, however, only 100 copies of this handsome book made. Any student is welcome to consult my copy. B.F.

James, Tho. Age 50 yrs or th-abts. Says in 1703 he appraised the est of Wm Fletcher late of this Co dec'd. etc. 18 July 1711. 18.91

Keeve see Quiffe. The same name circa 1700

Knight, Leonerd. Age 45 or th-abts. Deposition re survey of land. 21 Nov 1711. 18.112

Layland, Jno. of Wicco par. Age 30 or th-abts. Some time since carried the chain in survey made by Col Geo Cooper for Mr Richd Nutt, etc. 20 June 1711. 18.61

Spicer. See Helder entry just above on this page.

Woodamore. Wm Bascuth alias Woodamore was servant to Mr Peter Knight. 16 July 1685. 4.287

My Goodness ! - I hope the Lord in His Mercy will divert me from ever attempting to construct an imitation register again. Beverley Fleet.

www.ingramcontent.com/pod-product-compliance
Lightning Source LLC
Chambersburg PA
CBHW020646300426
44112CB00007B/264